Introduction
to
Planning History
in the
United States

Introduction
to
Planning History
in the
United States

Edited by

Donald A. Krueckeberg

The Center for Urban Policy Research
Rutgers University
Building 4051 — Kilmer Campus
New Brunswick, New Jersey 08903

© Copyright 1983, Rutgers — The State University of New Jersey
All rights reserved.
Published in the United States by the Center for Urban Policy Research
Rutgers University, New Brunswick, New Jersey 08903
Manufactured in the United States of America

Library of Congress Cataloging in Publication Data
Main entry under title:

Introduction to planning history in the United States.

    Bibliography: p. 280
    Includes index.
    1. City planning — United States — History — Addresses, essays. lectures.
I. Krueckeberg, Donald A.
HT167.I57   1983   307′.12′0973   82-14572
ISBN 0-88285-083-0

Contents

List of Plates

Acknowledgments

I wish to express my deep appreciation to Robert W. Burchell, James Hughes, and George Sternlieb, whose idea of this book and enthusiasm for it got it all started and kept it going. I am also very grateful to each of the contributing authors and their publishers for their cooperation and support.

As usual, I received helpful suggestions from many friends and colleagues, especially Robert Beauregard, Lee Krueckeberg, John Pucher, and David Listokin. I am also very grateful to my friend and colleague, Richard Brail, who shouldered Atlas' share of a course we jointly taught while the book was in preparation. I am also greatly indebted to Warren I. Susman, professor of American History at Rutgers, whose lectures have been a rich source of ideas and insights into American intellectual development.

I also wish to thank Vera Lee for her endless assistance and good spirits and Mary Picarella and Barry Jones and the staff of the Center for Urban Policy Research — particularly Lydia Lombardi and Joan Frantz — for their professional management of the book's production.

Donald A. Krueckeberg
New Brunswick, New Jersey
May 1982

About the Contributors

Alan A. Altshuler is professor of political science at the Massachusetts Institute of Technology, Cambridge, Massachusetts.

John F. Bauman is professor of history and urban affairs at California State College, California, Pennsylvania.

Eugenie Ladner Birch is professor of urban planning at Hunter College, New York City.

Allen F. Davis is professor of history at Temple University, Philadelphia, Pennsylvania.

Phillip J. Funigiello is professor of history at the College of William and Mary, Williamsburg, Virginia.

Allan B. Jacobs is professor of city and regional planning at the University of California, Berkeley.

Donald A. Krueckeberg is professor of urban planning and policy development at Rutgers University, New Brunswick, New Jersey.

Norman Krumholz is professor of urban affairs at Cleveland State University, Cleveland, Ohio.

Jon A. Peterson is professor of history at Queens College, City University of New York, New York City.

William H. Wilson is professor of history at North Texas State University, Denton, Texas.

Robert L. Wrigley, at the time of the first publication of his paper, was a member of the staff of the Area Development Office, U.S. Department of Commerce.

1

The Culture of Planning

Donald A. Krueckeberg

Considering the immense importance of a right location, and a right planning for cities, no step should ever be taken by the parties concerned, without employing some person who is qualified by a special culture, to assist and direct. Our engineers are trained for a very different kind of service, and are partly disqualified for this by the habit of a study more strictly linear, more rigidly scientific, and less artistic. The qualifications of surveyors are commonly more meagre still .... Nothing is more to be regretted, in this view, than that the American nation, having a new world to make, and a clean map on which to place it, should be sacrificing their advantage so cheaply, in the extempore planning of towns and cities. The peoples of the old world have their cities built for times gone by, when railroads and gunpowder were unknown. We can have cities for the new age that has come, adapted to its better conditions of use and ornament. So great an advantage ought not to be thrown away. We want, therefore, a city planning profession .... [1]

Horace Bushnell
"City Plans," 1864

Introduction: Purpose, Scope, and Organization of the Book

The American professions began to multiply rapidly in the 1860s. The architects formed the American Institute of Architects in 1866. The engineering professions organized in 1871. Seventy-nine societies for professional service were chartered in the 1870s. In the next decade 121 more were established.

1

Another forty-five were added in the 1890s.[2] City planning was not one of these.

The city planning profession came later in this process of institutional development. The emergence of a "special culture," a special knowledge and training for city planning, might be dated as early as 1893 with the opening of the World's Columbian Exposition in Chicago and the model city it presented to the nation. Several significant beginning events coincided in 1909 with the publication of the famous Plan of Chicago, the first university course of instruction in city planning, at Harvard, and the first National Conference on City Planning. With the founding of the American City Planning Institute in 1917 the professional society was finally formed.

This book is an introduction to the history of the city planning profession in the United States, from its roots in the middle of the nineteenth century, through its emergence around the turn of the century, to the present day. Through a collection of papers by various authors, it introduces the reader to some of the important questions of American planning history. Why did city planning develop in the manner it did in the United States? What did it set out to achieve and how have those goals changed? Where did planning thrive and who were its leaders? What have been the most important ideas in planning and what is their relation to the major streams of American thought and social development? What has been the real impact of the planning movement on urban development in the United States? What have planners achieved? No single book could answer all of these questions. What this book provides is a general understanding upon which further study of the extensive literature of planning history, and of the broader field of urban history, can build.

The readings in this collection are divided into three historical periods: an initial period of independent but gradually converging concepts of a planned city; a second period of national organization, experimentation, and development; and a third period of implementation of planning ideas in nearly all levels and areas of urban policymaking. The first part of the book treats the period from 1840 to 1914. It includes four papers that reveal the origins of modern planning in the movements for sanitary reform, civic art and beautification, classical revival in civic design, and neighborhood settlements and housing reform. The second group of papers treats the period from 1914 to 1945. It covers the institutionalization of the profession; the rise of zoning and comprehensive planning; several influential figures of the period, including Robert Moses, Lewis Mumford, and Frank Lloyd Wright; and the new communities program of the New Deal. Also included in this period are the planned community of Radburn and its special influence on the planning movement, an account of the experiments in planning process and method conducted by the National Resource Planning Board, and an assessment of the alternative visions of the future held by planners at the end of World War II.

Part three contains case studies of planning since the war that focus on the role of the planner and the effectiveness of the profession. The first is a study of St. Paul, Minnesota in the 1950s, focusing on a highway location dispute and the planner's relation to the community and the political decision process. The second case reveals the work of planners for the city of San Francisco, California in the 1960s, chronicled by the director of the planning commission. The final study is a retrospective view of a decade of planning in Cleveland, Ohio from 1969 to 1979, assessing the impacts of a highly regarded new model of planning for equity. Each of these scenarios of post-war planning has connections with the field's deeper roots. The book concludes with a bibliography of planning history in the United States selected for further reading and reference.

The Origins of Urban Planning 1840-1914

The patterns of city development in the nineteenth century were overwhelmingly the result of free enterprise. Cities were laid out as often by real estate developers, engineers, surveyors, and even amateurs as government officials. The plan was most often a simple plotting of streets in a gridiron pattern and the subdivision of blocks into lots for sale. This atomistic system of city development was fed by rapidly changing technology and a swelling population, driven by great waves of immigration. The resulting basic and persistent American pattern of urbanization has been likened by William H. Wilson to vast "seas of unplanning." On this map of entrepreneurial activity we see three independent ideas arise and gradually begin to converge toward the concept of city planning. Those ideas are "scientific efficiency," "civic beauty," and "social equity."

Throughout the nineteenth century the railroad gradually tied the cities of the nation into a functional system of rapid transportation. The engineering of water and sanitary sewerage systems similarly came to join the elements of a single city into a centralized system based on two major scientific inventions responsive to the chaotic conditions of the nineteenth century. The first of these was the technical discovery in England in the 1840s that water flowing through a small-diameter pipe could function as the basis of a self-cleansing system of sewage removal that might service an entire city. Connected with the already feasible centralized supply of water, this new device of "water carriage sewerage" completed the urban water delivery-waste collection cycle and provided the technology to transform a city from an unsanitary aggregation of private lots, each with its own well and privy, to an integrated system of water and waste flows at higher (yet more sanitary) densities of development.

The second invention was a planning procedure that entailed the systematic mapping and recording of sanitary conditions on every parcel of land. The sanitary survey was devised to provide planning information for the treatment of cities under siege of epidemic yellow fever. It was among the first efforts to collect detailed data on an entire city for the purpose of formulating and implementing plans for the common good. In this case the common good was the most fundamental of all — human survival.

These new ways of portraying the city, as a system of interdependent parts and as an object of scientific survey, led to a new consciousness of city building, though not immediately to the concept of comprehensive city planning. This new "townsite consciousness" was most fully absorbed into the parks movement and particularly the work of the great landscape architect Frederick Law Olmsted. His work reflected the careful selection of sites and their painstaking development according to principles of good drainage, plentiful sunlight, pure water, clean air, and, of course, pleasing design. Many important contributions were made to the city planning movement by Olmsted, such as Central Park in New York and the suburb of Riverside, Illinois. These early planning concepts, participants, and activities are discussed by Jon A. Peterson in *The Impact of Sanitary Reform upon American Urban Planning, 1840-1890*, chapter 2.

The idea of the "City Beautiful" came on the heels of sanitary reform. It was not a simple social whim for cosmetic veneer, as it is often misrepresented, but a complex set of forces bidding to expand civic consciousness as well as raise standards of public design. There were four major branches of the city beautiful movement, three of which focused on either small public spaces or more comprehensively on medium and smaller sized cities. These were the movements to promote "municipal art," "civic improvements," and "outdoor art." These are treated in chapter 3, *The City Beautiful Movement: Forgotten Origins and Lost Meanings*, also by Jon A. Peterson.

The idea of "municipal art" was to make the cities into patrons of the arts. This involved the promotion of decoration, sculpture, collaborative works for public display, the planting of street trees, the use of color in civic design, and campaigns against billboards and smoke. These causes were backed by municipal art commissions, and often incorporated into broader programs of city beautification and public housekeeping called "civic improvement" that sought to counterbalance the heavy hand of industrialization. Civic improvement societies sprang up in hundreds of small and medium-sized cities, spurred by the influential writings of Charles Mulford Robinson, pioneer planner and planning publicist. Frequently led by women, these local societies formed a national network of civic organizations. Much of the popular national support for the idea of planning, when it emerged as a profession, was to be found in this powerful national movement.

The third branch of the City Beautiful movement, "outdoor art," was led by the American Park and Outdoor Art Association (APOAA) in which Frederick Law Olmsted was a major figure. In 1904 the civic improvement associations merged with the APOAA to form the American Civic Association, bringing into one organizational body programs of land planning that ranged from the promotion of a national park system in the wilderness to an agenda of city parks, planned urban development, better housing, civic art, sanitation, and traffic safety. By 1905 there were 2,426 affiliated civic improvement societies supporting the American planning movement.

THE PLAN OF CHICAGO; PROPOSED CIVIC CENTRE SQUARE, SHOWING THE GROUP OF SURROUNDING BUILDINGS

1.1   Illustration from the *Plan of Chicago,* 1909, p. 117.

The fourth branch of the City Beautiful movement, "classical design," came in its purest form in the attempt by architects to integrate traditional Grecian-Roman architectural themes into monumental city plans. Usage of grand design in the United States already had important precedents, especially in Pierre L'Enfant's spiderweb streetplan for Washington, D.C. in the 1790s. Daniel Burnham of Chicago became the acknowledged leader of this movement a century later, and organizer of the design team for the Chicago Columbian Exposition in 1893. Design themes of grouped public buildings in the neoclassical style, great boulevards, and monuments anchoring grand perspectives were repeated throughout the following two decades, culminating in the 1909 *Plan of Chicago* which is presented in chapter 4, *The Plan of Chicago,* by Robert W. Wrigley, Jr. One can see from his portrayal that the plan was not only a great performance of the artistic process. It was also the beginning, in the promotional work of Walter D. Moody and others who tried to implement the plan, of a movement toward a governmental process that was regional in scope and participatory in style.

Upon these foundations of sanitary reform and civic beauty arose yet a third level of planning culture whose goals were neighborhood building and housing reform. Neighborhood settlement workers and housing reformers brought to the city planning movement humanitarian concerns for children, their schools and playgrounds, their home environments, sound housing, and a spirit of community life. They were devoted to the amelioration of slum tenements and their overcrowded and unsanitary conditions. This third level of planning interests is presented in chapter 5, *Playgrounds, Housing, and City Planning,* by Allen F. Davis.

Housing reform throughout most of the nineteenth century had been a wholly private-sector and largely unsuccessful effort. The problem was very challenging. Philanthropists and other idealists had been attempting to create good housing for the poor as a sound investment of private capital yielding a return. Toward the end of the century these efforts were largely supplanted by the promotion and adoption of various housing laws regulating minimum standards of space, light, air, and plumbing through controls on building design. As Davis suggests, however, many planners and housing reformers saw that these regulatory measures also were inadequate to produce sound housing in sufficient supply. By 1909, when the various strains of planning interest came together in the first National Conference on City Planning, it was clear that more direct governmental intervention would be required.

Thus we see on the 19th century landscape of individualism and industrial enterprise three converging ideas of urban planning: one of sanitation and scientific efficiency, a second of civic beauty and the building arts, and a third of social equity and charity. Enterprise alone bred chaos. Cooperation for efficient development was essential to the survival of city life. The City Beautiful movement implied, however, that even an efficient mode of enterprise was not enough. There were higher values than making money and being connected to the sewer system, valves such as art, community appearance, and nature. Humanitarian concerns for those whom Jacob Riis called, "the other half" completed the tripartite city planning concept.

The Growth of Planning between the Wars

William H. Wilson presents the achievements of planning between the wars as the product of two extremes, the down-to-earth realists and the high-flying idealists. These are his *Moles and Skylarks* of chapter 6. On the front of realism we find the formation of the professional organizations, schools of formal instruction, and the institutionalization of the planning function within local, and later, regional and national government. The tools of practice were developed and refined. Zoning and the master plan contributed to a new version of civic efficiency, aspiring to scientific city building. Wilson shows us, in the figure of Robert Moses of New York, an entrepreneur of the public dollar and builder of a civic empire.

The idealists built a city of utopian concepts and values that left a permanent imprint on the development of planning thought. Lewis Mumford, one of America's most eloquent critics of pragmatism and technology, developed a philosophy of city development for humanistic ends, in association with New York City area architects, housers, planners, and economists. Their collaboration led ultimately to one of the great symbols of the American planning movement — the town of Radburn. On other fronts, idealists such as Frank Lloyd Wright, the architect, and Rexford Tugwell, the economist, challenged America with their ideas of new towns for the prairie and new programs for the rural poor.

The design of Radburn, New Jersey, a "new town for the motor age" as it was called, was a major new synthesis of planning ideas. The historical impact of this phenomenon is analyzed by Eugenie Ladner Birch in chapter 7, *Radburn and the American Planning Movement: The Persistence of an Idea*. Many of the best minds in the field contributed to this plan as a model of urban decentralization, self-containment, environmental sensitivity, common open space, community services, and automotive safety. The integration of all these ideas into one scheme backed by a private investor destined Radburn for historic importance of classic proportions.

From 1933 to 1944 the most significant new dimension of the planning world was embodied in Roosevelt's National Planning Board (successively renamed National Resources Board, National Resources Committee, and National Resources Planning Board). The Board, staffed with city planners from across the nation, undertook several pathfinding programs to advance planning in the United States. One of the most important was a series of experiments in planning process and methods applied to a sample of cities. These experiments are described by Philip J. Funigiello in chapter 8, *City Planning in World War II: The Experience of the National Resources Planning Board*. The emphasis here was not on physical design but rather on a systematic and linked process of study, analysis, and public participation in policymaking. Tests of the process in Corpus Christi, Texas; Tacoma, Washington; Salt Lake City, Utah; and Buffalo, New York, resulted in a variety of successes and failures. Later embodied in a widely utilized handbook, *Action for Cities*, this model of the planning approach has dominated the field.

The war years, 1940-1945, provided a recess in domestic affairs during which choices about the directions of post-war urbanization could be made.

John Bauman delineates the major alternatives in *Visions of a Post-war City: a Perspective on Urban Planning in Philadelphia and the Nation, 1942-45*, chapter 9. As long as the war diverted national resources and energies, the reinvestment needed to improve deteriorating cities would not be available. There were two major visions of how resources ought to be concentrated after the war. One choice was the massive problem of improving the housing of slum dwellers; the other was redeveloping the commercial cores of the cities. Bauman's analysis suggests that the housing reformers became divided over the question of suburban vs. central city housing, and the divided camp was conquered by the downtown renewal interests who captured the central city housers and founded a new school of "urban redevelopment." Urban redevelopment became the urban renewal program. Philadelphia seems to demonstrate this phenomenon almost perfectly.

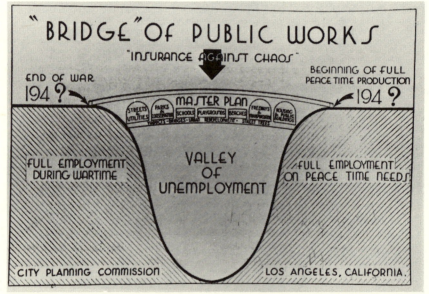

1.2   Illustration of planning for the post-war period. From the *ASPO Newsletter*, Vol. 9, No. 7, July 1943, p. 59.

Bracketed by two world wars and punctuated by the great depression, the period from 1914 to 1945 was in many ways a period of preparation — organizing, training, testing alternatives, and synthesizing differences. It was a period of nationalizing and standardizing the planning movement and many of its inventions: zoning, the master plan, the planning commission, neighborhood design, public housing, the planning process, and state and federal roles. In contrast to the previous period, 1840-1914, the planning profession was now quite visible and its culture was extensive, including a substantial literature, widespread graduate university training, prominent national leaders, and important governmental planning institutions. The American Institute of Planners, the main professional body, was still relatively small, having grown to no more than a few hundred members. But it was destined to mushroom in the next three and one-half decades to over twenty thousand individuals.

Planning since World War II

One of the interesting characteristics of the way in which the planning field has changed over the years is that it has experienced successive additions but virtually no deletions. Many new causes were taken on but few were ever abandoned. There are exceptions, of course. The campaign against the common housefly, dreaded as a carrier of disease, was prominent in the planning agenda of the turn of the century. In its place today are more sophisticated enemies like carcinogenic substances and nuclear wastes. But the point is that nearly all of the interests and activities initiated in earlier periods persisted after the war, as the last three chapters confirm.

The initial impact of post-war suburbanization and urbanization on the planning field was more quantitative than qualitative and stemmed largely from the expanded influence of federally initiated programs. There were four programs of major significance: public housing, urban renewal, home mortgage insurance, and highway building. Public housing had become national policy by 1937 and, though never sufficiently adequate to meet the estimated demand, its trickle of units began to leave a distinct mark on the urban landscape by the late 1950s. Urban renewal began as a federal program in the Housing Act of 1949, aimed at fulfilling those needs for improved housing quality and downtown renewal described by Bauman in chapter 9. The impact of the federal home mortgage insurance programs, initiated in 1934 and administered by the Federal Housing Administration, was no doubt greater than the first two combined, as it facilitated the massive growth of the suburbs around what *Fortune* magazine called "the exploding metropolis."

The fourth great federal force in this era, and probably the greatest of them all, was the Interstate Highway System built by the Highway Act of 1956. Its influence was overpowering because it represented not only its own billions of dollars of capital investment, altering patterns of national accessibility and local land use, but it acted as a catalyst that sped the interaction of the other three big programs in one great concerted metropolitan transformation. Its pathways through cities often displaced the poorer residents by demolishing their housing and thus increasing the need for public housing development. The joint planning of highways and urban renewal projects accelerated both programs and made possible the taking and remaking of ever larger quantities of central city land, as well as providing a private transportation system that supported the insured-mortgage suburbs. They in turn fostered new suburban shopping centers that were less dependent on public transportation systems. By now the syndrome is familiar.

Many planners, of course, facilitated these programs. Others struggled against their manner of application if not their objectives. The greatest and bloodiest of these battlefields was the urban highway. In chapter 10 Alan Altshuler portrays this episode in planning history in his study, *The Intercity Freeway,* in St. Paul, Minnesota. Here we see how the values and methods of the highway engineers and the city planners differed sharply. While the interest of the downtown merchants, the local neighborhoods, and the highway users were often the stakes, it was invariably the engineers who in the end won out. They had the "habit of a study," as Horace Bushnell diagnosed it 100 years earlier, "more stictly linear, more rigidly scientific, and less artistic." As Altshuler concludes, the greatest lesson learned from these decades of battles was that these characteristics added up to political effectiveness.

As the 1960s unfolded, national attention focused on "the urban crisis." Racial and class inequalities were addressed by the civil rights movement, the federal programs for the great society, model cities, and the anti-war movement. The national government formed a new cabinet level Department of Housing and Urban Development in 1965. Hundreds of colleges and universities opened new programs in planning and urban studies. In the midst of this period of activities, experimentation, and an unprecedented level of national interest in cities, Allan Jacobs took on the job of director of planning for the city of San Francisco. He describes his activities in the first year in chapter 11, *Getting Going, Staffing up, and Responding to Issues.* Jacobs's chronicle reflects a new level of technical confidence as well as a new style of political savvy and boldness. The historical roots of the planner's work are still there: zoning cases, development designs, neighborhood planning, long-range plans, and battles with other professionals and civic agencies. But it is clear that Jacobs and his planners had developed a politically effective style, backed by technical skills and clear objectives for which the planners in St. Paul, a decade earlier had still been groping.

Lest this upbeat representation of the role of modern urban planning be attributed to the unique talents of an Allan Jacobs and the romance of San Francisco, we turn in the final chapter to the comparatively grim and difficult circumstances of declining industrial Cleveland, Ohio. Through the eyes of Norman Krumholz, Cleveland's planning director from 1969 to 1979, we see an unusual commitment in action that has captured the imagination of the profession and is a symbol of the reform spirit of planning in our time.

The Cleveland model of the planner is of an activist, an interventionist, and an advocate of public actions that will increase the choices and opportunities of the city's residents. Compared with its suburbs, Cleveland is largely poor,

Black, and failing as an economically viable enterprise. The heroic issues of
this decade turn on financing mass transit, the ownership of public utilities,
and the distribution of the benefits of downtown revitalization. The planners
approached these activities with a clear sense of ethical imperative. They
learned well the lessons of St. Paul — the need for clearly stated normative
standards, a clear understanding of the political decision process, and a
rigorous analytical attack on the problem. We must not lose sight of the fact,
of course, as Krumholz reminds us, that the greater number of issues they
dealt with were more routine, less heroic, and had little or nothing to do
directly with the moral imperatives of their position of advocacy. The keys to

1.3 Citizen involvement in Cleveland — the Buckeye Woodland Community
Congress in 1978 (photo by Susan C. Kaeser).

successful planning are molded in the conclusions of Krumholz's story; that
planning *can* do something about the very core moral problems of our society
— poverty and racial discrimination; that there is more than sufficient
freedom in the system for planners to act in accord with their own vision of a
better society; that the essential step is to define a clear goal and to commit
oneself to it; that success requires hard information, skilled persuasion, and
substantial amounts of time; and, as is also seen in the San Francisco case, that

with leadership and discipline we will never fail to attract bright, hard working young people to carry on this profession. Norman Krumholz's personal reflections and conclusions express, as rigorously and as eloquently as any historian could hope to, the promise of the past: that there will be a future that will be worthwhile if we are committed to making it so.

NOTES

1. Horace Bushnell. 1864. "City Plans." In *Work and Play,* Horace Bushnell, pp. 196-97. London: Alexander Strahan.

2. See John William Ward. 1966. "The Politics of Design." In *Who Designs America?*, ed. Lawrence B. Holland, pp. 68-71. New York: Doubleday and Company.

2

The Impact of Sanitary Reform upon American Urban Planning, 1840-1890

Jon A. Peterson

The changing make-up of the human physical environment represents a significant, if relatively unstudied, aspect of modern social history. Population growth, new technologies, changes in social and economic organization, shifting cultural norms, the expansion of socially instrumental knowledge, and other developments have repeatedly disrupted existing physical arrangements and also necessitated or suggested new configurations. Thus, any society that has experienced the complex transformations that we identify by such terms as modernization, urbanization, and industrialization has inevitably recast not only its social relationships but its material environment as well. For this reason, the human habitat should not be regarded as simply the context of social history. Instead, it should be seen as an integral element of any major social transformation.

The interactions between environmental and social change are complex and varied. This paper explores only one such relationship and views its implications for urban planning, namely, the relationship between the increasingly scientific understanding of infectious disease which made headway in the United States in the middle decades of the nineteenth century and the experience of urbanization, especially the felt sense that rampant city growth had produced socially intolerable conditions. These two currents came together in a broadly focused movement for preventive sanitation, then known as sanitary reform. Together they yielded a virtual city planning agenda for nineteenth-century American cities. Begun fitfully in the 1840s, sanitary reform flourished briefly on the eve of the Civil War. It then regained

From the *Journal of Social History* **13**, 1 (Fall 1979), pp. 83-103. Copyright © 1979 by Peter H. Stearns, editor. Reprinted by permission.

momentum after the conflict, achieving its peak strength in the years around 1880 — only to be undercut by bacteriologically based concepts of public health from the 1890s onward.[1]

Sanitary reform rested squarely upon an empirically grounded explanation of infectious disease, often dubbed the filth theory by medical historians. An elastic conception, it accommodated many varied opinions. Those holding anticontagionist views, for instance, pointed to filth — generally meaning putrefactive odors arising from decomposing organic wastes — as a cause of numerous scourges, among them yellow fever, Asiatic cholera, typhoid, typhus, scarlet fever, and diphtheria. Also suspect, depending upon the disease and the observer, were stagnant water, sodden ground, vitiated air, and the absence of sunlight. Others upheld a contingent contagionist viewpoint, arguing that a contagious agent spread under filth conditions, a compromise opinion that perpetuated concern for crude environmental factors well after the arrival of the germ theory in the United States in the mid-1870s.[2]

The social costs of urbanization to which sanitarians reacted stemmed from the rapid, often chaotic physical growth characteristic of mid-nineteenth century cities. As is well known, American municipalities then exerted few significant controls over their development. Private interests continually reshaped the city, erecting all manners of buildings, introducing drastically innovative modes of communication and transportation, and repeatedly extending suburban limits — virtually unconstrained except by forces registered through the market place. City growth, in short, was a helter-skelter process — haphazard, unregulated, and uncoordinated. Municipal officials commonly reinforced this pattern, ordering streets widened, sewers and water mains laid, and other public works undertaken on a piecemeal basis as need arose.

Witnessing the consequences of such growth for public health, armed with statistics that linked disease and death to unsanitary conditions, and unaware, as yet, of the still-crude nature of their environmental premise, sanitary reformers often demanded a fundamental restructuring of the physical basis of urban life.[3] They did so in an era when neither a city planning profession nor a widely recognized body of city planning doctrine existed in the United States. Thus, to the extent that they advocated systematic, large-scale reshaping of cities, sanitary reformers functioned as city planners. Like their twentieth-century counterparts, they became agents through which an evolving society sought to align its instrumental knowledge and its habitat.[4]

This paper will examine three major ways in which sanitary reform yielded urban planning alternatives to the dominant pattern of piecemeal urban growth. The first was water-carriage sewerage, an English innovation that ultimately restructured the basis of city sanitation in the United States. The second was sanitary survey planning, an elaborate procedure that best exemplifies the potential of sanitary reform as a stimulus to city planning. Finally, there was townsite consciousness, a generally heightened sensitivity to the health implications of a city's site and structure. This outlook became deeply embedded in the public thought of the Gilded Age, strongly influencing the era's most celebrated instances of urban design, notably the public parks and suburbs of Frederick Law Olmsted.[5]

None of these developments should be equated with city planning as conceived and advocated in this century. Rather, they should be viewed as responses to urbanization peculiar to the nineteenth century, responses made possible by the new understanding of environmental health. Nevertheless, the city planning inspired by sanitary reform anticipated certain broad features of twentieth-century practice and also had far-reaching impacts upon urban land use, as will be noted at the close of the paper.

I. Water Carriage Sewerage

Water-carriage sewerage represented a specialized form of urban planning. Introduced in the 1850s, it gradually supplanted long-accepted, piecemeal methods of waste removal, particularly the reliance upon privately built cesspools and privy vaults and the common municipal practice of constructing sewers without reference to a larger, citywide plan. Properly designed, water-carriage sewerage required an integrated system of underground channels fitted to the natural drainage contours of a city. Within this complex, individual sewers had to be sloped to facilitate the gravity flow of waterborne wastes to outfall points located beyond the immediate environment of the urban dweller, and they had to be sized and shaped both to accommodate rainstorms and to encourage dry-weather flow. The engineers who created these elaborate works mastered one of the major planning arts that emerged out of the nineteenth-century reaction to urbanization.

The concept of water-carriage sewerage evolved from the attack by sanitary reformers upon what will here be identified as private-lot waste removal. Under this long-conventional method of city sanitation, nearly all urban households and businesses in American towns and cities discharged their wastes upon the land adjoining their dwellings and shops, principally within the confines of the private lot but also into the streets, especially in areas where little yard space existed. The procedure imposed a heavy sanitary burden upon the immediate habitat of the city dweller. Water spilled from pumps or cisterns muddied the ground, while privy vaults, sometimes lined with brick or stone and called "cispools" and "sinks," functioned as receptacles for excrement. Kitchen slops and wash water from a dwelling or shop either drained into these pits or into the street. Yards and, not infrequently, alleys and streets became holding areas for rubbish and garbage until removed by workmen (often licensed as scavengers) or consumed by pigs, goats, cows, and other domestic animals.[6]

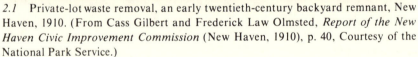

2.1 Private-lot waste removal, an early twentieth-century backyard remnant, New Haven, 1910. (From Cass Gilbert and Frederick Law Olmsted, *Report of the New Haven Civic Improvement Commission* (New Haven, 1910), p. 40, Courtesy of the National Park Service.)

Under private-lot waste removal, house drains and common sewers served a different purpose from that of their counterparts today. Intended strictly as water drains, they prevented the flooding of yards, cellars, and streets from rainstorms or household wash water. Indeed, many large sewers began as bridged-over gullies and brooks. Looking back from the vantage of the post-Civil War era, American engineers often characterized early nineteenth-century sewers as crude, boxlike constructions built variously of wood, stone, or mortarless brick and laid with flat or curved bottoms. As a rule, their builders had made them large enough for a man to enter for cleansing and repair.[7]

In general, these physical arrangements, while nominally regulated by municipal governments, required no centralized planning.[8] As a city grew, each household or business added any privies or cesspools it needed. Whatever drains or sewers were built reflected local circumstances, especially the needs of this or that district, block, or street to rid low areas of stormwater. No one yet perceived the elimination of waste and water as an interlocking problem that might be resolved by large-scale physical planning. Private-lot waste removal, in short, epitomized the piecemeal, decentralized approach to city building characteristic of the nineteeth century.

The failure of private-lot waste removal first became apparent in England, where similar arrangements existed. Because the English response would influence American reactions to comparable predicaments, it deserves special attention. In England during the first half of the nineteenth century, the once-sharp distinction between sewers as surface-water drains and cesspools and privies as waste receptacles broke down with disastrous results. As early as 1815 Parliament revoked its ban against draining excremental wastes into common sewers, and in 1847 it made this practice mandatory.[9] Behind these changes lay the pressures of urbanization. The fast-growing, densely packed towns of England could no longer cope with wastes by confining them to the immediate habitat of the city resident. By officially opening sewers to fecal matter, English authorities acknowledged the necessity of removing human ordure beyond the confines of the household lot. But this expedient only made matters worse; the established channels, built to man-size dimensions and sluggish in their flow, often clogged with fecal debris, to say nothing of animal carcasses, garbage, and other refuse that had never been easily excluded from sewers. English sanitarians of the 1840s denounced the results, condemning sewers as "elongated cesspools." In crowded, impoverished districts, the breakdown of private-lot waste removal easily transcended that epithet. Wastes of all sorts disfigured the cramped housing courts of the workers, accumulated in cellars, collected and pooled in the streets, and choked up ditch-drains.[10]

As early as 1842-1844, Edwin Chadwick, England's brilliant though abrasive champion of sanitary reform, conceived an extraordinary remedy for this situation. From John Roe, an engineer of London's Holborn and Finsbury sewer district, he learned that modest amounts of water when passing rapidly through a small, egg-shaped sewer would free it automatically of solid deposits, including dead cats. Why not, Chadwick asked in effect, remove all rainwater and household wastes by means of self-cleansing, inexpensive, small-pipe sewers? His answer involved nothing less than a vision of the city as a self-flushing mechanism powered by water. If water were delivered continuously to households, then water closets could replace privies; and self-cleansing sewers, powered by the resultant flow, could supplant cesspools. The sewers, if designed as an integrated system that fitted to the terrain, could remove by gravity flow all the household wastes beyond the city limits, where their agricultural use might yield monetary returns (a vain hope). In addition, if the streets were properly paved, sloped, and guttered, rainwater

could wash street debris into the sewers and out of the city.[11] The ruling
principle of this proposal eventually became the immediate removal from the
city of all waste before its decomposition would cause disease.[12]

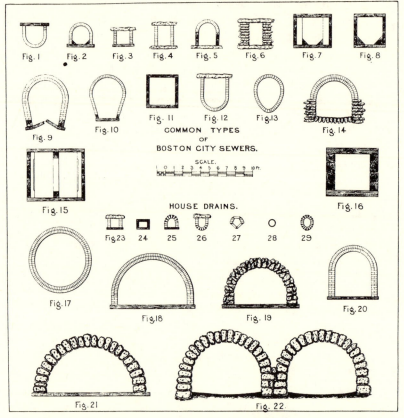

2.2   Cross-section of stone, wood, and brick common-sewers used in nine-
teenth-century Boston, including an egg-shaped sewer (no. 13) inspired by
English sanitary technology. (From Eliot Clarke, *Main Drainage Works of the
City of Boston* (Boston, 1888), opp. p. 20.)

Viewed as a whole, Chadwick's conception entailed the coordinated
reconstruction of urban places on a citywide scale. Abundant water supply,
well-engineered sewers, and carefully designed streetbeds were all involved.
Only once in the United States between 1840 and 1890, in Memphis,
Tennessee, would planning of this complexity be attempted in an established
city. That incident will be reviewed later. Chadwick's sewerage — the central
component of his program — proved far more influential. Chadwick labeled
his pipes the "arterial-venous system;" it was the first version of what came to

be called water-carriage sewerage. Nothing like it then existed in the United States or continental Europe.[13]

Inspired by the English reformers, the pioneer generation of American sanitarians often called attention to the health value of systematic sewerage. John H. Griscom, the New York City physician who began his now-famous battle to reorganize his city's health administration in 1842, was among the first.[14] A great admirer of Chadwick, he noted as early as 1844 that sewerage would be "not only the most economical, but the only mode, in which the immense amounts of filth daily generated in this large city, can be effectively removed." Abroad, he observed, the building of sewers "on the most scientific and substantial plans" had had "decidedly beneficial results upon the general health and comfort."[15] In the dozen years before the Civil War, virtually every major exposition of American sanitary reform echoed Griscom's views.[16]

In the United States the introduction of public water supplies contributed significantly to the breakdowns of private-lot waste removal, giving urgency to the warnings of sanitarians and additional reason for adopting the English innovation.[17] New York City and Boston provide examples. Before the 1840s both cities had relied upon a wide variety of water sources — wells, springs, cisterns, and also water piped from more distant sources by private companies.[18] Then both cities converted to public supplies, experiencing drastically increased per capita water usage as a result. In 1842, New York began drawing water from the Croton River reservoir, forty miles north of the city, and by 1850 its inhabitants were using three times more water than engineers had originally predicted. Boston opened its Cohituate Aqueduct in 1848, and by 1851 Bostonians were consuming over twice as much water as first expected.[19] As early as 1844, Griscom had foreseen the health consequences. Property owners, he then predicted, would convert their rainwater cisterns into cesspools to handle the excess water. The ground would soon collect "an immense mass of offensive material" that would generate "miasmatic effluvia" perilous to health. Subsurface water, augmented by rains, hydrants, and unused wells, would penetrate "many basements and cellars, rendering them very damp and unhealthy."[20]

Such conditions drove New York and Boston to build sewers but not to plan them as integrated systems. Between 1849 and 1865, New York built about 125 miles of lines; while between 1849 and 1873, Boston installed about 100 miles.[21] But none of this construction reflected a unified plan. The New York City government authorized new lines in response to landowners' petitions and political pressures, despite attempts at planning. In Boston a similar process yielded the same outcome: a hodgepodge, additive pattern of growth typical of nineteenth-century city building.[22] George E. Waring, Jr., the flamboyant engineer and publicist of American sanitary reform, later caricatured the results:

The older sewers of New York and Boston . . . have fitly been desribed as being highest at the lower end, lowest in the middle, biggest at the little end, receiving branch sewers from below, and discharging at their tops; elongated cesspools, half filled with reeking filth, peopled with rats, and invaded by every tide; huge gasometers, manufacturing day and night a deadly aeriform poison, ever seeking to invade the houses along their course; reservoirs of liquid filth, ever oozing through the defective joints, and polluting the very earth upon which the city stands.[23]

Waring overstated the chaos, but every fault he ridiculed can be documented.[24]

The first efforts to plan sewers — as distinct from building them piecemeal — resulted directly from the application of the new technology generated by English sanitary reform.[25] Three major attempts to introduce systematic sewerage before the Civil War, in Jersey City, in Chicago, and in Brooklyn —all demonstrate this influence. In each instance the engineers, all novices to the technology, borrowed directly from English experience. For example, as early as 1851 the water commissioners of Jersey City recognized that a public water supply, if developed, would require sewers to remove the water. Failure to build them would not just inconvenience Jersey City but menace its health.[26] Acting on this premise, the commissioners requested their engineer, William S. Whitwell, former chief engineer of the eastern division of the Cochituate Aqueduct, to devise a sewer system. His report of 1853, the first of its kind in the United States, drew explicitly on the major English sanitary investigations of the era: the Health of Towns commission of 1844-45; the Metropolitan Sanitary Commission of 1847; and the reports of the General Board of Health, an administrative body created in response to the 1848 cholera epidemic.[27] In 1855-1859, Jersey City built much of Whitwell's system but not the canal he had recommended for flushing out his shallow-sloped sewers.[28] An unsuccessful venture, its pioneering role has been forgotten.

Chicago also drew heavily upon English experience. There a health crisis prompted action. By 1855, local opinion had concluded that the city's flat, muddy, poorly drained site bore major blame for six successive yearly epidemics, five of cholera and one of dysentery, and for a mortality rate believed to be the highest in the nation.[29] Looking for technical assistance, the newly established Board of Sewerage Commissioners hired Ellis Sylvester Chesbrough, former chief engineer to the western division of the Cochituate Aqueduct, to plan the works. Chesbrough, like Whitwell, drew heavily upon English sanitary reports for technical data, remarking that "most of those published by Parliament were in the Commission's office."[30] After studying Chicago's plight, Chesbrough proposed that the city raise many of her streets above her all-pervasive mud so that her new sewers might have workable gradients. This bold and, eventually, celebrated scheme helped establish Chesbrough's reputation as the nation's preeminent sanitary engineer.

A third major system of sewerage built in the United States, that planned for Brooklyn in 1857-1859, also utilized English sanitary technology. Its designer, Julius W. Adams, had worked on the Cochituate Aqueduct, but his reputation lay in railroad construction and bridge design.[31] After close study of English data, including correspondence with Robert Rawlinson, an English engineer then loyal to Chadwick, Adams opted for a pipe system. But to avoid the polluting of a shallow, tidewater area, he also recommended large, intercepting sewers, a technique borrowed from English critics of Chadwick's pipe who were then urging interceptors as the best way to rid London of the infamous stench of the Thames River.[32]

In the fifteen years following the Civil War — especially the 1870s — the principle of water-carriage sewerage gained a permanent foothold in the United States. In New England, where urbanization had advanced furthest, engineers devised major systems for Providence in 1869, New Haven in 1872, and Boston in 1875. In Massachusetts numerous industrial cities implemented plans in the 1870s — Fall River, Haverhill, Lawrence, Lowell, Pittsfield, Springfield, and Worcester. Many other Massachusetts cities commissioned reports but failed to execute them. Outside of New England other cities considered action — Cincinnati and Indianapolis in 1880, San Francisco in 1876, Washington in 1878, and Baltimore in 1881.[33] All but Washington and Baltimore carried out their plans. Little wonder that Joseph Toner, president of the newly formed American Public Health Association, remarked in 1875 that sewerage, "the great problem in Sanitary Science," had become as fundamental an engineering art in this country as in Europe; and that five years later a prominent Massachusetts engineer observed that "our country-men have seized upon the water-carriage system with great unanimity" — sometimes even adopting it ahead of adequate water supply.[34]

Sanitary engineers, as the designers of sewer systems became known in the decade following the Civil War, presided over one of the most fundamental planning arts introduced in the nineteenth century. But they did not engage in city planning in the twentieth-century sense. Professionally, they advised cities and private clients about whatever "mechanical devices or works" were needed to remove "effete substances" from immediate human surroundings. To them this meant sewerage, house drainage, building ventilation, water closet design, and the like.[35] Sanitary engineers should be seen as civic servants, not municipal technocrats. For example, while they fully understood the connections between water supply, sewers, streetbed design, and house drainage and thus perceived the city as an interrelated mechanism in ways that previous generations had not, they generally devised their sewerage plans well after the installation of water supply, not because they approved the procedure but because that is how most city officials proceeded. Thus as planners, sanitary engineers operated as technical specialists, and their reports

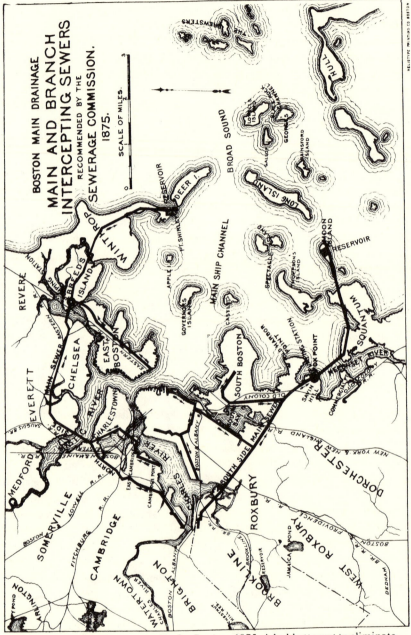

2.3 Metropolitan sewerage plan for Boston, 1875. A bold attempt to eliminate sewage pollution of the tidal flats and estuaries adjacent to central Boston. (From *Main Drainage,* Clarke, *op cit,* opp. p. 24.)

to localities consistently focused upon the precise workings of their proposed schemes, not broad issues of civic layout.[36] Being able, for example, to fit their sewers, catch basins, and manholes to existing streets, they rarely questioned street arrangements; and when they did, they adjusted the grades, not the pattern.[37] Sanitary engineers, in short, did not voice an expansive urban planning vision.

II. Sanitary Survey Planning

While sanitary engineers of the Gilded Age never became general urban planners, public health advocates in another dimension of their work evolved a comprehensive planning procedure which they applied to cities. Here called sanitary survey planning (no contemporary term for it existed), this forgotten technique represents a remarkable achievement unique to the peak years of sanitary reform around 1880. Proceeding from a rigorous application of sanitary principles, it reflected the special nature of the planning impulse within sanitary reform. Fully implemented, it required the study of every street, lot, and building in a city to determine the precise location of any prevalent diseases and all suspect environmental conditions. The composite data then yielded a sanitary portrait that became the basis for a complex remedial program, or plan.

The sanitary survey itself predated its use as a planning tool. The employment of surveys to identify the locus and possible causes of disease went back to the investigations of Edwin Chadwick in England in the 1840s and Louis Rene Villerme in France in the 1820s, among others, and had still deeper roots in the medical topography of the eighteenth century.[38] In the United States John Griscom, Lemuel Shattuck, and the American Medical Association had conducted limited surveys in the 1840s.[39] No one then described them as plans. But the root process of investigating the diseases of a locale and the associated physical conditions and then formulating solutions entailed a rational effort to fit remedies to a specific setting.

The first American survey sufficiently massive to resemble a planning process occurred in New York City in 1864. That year the Citizens' Association, a municipal reform group led by some of the city's wealthiest merchants, sponsored a building-by-building investigation of the entire city by collaborating physicians, engineers, and chemists.[40] Although the inquiry yielded numerous administrative and environmental proposals, another fifteen years passed before sanitarians consciously described this procedure as planning. That happened in Memphis, Tennessee, in 1879. Because this last episode marks the greatest practical advance of sanitary reform in this direction, it merits special attention.

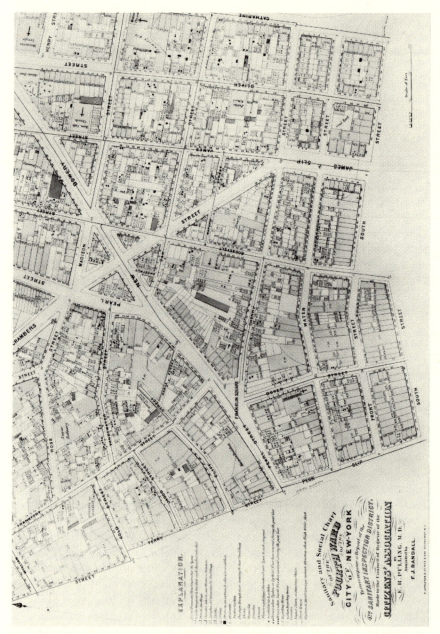

2.4 A sanitary survey map for New York City, 1865, color coded in the original, with black squares indicating "extremely offensive" privies, double stars recording typhus or typhoid fever, and triple stars, smallpox. (From the Museum of the City of New York.)

In the summer of 1878 a devastating yellow fever epidemic swept the lower Mississippi Valley. No place suffered more grievously than Memphis: out of approximately 45,000 people, 5,150 died.[41] The U.S. Congress, reacting to the panic, created in March, 1879, a National Board of Health to regulate quarantines and advise state governments. The following summer yellow fever revisited Memphis, and in October, Tennessee authorities requested the National Board to produce a "plan of future operations" based upon a thorough and complete sanitary survey." "Proper sanitation," they observed, "can only be accomplished through the means of a thoroughly systematized and comprehensive plan."[42]

Rarely has an appeal for planning been so swiftly and so fully answered. The National Board of Health, drawing upon intense discussions of sanitary survey procedures then recently conducted by the American Public Health Association, decided to treat Memphis as a model of the technique.[43] Between November 3, 1879, and January 3, 1880, the Board's investigators conducted an exhaustive, house-to-house survey. Their collected data filled ninety-six folio volumes, and the tabulations presented in four massive books described "every structure and individual lot of ground within the corporate limits." For each ward the investigators recommended specific remedial actions — 12,390 all told, mostly nuisance abatements. Meanwhile three special studies went forward. Major W. H. H. Benyaurd of the United States Engineers examined the scandalously polluted bayou that cut through the heart of Memphis: Dr. Charles Smart, U.S. Army Chemist, tested for water purity throughout the region; and the irrepressible George E. Waring, Jr. designed a sewerage system so novel that it would spark controversy for decades to come.[44]

The major recommendations, issued well before completion of the survey, outlined a sweeping program. There were nine proposals: *(1)* employment of a sanitary officer to superintend all sanitary work, *(2)* systematic ventilation and chilling of all city houses and their furnishings, *(3)* replacement of polluted wells and cisterns with a public water supply, *(4)* condemnation and destruction of numerous buildings ranging from shanties to large central city structures, *(5)* closing of privies and introductions of sewerage, (6) damming of the bayous and the park-development of its shoreline, *(7)* enactment of a sanitary code requiring the lifting of all buildings with floors less than two feet from the ground, *(8)* abatement of all nuisances discovered by the survey and *(9)* the repaving of streets.[45] Here then was a comprehensive reconstruction plan designed to free Memphis from its scourge, a plan surpassing in complexity even the sanitary idea of Chadwick in the 1840s.

How should this remarkable scheme be judged? One standard for evaluation is offered by twentieth-century urban planning with its emphasis upon comprehensiveness — that is, upon attempts to guide the future devlopment of cities by means of multipurpose, citywide, integrated plans.

From this vantage, the Memphis program should not be equated with twentieth-century methods. The sanitary survey was strictly limited to the identification of local disease factors and the formulation of appropriate remedies, and within this context it yielded an integrated, citywide plan with each element harmonized by the then prevailing epidemiology of yellow fever.[46] But from a twentieth-century perspective, such planning looks specialized in purpose, and its goals appear random and skewed. Thus, details such as building ventilation merited as much attention as such fundamental public works as sewerage and water supply. The woodblock paving was condemned as filthy, but the streets were ignored as a circulatory system. The park proposal represented an anti-pollution device more than a public space concept. In short, the comprehensiveness sought pertained to health factors, not to the city's commercial, circulatory, recreational, or domestic requirements.

This comparison highlights the fact that sanitarians had evolved a form of health planning applicable to cities, not a procedure concerned with all the major structural features of urban places in addition to those bearing upon health. The sanitary environment, not the urban environment, represented the root concern; and sanitarians were accordingly as anxious to apply their survey technique to rural areas, to states, and even to the nation as they were to cities.[47] Thus, in their relentless pursuit of disease, sanitary reformers should be seen as health planners by design and as urban planners by historical necessity — namely the fact that nineteenth-century urban populations suffered so often from epidemics attributed to filth conditions.

Nevertheless, the sanitary survey when applied to cities had yielded an extraordinary conception of city planning. Just how far-reaching it was is suggested by a major inquiry into yellow fever in Cuba conducted by the National Board of Health in 1879 and known as the Havana Commission. The filth of the island shocked and repelled the investigators — even the paper currency was "so dirty that it stinks." Powerless to act, the Commission sketched an ideal solution, and for Havana this meant total renovation:

> Pure water must be supplied in unusual abundance to the poor as well as to the rich: the swamps and the lowlands must be drained and raised with rock and earth instead of with garbage; old sewers must be reconstructed and new sewers be constructed to diminish subsoil moisture and subserve all other sanitary purposes which sanitation requires of them: the streets must in large number be widened, regraded, and so paved or repaired that they can be readily kept clean; the houses must be in very large proportion torn down and reconstructed on a different plan; the excavations for privies and for refuse water must be filled up and abandoned and a new system introduced; the stables must be removed, at least from close proximity to sleeping apartments; the harbor and its shore must be cleansed and kept so; and finally, the filthy habits of the common people generally must be reformed . . . .[48]

This drastic program demonstrates that sanitarians had evolved a concept of comprehensively guided environmental reconstruction addressed to the urban predicament as they understood it. But in the Gilded Age, with its inhibitions against strong government intervention, only an acute emergency, such as the Memphis crisis, justified action.

III. Townsite Consciousness

Because sanitary reform proceeded from an environmental premise about the causation of disease rather than from a root interest in the urban setting, its spokesmen never produced a model city concept or theorized much about the overall design of cities.[49] To have done so would have raised issues that would have been irrelevant to sanitary betterment. Questions about traffic circulation and public architecture are examples. But the rigorous search for environmental preventives to ill-health inevitably produced numerous insights into the site arrangements and structure of cities. These attitudes are here called townsite consciousness. Their importance — and indeed the best indication of their reality as a sanitary reform perspective — lies in their profound influence upon the most innovative urban planning undertaken during the generation following the Civil War, notably the landscape work of Frederick Law Olmsted.

Townsite consciousness did not exist as a systematic doctrine. Typically, sanitary reformers displayed their sensitivity to the site and structure of cities through passing observations and tangential remarks. For example, Egbert L. Viele, a sanitary activist and engineering authority on the natural drainage of Manhattan, criticized New York in 1865 for having adopted "the rectangular system of streets and avenues" heedless of the island's "original topography."[50] But Viele offered no further comments upon gridiron street design. His interests centered upon faulty land drainage, a site-related issue much discussed by sanitarians. Road embankments, he noted, too often dammed up water, causing stagnant and pestilent spots all over the island. Elisha Harris, a nationally prominent public health leader, offers another example. In the mid-1870s, he made important townsite observations while comparing the health conditions of several major cities. Brooklyn's "great hygienic advantages" he attributed to its higher elevation than Manhattan, its "greater extent of dwelling area," and the open tree-planted grounds about its buildings.[51] These too were passing remarks.

On the basis of such views the attitudes characteristic of townsite consciousness can be characterized as follows. A city, most sanitarians would have agreed, should be arranged as an airy, verdant setting free from the excessive crowding and physical congestion then common in major urban centers. Its site should be dry and readily drained of stormwater. Parks and trees should be abundant enough to refresh the air. There should be ample opportunities for outdoor exercise. A pure water supply should be available as well as a water-carriage sewer system. Nuisance trades, such as slaughter-houses, should not operate within built-up districts. Sunless, ill-ventilated tenements, dark, moist cellar dwellings, and backyard privies and cesspools should be avoided.[52] In other words, freedom from organic wastes, stagnant water, ground moisture, and human congestion and the presence of abundant clean water, fresh air, and sunlight formed the basis of townsite consciousness.

Many of these ideas became fundamental to the urban planning of Frederick Law Olmsted following the Civil War. A man of many attempted careers — farmer, foreign travel writer, social commentator, publisher, park administrator, U.S. Sanitary Commission director, and mining estate manager — Olmsted concerns us here in his final, most durable role as a landscape architect.[53] In this capacity he recognized the natural landscape not only as an aesthetic and cultural resource but as a sanitary one as well. Much of his thinking pivoted upon this insight.

This fact is clearly demonstrated by the theory of urban progress which Olmsted formulated in 1868-1871 to undergird his thinking about parks, parkways, and suburban neighborhoods. Sharing the common distrust of sanitarians for human crowding, Olmsted judged urban progress since the Middle Ages largely in health terms. The closely-built walled cities of medieval Europe had been sickly places, he argued, their congested conditions reflecting the requirements of military defense. In more recent times, however, "the abandonment of the old-fashioned compact way of building towns, and the gradual adoption of a custom of laying them out with much larger spaces open to the sunlight and fresh air" had yielded greater immunity from "the plague and other forms of pestilence." A major reason for this was that human respiration generated "a certain gas, which, if not dissipated, renders the air of any locality at first debilitating, after a time sickening, and at last deadly." Thus stagnant air and insufficient sunlight and foliage to disinfect it had caused much of the higher mortality of cities in the past and still accounted for variations within many nineteenth-century urban settings — for example, between the "closer built parts" of Brooklyn and those sections with wider streets and numerous gardens.[54]

Olmsted believed that his parks, parkways, and suburban neighborhoods extended the historic trend toward more healthful cities. Immense scenic grounds such as Central Park in New York, Prospect Park in Brooklyn, and Franklin Park in Boston further opened up the city and also offered sufficient trees and space to permit the disinfecting power of sunlight and foliage to modify the city's air.[55] The broad, tree-lined streets that Olmsted designed as access roads and as devices for thrusting park scenery into the city proper also fulfilled sanitary purposes by fixing the basis for residential neighborhoods of unusually "open, elegant, and healthy character."[56] Olmsted also held strong convictions about mental hygiene, another facet of the public health movement. Congestion depleted nervous energies, he repeatedly argued, and he believed strongly that spacious, restful parks and low-density neighborhoods helped counteract this deprivation.[57]

These claims were not idle rationalizations but integral elements of Olmsted's experience and outlook. As a leader of the U.S. Sanitary Commission during the Civil War, as a friend of Elisha Harris and George E. Waring, Jr. — both of whom collaborated with him on various planning projects — Olmsted enthusiastically supported the public health movement. He joined the American Public Association in 1872, the year of its founding, and became chairman of its committee on the "sanitary value and uses of shade trees, parks, and forests."[58] Indeed, Olmsted's interests in sanitation were part of a general outlook common among established "liberal" reformers and intellectuals of his era.[59]

Olmsted's suburban planning also embraced the topographical concerns of sanitarians. Realizing that slapdash development of outlying districts by conventional subdividers often created health hazards — for example, malaria, as a consequence of inadequate drainage — Olmsted emphasized thorough site preparation and design. He fitted roadways to the natural terrain not only with an eye to picturesque effects but with a view to natural drainage contours as well.[60] In the most extraordinary residential plan he ever formulated — now forgotten because it was never implemented — he drew upon the best-available knowledge of land drainage in hopes of freeing Staten Island from malaria and turning it into a suburban paradise.[61] The now-famous plan for Riverside, Illinois, drawn by Olmsted and his partner Calvert Vaux in 1868, included careful provision for water supply and land drainage.[62] In fact, Olmsted believed sanitary matters to be so important that by the late 1880s he regularly advised tract-owner clients to hire a sanitary engineer and insisted that preliminary topographic surveys for suburban sites include data about the characteristics of the soil, the position of swamps, and the location of creeks, brooks, ditches and other water courses.[63] Such information was as vital from a health perspective as it was from the vantage of taste and convenience.

Thus Olmsted integrated into his work the sundry insights of sanitary reform. He did this not because he was a health planner but because he was a broad-minded landscape architect keenly engaged in the public thought of his era. His commitment to urban planning had numerous roots apart from public health, but the townsite consciousness of sanitarians invigorated and gave substance to that commitment, encouraging in this way the emergence of planned development as an alternative to piecemeal urban growth.

Olmsted's parks and suburbs, the survey plans of Memphis, and water-carriage sewerage all exemplify how an urbanizing nation gave rise to environmental planning as a specialized art. In each instance society reacted to its own growth in terms of the socially instrumental knowledge available to it. Neither the experience of urbanization alone nor the knowledge of infectious disease alone yielded the resultant pleas for a reconstructed city. These two factors, along with others continually interacted, the experience justifying the invocation of the new theory of disease and the new etiology shaping both the way in which the experience was judged and the character of the remedies proposed.

Sanitary reform not only generated novel forms of urban planning, it also prefigured the fragmentary quality of much twentieth-century planning in practice. This outcome, it must be stressed, was not what the American city planning profession had hoped to achieve in its formative years during the Progressive Era and up to the 1950s. Throughout that time span, its spokesmen commonly sought to control city growth as a totality. They addressed themselves to all the major physical aspects of a metropolis — its circulatory system, its land uses, its community facilities, its utilities, and its visual amenities — and asked that all relevant proposals be dovetailed into one interlocking program or master plan.[64]

This comprehensive vision never became a reality. Actual authority over environmental change remained the province of numerous specialists who often worked in ignorance of one another — architects, engineers, traffic consultants, landscape designers, housing experts, and many others. In addition, the parcellation of urban political power among rival municipalities and diverse local, state, and federal agencies stymied any broad, integrated conception of planning. Thus, the plans that have palpably altered the metropolis have commonly dealt with its parts, not the whole. Recent examples include programs for urban renewal, belt highways, industrial parks, downtown malls, rapid transit, and even the much-vaunted new towns. All of these undertakings, even when thoroughly planned in themselves, have either treated limited geographic areas or addressed specialized functions within an urban territory. By contrast the numerous master plans that have attempted to shape entire cities and their regions as unified entities, have become notorious among present-day planners as costly, end-state conceptions that have rarely been fulfilled, except, significantly, in fragments.[65] Well-known instances include the regional plan for New York in the late 1920s and the Year 2,000 Plan for Washington, D.C., in the early 1960s.

Sanitary reform foreshadowed this experience. Like the planning profession before World War II, its leaders had harbored an impulse toward sweeping reconstruction and development as seen in the Memphis and Havana proposals. But in terms of actual achievements, sanitary reform had proved far more decisive in promoting sewerage planning, an exacting art entrusted to engineers, and in influencing the ongoing design of other fragments of its cityscape, such as Olmsted's parks and suburbs. Sanitary reform, in short, had anticipated the triumph of specialized, limited-purpose urban planning over a more comprehensive vision.

A final judgment of the impact of sanitary reform upon urban planning cannot stop with the conclusion that it realized its goal on a less than comprehensive basis. After all, most social change in the American past has occurred incrementally. Thus the critical question to answer in closing this inquiry should be: did planned sanitary works, whatever their scale or complexity, have important consequences for the physical city? An answer will be sketched in terms of urban land use, a classic dimension of city planning throughout its history.[66] Significantly, the evidence sustaining this answer also bolsters the viewpoint asserted at the outset of this paper, that environmental change must be viewed as integral to other social transformations now conventionally associated with modern history.

One illustrative but little appreciated impact of sanitary reform upon urban land use can be seen in terms of the amenity value of the residential lot. The substitution of planned sewerage for private-lot waste removal, itself a momentous development, did more than end a health-threatening custom incompatible with new knowledge of infectious diseases. It also freed much household yard space for new social functions, such as family recreation. The now commonplace above-ground swimming tanks found in small backyards throughout many cities symbolize this change. These so-called "pools" preempt the very ground that a mid-nineteenth century family would have allocated, of necessity, to a privy, a cesspool, or a well and thus represent a land use option facilitated by sanitary reform. Such connections between private amenity and sanitary change have not always been after-the-fact developments. For example, many of the civic improvement organizations that gave force to the city beautiful movement at the opening of the twentieth century urged small-lot householders to plant flowers, vines, and grass in their backyards in place of the waste and rubbish then customarily dumped there. This swap of gardenesque beauty for squalor typified the City Beautiful. Improvement enthusiasts often idealized the "spotless town," a utopian image derived from the filth theory of disease.[67] For them, beauty and cleanliness went hand in hand; for us, looking back, the association suggests the subtle ramifications of sanitary reform.

More spectacular impacts upon land use can be demonstrated with respect to public open space in American cities. Certain parks that have become synonymous with their city's identity exist by virtue of attacks on now-forgotten nuisances. Bushnell Park in Hartford, Connecticut, built in the late 1850s, displaced an obnoxious central-city dump, an old railroad depot, an

ancient grist mill, two derelict tanneries, a soap works, and eight or ten "filthy"
tenements and as many pig sties. This redemption had major consequences for
downtown Hartford. Along one park border "costly residences" crowded out
"cheap buildings" and "shanties," while along another edge "fine business
blocks . . . superseded cheaper ones," and within the park the state of
Connecticut erected a new capitol building.[68] In Boston the creation of the
Back Bay Fens produced similar results. Constructed in the early 1880s in
accord with a plan by Frederick Law Olmsted, it redeemed "the foulest marsh
and muddy flats to be found anywhere in Massachusetts."[69] With its
completion "fine residences, churches and institutions" occupied the adjoining
land, "making it in some respects the most attractive section of the city."[70] As
in Hartford, the resolution of an acute nuisance triggered basic changes in
land use.

Sewerage planning and sanitary land reclamation have also had dramatic
although delayed impacts upon urban development, spanning generations. In
Boston, the Charles River Basin, "generally regarded as one of the finest water
parks in the world," resulted as much from the construction of two vast
intercepting sewer systems, one for Boston to the south of the river, the other
for cities lying to the north, as from civic design. These interceptors, conceived
in 1875 and executed at different times over the next quarter century, diverted
raw sewerage that had once befouled the Charles, making feasible both the
damming of that estuary in 1910 to create the Basin and the construction of
the esplanade-lined Boston shore after 1929.[71] In Chicago, the Sanitary and
Ship Canal had similar consequences. Dug in the 1890s after years of talk, it
reversed the flow of Chicago sewage away from Lake Michigan toward the
Mississippi River, thereby enhancing the recreational potential of Chicago's
lakefront and making possible that city's new immense lakeshore park belt, as
realized in this century.[72] Finally, in Washington, D.C., the monumental
landscape of the Mall, a strictly twentieth-century creation, owes its existence
to late-nineteenth-century sanitary action. The channeling of the fetid Tibert
Creek into a trunk sewer in 1872-1873 along what is now the northern
boundary of the Mall (Constitution Avenue) helped to release that area from
its unsavory reputation, and the reclamation of the malarious Potomac Flats
to the west and south of the Washington Monument, begun in 1882, created
the physical setting for the western end of the Mall as we know it.[73] The
Lincoln Memorial, the climax of that scene and probably the most authentic
shrine this nation possesses, stands in what Speaker of the House of
Representatives Joseph Cannon once derided as "that God damned swamp."[74]

Clearly, nuisance abatement, landfill operations, and sewerage facilitated
the reorganization of urban space, accommodating new functions demanded
by an evolving social order. Residential lots were put to new use, constraints
upon urban development were broken, new modes of public recreation were

encouraged, and the very image of the American city was recast, including the capital-city vistas that symbolize American nationhood today. Of course, none of these transformations, whether in Hartford, Boston, Chicago, or Washington or even in one's own backyard, was necessitated by sanitary works per se, but without such undertakings many now prized amenities of urban life would have been physically impossible.

NOTES

The author wishes to thank the Charles Warren Center for Studies in American History for fellowship assistance which supported a portion of the work in this article. The author also wishes to thank the American Philosophical Society and the American Council of Learned Societies for funding the collection of photographs used.

1. For brief overviews of sanitary reform beginning with John Griscom's effort in New York and running through the work of the National Board of Health, 1879-1883, see George Rosen, *A History of Public Health* (New York, 1958), 233-248; and Richard H. Shryock, "The Organizations and Significance of the Public Health Movement in the United States," *Annals of Medical History*, n.s. 1 (1929), 645-653. For a sophisticated account dealing with a pioneering state, see Barbara Gutmann Rosenkrantz, *Public Health and the State: Changing Views in Massachusetts, 1842-1936* (Cambridge, 1972), 1-96.

2. For a discussion of how environmentalist assumptions unified sanitary reformers, see Barbara Gutmann Rosenkrantz, "Cart before Horse: Theory, Practice and Professional Image in American Public Health, 1870-1920," *Journal of History of Medicine and Allied Sciences*, 29 (1974), 58-60.

3. A few historians have recognized the impact of public health ideas upon the large-scale layout of cities. For example, see Michael H. Frisch, *Town into City: Springfield, Massachusetts, and the Meaning of Community, 1840-1880* (Cambridge, 1972), 170-172, 231-237; and Sam Bass Warner, Jr. *The Urban Wilderness: A History of the American City* (New York, 1972), 198-207.

4. Most American urban planning before the twentieth century addressed townsite design, i.e., the layout of the towns and cities on previously unsettled or sparsely occupied lands. Because such planning commonly relied upon elemental gridiron plats, it rarely required the services of more than conventional surveyors. For a history emphasizing townsite design, see John Reps, *The Making of Urban America: A History of City Planning in the United States* (Princeton, 1965). For the emergence of the twentieth-century idea of planning as the expert formulation of a unified multipurpose program for shaping the physical development of already established cities, see Jon A. Peterson, "The Origins of the Comprehensive City Planning Ideal in the United States" (Ph.D. diss., Harvard University, 1967). For the evolution of the planning profession in this century, see Mel Scott, *American City Planning Since 1890* (Berkeley, 1969).

5. Another consequence was interest in tenement housing. Detailed discussion of this subject is omitted because sanitarians focused most of their attention upon the physical condition and arrangement of the dwelling and its lot, not upon the larger design of working-class neighborhoods or districts. Their broadest idea, that of tenement house regulation, has been discussed by Roy Lubove. *The Progressives and the Slums: Tenement House Reform in New York City, 1890-1917* (New York, 1962), 1-48. Detailed discussion of public water supply planning has been omitted because that concept predated sanitary reform. See Nelson Manfred Blake, *Water for Cities: A History of the Urban Water Supply Problem in the United States* (Syracuse, 1956).

6. Neither urban nor public health historians have focused upon the private lot in the sanitary arrangement of cities. Its waste removal function may be glimpsed in John B. Blake, *Public Health in the Town of Boston, 1630-1822* (Cambridge, 1959), 165-170, 207-212; Sidney I. Pomerantz, *New York: An American City, 1783-1803* (New York, 1938), 269-277; and Williams Travis Howard, Jr., *Public Health Administration and the Natural History of Disease in Baltimore, Maryland* (Washington, 1924), 142-144. For use of the terms "cispool" and "sink," see John H. Griscom, *The Sanitary Condition of the Laboring Population of New York* (New York, 1845), 48-52.

7. For the early history of sewers in America, see Carl Bridenbaugh, *Cities in the Wilderness: Urban Life in America, 1625-1742* (New York, 1938),159-161,318-319; idem., *Cities in Revolt: Urban Life in America, 1743-1776* (New York, 1955), 28-30, 237-241: and Leonard Metcalf and Harrison P. Eddy, *American Sewerage Practice* (New York, 1914), 1:14-20. For historical comments by engineers who witnessed the beginnings of water-carriage sewerage, see Edward S. Philbrick, *American Sanitary Engineering* (New York, 1881), 53: J. Herbert Shedd, "Report on Sewerage in the City of Providence," City Doc. No. 56 (Providence 1874) 21-27; and James P. Kirkwood, "Sewerage Works," The Board of Water Commissioners, *The Brooklyn Water Works and Sewers: A Descriptive Memoir* (New York, 1878), 72-73.

8. For characteristic regulations, see Howard, *Public Health Administration,* 66-67.

9. Philbrick, Sanitary Engineering, 53. For English sewerage, see *First Report of the Commission Inquiring into Health of Large Towns* (London, 1844). I:xii-xv; Metcalf and Eddy. *American Sewerage*, 1:3-9.

10. These conditions are documented by Edwin Chadwick. *Report from the Poor Law Commissioners on an Inquiry into the Sanitary Condition of the Labouring Population of Great Britain* (London, 1842), 26-28, 30-31, 38-39, 44-46.

11. *Ibid.,* 36-37, 48-63, 373-379; S.E. Finer, *The Life and Times of Sir Edwin Chadwick* (London, 1952), 220-224, 236; R.A. Lewis, Edwin Chadwick and the Public Health Movement, 1832-1854 (London, 1952), 53-55.

12. Kirkwood, "Sewerage Works," 74.

13. E.S. Chesbrough, *Report of the Results of Examinations Made in Relation to Sewerage in Several European Cities, in the Winter of 1856-1857* (Chicago, 1858). Significantly, the only European city that became an exception before the mid-1860s was Hamburg. In 1842 William Lindley, an English engineer, designed a water-carriage system directly based upon Chadwick's principles — the first such system in modern time. See Ibid. 29-33; and Lewis, Edwin Chadwick, 61. The famous sewers of Paris did not remove fecal matter. See Metcalf and Eddy. *American Sewerage,* l:10-14; and Shedd, "Report on Sewerage," 12.

14. Duncan R. Jamieson, "Towards a Cleaner New York: John H. Griscom and New York's Public Health, 1830-1870" (Ph.D. diss., Michigan State University, 1971), 2-3.

15. Griscom, *Sanitary Conditions,* 52. Since Chadwick's pipe system was not carried out in England until after 1848, Griscom may have known of Lindley's Hamburg scheme (see note 12) or he may have had rough impressions of the Parisian sewers. For the English situation, see Finer, *Sir Edwin Chadwick,* 442-452.

16. "First Report of the Committee on Public Hygiene of the American Medical Association," *Transactions of the American Medical Association,* 2 (1849), 432-433; [Lemuel Shattuck] *Report of a General Plan for the Promotion of Public and Personal Health* (Boston, 1850), 160; Association for Improving the Condition of the Poor. *Fourteenth Annual Report* (New York, 1857), 25-26, 37: John Bell, "Report on the Importance and Economy of Sanitary Measures to Cities," *Proceedings and Debates of the Third National Quarantine and Sanitary Convention* (New York, 1859), 478-479; and Egbert I. Viele, "Report on Civic Cleanliness and the Economical Disposition of the Refuse of Cities," *Proceedings and Debates of the National Quarantine and Sanitary Convention* (Boston, 1860), 253.

17. Joel A.Tarr and Francis Clay McMichael, *Decisions about Wastewater Technology, 1800-1932*. American Society of Civil Engineers, Reprint 2792 for ASCE Convention, September 27-Oct. 1, 1976, 5-8. See also George E. Waring, Jr., *The Sanitary Drainage of Houses and Towns* (New York, 1876), 107-114.

18. Charles Weidner, *Water for a City: A History of New York City's Problem from the Beginning to the Delaware River System* (New Brunswick, 1974), 14-23; Blake, *Public Health in the Town of Boston*, 156-157. See also Blake, *Water for Cities.*

19. New York: from a projected use of 26.4 U.S. gallons daily per capita to an actual use of 78 gallons by 1850. Weidner, *Water for a City*, 48, 56. Boston: from about 30 gallons to about 66 by 1851. Blake, *Water for Cities*, 237; William J. McAlpine, *Report Made to the Water Committee of the City of Brooklyn* (Brooklyn 1852), 25.

20. Griscom, *Sanitary Conditions*, 52.

21. Boston in 1849 had 25 miles of sewers and in 1873, 125 miles. See "First Report of the Committee on Public Hygiene," 433; and Eliot C. Clarke, *Main Drainage Works of the City of Boston* (Boston, 1885), 11. New York had about 69 miles in 1849 and in 1865, about 194 miles. See George E. Waring, Jr., *Report on the Social Statistics of the Cities* (1886; reprinted, New York, 1970), 2:570-571.

22. For New York, see *ibid.* 2:571; and John Duffy, *A History of Public Health in New York City, 1625-1886* (New York, 1968), 405-418. For Boston, see Clarke, *Main Drainage,* 14-15.

23. George E. Waring, Jr., "House Drainage and Sewerage," *Philadelphia Social Science Association* (Philadelphia, 1878), 11. For biographical information about Waring, see James H. Cassedy, "The Flamboyant Colonel Waring," *Bulletin of the History of Medicine*, 36 (1962), 163-176; and Martin V. Melosi. *Pragmatic Environmentalist: Sanitary Engineer, George E. Waring, Jr.*, Public Works Historical Society. Essay No. 4 (Washington 1977).

24. Many of these failings are reviewed by Metcalf and Eddy, *American Sewerage*, 1:16-19. See also the reported comments of Edward S. Philbrick in "Report of the Eleventh Annual Convention of the American Institute of Architects," *The American Architect and Building News* 3 (1878), 51.

25. Joel A. Tarr and Francis Clay McMichael have recently criticized the "conventional explanation" for the adoption of water-carriage sewerage as overemphasizing public health. They argue that the introduction of a prior technology, namely abundant water supply, should be seen as far more crucial. It caused the breakdown of the old cesspool and privy vault arrangements and produced consequences that only sewers could remedy. See Tarr and McMichael. *Decisions about Wastewater*, 3. Tarr and McMichael's criticism, however, establishes a false dichotomy between their viewpoint and the "public health" interpretation by reducing the latter to a crisis hypothesis, namely an argument that yellow fever and cholera epidemics caused cities to adopt sewerage. Still more recently, Tarr and McMichael have reformulated their argument, still minimizing public health but discussing it more realistically as a more pervasive concern, not simply as a crisis consideration. See Joel A. Tarr and Francis Clay McMichael, *Retrospective Assessment of Wastewater Technology in the United States: 1800-1972* (Pittsburgh, October, 1977), Chp. 1, 6-15. In truth few public health historians have written in any detail about the introduction of water-carriage sewerage in the United States. One who has, Duffy, *Public Health in New York City*, 405-408, acknowledges the importance of waste supply. This paper assumes that public health concerns and efforts to cope with abundant water were inextricably related and that neither consideration alone adequately explains the adoption of water-carriage sewerage. This paper does assert, however, that health considerations play a dominant role in certain phases of this development, notably in originating the concept of water-carriage sewerage in identifying many of the ill consequences of increased water usage as sanitary ones, and in emphasizing the value of planned as opposed to piecemeal sewerage in identifying many of the ill consequences of increased water usage as sanitary ones, and in emphasizing the value of planned as opposed to piecemeal sewerage.

26. Jersey City, Board of Water Commissioners, *Acts of the Legislature in Reference to Water Supply and Sewerage and Reports of the Water Commissioners* (Jersey City, 1864), 67-70.

27. *Ibid.*, 47, 123, 150: William S. Whitwell, *Report made to the Water Commissioner of Jersey City, April 11, 1853, upon a Plan of Sewerage* (New York, 1853), 5. Whitwell favored the small-pipe sewers advocated by Chadwick.

28. Jersey City, Board of Water Commissioners, "Eleventh and Tenth Annual Reports," in *Acts of the Legislature in Reference to Water Supply*, 11-20.

29. John Rauch. "The Sanitary Problems of Chicago, Past and Present," American Public Health Association. *Public Health Reports and Papers*, 4 (1877-1878), 10. Hereinafter cited as APHA, *Reports and Papers*.

30. Board of Sewerage Commissioners. *Report and Plan of Sewerage for the City of Chicago, Illinois* (Chicago, 1855), 9. For biographical data on Chesbrough and a history of his plan, see Louis P. Cain. "Raising and Watering a City: Ellis Sylvester Chesbrough and Chicago's First Sanitation," *Technology and Culture*, 13 (1972), 353-365.

31. For biographical data, see *The National Cyclopedia of American Biography* (New York, 1907), 9:33; and Henry R. Stiles, ed. *The Civil, Political, Professional, and Ecclesiastical History and Commercial and Industrial Record of the County of Kings and the City of Brooklyn, New York* (New York, 1884), 1325-1326.

32. For Brooklyn sewers, see Kirkwood, "Sewerage Works," 71-73: Julius W. Adams, *Report of the Engineers to the Commissioners of Drainage of Wards First, Third, and Sixth*, Sept. 10, 1857 (Brooklyn, 1857): Julius W. Adams. *Report of the Engineer to the Commissioners of Sewerage of the City of Brooklyn, upon the General Drainage of the City* (Brooklyn, 1859); and Waring, *Social Statistics of Cities* 1:476-479.

33. These dates are taken from sewerage reports of the era. Collections of such reports exist at the Massachusetts Institute of Technology and the New York Public Library. For a thorough list of early reports, see Rudolph Hering, "Catalogue of Publications Relating to Sewerage" in "Report of the Results of an Examination Made in 1880 of Several Sewerage Works in Europe," National Board of Health, *Annual Report, 1881* (Washington, 1882), 200-212. See also the descriptions of "drainage" for particular cities. Warings. *Social Statistics of Cities*, vols. 1,2.

34. Joseph M. Toner, "A View of Some of the Leading Public Health Questions in the United States," *APHA, Reports and Papers* 2 (1874-1875). 40: Philbrick, *Sanitary Engineering* 72.

35. For this definition and topical coverage, see *ibid.* 1. passim.

36. For representative sewerage-plan reports, see Shedd. "Report on Sewerage," and David W. Cunningham, *Report of the Engineer to the Committee on Sewers and Drains of the City of Lowell on a General System of Sewerage, 1873* (Lowell, 1874). For an interpretation of engineers as municipal technocrats, see Stanley K. Schultz and Clay McShane, "To Engineer the Metropolis: Sewers, Sanitation, and City Planning in Late Nineteenth-Century America." *The Journal of American History*, 55 (1978), 389-411.

37. Chicago's extensive street raising, required by Chesbrough's plan of 1855, is the best known instance of grade changing. Less spectacular, small-area adjustments were not rare. By contrast engineers almost never required new street alignments. For an unusual exception, see William P. Humpreys. *Report on a System of Sewerage for the City of San Francisco* (San Francisco, 1876), 17.

38. Rosen, *History of Public Health*, 176-280.

39. Wilson G. Smillie, *Public Health, Its Promise for the Future: A Chronicle of the Development of Public Health in the United States, 1607-1914* (New York, 1955), 228-232.

40. Rosen. *History of Public Health*, 243-245; Report of the Council of Hygiene and Public Health of the Citizens' Association of New York, upon the Sanitary Conditions of the City (New York, 1866).

41. Gerald M. Capers, *The Biography of a River Town: Memphis, Its Heroic Age* (Chapel Hill, 1939), 195, 198.

42. "Report on Sanitary Survey of Memphis, Tennessee," National Board of Health, *Annual Report, 1879* (Washington, 1879), 237.

43. For the discussion of surveys by the American Public Health Association, see John S. Billings. "Report of Committee on the Plan for a Systematic Survey of the United States: with Remarks on Medical Topography," APHA. *Reports and Papers* 2 (1874-1875), 41-46; and Elisha Harris, "Report on the Preparation of a Plan for a Sanitary Survey of the United States," *ibid.* 3 (1875-1876), 106-108.

44. For the beginning date of the survey, see letter from F.W. Reilly, Memphis, Dec., 1879 to R.W. Mitchell. National Archives: National Board of Health, State Reports—Tennessee. Item 3875. For description, see "Sanitary Survey of Memphis," 245.

45. *Ibid.*, 239-240.

46. The Council of Hygiene of the Citizens' Association of New York stated this pattern of thought concisely, "Sanitary science . . . takes cognizance of disease, mortality, all dangers to health; and its inquiries as well as its applications descend directly to causes. From investigation of causes it brings forth remedial suggestions and projects sanitary works." *Report of the Council of Hygiene*, civ. Italics in original.

47. Elisha Harris, "Report on a Sanitary Survey of the United States," APHA. *Reports and Papers*, 4 (1877-1878), 27-30.

48. S.E. Chaille and G.M. Sternberg, "Preliminary Report of the Havana Yellow Fever Commission of the National Board of Health." National Board of Health. *Annual Report, 1879* (Washington, 1879), 45-54. 49. Before the 1980s American Sanitary reformers never produced an analog to the utopian city of health imagined by the English sanitarian, Benjamin Ward Richardson. See James H. Cassedy, "Hygeia: A Mid-Victorian Dream of a City of Health." *Journal of the History of Medicine and Allied Sciences* 17 (1962), 217-228. A few sanitarians argued that state boards of health should make the layout of new towns a public health concern, but this viewpoint was only rarely expressed. For examples, see [Shattuck], *Report of a General Plan*. 153-162; Benjamin Lee, "A Plea for a State Board of Health." *Philadelphia Social Science Association* (Philadelphia, 1878). 11.

50. Egbert I. Viele, *The Topography and Hydrology of New York* (New York, 1865), 6.

51. Elisha Harris, "Observations on the Sanitary Condition and Public Health-Care of the Principal Cities in the United States." APHA. *Reports and Papers* 2 (1874-1875). 166.

52. For the importance of airy settings, see [John H. Griscom], *The Uses and Abuses of Air: Showing its Influence in Sustaining Life and Producing Disease: with Remarks on the Ventilation of Housing* (New York, 1848). For reactions to crowding and physical congestion, see Association for Improving the Condition of the Poor. *Fourteenth Annual Report*, 27, 40, 44. For the sanitary value of trees and parks and the importance of outdoor exercise, see John Rauch, *Public Parks: Their Effects upon the Moral, Physical, and Sanitary Condition of the Inhabitants of Large Cities* (Chicago, 1869), 32-50, 80-84. For discussion of slaughterhouses, see Gustavus Devron, "Abattoirs." APHA. *Reports and Papers*, VI (1880), 217-224. For housing, see Lubove, *Progressives and the Slums*, 1-48.

53. The basic biography of Olmsted is Laura Wood Roper, *FLO: A Biography of Frederick Law Olmsted* (Baltimore, 1973).

54. For quoted remarks, see Frederick Law Olmsted and Calvert Vaux, "Report of the Landscape Architects and Superintendent to the President of the Board of Commissioners of Prospect Park. Brooklyn (1868)," in Albert Fein, ed., *Landscape into Cityscape: Frederick Law Olmsted's Plan for a Greater New York* (Ithaca, 1967), 147-148. For his theory of progress, see *ibid.*, 135-149; and Frederick Law Olmsted et al. "Report to the Staten Island Improvement Commission of a Preliminary Scheme of Improvements (1871)," in *ibid.*, 181-184.

55. Frederick Law Olmsted. *Public Parks and the Enlargement of Towns* (1880; reprinted ed., New York, 1970), 15.

56. Olmsted and Vaux. "Report of the Landscape Architects (1868)," 160. For Olmsted's belief in the health-value of low density suburbs, see especially Olmsted, Vaux & Co., *Preliminary Report upon the Proposed Suburban Village at Riverside, Near Chicago* (New York, 1868), 6.

57. Olmsted, *Public Parks*, 9-25.

58. Stephen Smith, "Historical Sketch of the American Public Health Association," APHA. *Reports and Papers*, 5 (1878-1879), xv; "List of Members of the Associations," *ibid.*, 252.

59. Peterson, "Origins of the Comprehensive City Planning Ideal," 34-38.

60. *Prospectus of the New Suburban District of Tarrytown Heights with Plan and Report of Messrs. Olmsted, Vaux & Co., Landscape Architects* (New York, 1872), 19.

61. Olmsted, et. al., "Reports to the Staten Island Improvement Commission (1871)."

62. Victoria Post Ranney, *Olmsted in Chicago* (Chicago, 1972), 13.

63. Letter from F.L.O. & Co., May 31, 1892 to J.J. Albright (President, Deprew Land Co., Buffalo, New York), Library of Congress: Olmsted Papers, Box 36.

64. For the roots of this conception, see Peterson, "Origins of the Comprehensive City Planning Ideal."

65. Richard S. Bolan. "Emerging Views of Planning." *Journal of the American Institute of Planners*, 33 (1967), 234. Melville C. Branch, "Critical Unresolved Problems of Urban Planning Analysis," *Journal of the American Institute of Planners*, 44 (1978), 58.

66. Another approach might discuss the impact of sanitary reform upon health. Recently, for example, Edward Meeker has argued that "the advent of the public health movement led to a reduction in the incidence of several infectious diseases in cities." Edward Meeker. "The Improving Public Health of the United States, 1850-1915." *Explorations in Economic History*, 9 (1972), 372. This may be true but not for the reasons Meeker offers. Meeker argues that public health improved rapidly beginning in the 1880s, and he attributes much of this gain to the introduction of sewerage and water filtration. *Ibid.*, 354-369; and Edward Meeker, "The Social Rate of Return on Investment in Public Health, 1880-1910," *The Journal of Economic History*, 34 (1974), 392, 394. This explanation is dubious for the 1880s and most of the 1890s. In those years many new sewer systems disseminated typhoid fever by polluting the water supply of downstream or lakeside communities. Water filtration, itself a remedy for this predicament, did not win widespread municipal acceptance until after 1897. Tarr and McMichael, *Retrospective Assessment of Wastewater Technology*, Chp. IV, 5-6, 9-10. That other causes were at work can be proven for Baltimore; between 1880 and 1910 that city's crude death rate from infectious diseases fell rapidly as Meeker demonstrates in "Improving Public Health," Table 4, 364, but not until 1911-1915 did Baltimoreans enjoy the benefits of sanitary sewerage or water filtration. Howard, *Public Health Administration*, 121, 132. In general, most gains in public health followed the era of sanitary reform (1840-1890), but those achieved in the 1880s occurred before bacteriologically based preventive measures became widespread and probably resulted from the earlier movement.

67. For the connections between beauty and cleanliness in the City Beautiful movement, see Jon A. Peterson, "The City Beautiful Movement: Forgotten Origins and Lost Meanings," *Journal of Urban History*, 2 (1976), 420-425. For references to backyard efforts, see Jessie M. Good, *The Work of Civic Improvement* (Springfield, 1900), 8, 14; and Dorothy N. Law, "Woman's Work for Civic Beauty," *Home and Flowers*, 11 (1902), 5-7. For the "spotless town" image, see Charles Mulford Robinson, "The Plan of the Model City," *The Criterion*, 2 (1902), 37: for its linkage to the filth theory, see Charles V. Chapin, "Dirt, Disease, and the Health Officer," APHA, *Reports and Papers*, 27 (1902), 296-299.

68. "Bushnell Park, Hartford — Its History," Public Park Association of Providence, *Parks of Providence*, 8 (1889), 17-22.

69. E.W. Howe, quoted in Walter Muir Whitehill. *Boston*: A Topographical History (Boston, 1963), 180.

70. Frederic H. Fay, "The Planning of a City," Boston Tercentenary Committee. *Fifty Years of Boston: A Memorial Volume* (Boston, 1932), 56. For the Fens development, see Roper, *FLO*,

385-386. The best account of Back Bay planning is Bainbridge Bunting, *Houses of Boston's Back Bay* (Cambridge, 1967), 361-399.

71. For the quotation, see Charles W. Eliot, 2d. "The Boston Park System," Boston Tercentenary Committee. *Fifty Years*, 671. For a brief account of the sewer projects, see Charles M. Spofford, "Engineers and Engineering in Boston," *ibid.*, 441. For a full history of the southern system, see Clarke, *Main Drainage*. The connections between the intercepting sewers and the Charles River Basin are noted by Eugene C. Hultman, The Charles River Basin," The Bostonian Society, *Proceedings* (Boston, 1940), 48.

72. For a history of the sanitary canal, see James C. O'Connell, *Chicago's Quest for Pure Water*, Public Works Historical Society, Essay No. 1 (Washington, 1976). For the connections between the canal and lakeshore cleanliness and recreation, see Carl Condit. *Chicago, 1910-1929: Building, Planning, and Urban Technology* (Chicago, 1973), 18.

73. For the filling of Tiber Creek, also known as the Washington Canal, see William M. Maury. *Alexander "Boss" Shepherd and the Board of Public Works*, G.W. Washington Studies No. 3 (Washington, 1975), 30-32. For the sanitary reclamation of Potomac Flats, see Constance McLaughlin Green, *Washington: Capital City, 1879-1950* (Princeton, 1963), 18, 20-21.

74. Joseph Cannon, quoted in John W. Reps. *Monumental Washington: The Planning and Development of the Capital Center* (Princeton, 1967), 158. Reps describes the origins and development of the Mall in detail.

3

The City Beautiful Movement

Forgotten Origins and Lost Meanings

Jon A. Peterson

Historians have paid little attention to the quest for the City Beautiful at the opening of the twentieth century. The subject has mainly attracted commentators upon urban and architectural design who have emphasized two themes, the City Beautiful's devotion to classic-renaissance taste in the building arts — the Boston and New York Public Libraries are noted examples — and its commitment to monumental city planning. The McMillan Plan for Washington, D.C., issued in 1902, epitomizes the latter. An updated version of the then neglected L'Enfant layout, the McMillan Plan made possible the Washington so familiar to tourists today — the vast, tree-lined Mall; the Lincoln and Jefferson Memorials, each terminating grand vistas; and the cluster of classic-style buildings near the U.S. Capitol. The ascendancy of this pattern of taste, observers have repeatedly asserted, derived largely from the Chicago World's Fair of 1893, the famous White City. That spectacle with its great water basin framed by white palaces reminiscent of ancient Rome and renaissance Italy dazzled the multitudes, stamped the new style upon the nation and unveiled the virtues of large-scale civic design.[1]

This paper seeks to open fresh perspectives upon the City Beautiful. That it embraced classic-renaissance architecture and monumental planning is not questioned. What is claimed is that the City Beautiful had other meanings and

Reprinted from Jon A. Peterson, "The City Beautiful Movement: Forgotten Origins and Lost Meanings. "*Journal of Urban History,* Vol. 2, No. 4. pp. 415-434. © 1976 Sage Publications, Inc., with permission.

origins and that their recovery enables us to recognize the phenomenon as a complex cultural movement involving more than the building arts and urban design. Three concepts are essential to this reconstruction: municipal art, civic improvement, and outdoor art. Each played a vital, if now forgotten, role in launching the movement; each had distinct historical roots predating the Chicago World's Fair; and each began with different constituencies.

The origins and nature of these three causes, their fusion into a movement, and the special flavor they imparted to that outcome represents the main concerns of this inquiry. The formative years of the City Beautiful were 1897 to 1902. In this period the three causes developed national expression. Their leaders recognized each other's common interest in civic beauty, joined forces at major conferences, and blended their once distinct goals. By 1902 local campaigns seemingly mushroomed across the nation—in small towns, medium-sized cities, and metropolitan centers; in the Northeast, Midwest, South, and Far West—and a nationally coordinated promotional strategy crystallized. Pursuit of monumental city plans, though advocated by some architects, did not characterize these years. The local groups that gave the new movement so much of its force commonly pursued piecemeal programs, sometimes favoring big projects but often stressing small, feasible goals.

Municipal art began in New York City in the 1890s. Only recently recognized as a root of the City Beautiful, it included meanings not commonly associated with that slogan, notably a zeal for decorative art and an advocacy of small-scale adornment.[2] Decorative art referred to artistic works, especially sculpture, murals, and stained glass, designed to complement the forecourts, facades, and the public interiors of major buildings. All this required close cooperation between architect, sculptor, and painter and was often known as collaborative or allied art. H. H. Richardson of Boston, the most innovative architect of the Gilded Age, pioneered the concept in the early 1870s and through his famous Trinity Church project instilled the goal in three influential New Yorkers, architects Stanford White and Charles McKim and sculptor Augustus Saint-Gaudens.[3] From 1886 onward the Architectural League of New York, itself constituted as a body of allied artists, staged annual exhibits featuring decorative work.[4] In 1887 McKim advanced the cause dramatically by insisting that murals and sculpture adorn the public library he would design for Boston.[5]

The Chicago World's Fair clearly did not initiate American artists to decorative art, but it gave such work unprecedented recognition. The terraces, rostral columns, and fountain basin of the Court of Honor bristled with sculpture while frescoes enlivened the entryways to the exhibition halls. This lavish fulfillment of what Richardson had begun, albeit in a wholly different setting, lay behind the creation of the Municipal Art Society of New York in March 1893, on the eve of the Fair's opening. Richard M. Hunt, dean of the

American architectural profession, builder to the Vanderbilts, and designer of the central edifice of the White City, oversaw the founding. He and the artists who joined him, many just back from Chicago, defined their goal as providing "adequate sculptural and pictorial decorations for the public buildings and parks in the city of New York."[6] They sought, in short, to municipalize decorative art, to convert city government to art patronage.

No one then labeled this aspiration the City Beautiful nor did the Municipal Art Society contemplate city plans. In fact, their modest goals faltered amid the severe mid-1890s depression. Anticipating 2,000 members, the Society claimed only 350 five years later. Announcing it would stage annual contests for decorative works and donate the winning design to the city, it held only one with its own funds, in 1894, for a set of courtroom murals. The organization apparently lacked the resources its original goals required.[7] Elsewhere, its example inspired only one similar society begun in Cincinnati in 1894.[8]

By 1897 as the depression lifted, the New York art establishment—the most sizable in the world this side of Paris and the most influential in the United States—gave every sign of heightened collective confidence, increased assertiveness, and intensified interest in municipal art. In 1893 and 1895 sculptors and then mural painters created national societies based in the city. Each kept a weather eye open for decorative art opportunities. In 1895 the major art societies formed the Fine Arts Federation to secure united action on common issues and loudly protested an official site choice for a major patriotic monument and agitated successfully to include in the new charter for the Greater City of New York a municipal art commission to oversee art acquisitions by the city.[9]

Furthermore, architects in New York and elsewhere during the depression had dreamed of large-scale civic embellishments, though not comprehensive city planning. Design contests among architectural clubs in various cities reflected this new aspiration: in Boston, a competition for the design of Copley Square; in Cleveland, for a public building group; in New York City, for a plaza entry to a terminal passenger station. The Chicago Fair had probably stimulated these essays in public art. It had certainly inspired the Cleveland project as well as Daniel Burnham's personal scheme for a vast Chicago lakefront park, drawn in 1896.[10] From the public's perspective, however, these developments had been off stage; even architectural publications had paid them minimal heed.

Once prosperity returned, the artists' mood shifted. Municipal art in New York from 1897 onward became an aggressive, expansive, much-proclaimed enthusiasm. Decorative art made new conquests and the term "municipal art" expanded to embrace virtually every proposal—small or large—for enhancing the city's appearance. European urban scenes—the great boulevards, plazas,

3.1 The Dewey Arch at Madison Square, New York, 1899, evoking the patriotic classicism and cosmopolitan urbanism of the municipal art movement. (Courtesy of the Francis Loeb Library, Graduate School of Design, Harvard University.)

monuments, bridges, and esplanades—familiar to artists from student days
and later travel, inspired many recommendations. Municipal art became as
broad as the artists' revulsion for New York was wide. They deplored the
destruction of colonial houses and the quarrying of the Palisades. They
condemned advertising monstrosities, crass sidewalk fixtures, and banal
business streets.[11] Less an ideology than an activated urbanity, municipal art
was rooted in the jarring contrasts between the artful civic scenes of Europe
and the artless cityscapes of America. Its proponents spoke far more often of
Paris, Rome, and Florence than of the White City.

With greater enthusiasm came greater visibility. The civic-minded Reform
Club of New York aired the artists' views in their new quarterly, *Municipal
Affairs*, from 1897 onward. In 1898-1899, the Architectural League of New
York staged public discussions of "The Plan of the City," featuring
monumental bridge-approach schemes, a seven-mile Hudson River terrace,
and other major embellishments.[12] The National Sculpture Society made the
deepest popular impression, tapping the exuberant patriotism that closed the
century. Waiving professional fees, they erected a stunning, white, sculpture-
laden triumphal arch in Madison Square as the visual climax to a stupendous,
two-day welcome-home celebration for the Hero of Manila. A spectacular
success, the Dewey Arch raised new hopes for a transformed New York.[13]

By 1899 the City Beautiful metaphor symbolized this new enthusiasm. And
it was New York artists and art critics who first used the term. They lifted it
from the arts and crafts movement in England. In 1896 the Arts and Crafts
Exhibition Society of London sponsored five lectures on "the application of
the idea of beauty as well as of utility to the organization and decoration of our
greater cities." T. J. Cobden-Sanderson, a book illustrator and friend of
William Morris, emphasized the phrase in his introductory talk. Published
under the title *Art and Life, and the Building and Decoration of Cities*, the
lectures became available in 1897.[14] The new slogan, never before used in
municipal art discussion, quickly took hold. By March 1898, Charles R.
Lamb, an architect active in New York art circles, was exhorting his city to
realize "the dream of the idealist, 'THE CITY BEAUTIFUL.'"[15] *Municipal
Affairs* conferred full blessing upon the term in its December 1899 issue,
splashing the words across its front cover.

Other events in 1899 revealed the spread of municipal art beyond New York
to other major cities. In Cleveland a national convention of architectural
clubs, the first of its kind, organized the Architectural League of America.
Nearly all members were young professionals. The great excitement of their
meeting focused upon the Cleveland Chamber of Commerce and its recent
endorsement of a "group plan" for public buildings. Within a year the League
had formed a National Committee on Municipal Improvements and Civic
Embellishments to encourage public art elsewhere.[16] Meanwhile, in Chicago

several dozen artists struggled to organize what would become, in 1901, the Municipal Art League.[17] And in December, the Municipal Art Society of Baltimore, begun earlier in the year, sponsored the first municipal art conference in the United States. Speakers—mainly artists and art critics—came from New York, Boston, Chicago, Philadelphia, Washington, and Rome, Italy.[18]

Municipal art did not yet mean planning. Its implicit ideal of the city as a work of art honored many impulses. Certain architects by 1898-1899 favored large plans, and their thinking pointed toward the scheme for Washington in 1902 and other grand designs celebrated as part of the City Beautiful.[19] Others along with most artists urged more minute changes in the cityscape. George Kriehn, a Chicago art historian, articulated the prevalent view in an address to the Baltimore conference. "Of all modern cities," he said, "Paris, more than any other, deserves the title of 'The City Beautiful.'" But he favored a particularistic approach, not a Haussmannic one. He condemned the inartistic condition of American cities and the "hideous signs and billboards" that disfigured them. He advocated "enforcement of smoke ordinances," the "judicious use of color" to enliven business streets, the display of trees, fountains, and statues in public places, and the creation of splendid civic buildings adorned with murals and massed in groups. "If we take every element of ugliness one by one, and try to root it out," he declared, "the task will not be difficult."[20]

Small-scale, piecemeal projects played an even more dominant role in civic improvement. This second, little known source of the City Beautiful discloses still other meanings and origins of the movement and helps recover the significance of Charles Mulford Robinson as prophet to the cause. Unlike Daniel Burnham, who personified the big side of the City Beautiful, especially its penchant for grand plans, Robinson knew the small side intimately. He became the first to recognize fully the underlying unity of the movement and to provide in his prolific writing a mirror by which the disparate groups could perceive their common identity.

Civic improvement began as a laymen's cause and flourished initially in small- to medium-sized cities. The organization that gave it national leadership originated, somewhat improbably, in Springfield, Ohio, a college town and publishing center forty-four miles west of Columbus. D. J. Thomas, a local publisher of floral and pet magazines, had become interested in village improvement societies in 1899 and had printed reports about some in New England, the South Atlantic states, California, and elsewhere in his magazine, *Home and Flowers*. Neither he nor Jessie M. Good, the energetic spinster who wrote the accounts, anticipated their appeal. Letters poured in, many requesting an information center on improvement work and others asking "why not start a national movement for civic beauty?"[21] In response, *Home and Flowers* staged a convention of associations in Springfield, October 10, 1900. Ohioans predominated, but some individuals arrived from St. Paul, Minnesota, Oakland, California, and Pensacola, Florida. Professor Charles Zueblin, a University of Chicago sociologist and skillful popular lecturer, attended as did Frank Chapin Bray of Cleveland, editor of the influential *Chautauqua* magazine, and Samuel "Golden Rule" Jones, mayor of Toledo. Together they created the National League of Improvement Associations and resolved to urge "all organizations interested in the permanent improvement and beautifying of American homes, and their surroundings, whether in country, village, or city, to unite with us in membership."[22]

Like the decorative art theme within the City Beautiful, village improvement had roots predating the Chicago World's Fair. As far back as 1848, Andrew Jackson Downing, the preeminent popularizer of English landscape gardening in America, had called upon urbanites who aspired to "country life" to establish "rural improvement" societies for encouraging tree planting and tasteful architecture.[23] Downing's famous books on country houses and their landscaping inspired a succession of works that provided the aesthetic rationale for village improvement in its early years.[24] The first society to fulfill it, the Laurel Hill Association, began in Stockbridge, Massachusetts, in 1853 and became the prototype for all that followed. At the outset Stockbridge was a neglected Berkshire mountain town with rutted streets, treeless roadsides, a tumble-down cemetery, and an unkempt commons. By the 1870s Stockbridge was famous. Its residents walked along neat gravel sidewalks, enjoying the shade and well-kept lawns. The streets, long since regraded and paved, offered quiet rides for the wealthy families who sought summer respite from the city.[25] By 1880 Massachusetts had twenty-eight associations and Connecticut between fifty and sixty, many in country towns anxious to capture the summer trade.[26] Cleanliness, order, and cultural activity as well as picturesque landscape amenities gave substance to the village ideal under these conditions.

In the 1890s the concept spread beyond New England, disseminated in part by articles in *The Atlantic Monthly Forum*, and other national magazines.[27] Societies begun in Honesdale, Pennsylvania, in 1892, and in Montclair, New Jersey, in 1895, received wide publicity. Women dominated many groups. The Honesdale Improvement Association with 230 members, for example, admitted men only on an honorary basis. Many associations, thus, belonged to state federations of women's clubs through which they kindled further interest. In the South Atlantic states the Seaboard Airline Railroad, running from Portsmouth, Virginia, to Atlanta, Georgia, attempted to organize an improvement society at every stop on its line in the late 1890s with a view to attracting northern industry. By 1900 California had "several dozens" of associations, the greatest concentration outside of New England and many but one or two years old.[28]

3.2/3 Piecemeal civic improvement, Harrisburg, Pennsylvania, before and after. A typical swap of gardenesque beauty for unsanitary backyard sheds and eyesore signs and placards, about 1900-05. (Courtesy of the Francis Loeb Library, Graduate School of Design, Harvard University.)

The National League of Improvement Associations approached improvement as a crusade. Unsophisticated, well mannered, and very much in earnest, its founders preached, in their own words, "the gospel of Beauty and the cult of the god sanitation."[29] Jessie Good, the national organizer and unofficial propagandist, captured the zealous enthusiasm of many local groups, especially those led by women, whether in the League or not:

> No task is too great for these associations to undertake. They will direct the digging of anything from a sewer to a flower bed. They will order down your front fences and order up electric lights with equal sangfroid. Water flows at their command. They create sentiment in favor of ornamental back yards and tidy alleys. Indeed, they offer you prizes for the prettiest back yard and neatest alley.[30]

For Charles Zueblin, the second president, how to direct these local energies became the critical issue.

The answer unfolded in 1901-1902: it was to identify improvement effort with the mainstream of Progressive reform. At its second convention in August 1901, the organization renamed itself the American League for Civic Improvement and defined its goals as "the promotion of outdoor art, public beauty, town, village, and neighborhood improvement."[31] By emphasizing "civic improvement" over "village improvement" in its new title, the League aligned itself with the reform ethos of the era or what Zueblin repeatedly called "the new civic spirit."[32] In its second year the League won full support from the Chautauqua institution, which soon showered its members with improvement study-guides.[33] By its third convention in September 1902, the League had created fourteen advisory councils of nationally known experts in such areas as municipal art, municipal reform, social settlements, sanitation, and recreation and championed itself as a "federation of organizations and individuals aiming to promote the higher life of American communities."[34] The implicit goal of building a roof organization for Progressive reform never came to pass, but the League did prosper. By 1902 it had six times as many individual members (232)—many of them important opinion leaders—and three times as many association members (148) as the year before. And it had shifted its headquarters from Springfield to Chicago.[35]

The aesthetic goals of improvement societies, whether in or out of the League, blended images of small-town beauty with order, cleanliness, and moral uplift. A Dayton, Ohio newspaper captured the vision nicely: "The town which has well kept streets, beautiful parks, attractive home grounds, plenty of fresh air and generally favorable sanitary conditions is the town the moral development and industrial progress of which will always commend it."[36] Dozens of reports for 1902 alone confirm this description. The civic committee of the Nebraska Federation of Women's Clubs, for example, started a "vigorous campaign" for "rest rooms in towns and cities; forestry; vacant lot cultivation; improvement of church exteriors and surroundings;

and cemetery improvement." The Society for Beautifying Buffalo, led by a park commissioner, instituted "a crusade against the flaring billboard" then defacing "too many neighborhoods." The Village Improvement Society of Idaho Falls, the second largest club in the state comprising seventy "leading women" of the city, agitated successfully for "fifty rubbish boxes of uniform size, painted white and neatly lettered" and for tree planting on residential streets. In Louisville, Kentucky, the Women's Club "began with the passing of an anti-expectoration ordinance" and then took up the questions of "tree-planting, street wires, the smoke nuisance, vacant lots, signs, and playgrounds."[37]

Civic improvement also spread to metropolitan centers such as Chicago, St. Paul, and Milwaukee. The Civic League of St. Louis won the most acclaim. Begun early in 1902, the League sought to revamp St. Louis in time for the Louisiana Purchase Exposition of 1904. It gained nearly 2,000 members in ten months and in the same period built three public baths in poor neighborhoods, became the watchdog of the billboard and health ordinances, supported a major cross-city boulevard proposal, helped activate a "keep our city clean" campaign, secured appointment of a woman sanitary inspector, encouraged tree planting and children's gardens, and demanded clean water in a city where liquid mud too often ran from the taps. "In short," said Mrs. Louis Marion McCall, an officer in both the Civic League and the American League for Civic Improvement, "there is such an incipient renaissance on in the staid old city of St. Louis as is to be found nowhere outside of the national capital with its stupendous and colossal scheme of beautifying the city of magnificent distances. It touches everything in the city's life."[38] Her comparison was apt, for St. Louis and Washington both exemplified the City Beautiful at that time, St. Louis the project-upon-project approach then dominant and Washington with its comprehensive plan (the McMillan Plan of 1902) the wave of the future.

By the years 1900-1901 a remarkable variety of groups favored some form of aesthetic betterment. Apart from those already noted—municipal art societies, village and civic improvement associations, various architectural and art organizations, the Chautauqua institution, local and state women's clubs—there was one of special importance, the American Park and Outdoor Art Association. Begun in 1897, it championed the third neglected element of the City Beautiful, outdoor art or the cultivation of landscape beauty especially as found in great city parks.

Rooted in the romantic ethos of the pre-Civil War era and given physical expression by Frederick Law Olmsted and other landscape designers from the 1850s onward, outdoor art enjoyed widespread but unorganized and often naive public sympathy by the 1890s. The Association sought to educate, intensify, and focus this support. Its members, numbering 237 by 1900,

3.4 The outdoor art ideal of the parklike residential street, also shared by village improvement advocates. Buffalo, New York. (Courtesy of the Francis Loeb Library, Graduate School of Design, Harvard University.)

consisted mainly of landscape architects, park superintendents and commissioners, and highly knowledgeable laymen. Priding themselves as guardians of landscape taste, they met annually in cities with major park systems, partly to draw attention to these great works and to expound the "proper" principles of park development. To advance outdoor art they repeatedly promoted the landscaping of factory grounds, school yards, railroad-station sites, and city streets; attacked the mounting billboard nuisance; and pleaded for state parks and forest preservation. Like others who favored beautification, they emphasized piecemeal, practical projects. Even children's gardens, a favorite objective, fulfilled their purposes, they believed, by nurturing a love of nature and with it hopes for a more beautiful America.[39]

In 1900-1901 the City Beautiful movement completed its gestation. The organizations supporting municipal art, civic improvement, and outdoor art began interacting and sharing ideas as never before. At national conferences landscape enthusiasts entertained speeches on municipal art; civic improvers claimed outdoor art as a formal goal; and municipal art societies supported park development and advertising regulation. The possibility of merging the American Park and Outdoor Art Association with the American League for Civic Improvement arose; fulfilled in 1904, this union produced the American Civic Association.[40] The key national organizations also evolved a common strategy, notably the promotion of an elaborate "model city" exhibit for the St. Louis World's Fair.[41] Through such interchanges and programs, the City Beautiful metaphor ceased to express municipal art enthusiasm alone and became everybody's slogan, as applicable to tree planting as to architectural adornment.[42] This mingling of organizations and ideas gave the City Beautiful its complexity as an ideal and its vitality as a cause. With the process begun, the birth of the new movement could be proclaimed.

The man who wrote the birth certificate was Charles Mulford Robinson. Born April 30, 1869, he had grown up in Rochester, New York, in the historic and sedate Third Ward whose "quaintness" and "village-like" atmosphere he would later celebrate in several small books.[43] Graduated from the University of Rochester in 1891, he became a reporter for the Rochester *Post-Express* and eventually an associate editor. Even-dispositioned and optimistic by temperament, he had a gentle wit and engaging personal manner. A lucid and prolific writer, he would bring to the City Beautiful movement an inimitable talent for elucidating its inchoate events. Travels in Europe in 1891 and 1894 aroused his first interest in civic scenes, and in 1899 when *The Atlantic Monthly* published three articles of his on "Improvements in City Life," one discussed "Aesthetic Progress." *Harper's Monthly* liked it and sent Robinson to Europe to write of comparable developments. From this point onward, Robinson's role as a civic art publicist was set.[44]

Robinson's first major book, *The Improvement of Towns and Cities*, not only appeared amidst the burgeoning City Beautiful movement, it overviewed all the varied endeavors and declared that they represented not many efforts but one. In his preface Robinson listed over 110 societies then active, many of them roof organizations, some of them in England and Belgium, portrayed them as "one brotherhood in the joyous and earnest new crusade for beauty of town and city."[45] He intended his work as a manual for all the groups, seeking to reduce the isolation between each and instill a consciousness of interdependence. Presenting all the goals of the movement in a logical order, he hoped that the entire pattern of activity might be perceived and a harmonious result encouraged.

The City Beautiful for which Robinson spoke was still in its preplanning phase. His book, subtitled "The Practical Basis of Civic Aesthetics," stressed piecemeal projects suited to every known form of betterment effort. The opening chapter discussed the city's site without emphasizing planning. Site-selection principles merited attention, Robinson argued, so that the few locational advantages remaining to cities might be exploited, such as neglected hilltops and waterfronts.[46] Next he outlined ideal street systems, including Vienna's famous ring streets, but he found such models serviceable mainly in suggesting how to mend existing arrangemens.[47] Five chapters on street beauty followed, each a civic improver's delight. They touched everything from tree planting and burial of overhead wires to beautification of street fixtures, smoke abatement, and advertising regulation. Another four chapters on the "Aesthetic Phase of Social and Philanthropic Effort" honored outdoor and municipal art, by taking up parkways, parks, ornamental squares, playgrounds, and architectural concepts such as building decoration and historic preservation. Chapters on sculpture, art education, and the methods of securing civic art closed the book.

The prophetic nature of Robinson's work fast became apparent. He had drafted it in 1900 before the cause he proclaimed had attracted general notice. His publisher, G. P. Putnam's Sons, skeptical that a market existed, forced him to meet printing costs. Issued in May 1901, *The Improvement of Towns and Cities* sold immediately and well. In November, Putnam's reprinted it. By 1916 it had passed through eleven editions. Key opinion leaders saw its value and elevated Robinson to the top ranks of City Beautiful organizations. Within a year and a half of publication, Robinson had become recording secretary of the American League for Civic Improvement, acting secretary of the American Park and Outdoor Art Association, and member of the inter-association committee charged with planning the "model city" exhibit for the St. Louis World's Fair.[48] Hailed by Zueblin as "the leading authority in the country," Robinson had written what one improvement official dubbed the "bible of the believers in the city beautiful."[49]

Only after 1901 did the movement which Robinson's book so perfectly mirrored gradually shift toward city planning. In 1902 the McMillan Plan for Washington and a now-forgotten scheme for Harrisburg, Pennsylvania provided the nation its first usable examples of comprehensive city planning.[50] Robinson, Zueblin, and other City Beautiful spokesmen—even the Chautauqua institution—seized the meaning of these events and thereafter promoted planned civic betterment.[51] Even small towns, Robinson argued in 1902, should seek an expert to "suggest a general scheme" of action. "Instead of having spotty improvements here and there, that have no connection with one another and no permanent character," the advisor would "make every effort count as a step toward the consummation of a harmonious general plan. There will be nothing wasted and nothing duplicated."[52] He emphasized this new perspective in his second major book, *Modern Civic Art*, issued in 1903.[53]

The conversion of the City Beautiful to planning came slowly and never fully succeeded. As late as 1904 only New York and San Francisco had taken steps to secure comprehensive plans.[54] Thereafter, sustained planning activity commenced, at least a dozen cities acquiring plans in 1905-1908. By the latter date New York, San Francisco, and St. Louis had reports. So did many lesser places: Columbus, Ohio; Columbia and Greenville, South Carolina; Roanoke, Virginia; Denver, Colorado; San Diego and Oakland, California— even distant Honolulu and Manila.[55] By this point the equation of the City Beautiful with city planning had far more truth, but it remained a partial truth. In 1901 nearly 1,000 improvement organizations existed. An inquiry in 1905 counted 2,426 "improvement societies," and impressionistic evidence for 1908 suggests no diminution of activity.[56]

We can now summarize the forgotten origins and lost meanings of the City Beautiful. Contrary to conventional wisdom, the movement began between 1897 and 1902 as interest in municipal art, village and civic improvement, and outdoor art found organized, interconnected expression and gained its best spokesman in Charles Mulford Robinson. Those who have overlooked the small-scale side of the City Beautiful have not merely passed over a curious interest in ornamental lampposts, street trees, public murals, or rubbish cans; they have ignored a pattern of activity sustained by thousands of civic groups across the nation. Unlike commentaries that trace the origins of the City Beautiful to the Chicago World's Fair, this account insists upon additional influences, notably decorative art, concepts of small town beauty, and landscape design ideas. Also emphasized is the movement's congeniality to piecemeal change; only after 1901 did comprehensive city planning become a widely advocated goal.

This altered perspective upon the City Beautiful suggests new judgments of its significance. These can only be sketched. The prosperous middle- and upper-class elements of towns and cities who gave the movement its force seized the long-established belief in the morally uplifting value of beauty and placed fresh energies behind it. Exuding the social optimism of the Progressive era, the national spokesmen for the cause repeatedly claimed that beauty would evoke or at least express a regenerated civic life. The prominence of this theme suggests that for many the City Beautiful was the aesthetic expression of turn-of-the-century urban reform. The small-scale side of the movement also helps explain its vitality. A comely park, a clean street, a dignified city hall: these and dozens of other practical goals kept local organizations active and larger dreams alive. They also enabled City Beautiful proponents to blend civic boosterism with reform. A more attractive city, they claimed, would promote tourism, enlarge trade, and generally revitalize the local economy.

Finally, the City Beautiful may also be seen as a never-very-systematic cluster of environmental norms popularized among the middle and upper classes. The standards had been in the making before the Chicago World's Fair as the previous discussion of municipal art, civic improvement, and outdoor art reveals. But not until 1897-1902 had these disparate goals been commonly fused together, celebrated with a slogan, and championed so widely and vigorously. Inspired by the Fair and European civic art as well, this newly constituted demand for beauty, order, and cleanliness may have left more enduring marks than commonly appreciated. Today at the prosperous fringes of American cities sidewalks are straight, utility wires are often buried, advertising signs are confined to commercial areas, civic buildings are attractive by many standards, streets are swept. If not, community sentiment holds that they should be. Many aspects of the City Beautiful persist in zoning codes, subdivision regulations, and local ordinances and, more profoundly, in the culture of suburbia. The movement died long ago, but its legacy may be so commonplace that we have overlooked it.

NOTES

The author wishes to thank the American Philosophical Society and the American Council of Learned Societies for funding the collection of photographs used.

1. The most complete acount of the City Beautiful to date is Mel Scott, *American City Planning Since 1890* (Berkeley, 1969), 47-109. For critical commentaries, see Lewis Mumford, *Sticks and Stones: A Study of American Architecture and Civilization* (New York, 1924), 123-151; Thomas Adams, *Outline of Town and City Planning: A Review of Past Efforts and Modern Aims* (New York, 1935), 179-182, 197-205; Robert Averill Walker, *The Planning Function in Urban Government* (Chicago, 1941), 12-16; John Burchard and Albert Bush-Brown, *The Architecture of America: A Social History and Cultural Criticism* (Boston, 1961), 246-250; and Norman Newton, *Design on the Land: The Development of Landscape Architecture* (Cambridge, 1971), 413-426. For a more favorable assessment, see Christopher Tunnard, *The City of Man* (New York, 1953), 303-313; Christopher Tunnard and Henry Hope Reed, *American Skyline: The Growth and Form of Our Cities* (New York, 1953), 136-153; and Christopher Tunnard, *The Modern American City* (Princeton, 1968), 36-66. The only historian to overview the movement is

Roy Lubove, *The Progressives and the Slums: Tenement House Reform in New York City, 1890-1917* (New York, 1962), 217-221; and *The Urban Community: Housing and Planning in the Progressive Era* (Englewood Cliffs, 1967), 59. For a case study demonstrating the importance of park promotion to beautification but applying the term City Beautiful partly to the 1870s and 1880s before it came into use, see William H. Wilson, *The City Beautiful Movement in Kansas City* (Columbia, 1964). For the contributions of Daniel H. Burnham to City Beautiful planning, see Thomas H. Hines, *Burnham of Chicago: Architect and Planner* (New York, 1974), 74, 158, 166, 368.

2. For brief sketches of the relationship of municipal art to the City Beautiful, see Scott, *American City Planning*, 43-46; and Harvey A. Kantor, "The City Beautiful in New York," *The New York Historical Society Quarterly*, 57 (1973), 149-171.

3. Royal Cortissoz, *John LaFarge: A Memoir and a Study* (Boston, 1911), 152-160; Charles Baldwin, *Stanford White* (New York, 1931), 45-46.

4. The Architectural League of New York, *Officers, Committees, Members, Constitution and By-Laws, 1905-1906* (New York), 3-5.

5. Walter Muir Whitehill, *Boston Public Library: A Centennial History* (Cambridge, 1956), 142, 148-149.

6. Lillie H. French, "Municipal Art," *Harper's Weekly*, 37 (1893), 371.

7. *Ibid.*; Edward Hamilton Bell, "Art in Municipal Decoration," ibid., 38 (1894), 401; *Yearbook of the Art Societies of New York, 1898-1899* (New York, 1899), 87-91.

8. The Municipal Art Society of Cincinnati, *Constitution and By-Laws, Adopted on the Thirty-first of May, 1894.*

9. *Yearbook of the Art Societies*, 108-109, 146-148, 155-156; Editorial, *The American Architect and Building News*, 50 (1895), 141; Editorial, *ibid.*, 55 (1897), 25.

10. For examples of contents, see *Catalogue of the Eleventh Annual Exhibition of the Architectural League of New York* (New Rochelle, 1896), 10: "The Society of Beaux–Arts Architects." *The American Architect and Building News*, 51 (1896), 78-79; "T-Square Club of Philadelphia," *ibid.*, 52 (1896), 39; Herbert B. Briggs, "Cleveland Architectural Club," *ibid.*, 48 (1895), 7. For the genesis of the Cleveland and Chicago-lakefront schemes, see Hines, *Burnham of Chicago*, 159-160, 313-314.

11. Frederick S. Lamb, "Municipal Art," *Municipal Affairs*, 1 (1897), 674-688. See also entire issue, *ibid.*, 2 (1899).

12. *Yearbook of the Art Societies*, 56, 61, 63-69.

13. Barr Ferree, "The Dewey Arch," *The American Architect and Building News*, 67 (1900), 11-12, 19-20; "Celebrating a New Era," *Harper's Weekly*, 43 (1899), 954.

14. Arts and Crafts Exhibition Society, London, *Art and Life, and the Building and Decoration of Cities* (London, 1897), 5, 43.

15. Charles R. Lamb, "Civic Architecture," *Municipal Affairs*, 2 (1898), 72. Capitalized letters as in the original text.

16. The Architectural League of America, *The Architectural Annual* (Philadelphia, 1900), 52, 118-120, 197-212, 279; "Topics of the Day," *Architects' and Builders' Magazine*, 1 (1900), 337.

17. Charles Mulford Robinson, "Among the Improvement Clubs," *Municipal Journal and Engineer*, 12 (1902), 112.

18. George Kriehn, "The Baltimore Conference on Municipal Art," in Architectural League, *Architectural Annual*, 47.

19. Most architects who promoted the big side of the City Beautiful in 1898-1899 has not yet settled upon the concept of a comprehensive city plan. The Architectural League of New York exemplified the most advanced thinking. One architect-member, Julius F. Harder, voiced the principle of a general plan early in 1898, but when the League discussed "The Plan of the City" in the winter of 1898-1899, its members outlined a series of distinct, large-scale projects, not an

integrated program for reshaping New York. Julius F. Harder, "The City's Plan," *Municipal Affairs*, 2 (1898), 24-25; *Yearbook of the Art Societies*, 63-69.

20. Kriehn, "Baltimore Conference," 47; George Kriehn, "The City Beautiful," *Municipal Affairs*, 3 (1899), 595.

21. "The National League of Improvement Associations: A Short History," in Jessie Good, *The How of Improvement Work* (Springfield, 1901), 44; Benjamin F. Prince, *A Standard History of Springfield and Clark County, Ohio* (Chicago, 1922), 178-179; Clifton M. Nichols, "The Printing and Publishing Interests of Springfield, Ohio, 1800-1900," in Benjamin F. Prince, ed., *The Centennial Celebration of Springfield, Ohio, Held August 4th to 10th, 1901* (Springfield), 224. Nicholas reported *Home and Flowers* circulation as 125,000 for 1901.

22. *Dayton Daily Journal*, Oct. 12, 1900.

23. Andrew Jackson Downing, "On the Improvement of County Villages" (1849) in George William Curtis, ed., *Rural Essays* (New York, 1869), 229-235.

24. Warren H. Manning, "The History of Village Improvement in the United States," *The Craftsman*, 5 (1904), 423-432.

25. Nathaniel Hillyer Egleston, *Villages and Village Life with Hints for their Improvement* (New York, 1878) 60-67.

26. Birdsey G. Northrup, "Address of Hon. B. G. Northrup" in The West Ewing Improvement Association, *Proceedings of Anniversary Meeting* (Trenton, 1880), 15; Editorial, *The American Architect and Building News*, 8 (1880), 278.

27. "The National League. . . . : A Short History," 42.

28. Mary Caroline Robbins, "Village Improvement Societies," *The Atlantic Monthly*, 79 (1897), 217, 221; Birdsey G. Northrup. "The Work of Village Improvement Societies," *Forum*, 19 (1895), 100-102; and Jessie M. Good, *The Work of Civic Improvement* (Springfield, 1900), 6-10, 16, 20-26.

29. "The National League. . . "A Short History," 42.

30. Good, *Work of Civic Improvement*, 10.

31. "Successful Civic Beauty Rally," *Home and Flowers*, 10 (Sept., 1901), 9.

32. Charles Zueblin, "A Decade of Civic Improvement," in *Nation-Wide Civic Betterment: A Report of the Third Annual Convention of The American League for Civic Improvement* (Chicago, 1903), 14; Charles Zueblin, "The New Civic Spirit," *The Chautauquan*, 38 (1903), 55-59.

33. For the close relationship of the League and Chautauqua, see "Two Notable Civic Betterment Events," *Home and Flowers*, 12 (1902), 143-145.

34. *Nation-Wide Civic Betterment*, inside front cover. Other advisory councils dealt with arts and crafts, civic, church, libraries and museums, parks, public nuisances, preservation of nature, rural improvement, school extension, and village improvement.

35. In August 1901, there were 46 association members and 35 individual members. See "Treasurer's Report," *Home and Flowers*, 10 (Sept., 1901), 9; and membership-fee data in "Plans for a Year of Active Work" in *ibid.*, 10 (Oct. 1901), 12. For September 1902 membership, see *Nation-Wide Civic Betterment*, 97-103. The League also listed 29 firms as commercial members.

36. *Dayton Daily Journal*, May 16, 1901.

37. For Nebraska, see "Beautiful American Cities," *Home and Flowers*, 12 (1902), 33. For Buffalo, see "More Beautiful American Cities," *ibid.*, 11 (1902), 24-25. For Idaho Falls, see "Civic Improvement Progress," *ibid.*, 12 (1902), 60. For Louisville, see *Nation-Wide Civic Betterment*, 3.

38. Mrs. Marion Louise McCall, "What Organization Has Done for St. Louis," in *ibid.*, 50-56; "St. Louis Still Brushing Up," *Home and Flowers*, 13 (1903), 252.

39. The American Park and Outdoor Art Association, *Proceedings and Annual Reports* (various titles), 1897-1903, and throughout.

40. For examples of interaction, see "Two Notable Civic Betterment Events," 143-146; "An Object Lesson in Modern City Making" in *The Twentieth Century City: Proceedings of the Annual Convention, 1901, of The American League for Civic Improvement* (Springfield, 1901), 68-69; and The American Park and Outdoor Art Association, *Proceedings of the Fourth Annual Meeting held at the Art Institute, Chicago, Illinois, June 5, 6, and 7, 1900*, 22-24, 26, 84-95.

41. For the beginnings of the "model city" project and of merger talk, see "Successful Civic Beauty Rally," 10. Organizations collaborating on the "model city" were the Municipal Art Society of New York, The American Park and Outdoor Art Association, The American League for Civic Improvement, the National Municipal League, and the American Scenic and Historic Preservation Society; see "Object Lesson in Modern City Making," 68-69.

42. For examples of such usage, see "The City Beautiful, Recent Endeavors toward Civic Improvement," *Current Literature*, 32 (1902), 418-432; and Charles Mulford Robinson, "Among the Improvement Clubs," *Municipal Journal and Engineer*, 11 (1901), 267.

43. Charles Mulford Robinson, *Third Ward Traits* (Rochester, 1899), 5-8; *Third-Ward Catechism* (Rochester, 1908).

44. "American Society of Landscape Architects, Minutes on the Life and Services of Charles Mulford Robinson, Associate Member," *Landscape Architecture*, 9 (1919), 180-189.

45. Charles Mulford Robinson, *The Improvement of Towns and Cities or the Practical Basis of Civic Aesthetics* (New York, 1901), viii-xii.

46. *Ibid.*, 3-17.

47. *Ibid.*, 8, 20-25.

48. "Successful Civic Beauty Rally," 8; "Two Notable Civic Betterment Events," 164; *The Twentieth Century City*, 62, 68.

49. "Inaugural Address of President Charles Zueblin," in *ibid.*, 65; McCall, "What Organization has Done for St. Louis," 50.

50. For the importance of the Harrisburg scheme, see Charles Zueblin, "Harrisburg Plan of Municipal Improvement," *The Chautauquan*, 39 (1904), 60-68.

51. "Making Chautauqua a Model," *ibid.*, 37 (1903), 449-462; Zueblin, "Decade of Civic Improvement," 16-17.

52. Charles Mulford Robinson, "What the Smallest Town Should Do," *Public Improvements*, 7 (1902), 108.

53. Charles Mulford Robinson, *Modern Civic Art or the City Made Beautiful* (New York), 1903), 32-35, 271-286.

54. Charles Mulford Robinson, "New Dreams for Cities," *The Architectural Record*, 12 (1902), 410-421. In 1904 the federal government also arranged for a comprehensive plan for Manila in the Philippines.

55. For a list that includes nearly all plans drawn up in three years, see Theodora Kimball, ed., *Municipal Accomplishment in City Planning and Published City Plan Reports in the United States* (Boston, 1920).

56. "Successful Civic Beauty Rally," 8; "The American Civic Association Convention in Cleveland, O., October 4-6," *Park and Cemetery and Landscape Gardening*, 15 (1905), 372. For 1908 see Charles Mulford Robinson's monthly column "Civic Improvement" in *Charities and The Commons*, 20-21 (1908).

4

The Plan of Chicago

Robert L. Wrigley, Jr.

In the spring of 1893, the World's Columbian Exposition opened in Chicago's Jackson Park. In this "White City" of almost 700 acres, Chicagoans and millions of visitors, accustomed to urban ugliness, saw for the first time a splendid example of civic design and beauty in the classic pattern and on a grand scale, and they liked it. Indeed it marked the beginning in this country of orderly arrangement of extensive buildings and grounds. Throughout the nation people began to wonder why cities couldn't be as orderly and beautiful as the Columbian Exposition and nowhere was this matter discussed more than in Chicago. The first suggestion was to preserve the exposition site and make it permanently attractive. Then the possibility of extending a park north from the fair grounds seven miles to Grant Park by filling in part of the lake front was debated. The famous architect and leading spirit of the fair, Daniel H. Burnham, working with the South Park Commission, completed plans for such a park in 1896.

The 1893 World's Fair and the Chicago Plan

That the first comprehensive plan for the orderly development of a great American city should come out of Chicago seems rather surprising. Having grown enormously during the last quarter of the nineteenth century as a center of transportation, commerce, and manufacturing, Chicago was typically a city of rugged individualism. Its pattern of development over the lake plain

The author appreciates the assistance of Miss Helen Whitehead of The Chicago Plan Commission, who furnished needed information and photographs.

Reprinted from Robert L. Wrigley, Jr. "The Plan of Chicago: Its Fiftieth Anniversary," *Journal of the American Institute of Planners* 26, 1 (February, 1960), 31-38, copyright © 1960, *Journal of the American Institute of Planners,* reprinted with permission.

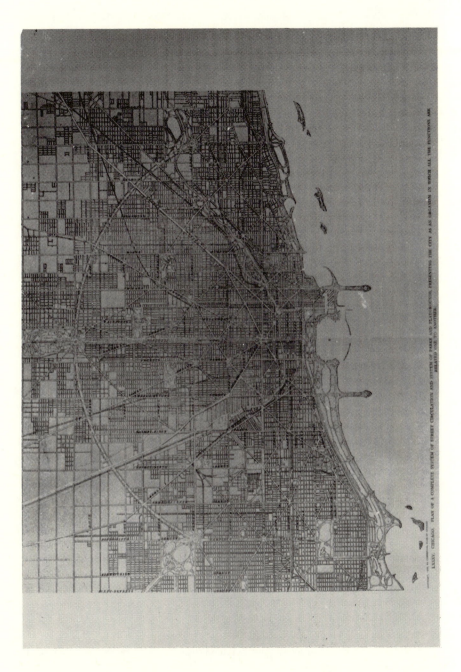

4.1 Overview of the Major Proposals of the *Plan of Chicago* (from the *Plan of Chicago*, 1909, p. 80).

included a mixture of land uses unparalleled in any urban area. The earmarks of rapid expansion without guidance were found everywhere, and vast slums extended outward from the core area. Like most American cities, especially great industrial centers, Chicago could hardly boast of civic improvements and beautification although it did have a number of distinguished cultural institutions and the beginning of a splendid park system. But the problem of city betterment received a great deal of thought and reevaluation during the last decade of the century.

Various individuals and groups, especially the Commercial Club and the Merchants' Club, whose members were leaders of the business community, had been closely associated with the fair and were keenly interested in the lake-front park. They kept the idea of municipal improvement alive, eventually raising the possibility of preparing a comprehensive plan for the entire city.

The Plan of Chicago

Between 1901 and 1905 the need for a General Plan was discussed in both clubs, with Franklin MacVeagh, Frederic A. Delano, Charles D. Norton, Edward B. Butler, and other club members pressing for some positive action. Finally in June 1906 the Merchants' Club invited Mr. Burnham, who was one of the club members, to prepare a plan for Chicago. In the following year the Merchants' Club and the Commercial Club merged under the name of the latter, so the plan was completed and eventually published, in June 1909, by the Commercial Club, whose plan committee was headed by Charles D. Norton as chairman and Charles H. Wacker as vice-chairman.[1] As for interest and support by club members, Wacker later reported that "no time was spared, no money was stinted and the best talent was secured." Specifically the plan and its subsequent history is a landmark in city planning because:

- Its conception and preparation were initiated and paid for by private individuals.
- It was the first comprehensive plan for a great American city.
- It was a brilliantly conceived and executed plan with proposals covering area beyond the central city.
- The gift of this plan to the city of Chicago brought about the organization of the planning commission.
- For over a decade the Chicago Plan Commission was financed largely by those individuals who initiated and paid for the plan.
- The educational program aimed at winning citizen support for the plan and effectuating its recommendations was the most successful in the history of the American planning movement.
- The record of accomplishments based on the plan has long been the envy of city officials and planners.
- *The Plan of Chicago* had a significant impact on city development far and wide. As Robert A. Walker stated in 1940, the plan

". . . . established a pattern for American city planning. Its influence is manifest in the grand perspective sketched in every important planning report of the last thirty years. . . and the public works program undertaken in conformity with the recommendations of the plan has stimulated innumerable favorable comments in the literature of the field."[2]

Daniel H. Burnham and the Chicago Plan

It was appropriate that Daniel H. Burnham should prepare the *Plan of Chicago*, commonly called "the Burnham Plan." As one of the nation's foremost architects and a Chicagoan, he had taken a leading role in the World's Columbian Exposition, serving as Director of Works. He had also

4.2   Daniel H. Burnham, about 1910.

planned the lake-front park and participated in other civic improvements. He was one of the two original members appointed in 1901 to serve on the Commission for the Improvement of the District of Columbia, better known as the McMillan Commission. Moreover, in 1905-06 he prepared plans for Manila and San Francisco, thereby enhancing his reputation as a city planner.

A man of great vision and courage, Burnham followed his own admonishment to planners everywhere to "make no little plans." With the aid of his associate, Edward H. Bennett, with the all-out backing of the Commercial Club, which financed the project to the tune of $85,000, and with the assistance of numerous public and business officials, the work as finally completed was imaginative, far-reaching in its proposals, and outstanding in its physical presentation.

It was indeed a "big plan," a labor of love which Burnham, who freely gave his own time for a project that took thirty months to complete, later looked back on as the "supreme effort" of his life.[3] The notable volume with beautiful illustrations and splendid text edited by Charles Moore, who had prepared the McMillan report for Congress, had an air of confidence and quality that has never been surpassed in planning literature. Compared to earlier plans, which were restricted largely to planning civic centers, parks, and thoroughfares, the *Plan of Chicago* was a significant step forward. Walker observes:

> In it one finds appreciation of the broad objectives of planning found in few of the many plans which preceded or immediately followed it . . . despite a predominant architectural emphasis, the Chicago Plan expressed an appreciation of the objectives of planning which put it well in the vanguard of the trend toward comprehensiveness.[4]

The plan also was a long-range proposal; Mayor Fred Busse, in his message recommending it to the City Council, said "the . . . plan does not contemplate the remodeling of Chicago in a year or a decade. It is a suggestion of a plan for the far future, as a suggestion of something to grow to."[5]

Concern for development beyond the central city was expressed in the plan as follows:

> In every town a public-improvement commission should be formed to bring about the most orderly conditions within the town itself, and especially to act in cooperation with similar bodies in neighboring towns so as to secure harmonious, connected and continuous improvements.[6]

Burnham's *Plan of Chicago* touched on many urban problems. Major recommendations were:

- Create a system of regional highways extending up to sixty miles outside the city. In this respect the plan had a metropolitan approach.
- Develop a systematic arrangement of streets and avenues within the city, especially diagonal boulevards to facilitate the flow of traffic to and from the central business district. Many of the existing streets were proposed for widening.

- Improve railway terminals by consolidating facilities within the city and by building a great freight and warehousing center southwest of the city for handling through freight. Many of these proposals were based on Frederic Delano's 1904 railway plan for Chicago.
- Construct extensive new docks at the mouth of the Chicago River and in the Calumet Lake area.
- Improve the Lake Michigan frontage by developing parks, beaches, and a series of off-shore islands.
- Extend the outer park system, chiefly forest preserves, and develop more parkways to connect existing and proposed parks. A special Park Commission in 1904 recommended a forest preserve system of 37,000 acres. Burnham proposed 40,000 to 50,000 acres which would give the Chicago area a total park system of about 60,000 acres.
- Create centers of intellectual life and of civic administration so related as to give coherence and unity to the city. Great emphasis was laid on a civic center for Chicago; also recommended were community centers for each suburban town.

4.3   The development of Burnham Park along the lake front.

Those who prepared the plan and attempted to carry out its proposals admitted that it was far from perfect. However, they had secured the best advice possible and they always maintained that its basic recommendations were sound. Early in the text they noted:

> The real test of this Plan will be found in its application; for such is the determination of the people to secure more perfect conditions, it is certain that if

the plan is really good it will commend itself to the progressive spirit of the times and sooner or later it will be carried out.[7]

4.4 Chicago's southside lakefront park today (1960).

Winning Citizen Support

The men responsible for the creation of the *Plan of Chicago* realized "that to cast it unheralded and unsupported upon a disinterested city would be to condemn it to early oblivion."[8]

Charles H. Wacker, a leader in the Chicago planning movement from the very beginning, was especially aware of the importance of winning citizen support for urban planning. He later wrote:

> Without hesitation, because we knew our plan was right, that it was basically sound and that its adoption and completion would benefit every citizen of our city immeasurably, we tackled the tremendous task of arousing the interest and awakening the desires of our great cosmopolitan mass of two and a half millions of people.[9]

Needing an outstanding executive officer, Wacker persuaded Walter D. Moody, the hard-driving Executive Secretary of the Chicago Association of Commerce, to take the job of Managing Director of the Chicago Plan Commission, a job he assumed in January 1911.

In his promotional work Moody had the support of the 328-member Chicago Plan Commission as well as that of Wacker, its permanent Chairman. This Commission, established by the City Council on November 4, 1909, shortly after the plan had been given to the city by the Commercial Club, was primarily a citizens' promotional group whose effective work was accomplished by a small committee.

4.5   Charles H. Wacker.

The new commission also gave the plan added stature, finally adopting it as the official General Plan of Chicago on July 10, 1911. But it was the Commercial Club, with its many distinguished and powerful personalities, and not the city, that enthusiastically pushed the plan during this period. How Moody, with this vigorous assistance developed his campaign for winning citizen support for the Plan of Chicago is one of the most brilliant episodes in American planning history.

Walter D. Moody — Master Salesman of City Planning

In his book *What of the City?* Moody sounded the keynote of successful accomplishment in urban improvement as he saw it:

City planning work in all its practical essentials is a work of promotion-salesmanship . . . It is a problem of arousing interest, creating human desire, stirring the spirit for better things and inspiring human action. . . . Primarily to that end all efforts should be devoted. New methods should be employed.[10]

And upon assuming office as Managing Director of the Commission in January 1911 he observed:

Naturally the plan must be worked out piece by piece. Those who have contemplated it as a whole have said "Impossible," forgetful of the all-important fact that every great structure must first have a plan before it can be reared stone by stone. The idea as contained in the plan for creating order out of chaos in Chicago should be taken up by the entire clergy of the city, all school teachers, . . . by the professors in all . . . colleges, by clerks in stores and offices, by factory employees . . . of all classes. Every Chicagoan, neighbor to neighbor, should catch the *Chicago Plan* spirit and talk about it. It is the one Chicago issue that all Chicago can and should unite on.[11]

4.6   Walter D. Moody.

As with all new progressive ideas, the *Plan of Chicago* was subject to widespread criticism by those who said that it was impractical and idealistic. The idea of the "city beautiful," a term used at the time of the World's Fair, was ridiculed by many. Feeling that the "city beautiful" designation was unfortunate, Moody emphasized the "city practical" at every opportunity. And, to counteract unfavorable comment, the Commission centered its attention on one specific and highly important recommendation — widening 12th Street and carrying it by a viaduct across the railroad yards south of "the Loop." Completion of this major project, the Commission believed, would strengthen its argument that the plan was a very practical one.

Campaigning to win the bond issue for the 12th Street project was Moody's first promotional work for the Plan Commission. Wacker had admonished him to "establish the plan . . . with the people." The *Plan of Chicago*, however, was sold at $25 a copy and only 1,650 volumes had been printed. Obviously it could not be widely read, so Moody prepared a brochure called *Chicago's Greatest Issue — An Official Plan*. This 93-page booklet outlined the plan in simple language, using heavy type to drive home major points. To create greater interest, some of the plan's illustrations were reproduced. The book was addressed to the "owners of Chicago" and the 165,000 copies, published in June 1911 at a cost of $18,000, were distributed to all property owners in the city and to all persons paying a monthly rent of $25 or more. This direct approach, plus intensive use of the press, brought success. The bond issue was carried, the 12th Street improvement was soon underway, and the backers of the plan were able to point to a solid accomplishment.

Pushing ahead with its promotional work, the Plan Commission published *Wacker's Manual of the Plan of Chicago* late in 1911. Moody wrote this celebrated book in an elementary style and illustrated it profusely so that it would carry the message of the *Plan of Chicago* to eighth-grade students. These children were at a very impressionable age, and many of them would drop out of school after this grade. In reference to the *Manual's* use in schools, Moody wrote:

> The results of study of this book appear three-fold — attracting the attention and sympathy of the parents to the *Plan of Chicago* through the children as a medium; the training of a future citizenry to become responsible in matters of government control; the ultimate accomplishment of the whole *Plan* in future years through an enlightened citizenry.[12]

Wacker's *Manual*, adopted by the Chicago Board of Education in 1912, was used as an eighth-grade text, and some 50,000 copies eventually were printed. This was the first time a text in planning was admitted for studying by an American school board, and it was used for almost a decade with unusual success. Some schools reported that their students begged to have more of this subject, and even today many a Chicagoan looks back with nostalgia to the days when he studied this little book.

Realizing the importance of personal contact, Wacker and Moody early considered the possibility of developing a lecture bureau in their efforts to win public support. They aimed at developing a series of illustrated lectures on city planning with the same appeal as a Burton Holmes travelogue. Preparing an interesting lecture was comparatively easy, but preparing a fine collection of slides was indeed a problem in those days. At first there was much trial and error, but no expense was spared in getting the best. Eventually, leading photographers in twenty-four nations were hired to take specific pictures needed in the lecture series, since the presentation of examples of good planning from other lands was considered a desirable way to sell planning at home. Thus a splendid collection of 200 slides, most of them hand tinted, was secured. Lectures usually were held in school auditoriums before capacity houses, made up of people living in the general locality of the school. Each program was announced in a colorful three-page circular that told something about the plan and program. Two tickets were enclosed with each invitation, and the number of invitations mailed was double the seating capacity of the auditorium. This virtually ensured a full house. And for those who didn't come there was always the folder to read with its short message on planning in Chicago. As many as 90 lectures were given in a single winter season, and almost 400 over a seven-year period with a total attendance of approximately 175,000, more than half by invitation.

The motion picture, then in its infancy, also was used. A two-reel film, "A Tale of One City," was prepared and shown at a major downtown theater at a gala "first night," and later at 60 theaters throughout the city with a total attendance of more than 150,000.

By the summer of 1914 almost five years had passed since the organization of the Chicago Plan Commission, and during this period significant progress had been made in implementing Burnham's plan. To commemorate this advance and to build up community confidence and devotion to the planning program, in July 1914, the Commission published *Chicago's World Wide Influence in City Planning*. The introduction indicated the Commission's view of its importance:

> It may be rightfully stated . . . that the work of the Chicago Plan Commission is exercising international influence and carrying the frame of Chicago in this branch of civic endeavor to the farthest corners of the earth.

The publication is filled with letters and other comments from all parts of the world, many of an envious nature praising the *Plan of Chicago* and the program of public improvements based on it.

Another interesting and very effective pamphlet, *Fifty Million Dollars for Nothing*, was issued late in 1916 in an effort to win public support for a lake-front park. It pointed out that waste material, which was being taken into Lake Michigan and dumped, could be used to make 1,300 acres of new park by building land along the lake front. Within twelve years, at virtually no cost to the city, according to the pamphlet, a new park could be created. In later years this park was developed and appropriately named Burnham Park, one of the most significant improvements based on the 1909 plan. This pamphlet was only one of many Commission publications dealing with specific projects. Two major publications, prepared under Moody's direction as World War I drew to a close, were *Economic Readjustment from a War to a Peace Basis* and *Seed Thoughts for Sermons*. The latter was particularly unusual. It described in some detail the humanitarian aspects of the *Plan of Chicago*. All ministers in the city received copies of this pamphlet with the suggestion that they give at least one sermon based on the ideas outlined therein; and in due time the value of comprehensive city planning was preached from virtually every pulpit in Chicago.

Notable Achievements of the Plan

By 1920 the *Plan of Chicago* had been for almost ten years an effective instrument in guiding the city's growth. This period was Chicago's "golden age" of comprehensively planned public improvements, according to most authorities. The team of Wacker and Moody, aided by unusually fine citizen support, pushed ahead with the utmost vigor in promoting their educational activities, and in coordinating new development with the plan. Their efforts were financed in part by the city of Chicago, but mostly by the Commercial Club, whose total subscription above the cost of the plan passed the $200,000 mark. Moody, the dynamic salesman of a comparatively unknown product —city planning, died in 1920, and thereafter some of the steam was taken out of the promotional work. But under Wacker's chairmanship, which continued until November 1926, many other projects proposed by the plan were either started or completed. After Wacker resigned in 1926, planning responsibilities largely passed from the hands of the original officers and backers, and a brilliant chapter of American planning history was closed.

Wacker served as Chairman of the Plan Commission for seventeen years, and "through all the Commission's work in this period," according to Walker, "the *Plan of Chicago* was its bible. It was the source of inspiration and the key to the promised land."[13] Thus, in reporting on its first ten years of progress the Plan Commission noted that:

> No other city of modern times has been given a plan so comprehensive — one that proposes so many economic, hygienic, sociological, commercial and humanitarian benefits — and one so thoroughly calculated to meet the needs of a vast and growing population.[14]

The *Plan of Chicago* was basically a plan for public improvements, chiefly within the city, but for highways and parks, it was regional in scope. In the decade that followed its completion the plan was not "updated" from time to time as is the practice today. In fact, the Commission had no technical planning staff to speak of, but only a staff to push development in accordance with the plan which, it should be remembered, had been a gift to the city. And although the original plan was a far-seeing one, its proposals for solving a number of pressing problems were not very effective.[15] The time did arrive, in the 1920s, when its recommendations had to be reevaluated, and through the years its broad proposals have been adjusted to evolving technology and to economic and social change. Yet up to the present day most of the basic recommendations of Chicago's first great plan are incorporated in the city's General Plan, and affectionate reference frequently is made to Burnham, Bennett, and Wacker, as great leaders of the past. Not so well remembered is Moody and his outstanding efforts to win public support and carry bond issues, yet without his special talents the accomplishment might well have been far less notable and impressive.

In order to finance various public improvements, 86 bond issues, totaling 234 million dollars, were sold by 1931; in addition special assessments on property immediately affected by improvements came to 58 million. Thus over a period of 20 years almost 300 million dollars were invested by the municipality in improvements proposed by the *Plan of Chicago*.

In 1933, at the beginning of Chicago's second World's Fair, the Plan Commission published *The Chicago Plan in 1933 — Twenty-five Years of Accomplishment*.[16]

Among other things, the 1933 survey reported "some 85 public improvements outlined in the *Plan of Chicago* are today complete, or so far advanced that their early completion is assured."

These improvements ranged from the modest to the spectacular. Possibly no American city has had so much to show in such a short period of time. Included were scores of street-widening projects, such as that of Michigan Avenue north to Lake Shore Drive and the mile-long viaduct carrying 12th Street (Roosevelt Road) across the railroad yards south of "the Loop." The double-decked Wacker Drive and several large bridges were major improvements along the main stem of the Chicago River, west from Michigan Avenue. The weaving of Chicago's major road network into the regional system also was accomplished. Proposals for railroad consolidation were not highly successful; nevertheless, the large new Union Station was built as suggested by the plan. The South Branch of the Chicago River was straightened, and harbor facilities were enlarged both in the downtown area and at Lake Calumet. The famous Navy Pier was built far out into Lake Michigan. Now land was slowly built up as the lake was pushed back and over twenty miles of lake-front park and beaches resulted, including Burnham Park — all new land lying south of Grant Park and extending almost seven miles to Jackson Park. And within these lake-front parks notable museums and other institutions were developed, much as Burnham and his associates had suggested. The outlying forest preserves were vastly extended until by 1933 they included 32,400 acres, about 75 percent of it still in a natural state. Other accomplish-

4.7 Chicago's magnificent "front door" on Lake Michigan.

ments could be cited, but those mentioned include the major improvements. Surely an impressive list.

Why was so much achieved? Unusually fine work in winning citizen support was an important factor in this success. The intense interest and wholehearted backing of Chicago's top business leaders was perhaps of equal importance. Basic to everything, however, if significant achievements were to be secured, was a plan that would arouse the fighting enthusiasm of those responsible for community betterment. This they had in the *Plan of Chicago*. As Daniel H. Burnham had stated in 1907 when he was fully engaged in the Chicago study:

> Make no little plans; they have no magic to stir men's blood and probably will not be realized. Make big plans; aim high in hope and work, remembering that a nobler, logical diagram once recorded will never die, but long after we are gone will be a living thing, asserting itself with evergrowing insistency. Remember that our sons and grandsons are going to do things that would stagger us. Let your watchword be order and your beacon beauty.[17]

NOTES

1. D. H. Burnham and E.H. Bennett, *Plan of Chicago* (Chicago: The Commercial Club, 1909).

2. *The Planning Function in Urban Government* (Chicago: University of Chicago Press, 1941).

3. Charles Moore, *Daniel H. Burnham — Architect, Planner of Cities* (Boston: Houghton, Mifflin and Co., 1921).

4. Walker, *op. cit.*

5. *Chicago Tribune*, July 7, 1909.

6. Burnham and Bennett, *op. cit.* There were those in high office favoring an approach that surely must have seemed radical at that time. At a dinner on January 8, 1910 the *Plan of Chicago* was formally presented to the city and at that time Alderman B. W. Snow commented: "The first step toward the realization of the ideals presented in the plan . . . must be to create one governmental unit to direct the affairs of Chicago and its outlying territory. Not through cooperation between the various governing bodies affected but through the consolidation of such governing bodies and the placing of all their forces under the direction of a single intelligence, will results be obtained" (*Chicago Tribune*, Jan. 9, 1910).

7. Burnham and Bennett, *op. cit.*

8. Walker, *op. cit.*

9. Charles H. Wacker, "Gaining Public Support for Planning Movement," *Proceedings, 5th National Conference on City Planning.*

10. Walter D. Moody, *What of the City?* (Chicago: A.C. McClurg & Co., 1919).

11. Walter D. Moody, *Wacker's Manual of the Plan of Chicago* (Chicago Plan Commission, 1911).

12. Moody, *What of the City?*

13. Walker, *op. cit.*, p. 241.

14. Moore, *op. cit.*, p. 115.

15. For example, its plan for eradicating slums was to open up these areas by cutting wide boulevards through them, just as Baron Haussmann had done in Paris.

16. *The Chicago Plan in 1933 — Twenty-Five Years of Accomplishment* (Chicago: Chicago Plan Commission, 1933).

17. Moore, *op. cit.*

5

Playgrounds, Housing
and City Planning

Allen F. Davis

The settlement workers' educational experiment and their commitment to neighborhood reconstruction led them into a series of closely related reform movements. If one accepted Friedrich Froebel's idea of creative play, or the belief of G. Stanley Hall that each child reenacted the history of the development of the race and must be provided an outlet for his animal energies, then it was a logical step from kindergarten to campaigns for public playgrounds. But the settlement worker did not need to read Froebel and Hall, or even to have a consistent philosophy of neighborhood regeneration; all he had to do was to look around him. "If we want decent adolescent boys we must give playgrounds to ten year olds," Jane Robbins announced. Lillian Wald agreed that the "young offender's presence in the courts may be traced to a play impulse for which there is no safe outlet."[1]

To many settlement workers, however, the best and most creative kind of play was rural play: many remembered their own childhood, vacations spent romping in the woods, swimming, riding, and fishing, and imagined that if other boys and girls could get out to the country in the summer, even for a short time, they would find strength of purpose and character. Many settlements established summer camps, a few maintained farms, and South End House regularly sent neighborhood boys as caddies to White Mountain summer resorts.[2]

The pioneer settlement workers themselves often closed up shop in the summer to escape to the country. Ellen Starr was constantly irritated by the

From *Spearheads for Reform: The Social Settlements and the Progressive Movement, 1890-1914*, by Allen F. Davis. Copyright © 1967 by Oxford University Press. Reprinted by permission.

dust and dirt at Hull House and loved to go to a clean New England village. Robert Woods maintained that the city was no place even for a settlement conference, and Lillian Wald said of New York, "This is an awful city to live in."[3] The city was an awful place to live for most of those in settlement neighborhoods, and if the residents sometimes became nostalgic it was understandable. After a few years of leaving in the summer months, however, they became realistically concerned with the misery of life in a hot tenement. Much of their energy they then devoted to fresh air excursions and summer camps with the thought of giving the youngsters a better place to play than the city streets, and of providing some relief for the mothers of small children. But they also felt that getting close to nature built character and independence. "The city girl benefits most from holidays in which she experiences nature in its more primitive aspects," Robert Woods and Albert Kennedy wrote.[4]

Some settlement workers had a tendency to romanticize "the green of the grass, the smell of the fields . . . the whir of the insects and the lowing of the cattle" and a few of the early settlement residents spent time and energy collecting flowers to distribute to the tenement dwellers. John Gavit, editor of the *Commons*, even remarked on one occasion that this was one of the settlements' "most useful inventions."[5] Residents did not, however, spend all their time distributing flowers and exporting children to the country. Many set out to provide more and better play space in the city and pioneered in demonstrating to the public the need for planned recreation.

The residents of Hull House established the first public playground in Chicago in 1893. Florence Kelley, disturbed by the unsanitary and unsafe conditions of several tenements near Hull House, sat down one night and composed a letter to a Chicago newspaper describing the conditions of the property owned by "A.E. Kent and Son." The son, William Kent, who later became a prominent progressive politician, immediately went to Hull House, talked with Florence Kelley and Jane Addams, and offered to give the buildings to the settlement if they would be run as model tenements. The two women suggested tearing down the buildings instead and making a playground. Kent accepted.[6]

At about the same time, Lillian Wald turned the backyard of Henry Street Settlement into a playground. It served as a kindergarten in the morning, as a place for older children to play in the afternoon, and a dance and festival place for young adults in the evening. Only a short time later, East Side House opened a similar facility on the banks of the East River with sandboxes and play apparatus. Northwestern University Settlement organized a large playground in Chicago and, in Philadelphia, College Settlement and then Starr Center supervised a playground. One observer remarked about the play area near Greenwich House in New York: "If a tablet were to be erected to commemorate the service of Mary Simkhovitch and the settlement to this neighborhood, it might apppropriately be placed in Hudson Park."[7]

Settlement workers did not originate the idea of neighborhood playgrounds; as with kindergartens, they adopted the idea before it had become widely accepted, demonstrated the need and usefulness, and then helped sell the idea to the city and eventually to the nation. They did not fight alone, of course. Robert Woods and Helena Dudley worked closely with Joseph Lee and the Massachusetts Civic League in the attempt to provide better playgrounds and public gymnasiums in Boston. In New York Jacob Riis, author of *How the Other Half Lives*, was one of the first to suggest the need for play areas near every public school and was a leader in the campaign for small parks and playgrounds.[8]

Riis's ideas were in agreement with those of settlement workers: social reform had to begin by altering the environment of the neighborhood. He wanted to make parks not just places filled with trees and flowers to look at, but useful areas where old and young might come to relax and play. Like Riis, Charles Stover, one of the early residents at Neighborhood Guild, felt that "Keep Off The Grass" signs should be removed from the parks and replaced with play facilities. Stover led the battle in New York for neighborhood playgrounds, especially for Seward Park.

II

As early as 1887 a park act passed in New York City recognized the need not only for small parks, but more significantly for play apparatus in them. Yet the Park Department ignored this provision of the law. In 1890, Stover, influenced much more by what he saw on the Lower East Side than by what he read about the importance of play, enlisted the cooperation of ex-Mayor Abram S. Hewitt and organized the Society for Parks and Playgrounds in New York "to secure in public parks plots especially devoted to children's recreation." The Society ran a large playground for a time at Ninety-second Street and Second Avenue, but only a handful of settlement workers and the group of reformers associated with the New York Reform club seemed interested. Finally, during Mayor Strong's administration in 1895, a committee headed by James B. Reynolds of University Settlement selected sites for two parks on the Lower East Side. The city purchased the property and tore down the tenements, but the parks were somehow never built. Seward Park was still a vacant lot filled with rubble, stagnant water, and exposed sewers —hardly a place for creative play.[9]

Stover, who had an unlimited supply of moral indignations as well as an ability to organize reform, interested Lillian Wald, James K. Paulding, Elizabeth Williams, Mary K. Simkhovitch, and a few other settlement

workers and reformers, and in 1898 formed the Outdoor Recreation League.
Felix Adler, Nicholas Murray Butler, president of Columbia University,
Richard Watson Gilder, editor of *Century Magazine,* William Dean Howells
and Jacob Riis were among the prominent citizens on the advisory board;
Stover was the president, and J.G. Phelps Stokes the treasurer (replacing)
Josephine Shaw Lowell, who served during the first few months). Settlement
workers made up a majority of the executive committee, and the ORL
headquarters was at Elizabeth Williams's College Settlement.[10] Lillian Wald
used her influence with the Commissioner of Health to get the city to level the
land and erect a fence around the park. The League then went to work, raised
the money, and installed a playground which opened June 3, 1899. Thousands
of children poured in from the very first day, and the playground was a great
success. The money for equipment, repairs, and supervision came from
private donations; however, the Outdoor Recreation League made it clear
that it was the city's responsibility to operate the playground in Seward Park
and do the same elsewhere.

In February 1900 the ORL submitted to the Park Board suggestions for
permanent improvements. They asked for sandboxes, shelters, basketball
courts, and play equipment for both boys and girls. But the Park Board
ignored their request. Instead it recommended a small park in the natural style
covering as large an area as possible, "with a view to provide sufficient lawn,
shrubberies, promenades and shade trees to make the park really useful and
attractive for the hard-working people of the neighborhood."[11] The ORL
protested vigorously, pointing out that a nearby park with shrubs and trees
was nearly deserted while Seward Park with its playground was filled with
children and its fence lined with adults watching the children play. They
appealed to the council, the mayor, and the park commissioners. Finally, in
April 1903, the city agreed to take over and run the playground.[12]

The innovators won the battle of Seward Park and gained national
publicity. But their fight was merely one skirmish in a major campaign in
many cities. Like so many other reforms, the play movement became
organized on the national level in the first decade of the twentieth century. It is
not surprising that the National Playground Association of America, formed
in 1906, included Stover, Reynolds, and Jane Addams. J. G. Phelps Stokes
was elected a member of its executive committee, and Miss Addams and
Joseph Lee became vice presidents.[13] The settlement workers' contributions to
the recreation movement were significant: as practical organizers, reformers,
and initiators, they helped convince the nation that creative play was
important to the development of better citizens. They showed, also, how
small playgrounds could help reconstruct the urban social environment.

III

Settlement workers also took part in a long and frustrating attempt to improve the housing in tenement neighborhoods. The overcrowding and filth in the tenements was an oppressive and overpowering sight — the first reaction was simply shock. Many settlement workers described the "garbage-strewn streets," "pale, dirty, undersized children," and the dark, damp rooms where a whole family existed. One New York resident found eleven people living in two rooms, and another discovered a room on a hot summer day "crowded with scantily-clothed, dull-faced men and women sewing upon heavy woolen coats and trousers."

The settlement investigators were obsessed with the inadequate toilet and bathing facilities and the absence of light and ventilation, but they documented the incredibly bad housing conditions with precision and sympathy.[14] Joining a protest movement already under way, they made important contributions of their own to housing reform. They had, for example, intimate knowledge of the conditions in their neighborhoods, and often stressed the little amenities that the housing reformer overlooked, such as the need for a parlor or front room for respectability and status. From their point of view, the improvement of housing was not an end in itself, but only part of the larger movement to reconstruct neighborhoods and improve the total environment of the city.

Since the beginnings of cities, men have been critical of urban housing. The model tenement, inspired by John Ruskin and developed in England by Octavia Hill, was one popular solution in the late nineteenth century. Built by limited-dividend corporations, model tenements were designed to provide modest but attractive housing for workingmen and their families and to set a standard of excellence for other landlords to follow. Although many philanthropic citizens in New York, Boston, Philadelphia, and other cities supported the movement, most settlement workers rejected this answer. They suggested that a more fundamental solution was needed for the housing problem.[15]

Starting with their own neighborhoods and moving outward, they began to document the need for better and more effective tenement house laws, then joined others in presenting their case to city councils and state legislatures. Robert Woods and several other residents of South End House cooperated with the Tenement House Committee of the Twentieth Century Club, while Harold Estabrook, a young resident of South End House, made a detailed study of a tenement district, and then worked to have some of the worst buildings torn down.[16]

Mary Sayles, a young Smith College graduate and fellow of the College Settlement Association, conducted the first systematic study of housing conditions in Jersey City in 1902. Living in the city at Whittier House, she had

the enthusiastic cooperation of Cornelia Bradford. Twice she was arrested
and many more times she was threatened or driven away by landlords. Yet
when the results were published, Governor Franklin Murphy was so
overwhelmed by the story of squalor and filthy and dilapidated homes that he
appointed a special tenement house commission which had its first meeting at
Whittier House.[17]

Kingsley House in Pittsburgh, College Settlement in Los Angeles, Union
Settlement in Providence, Kingsley House in New Orleans, and other
settlements scattered around the country played similar roles in their cities.[18]
Northwestern Settlement and Chicago Commons held conferences and
conducted housing investigations. But Jane Addams of Hull House and Mrs.
Emmons Blaine, daughter of Cyrus McCormick and friend of the settlement
workers in Chicago, really launched the housing movement in that city with
the establishment of the City Homes Association in 1900. They persuaded
Robert Hunter, wandering settlement worker, charity expert, and radical, to
conduct a thorough investigation of housing conditions. Like most progressive
reformers, they believed that "accurate knowledge of existing conditions must
be the basis for future reform." Hunter's report shocked some loyal Chicago
citizens who had always believed that because their city had plenty of room to
expand, it would be saved from the evils of the New York tenements. "Chicago
is both uninformed and unprepared for the future," Hunter concluded, and
predicted that the evils he described could not possibly be prevented under
existing laws.[19]

In larger part because of the energetic leaders of the City Homes
Association, Chicago got a better tenement house ordinance in 1902. The new
law helped a little, but another investigation three years later disclosed that
there was need for further change. Settlement workers and other reformers in
the city continued to agitate and investigate, but over the years their success
seemed meager compared with the energy spent. Yet housing reformers in
Chicago attracted national attention with their investigations and reforms,
and many cities sent experts to copy their methods.[20]

It was in New York that the most important work was done, and there that
the outline of a national housing movement was drawn. The name Jacob Riis
is almost synonymous with housing reform in New York. Born in Denmark in
1846, he came to America in 1870 and wandered from job to job before
becoming a police reporter for the New York *Tribune*. He became the leading
authority on life in the urban underworld, and recorded what he saw with
notebook and camera. In 1890 he published *How the Other Half Lives: Studies
Among the Tenements of New York*, a series of impressionistic sketches of the
degradation and human pathos in the slums. It was a plea for sympathy and a
demand for justice. There was a note of nostalgic agrarianism in his writing,
but his ability to depict the human side of poverty came through stronger.

More than any other single person he made Americans aware of the urban housing problem in the late nineteenth century. For Riis housing was only one aspect of a larger reform movement to regenerate the city.[21]

In many ways the settlement workers had much in common with Riis, but they were also realists interested in passing and enforcing legislation. They became directly involved in a more scientific and limited housing movement that also developed in New York, concerned primarily with restrictive legislation. The major credit for that movement belongs to the Tenement House Committee of the Charity Organization Society, and especially to Lawrence Veiller.

After graduating from City College, Veiller had been a resident in the early 1890s at University Settlement. His experience there, together with his work for the East Side Relief Work Committee during the depression of 1893, convinced him "that the improvement of the homes of the people was the starting point for everything." In 1898 Veiller talked Robert W. DeForest of the Charity Organization into forming a separate tenement house committee (though Veiller really wanted a separate organization); this committee became an important pressure group for tenement house reform in the city and the state and was primarily responsible for the appointment of a state tenement house commission in 1900.[22]

Veiller was principally a technician and scientific reformer who believed that the housing problem could be solved by passing restrictive legislation and housing codes. Settlement workers, many of whom had aided Richard Watson Gilder, the editor of *Century Magazine*, in his intensive investigation of housing conditions in 1894, joined Veiller. And he, like Gilder, found their energy and knowledge very useful. This was especially true in his educational campaign to show how poorly workingmen were housed. For this he organized an exhibition in the Sherry Building, at Thirty-eighth Street and Fifth Avenue in New York, that opened in February 1900. Exhibits demonstrated the incredible crowding in individual blocks, and photographs showed the "dark, unventilated airshafts" which provided the only air many tenements had. There were also display models of better designed buildings to show possible alternatives. Many New York settlements copied the idea in their neighborhoods and cooperated on a graphic study showing the actual income and expenditures of a large number of workingmen's families; other cities did the same thing. The Hull House group helped to prepare a similar display for Veiller's exhibition, and the residents of South End House worked on one sponsored by the Boston Twentieth Century Club. Over 10,000 people viewed the show in two weeks, and many more saw part of it when it was loaned to other cities.[23]

The exhibition aroused a number of influential people —including Governor Theodore Roosevelt — to the need for tenement house reform. The direct result was the passage of a bill, drafted by Veiller, providing for a New York Tenement House Commission. Veiller became the secretary of the commission and James B. Reynolds one of its members. The new agency made use of settlement workers in its investigations and public hearings. Thus armed with information, Veiller and his co-workers drafted a new housing code to eliminate some of the worst evils and provide ventilation and toilet facilities in each apartment. This new code was adopted in 1901. In order to enforce it, the housing reformers obtained a Tenement House Department in the city government. While the new arrangement did not solve the city's slum problem, it did put an end to some of the worst abuses.[24]

The New York movement, especially the exhibition and the new code, had an impact on nearly every large city in the country. When a man was needed to fill the position of chief sanitary inspector in Chicago to enforce its tenement house laws, Jane Addams and Mrs. Blaine looked to New York and persuaded the city to hire Charles Ball, one of Veiller's close associates and the chief sanitary inspector in the New York Tenement House Department.

The Chicago City Homes Association also borrowed the idea of the New York Tenement House Exhibition and established a permanent Municipal Museum in Chicago. This institution, also patterned after the Hull House Labor Museum, was "devoted to the collection and interpretation of materials illustrating the physical and social conditions and the administration of cities." More than just housing reform concerned its originators, however; they devoted space to vacation schools, parks, playgrounds, municipal art, and urban transportation. Jane Addams hoped thus to make the museum a place where historical and contemporary material about cities could be gathered and also a clearing house for urban reform.

Other cities also looked to New York for personnel and for ideas to solve their housing problems. It was natural, then, that the leader of the New York movement should become a key organizer of the National Housing Association in 1910. It is also significant that at the Association's organizational meeting settlement workers from Boston, Chicago, New Jersey, New Orleans, and Pittsburgh played prominent roles.[25]

IV

Many reformers in 1910 optimistically believed that the end was in sight, that investigation and legislation would eventually solve the problem of urban housing. Many settlement workers agreed, but more than most in the progressive era, they saw that housing was part of a greater problem. Florence Kelley, who had spent two decades protesting child labor in New York and Chicago, was well aware of the need for housing reform. But as she observed disease, and death, and despair in the tenements, she was struck by an elementary idea: it was simply the congestion of people, the overcrowding itself, that created most other social problems in the city. Housing reform, child labor reform, and a few scattered playgrounds would do no good unless some way was discovered to reduce the density of the population. "Instead of assenting to the belief that people who are poor must be crowded, why did we not see years ago that people who are crowded must remain poor?"

It was not an original idea, but to Florence Kelley an idea was of little use unless it was put to work. She conveyed her analysis to Lillian Wald, Mary Simkhovitch, Gaylord White of Union Settlement, and a few other settlement workers. Her explanation was simple and straightforward, and soon her friends, especially Mrs. Simkhovitch, began to catch some of her excitement. In 1907 they formed a Committee on the Congestion of Population with Mrs. Simkhovitch as chairman. Borrowing a page from the New York tenement house movement, they planned an exhibit to show the dangers and results of congestion.[26]

The committee hired Benjamin C. Marsh, a resident of Greenwich House, as secretary. He was a persuasive young man who, before coming to New York, had been secretary of the Pennsylvania Society to Protect Children from Cruelty and a graduate student in economics at Chicago and Pennsylvania universities. Somewhere along the way he had been converted by the writings of Henry George, and had become interested in the relation of rents and taxes to congestion. In the summer of 1907 Marsh went to Europe to gather material on city planning and housing that might be useful for the congestion exhibit. When it looked as though the panic of 1907 might require a postponement of the project, Carola Woerishoffer, a wealthy and beautiful young graduate of Bryn Mawr College who had recently moved to Greenwich House, stepped forward with a check for $3,000 to cover the expenses of the exhibit. George Ford, a young architect and a resident of Greenwich House, advised the committee on technical matters, and the settlement became the organizational center of the Congestion Committee's work. The group enlisted support from many organizations and arranged a "varied array of maps, diagrams, charts, statistics, models, photographs, and pictures." They all carried one and the same message: there were too many people crowded into tenement rooms, too many people in the workingmen's districts, too many in the city, and the new tenement house law had barely touched the problem.[27]

The exhibit began on March 9, 1908, in the Museum of Natural History and ran for nearly three weeks. Governor Charles Evans Hughes opened it, and many important people saw it. Some of the exhibits were frankly anti-urban. The Children's Aid Society showed contrasting pictures of healthy, ruddy-faced, country children tending cattle, and anemic, sickly, urban slum children playing in the streets. Professor Liberty Hyde Bailey of Cornell and others suggested that the only answer to urban congestion was to move the city dwellers to the country. Benjamin Marsh saw the major problem as an economic one and found the remedy in the single tax. Florence Kelley, Lillian Wald, Mary Simkhovitch, and others suggested that a migration to the farms was no solution; instead, the need was for more parks, playgrounds, and schools for the city, improved tenement house laws, better transportation, and above all, comprehensive city planning to limit the number of people that could live in a given area.[28]

The New York Congestion Exhibit received generous publicity and then went on the road. It moved to Brooklyn first, then to Richmond for the meeting of the National Conference of Charities and Correction. The next year the Committee on Congestion, together with the Municipal Arts Society, organized another exhibit on city planning which traveled to Washington, D.C., Buffalo, Elmira, Rochester, and Boston. With each exhibit there were addresses and conferences on the problem of congestion and what could be done about it. The campaign paid off. Governor Hughes appointed a Commission on Distribution of Population, and a short time later Mayor William Gaynor of New York appointed a City Commission on Congestion. And the Committee on Congestion called the first national conference on city planning for May 21, 1909 in Washington, D.C. At this meeting the National Conference on City Planning was born.[29]

Benjamin Marsh presided at the Washington conference, which was attended by such authorities in the field as Charles Robinson and Frederick Law Olmsted, as well as by Secretary of the Interior Richard A. Ballinger, Speaker of the House Joseph Cannon, and Senator Francis Newlands from Nevada. Among the many speakers were such settlement workers as George Hooker, George Ford, Benjamin Marsh, and Mary Simkhovitch.

Many of the reports were filled with unexciting details and statistics, but Mrs. Simkhovitch began her presentation by describing a little pageant of Robin Hood that had been put on by the children in the neighborhood of Greenwich House. She then described the overcrowded conditions that no pageant could erase. Though she used statistics, she also explained the consequences of congestion in terms of disease and death, the demoralizing effect of noise, and lack of privacy. Congestion had many causes, she said; among them were high rents, which forced many people to live in a small space, and industrial conditions that made it necessary to live near work. But there were social as well as economic causes. The city had advantages and conveniences. Where else could one live so close to relatives and friends and near a wide variety of churches, stores and inexpensive theatres? "The reason the poor like to live in New York is because it is interesting, convenient, and meets their social needs. They live there for the reason that I do; I like it." With that one sentence Mrs. Simkhovitch cut through the assumption held by many people at the conference, that if given the chance the poor would move out of the city. She argued for reducing the density of urban population because she liked cities and wanted to make them more livable, not because she wanted to recapture the small town. She argued for better distribution of population, better transportation, restriction of the number of people who could live in a single area, and above all, city planning on a regional basis.[30]

Mrs. Simkhovitch and other settlement workers, and a few of the other social reformers who attended the first national conference on city planning, were primarily concerned with social and economic planning. When the conference met the next year, however, it was obvious that the architects and engineers — who were concerned most with the aesthetic aspects of planning — had taken over. George Ford, Benjamin Marsh, George Hooker, and a few others nevertheless continued to urge comprehensive economic and social planning, but the National Conference on City Planning came to be dominated by those who concentrated on making the city more beautiful rather than more livable. As a result, they were often more interested in planning for the benefit of the well-to-do than in making life bearable for the tenement dwellers.[31]

Most settlement workers rejected the City Beautiful Movement, even though they occasionally cooperated in grandiose plans to improve and beautify the city. J. G. Phelps Stokes and Charles Stover were for several years prominent members of the New York Municipal Arts Society, which sought to achieve urban beauty, order, and efficiency. In addition, Stokes was chairman of the Civic Center Committee, which tried to promote the effective grouping of public buildings. Graham Taylor served on the Chicago Plan Commission, and George Hooker, long a resident of Hull House, was an active and aggressive exponent of city planning in Chicago. The Boston settlement workers cooperated in the comprehensive and sometimes utopian "Boston 1915" movement, launched in 1909 by Edward Filene and Lincoln Steffens to make Boston a more beautiful and more livable city by 1915. Many settlement workers also played the role of admiring host to Patrick Geddes, the brilliant and eccentric Scottish planner and exponent of the Garden City Movement, which sought to bring some of the best of the country into the city.[32]

Settlement workers were not opposed to making the city more beautiful; sometimes they acted and talked as if they really wanted to bring the amenities of the country and the small town back into the city. Usually, however, they were more concerned with promoting playgrounds than elaborate, formal parks, and were more interested in clean streets and tenement house laws than in grand tree-lined boulevards or elaborate ceremonial buildings. The fact that they lived in a working-class neighborhood tempered their interest in elaborate, sweeping, "city beautiful" schemes, and made them seek "realistic" and "practical" programs.

V

The settlement workers were planners in a sense. Their planning activity often took the form of negative action to block a measure that they believed would make the city or neighborhood less livable. In 1903 and 1904 when Mayor McClellan and the tenement house department of New York sponsored a bill that would have allowed the erection of temporary school buildings in public parks, they were moved to protest. Well aware of the need of new schools, they also believed in the importance of the public parks and realized that temporary measures often became permanent. The Association of Neighborhood Workers and the Outdoor Recreation League, which had fought hard to win the parks and playgrounds, protested so vigorously and effectively that they were able to block the measure.[33]

In 1905 the New York settlement workers went into action again to oppose a projected elevated railroad loop to connect the Brooklyn and Williamsburg bridges. This might have improved transportation in the area, but the workers feared that the elevated loop along Delancey Street would cause needless blight and more congestion in the Lower East Side. Instead, they favored a subway and advocated widening Delancey Street into a boulevard. Lillian Wald and Lawrence Veiller led the campaign of protest that helped defeat the measure. Stover called the first meeting and enlisted the support of many organizations on the Lower East Side. They held mass meetings, sent out form letters, appealed to influential people, persuaded newspapermen to present their point of view, and bombarded the city council with letters and petitions. Henry Street, College, and University settlements handled the clerical work, gathered most of the names on the petitions, and encouraged their members and supporters to protest the measure. The settlements had a great deal of help in the campaign, the source of which they never suspected; only after they had won did they learn that an unknown businessman, who opposed the elevated loop because he feared it would ruin his business, had spent $50,000 to defeat the measure.[34]

But their action was not always negative. Often they advocated another, unique kind of city planning — the revival of the neighborhood as a way of restoring the city. "Neighborhoods are the source of civic strength for progress," Graham Taylor announced at one point, in a phrase characteristic of the others.[35] Robert Woods and Mary Simkhovitch were the two who put the greatest emphasis on the neighborhood in city planning. "A settlement aims to get things done for a given neighborhood," Mrs. Simkhovitch wrote.

"It proposes to be the guardian of that neighborhood's interest, and through identification of the interests of the settlement group with the local interests, it forms a steadying and permanent element in a community which is more or less wavering and in flux. To work out the method by which a neighborhood may become a consciously effective group is . . . the difficult task of the settlement everywhere."[36]

Even more than Mary Simkhovitch, Robert Woods preached revival of the neighborhood, or as he sometimes phrased it, "the recovery of the parish." In an age when industrialism and immigration made the city expand at a fantastic rate, some unit smaller than the city but larger than the family seemed necessary to prevent the collapse of public morality, good government, and civic loyalty. "The neighborhood is large enough to include in essence all the problems of the city, the State, and the Nation . . . ," Woods wrote. "It is large enough to present the problems in a recognizable community form. . . .It is large enough to make some provision for the whole variety of extra-family interests and attachments. . . It is large enough so that the facts and forces of its public life, rightly considered, have significance and dramatic compulsion. . . . " Woods preached his idea of neighborhood revival so insistently that, at one conference, Jane Addams, who argued that the settlement should appeal to the whole city, became annoyed and blurted out, "Mr. Woods, I do not believe in geographical salvation." Yet even Miss Addams on occasion talked about the need to restore loyalty to the neighborhood in the industrial city. Sometimes there was a tinge of nostalgia for the social unity of the small town in the settlement workers' argument for the need of city neighborhoods; but there was also a realistic appraisal of the dehumanizing forces at work in the city and recognition of the need, especially among the occupants of the dreary tenement districts, for pride and loyalty in something larger than themselves.[37]

NOTES

1. Woods, "Settlement Workers Get Together on Social Problems," *Survey*, XXXI (Oct. 11, 1913), 45; Wald, *House on Henry Street*, 95.

2. Woods and Kennedy, *Settlement Horizon*, 121-30; Addams, *Twenty Years*, 16-7; Charles F. Ernst, "South End House Cady Scheme," *Survey*, XXVII (Oct. 7, 1911), 969-75.

3. Notes by Miss Josephine Starr on Ellen Gates Starr, April 30, Starr MSS; Woods to Addams, May 23, 1898; Wald to Addams, Dec. 24, 1914, Addams MSS.

4. Simkhovitch, "Fresh Air Organization," *Charities*, X (June 20, 1903), 601-2; William Mathews, "Lillian House: Which Affords Its Guests Fresh Air, Farm Life and Every Country Joy." *Survey*, XXIV (June 4, 1910), 407-19; Woods and Kennedy, *Settlement Horizon*, 127.

5. "On Life's Farm," *Commons*, III (June 1898), 1-2; "Flower Mission Work," *Commons*, I (July 1896), 12.

6. Elizabeth Thacher Kent, *William Kent* (privately printed, 1950), 95-6; Addams to Kent, March 7, 1910, "Jane Addams," n.d., William Kent MSS.

7. Wald, *House on Henry Street*, 81-4; "Playgrounds for Children," *Charities*, VI (May 11, 1901), 46; Anne O'Hagan Shinn, "Where Barrow Street and Bleecker Meet," *Survey*, XXXIX (Dec. 1, 1917), 247.

8. Clarence E. Rainwater, *The Play Movement in the United States* (Chicago, 1922), 13-43; E. Woods, *Robert Woods*, 213 ff; Joseph Lee, *Constructive and Preventive Philanthropy* (New York, 1902); Riis, "Playgrounds for City Schools," *Century*, XLVIII (Sept. 1894), 657-66.

9. Stover, "Playground Progress in Seward Park," *Charities*, VI (April 27, 1901), 386; James K. Paulding, *Charles Stover*, 43 ff; J. G. Phelps Stokes, "Narrative," Stokes MSS; *University Settlement Annual Report*, 1896, 16.

10. Stokes, "Narrative"; Outdoor Recreation League letterhead, Stokes MSS.

11. William Potts, "Seward Park Playground," *Charities*, III (June 17, 1899), 3; quotation from Stover, "Playground Progress in Seward Park," *Charities*, VI (April 27, 1901), 391.

12. Seward Park at Last a Reality," *Charities*, X (Feb. 7, 1903), 127-133.

13. "Playground Association of America," *Charities and the Commons*, XVI (April 21, 1906), 116-7; Henry Curtis to Stokes, March 2, 1906.

14. Alvan Sanborn, "Anatomy of a Tenement Street," *Forum*, XVIII (Aug. 1898), 554-72; Florence Kelley, "Sweating System," *Hull-House Maps and Papers*, 27-45; Ernest Poole, "The Lung Block: Some Pictures of Consumption in its Stronghold," *Charities*, XI (Sept. 5, 1903), 193-9.

15. Bremner, *From the Depths*, 206-7; *Andover House Circular*, Dec. 1893, 7.

16. Eleanor Woods, *Robert Woods*, 49; Estabrook, *Some Slums of Boston* (Boston, 1898); Anne Withington, "Boston Tenement House Conditions," *Commons*, IX (Sept. 1904), 418.

17. Mary B. Sayles, "Housing Conditions in Jersey City," *Annals*, XX (July 1902), 139-50.

18. "To Improve Pittsburgh's Bad Housing," *Charities and the Commons*, XIX (March 28, 1908), 1783; Bessie B. Stoddard, "Courts of Sonoratoun; The Housing Problem as it is to be Found in Los Angeles," *Charities and the Commons*, XV (Dec. 2, 1905), 295-9; Bradley Buell, "Eleanor McMain: One of the Pioneers," *Survey Graphic*, XX (Jan. 1931), 374-8.

19. "Proposed Budget for City Homes Association," with sketch of founding, 1913-14, Blaine MSS: Robert Hunter, *Tenement Conditions in Chicago: Report of the Investigating Committee of the City Homes Association* (Chicago, 1901), 16, 162.

20. "To Re-Investigate Chicago Housing Conditions," *Charities and the Commons*, XV (Nov. 18, 1905), 229-30; Addams, "The Housing Problem in Chicago," *Annals*, XX (July 1902), 99-107.

21. Jacob Riis, *The Making of An American* (New York, 1901); Riis, "What Settlements Stand For," *Outlook* LXXXIX (May 9, 1908), 69-72. Here as elsewhere in this chapter, I am indebted to Roy Lubove, *The Progressives and the Slums: Tenement House Reform in New York City, 1890-1917* (Pittsburgh, 1962).

22. Lawrence Veiller, OHP, 3; "Settlement Contribution to Legislation," *Commons*, V (July 1901), 7; Lubove, *Progressives and the Slums*, 81-149.

23. Veiller, OHP, 11-13, Form letters from De Forest, May 6, 1899, July 19, 1899, Veiller MSS; Veiller, "Tenement House Exhibition of 1899," *Charities Review*, X (March 1900), 19-27.

24. Veiller, OHP, 13-15; Lubove, *Progressives and the Slums*, 117-49.

25. Mrs. Blaine to Veiller, July 29, 1904; Ball to Raymond Robins, Dec. 28, 1903, Blaine MSS; Charles Ball, "The Municipal Museum of Chicago," *Commons*, X (April 1905), 215-20; Veiller, "National Housing Association," *Survey*, XXIII (March 5, 1910), 841-8.

26. Kelley, "The Settlements: Their Lost Opportunity," *Charities and the Commons*, XVI (April 7, 1906), 81; Wald to Harry Van Dyke, July 9, 1908, Wald MSS; Simkhovitch MSS.

27. Benjamin Marsh, *Lobbyist for the People* (Washington, 1953), 17; Carola Woerishoffer: *Her Life and Work* (Philadelphia, 1912), 13, 59-60; Lubove, *Progressives and the Slums*, 231-4.

28. Kelley, "Congestion and Sweated Labor," *Charities and the Commons*, XX (April 4, 1908), 48-50; John Martin, "The Exhibit of Congestion Interpreted," *Ibid.*, XX (April 4, 1908), 27-39.

29. Simkhovitch, "Committee on Congestion and City Planning," Simkhovitch MSS; Charles M. Robinson, "The City Plan Exhibition," *Survey*, XXII (May 29, 1909), 313-18; Marsh, "The Congestion Exhibit in Brooklyn," *Charities and the Commons*, XX (May 9, 1908), 209-11.

30. Mary Simkhovitch, *Proceedings of the First National Conference on City Planning*, Washington, D.C., May 21, 22, 1909; Hearing Before Senate Committee on District of Columbia; 61st Congress, 2d Session; Senate Document 422, 101-4. See Robert A. Walker, *The Planning Function in Urban Government* (Chicago, 1941), 10-12.

31. Walker, *The Planning Function*, 11-16. On the City Beautiful Movement see John Burchard and Albert Bush Brown, *The Architecture of America: A Social and Cultural History* (Boston, 1961), 273 ff. From 1913 to 1916 Ford was consultant to the Commission on Building Districts and Restriction, and drafted the New York City Zoning Ordinance, the first such ordinance in America.

32. Stokes, "Narrative," 24-6, Stokes MSS; Hooker, "A Plan for Chicago," *Survey*, XXII (Sept. 4, 1909), 778-90; Kellogg, "The Reconstruction Era in Boston," *Survey*, XXIII (Oct. 2, 1909), 13-14. For a sympathetic account of the Garden City Movement see Lewis Mumford, *Culture of Cities* (New York, 1938), 392-6.

33. Gaylord S. White, "Legislation Opposed by New York Social Workers," *Commons*, IX (April 1904), 144-6; "Mass Meeting at Greenwich House," *Charities*, X (Feb. 21, 1903), *Settlement Journal* (Henry St.) I (April 1914), 8-9.

34. James H. Hamilton, "The Winning of the Boulevard," USSQ, II (Dec. 1906), 24-6; Lillian Wald, "The East Side in Danger," *Commons*, X (April 1905), 222; Wald, *Windows on Henry Street* (Boston, 1934), 3-4.

35. Taylor, "Survival and Revival of Neighborhoodship," *Survey*, XXVIII (May 4, 1912), 321.

36. *Greenwich House Report*, 1904, 8. See also Simkhovitch, "The Neighborhood Looks at Planning," March 25, 1944, Simkhovitch MSS.

37. Woods, "Neighborhood in Social Reconstruction," *The Neighborhood and Nation Building* (Boston, 1923), 148-9; "The Recovery of the Parish," *Ibid.*, 133-46; Jane Addams's remark recalled by Albert Kennedy in address, "The Settlement Heritage," at NCSW, June 4, 1953, copy NFS.

6

Moles and Skylarks

William H. Wilson

Whether realists or utopians, city planners from 1915 to 1945 were most successful when they planned comprehensively or built specifically. Realistic building comprised parkway systems and similar projects that were geographically inclusive but conceptually narrow. Utopian schemes involved totally planned, spatially restricted undertakings such as public housing or greenbelt suburbs — islands afloat in seas of unplanning. Metropolitan areas continued to grow, usually without the benefit of more than the flimsiest control. This should not suggest that all planning was futile. It does mean that a study of city planning is quite different from a study of planned cities.

The Realists

The realists' planning attitudes and activities of the early twentieth century cast long shadows. By 1915 City Beautiful plans were gathering dust, and City Beautiful planners were mostly aging landscape architects. Younger planners often scoffed at the City Beautiful legacy, charging its creators with a narrow concern for superficial and meretricious urban decoration in the midst of unplanned squalor and decay. The younger men prided themselves on their toughminded empiricism, their comprehensive view of urban problems, and their ability to merge their encyclopedic knowledge with their salesmanship in committing the public to the reconstruction of American cities. Their zest for fact-gathering and feasibility studies found expression in the phrases "city functional," "city scientific," and "city efficient." Everything urban —

Reprinted from William H. Wilson, 1974. *Coming of Age: Urban American 1915-1945.* New York: John Wiley. Copyright © 1974. John Wiley & Sons, Inc. Reprinted by permission.

housing, education, public health, recreation, and mass transit — was within their professional ken.

The resulting grand plans suffered stillbirths despite their authors' optimism and certitude. The movement for "Boston—1915," begun in 1909, was the first thrust for a comprehensive metropolitan plan. Youthful planners promised a blueprint for strengthening the complex interrelationships of urban living. What emerged was a metropolitan improvement scheme to be financed partly by Boston, partly by levies on the suburbs, partly by the state. It failed because of suburban indifference and hostility toward Boston's taxes and the lower-class elements in its population.

Planners already had taken up the fight for beliefs that would later become conventional wisdom. By 1915 most had been converted to zoning. Philip Kates, an attorney interested in urban problems, already had proposed an investigative federal Municipal Commission in a speech to the 1911 Conference on City Planning. The prospect of federal intervention horrified many planners. Yet the conviction that urban problems were national problems requiring federal involvement had begun to gather momentum. Planning already had become a profession, in the eyes of planners at least, with all that meant in the way of organizations, annual meetings, publications, special training, and expanding institutional relationships. The national conferences on city planning were (since 1909) drawing together planners, social and settlement-house workers, housers, architects, and sympathetic professionals in other fields for searching discussions of the urban crisis. In 1909 Harvard University offered the first course in planning, a harbinger of the departments of city planning to follow a generation later.

The 1913 planning conference anticipated the mushroom growth of city planning commissions with its model enabling act for a municipal "Department of City Planning." Planning commissions were the spawn of the same quest for efficiency and order that produced the city manager movement. They implied a similiar bureaucratic development, with the model "department" employing "engineers." The American City Planning Institute (later the American Institute of Planners) would be formed in 1917.

Planning literature mushroomed. The *Survey* magazine, *American City*, and other periodicals carried news of planners' activities and aspirations. Published plans such as *The Plan of Chicago* (1909) were a well-established means of disseminating planning ideas. A wealth of "how-to" books complemented the plans. They conceded greater social sophistication to European, especially German, cities with their careful land-use controls (zoning), their reservation of grounds for public purposes, and their restrictions on urban land speculation. Discussions of the problems of state enabling legislation and legal snares foreshadowed the time when impatient urban bureaucrats and civic leaders would rebel against statehouse control and constricting court decisions. Frank acknowledgment that many major improvements would cost more money than the cities' residents had previously raised forecast the day when urban projects would require federal financing. Benjamin C. Marsh's *An Introduction to City Planning: Democracy's Challenge to the American City* (1909) discussed the European successes while later books concentrated more on immediate problems, legislative and legal. They included John Nolen's *Replanning Small Cities* (1912) and Flavel Shurtleff's *Carrying Out the City Plan* (1914).

All these planners were realists; that is, they planned for the existing order. Their visions of the future embraced a society based on free enterprise, still individualistic and democratic if somewhat more malleable. Their realistic planning impinged on most of the physical growth of cities during the interwar period. Their victories, in the short run at least, were many. The zoning movement towers among the realists' great achievements. It also typifies their shortcomings.

Efforts to establish zoning, that is, to separate and restrict urban areas according to function, were ancient. The hyperdevelopment of industrial cities intensified the urge to control. City Beautiful planners of the nineteenth century, forced to work without serious limitations on land use, designed some parks and boulevards to divide retail from residential districts, inhibit industrial expansion, and segregate racial neighborhoods. Cities turned to nuisance regulations, but the courts sometimes limited them to prohibiting flagrant assaults on the senses. A relatively smokeless and noiseless factory, for instance, might be allowed in a residential neighborhood even though it violated the doctrine of separation of functions.

Deed restrictions on residential lots were a solution but only for higher priced developments. Besides, the Supreme Court was more friendly to municipal controls, approving Boston's heights of buildings ordinance in 1909 and Los Angeles's industrial zones in 1915. Professional planners, their eyes fixed on European cities, mostly ignored these domestic solutions. In 1913 the legislatures of New York, Minnesota, Wisconsin, and Illinois passed bills enabling cities to designate residential areas closed to industry. The governor of Illinois vetoed the bill presented to him but the other bills stood. Clearly, urban citizens were desperately determined to halt the blighting of residence districts. But the legislation did not even hint at the need for comprehensive zoning, to say nothing of comprehensive planning.

Zoning did not emerge from the plight of the citizen-as-resident, however much it might shape his future homebody role. Instead it was a response to threats against commercial and retail property in one place, New York City. The threatened property owners' economic and political power forced a solution, a solution rendered with such skill that it became the panacea for pell-mell urban growth. That a solution designed for one locality could be generally accepted may seem absurd, but its acceptance has a rational explanation.

Commercial and retail property owners on Manhattan Island faced property losses as threatening as any confronting the most harried middle-class homeowner. In lower Manhattan, the skyscraper loomed as the monstrous offspring of technological wizardry. Astronomical land values, structural steel, and a sophisticated life support system combined with egotism to shove buildings ever higher. In 1913 the dynamic merchant Frank W. Woolworth sent his gothic skyscraper to 60 stories, 792 feet above the pavement. It was a huge structure by standards of any time and place. The Woolworth and other tall buildings robbed their lesser neighbors of light and air, though their tower construction mitigated the damage.

Even while Woolworth opened his tower, General Thomas Coleman duPont was planning something more ominous, a new Equitable Building at 120 Broadway. When completed in 1915 the Equitable's 42 stories no longer were spectacular. But its dimensions were. Forecasting later slab-sided monsters, the Equitable covered a city block, crammed 13,000 workers into its 1,250,000 square feet of office space, and forced the surrounding streets and sidewalks to accept the 100,000 people who entered and left the building each day. Worse, the Equitable cast a noontime shadow four blocks long, sealing off buildings up to half its height from direct sunlight. Owners of buildings wrapped in the new gloom suffered a loss of tenants and received reduced tax valuations. Tenants who remained reported that their office workers were absent on account of illness more often than before.

Farther up Manhattan another land-use battle raged. Since the late nineties an expanding cluster of stores and specialty shops catering to the carriage trade had steadily shoved aside the millionaire's mansions on Fifth Avenue north of Thirty-fourth Street. The millionaires fought the encroachment. The avenue's soaring land values, its proximity to store and shop customers, and its safe distance from warehouses, loft factories, and immigrants were against them. By 1970 the battle between millionaires and stores was over and the defeated rich were in retreat up Fifth Avenue to make another stand on the margin of Central Park. Now the store owners turned to face a new foe — the garment industry with its thousands of poor Russian Jewish workers. The garment factories were moving north and west from the inefficient, over-crowded tenements of the lower East Side to newer buildings nearer the major railroad stations. In 1907 the Fifth Avenue Association was formed by merchants determined to hold their conquest for themselves.

A few years after its founding the Fifth Avenue Association began pressuring Manhattan's borough president, George McAneny, to persuade the city to set low maximum building heights on Fifth Avenue. No overt regulation could keep out the garment industry, but low buildings would be

too small, forcing the industry to look elsewhere for space. Nothing came of
the height regulations, but McAneny was the right man to pressure. A
newspaperman and reform politician, he was later to be a member of planning
agencies both public and private. At the same time that the Fifth Avenue
Association was at work, another reformer, Edward M. Bassett, was
discussing with McAneny the interrelated problems of building height,
congestion, and chaotic land use. Bassett was the father of zoning of America.
He had been influenced by various European schemes to deconcentrate urban
areas, and had already decided to devote his substantial legal talent to the
cause of city planning.

McAneny led the city council in establishing, in February 1913, a Heights of
Buildings Commission to study the problem of size limits on commercial
buildings. The Commission was to examine all aspects of the matter,
including zoning the city by function, and report to a specially designated
committee of the city council. Four circumstances surrounding the Heights of
Buildings Commission were especially noteworthy. First, its creation did not
commit anybody to anything. Second, its 19 members were mostly real estate
men or members of the Fifth Avenue Association; therefore any recommendations were almost certain to reflect what the dominant owners of
commercial and retail property wanted. Third, although zoning was, strictly
speaking, only a demarcation based on the functional status quo, McAneny
termed the commission "a wedge into the problem of city planning."[1] In later
years zoning rarely came within shouting distance of true planning for the
future. Yet McAneny had called zoning a part of planning, an identification
that grew until, in many minds, the part was mistaken for the whole. Fourth,
Bassett was chairman of the Heights of Buildings Commission. With a dogged
determination worthy of his name, Bassett set about drafting a zoning
ordinance that would serve property owners while it survived legal assaults.
Bassett was no tool of the rich. He was a reformer, one of those men who likes
to think of himself as a practical idealist.

The committee's report of December 1913 suggested that height regulations
on buildings, stated as multiples of street width, would admit sufficient light
and air. Unfortunately there were no existing standards of sufficiency for
either. Above the maximum height (300 feet was the highest) buildings would
be set or stepped back, revealing their neighbors to the sun and preventing any
more unconscionable overcrowding. Or so the theory went. Outside of the
heavily congested districts there were more severe building height and volume
limits. The next step after the report was to secure a zoning enabling act from
the legislature, done in 1914. In the summer of that year the council appointed
a second commission, the Commission on Building Districts and Restrictions,
to hold hearings and draft a zoning ordinance. Bassett was chairman once
more, and the membership was little changed from that of the first

commission.

The difference between the titles of the first and second commissions — Heights of Buildings versus Building Districts and Restrictions — indicated an increasing concern for the functional segregation of urban activities. In hearing after hearing the indefatigable Bassett promoted that concern. He reassured owners that their property values would be maintained, indeed enhanced, that broadly conceived zoning was legally secure, and that his careful, block-by-block ordinance would ratify the status quo. Bassett was convincing. With the New York commercial and financial community solidly behind it, the commission's draft became law on July 25, 1916.

In some ways the law was without precedent, in the United States at least. The ordinance divided New York into commercial, residential, and unrestricted districts, into five types of heights-of-building districts, and into five types of area districts that regulated the size of courts and yards. The height and area requirements really regulated the volumes of tall buildings by requiring in crowded districts, for example, either a set-back design or a tower that left a portion of the air above its lot unoccupied. Detailed maps showed the boundaries and extent of each type of district.

The ordinance was a beginning. If it had been used with a lively sense of its shortcomings and of the need for its improvement, its regulations might have been beneficial to New York and other cities. It was not so used. The second commission regretted the lack of comprehensive planning, and some shortcomings were confessed. But in the minds of Bassett and most of his associates their unprecedented labors outweighed any defects.

There were defects. The use, height, and area maps overlapped in confusing ways. Many builders of large speculative office buildings sought the maximum allowable volume for their structures. The result, in the maximum height districts, was a building "envelope" of ziggurat shape, like an awkward staircase for giants. The ziggurats were not always unlovely, although most of them were. In either case they stole light and air from surrounding buildings as before. A ziggurat could be avoided by sending up a slender tower, but tower construction sacrificed huge hunks of rentable office space to esthetics. Towers were possible only when their owners wished to satisfy desires for recognition and display.

The ordinance permitted — or omitted to control — much that begged for restriction. The report of the Height of Buildings Commission verged on the hysterical when it described the possibilities of a serious fire in a tall building. It conjured up horrible visions of the panic that would occur if a disaster disgorged the human contents of skyscrapers upon Manhattan's narrow streets. Such fancies were farfetched but they did dramatize the real problem of congestion in lower Manhattan. The obvious solution was to limit the heights of buildings in crowded areas. But only heights up to the first setback, not absolute heights, were regulated. Anyone with the money and the will could send a building up as high as he wished so long as he complied with the regulations.

The ordinance failed to limit any type of residence in commercial districts. Neither did it exclude all manufacturing. The city took no action against the garment industries crowding nearer to the fashionable stores along Fifth Avenue. Only the year before the Supreme Court had vindicated Los Angeles's ejecting factories from newly established nonindustrial areas. The timid New Yorkers were content to forbid any more factories near Fifth Avenue.

In the case of Fifth Avenue, indeed, the private action of the Fifth Avenue Association accomplished what the ordinance could not — it rid the area north of Thirty-Fourth Street of garment factories. The Fifth Avenue Association supported zoning, but it had three other, stronger strings to its bow. First, it persuaded the city's major lending institutions to withhold loans from the builders of loft buildings north of Thirty-fourth Street. The action made it clear to factory owners that they could not extend their beachhead in the fashionable retail district. Second, in March 1916, the Fifth Avenue Association ran full-page ads in the major dailies to announce a boycott of all garment manufacturers who refused to move by February of the following year. Third, the Association sweetened the pill. It offered help in relocation and promised not to enforce the boycott against firms agreeing to move when their leases expired. The result was a near-unanimous capitulation by the garment industry, even before the zoning ordinance became law.

Zoning contained no incentives to "upgrade" an industrial or commercial district to residential use, only a mechanism of "adjustment," or "rezoning" to open a residential neighborhood to commercial and industrial encroachment. Zoning, then, was narrow, partial, and socially defective. But its very shortcomings made its success. Enlightened real estate developers, store owners, and industrialists in city after city favored zoning because it officially endorsed their past activities and promised them more of the same. A few intelligent New Yorkers warned against the blind adoption of an imperfect scheme for one city, but to no avail. The largest, most sophisticated city seemed to be the most innovative. To harassed city planners, anxious for allies, zoning was an issue on which they could unite with forward-looking businessmen.

Enlightenment and progressivism produced zoning's ultimate folly, rigid segregation of districts by function. *Some* segregation, such as banning new single-family dwellings in industrial developments, was justified. It was left to the advanced intellectual community of Berkeley, California — on the suggestion of some local manufacturers — to ban *all* new residential construction in industrial districts. In contrast, the utopians of the day believed that workers' domestic and productive lives needed reintegration, not further separation. The utopians may not have hit upon a universal solution but at least their ideas were worth heeding. Suppose Berkeley's planners, industrialists, and landlords sat down together to refashion factories into clean, quiet places that could nestle side by side with humanely replanned workers' housing. That would have been a truly enlightened act, whether or not an entirely successful one. Nothing of the sort was considered. Instead, the Berkeley solution increased the psychic and physical distances between home and work, not to mention the cost of transportation. Suggestions that cities should establish semirural greenbelts by zoning out all building on their peripheries were equally ignored.

By the end of 1921 city planners and local elites had secured zoning enabling acts from almost half the state legislatures in the country. No less a personage than the indefatigable Herbert Hoover gave their efforts a boost during that year. Hoover, as Secretary of Commerce, appointed an advisory committee to draft a model state zoning enabling act. Hoover's passion for system, order, and planning through voluntary cooperation led him to proven methods. He appointed Bassett to head the committee, thereby insuring the transfer of New York's wisdom, or unwisdom, to the nation. The other members of the committee were realists in housing, planning, and real estate, men ready to follow Bassett's lead.

The committee was ready with a preliminary draft by September, 1921; by early 1924 the Government Printing Office was distributing the finished document, the Standard State Zoning Enabling Act. The model act gave the merest nod in the direction of comprehensive planning. There was nothing in it to prevent a city from making its zoning ordinance a substitute for a comprehensive plan. The energy of zoning's backers and the ease of its adoption sped acceptance. In his introduction to the model zoning ordinance Hoover boasted that 22 milion people lived under zoning, with their number growing month by month.

Even though Hoover had blessed zoning, it was not entirely secure until the United States Supreme Court had passed upon its constitutionality. By 1926 more than 400 cities and towns had zoning ordinances, and several state supreme courts had upheld zoning as a proper exercise of municipal police power. Only courts in states without state enabling acts had overturned zoning. The reiterated police power doctrine and the sheer number of zoned municipalities seemed to place zoning beyond danger. Bassett wanted it that way — to make Supreme Court justices blanch at the thought of unsettling the lives of the tens of millions of people who lived on zoned land.

Urban police power was safe from direct assault but not from an astute introduction of some equally valued principle in opposition. The lawyers for a Cleveland real estate firm hit upon such a principle — the loss of rights guaranteed by the Fourteenth Amendment to the federal Constitution. Euclid, Ohio, a suburb of Cleveland, was the other party to the suit. In 1922 Euclid adopted a zoning ordinance placing land owned by the Ambler Realty Company in a residential category. The Ambler firm was holding the property for commercial and industrial development, and was dismayed by the loss of values. It argued that its property, that is, the difference betwen the lower residential values, and the higher commercial and industrial values, had been taken from it without the due process of law guaranteed by the Fourteenth Amendment.

There was really no defense against Ambler's argument, except to say that it was irrelevant. The danger for zoning was that the conservative courts of the day zealously guarded property rights, especially those infringed by newfangled regulations. The United States District Court upheld Ambler, and Euclid appealed to the Supreme Court. The high court vindicated zoning in a landmark four-to-three decision, a decision owing much to a brilliant brief by Alfred Bettman, a Cincinnati lawyer and city planner. Bettman focused his attack on a secondary statement in the Ambler brief, that urban growth was too dynamic and spontaneous to foresee or control. Zoning, Bettman replied, "represents the application of foresight and intelligence to the development of the community."[2] He marshaled mountains of evidence and supporting briefs to show that zoning involved assigning various needed urban functions to their proper places, or as he expressed it, keeping the furnace out of the living room. He was careful to include the Bassett argument; if the high court undid zoning in this instance, the results would be catastrophic and nationwide. His arguments probably persuaded one of the court's conservatives, Justice George Sutherland, to abandon his beloved Fourteenth Amendment in favor of municipal police power.

Ironically, infatuation with zoning began to fade just as the Supreme Court affirmed its validity. Zoning had not abolished human nature. Reform groups in New York City attacked the Board of Standards and Appeals for corruption in the granting of variances. The full scandal was not revealed until 1931 and 1932, when it became an issue in the reform movement that triumphed in the mayoral election of Fiorello H. La Guardia. Often the bribery (usually accomplished by kickbacks and excessive fees) did not harm anyone in any tangible way. Sometimes, as when a block in a fine Manhattan residential district was opened to business over the residents' opposition, it did. Either way, the public became less enamored of zoning as other cities followed New York, not only in adopting zoning, but in establishing boards to grant variances.

Planners lost faith, too. At first they confined themselves to reiterations that zoning was not a substitute for planning. Bettman sounded the warning. So did Thomas Adams, a gifted British planner who frequently worked in the

United States during the twenties and thirties. Zoning was the end of the planning process, not the beginning, Adams told the national planning conference in 1920. Adams proposed a two-step planning exercise. First, he would have extended city planning to encompass regional planning. Second, he would have worked from the region back through general plans for population centers, through specific plans for housing, industries, and other basic elements, with zoning used to fix the final decision. The Standard City Planning Enabling Act of 1927, prepared under the aegis of Hoover's Department of Commerce, reflected the new concern. The zoning enabling act of three years before had nearly brushed planning aside, but the later act paid it exclusive attention. Without rigidly defining a master plan, the act's most influential authors — Bassett, Bettman, the younger Frederick Law Olmsted — suggested five areas of planning. These included streets, public grounds, public buildings, public utilities, and zoning, which brought up the rear in a distinctly subordinate position.

Planners' initial caution had become widespread disillusionment by the thirties. They complained of unsound zoning changes based on nothing more than the ignorance or venality of adjustment boards and city councils. They attacked overzoning, or the reserving of vastly more land for commercial and industrial purposes than could be used. Some of these projections for business use would have brought a gasp from the most sanguine of boosters. In this the zoning laws followed New York's famed 1916 resolution, which permitted, under full utilization, working space for some 300 million employees. (The population of New York City in 1920 numbered fewer than six million souls.) Los Angeles zoned enough business land for a population larger than the country's. Modest-sized Duluth established land uses and office building envelopes to house a highly improbable 20 million workers.

All this might have been dismissed as innocent Babbittry except for some pernicious results. The other side of the overzoning coin was the underzoning of residential property. In 1923 single-family residences occupied 12 percent of Chicago's land area. So did industry. The zoning ordinance doubled industry's allotment to 24 percent; it cut the area reserved for single-family residences to three percent. Commercial, two-family, and apartment uses all received bigger slices of the land pie than they occupied at the time. The zoning ordinance left three-fourths of Chicago's single-family residential land unprotected against encroachments. It also encouraged property taxation based on future, not present, uses. Heavier taxation sped the destruction of residential areas in favor of "more intensive uses," a euphemism for crowding. Those tendencies were not confined to Chicago, but were nationwide.

So-called "spot zoning" developed during the twenties. Spot zoning involved rezoning lots here and there, usually for some nonresidential purpose in a residential area. It was one result of the over-refinement of zoning classifications. Permissive adjustment boards conferred these ultrarefined classifications on patches of land all over cities. The result was practically the same as the granting of variances.

How much in favor of zoning may be rescued from this sordid tale? Not much. In some instances zoning probably saved investments, in others it provided landowners with windfall profits to offset higher taxes. In many aging residential areas it probably retarded helterskelter conversions to nonresidential use. These gains scarcely overcame the deficiencies.

Comprehensive or "master" planning resulted in no more definite improvement and even less superficial activity than did zoning. Much so-called master planning occurred in the understaffed offices of city planning commissions. Many commissions lacked the numbers and knowledge to construct comprehensive plans. They took refuge in an interpretation of the Standard City Planning Enabling Act (repeated almost verbatim in many state statutes) permitting the piecemeal development of comprehensive plans. Thus urban citizens of the late twenties and thirties were treated to one-at-a-time "master" plans of the single elements in a comprehensive plan — parks, streets, public transportation, and so on.

Independent professional planners often produced genuine comprehensive plans. Typically a city or some well-financed citizen group within it would hire a professional consultant and some of his staff to make surveys, draw maps and perspectives of projected improvements, and write up analyses and cost estimates. Frequently the outside planners worked with the local planning commission if there was one. Usually the plans incorporated revised versions of past proposals. New portions almost always included radial and circumferential highways for traffic relief.

Sometimes the plans were true supraurban schemes, such as Russel V. Black's inspired plan for the Philadelphia region. Harland Bartholomew wrote a perceptive study of the San Francisco Bay area. Like most city plans, the regional schemes foundered on the rock of expense; huge levies would be required to transfer the finger parks and the multilane highways from paper to ground. There were other problems. Because most regional plans seemed to work outward from their dominant cities, residents of the region feared urban imperialism. Then too, important interests might oppose or mishandle the plans. Black found his efforts frustrated because at least one businessman-member of the sponsoring organization attacked elements of the Philadelphia plan that clashed with the interests of his firm. Bartholomew's San Francisco plan was in the hands of a dedicated, sympathetic businessman who was genuinely concerned for the bay area. He failed, however, to approach the jealous, somewhat fearful leaders in the smaller communities with the required diplomacy and tact.

A street cut through here, a parkway built there, were the noticeable results of almost all such city and regional plans. But there were important if less tangible increments. The plans promoted thinking about class interdependence, about housing, about the separation or mixing of urban functions, about transportation, and about the symbiosis of city and region. They incorporated past ideas in park extensions, zoning, streets and housing, bringing them abreast of the current situation. If the older proposals were not realized in their revised form, they were available to still later planners.

The noblest of the era's comprehensive plans was the great Regional Plan of New York and Its Environs. "Monumental" is a tired word but the only adjective adequate to this interdisciplinary effort by the outstanding urbanologists of the day. Their cooperative labors cost more than a million dollars, lasted 10 years (although the full-scale effort took about seven years), and produced 10 books. The plan was a success in realistic terms, for many of its proposed highways, rail routes, parkways, and air terminals were built.

The RPNY sponsors and managers formed a roster of leading lights. Charles D. Norton, an enlightened banker, sold the Russell Sage Foundation on the regional scheme. Unofficially begun early in 1921, the RPNY was formally announced the next May with an initial $25,000 grant from the foundation. Luminaries including Herbert Hoover and Elihu Root graced the send-off banquet. Norton was the first chairman of the guiding Committee on the Regional Plan. Thomas Adams, early an advisor, became the general director of plans and surveys in 1923. Top professionals in planning, architecture, engineering, sociology, housing, economics, and other specialties joined the staff.

If realism and professionalism was the RPNY's strength, it was also its weakness. Three limitations marred the work of its dedicated planners. First, such men, working under such auspices, were not likely to consider plans requiring the modification of any existing economic and social arrangements. This is not a harsh criticism, for it implies neither that the RPNY was a spineless sellout to The Interests, nor that it should have been composed of bug-eyed radicals with brains on fire. It does suggest that the planners might have speculated on, say, the possibilities in the continued growth of special-purpose metropolitan districts and in new uses for the district idea. They might have suggested what changes in housing or transportation could be foreseen, given huge, if improbable, federal outlays for those purposes. They might have dwelt on the disadvantages of jealous localism and the possible gains from consolidating some of the over 500 incorporated cities and towns in the region. All of these "mights," and more, would have been compatible with a hardheaded statement of what could be done (and could not be done) given the existing situation. The RPNY looked only at what was, not at what could have been. Its failure to speculate, to cut itself adrift from its own present (except in certain population and economic projections) was an unfortunate limitation, no less arbitrary for being self-imposed.

Second, the RPNY was a scheme to save New York City by preserving its economic and cultural viability. Norton's thinking had begun with restoring the city's commercial areas — naturally enough, given his banking background — and had extended to transportation, recreation, and civic art. Adams and his co-workers accepted Norton's premises. According to Adams, the RPNY included three major purposes: (1) to promote lower densities through "diffused recentralization of industry" and planning for new industrial centers; (2) to reunify home and work by planning for new residential areas near industry; and (3) "sub-centralization" of business for greater consumer convenience.

Some of the plans derived from these principles were practical and sensible, such as the residential superblocks equivalent in size to four or six standard city blocks with their intervening streets. The word "superblock" later became associated with dehumanized skyscraper housing, but in the twenties it included even single-family residences. The land not given over to streets in the superblocks could be used for parking, for playgrounds, for houselots with garden spaces, and for wider, safer through streets on the perimeter. The irrationality of the village street pattern in an urban setting — giving some 40 percent of the land over to streets and jamming the people onto the remainder—was recognized in the nineteenth century. The RPNY intelligently planned a corrective within the metropolitan framework.

When all was said and done, however, the RPNY's three purposes boiled down to one: to decentralize and decongest New York enough for it to continue functioning in traditional ways. The humane intelligence of some specific plans did not alter the fact. The planners of the RPNY did not oppose all congestion and overcrowding; they opposed only the extreme agglutinations that carried the threat of death to the city's commercial, financial, and cultural institutions. Some traffic diversion, some retail decentralization was necessary to keep Manhattan from strangling to death. But the revivified Manhattan was not to be fundamentally altered.

For example, the RPNY's proposal for lower Manhattan consisted of a Washington Monument-type obelisk at the water's edge, with a semicircle of heavily wooded parkland beyond. The scheme was undoubtedly expensive, and was attractive, even allowing for its overblown formalism. But it was little more than a cosmetic application. Nothing basic changed in or about the forest of skyscrapers looming above the forest of park trees.

Third, the RPNY was really a plan for "New York and Its Environs," and not a true regional plan. The plan assumed the overriding importance of New York and its continued domination of its hinterland. Indeed Norton believed that planners would have to confine themselves to a radius of 40 miles from the center, a convenient commuting distance. The committee thrust out as far as 130 miles, but Norton's principle remained intact. The RPNY planned for the area palpably dominated by New York City. Of course there were verbal genuflections to local interests in the planners' essays. In 1929 the committee, its work largely done, was replaced by the proselytizing Regional Plan Association. The RPA sent emissaries to village and county boards by the dozen. They distributed copies of the RPNY volumes, exhorted their listeners to accept planning, and measured their success in planning boards established and zoning ordinances adopted.

The RPNY's limitations were hopeless defects in the eyes of Lewis Mumford, the utopian replanner. In two articles in the liberal *New Republic* during 1932 Mumford laid bare the sins, great and small, of the RPNY. Its manifold evils stemmed from its acceptance of the *status quo*, so that its talk of garden cities, land-use controls, farms nestled comfortably in the semiurban landscape, and so on were mere camouflage for continuing centralization. While Mumford's criticism was captious and possibly mistaken in some particulars, it did touch the basic flaw in the RPNY and in all such regional plans. For the RPNY was devoid of alternatives to the existing arrangements. It based its cautious projections upon "reasonable" expectations of public opinion or government policy.

In reply Adams quarreled over details, but he could offer no real refutation of Mumford's main attack beyond restating the RPNY's original purpose. What Mumford wanted, Adams wrote, was an economic and social revolution in the states of New York, New Jersey, and Connecticut, or else a "despotic" government to carry out a radical decentralization scheme. But Mumford was really criticizing Adams for doing half a planner's job, for providing many acceptable (and therefore obsolescent) plans but failing to supply a vision of a more just, equitable future.

Books and articles on planning more than kept pace with the plans themselves. The result was an expansion of knowledge beyond even an expert's ability to assimilate. Much of the literature was ephemeral or arcane, appearing in newspapers, newsmagazines, or in specialized publications including the *National Municipal Review*, the *Architectural Record*, and the *Journal of the American Institute of Planners*. Scholarly and semischolarly journals accepted articles on city and regional planning. The cascade of books included Harland Bartholomew's *Urban Land Uses* (1932), an early volume in the Harvard City Planning Series, Thomas Adams's erudite *Outline of Town and City Planning*, published by the Russell Sage Foundation in 1935, and Robert A. Walker's astute *The Planning Function in Urban Government* (1941).

Educational expansion continued. The 1928 Conference on Research and Instruction in City and Regional Planning at Columbia University asked for planning to be recognized as a profession requiring the usual educational reinforcement, full-blown schools on university campuses graduating young people trained in professional canons and techniques. The conference deplored inadequate preparation and narrow specialization in a field requiring both breadth of knowledge and integration of separate disciplines such as landscape architecture and sanitation. Harvard University was already preparing a School of City Planning. It opened in 1929, with a grant from the Rockefeller Foundation and an endowed Charles Dyer Norton Chair of Regional Planning. In that year more than 30 colleges and universities in the United States offered courses in city planning. Through the years to World War II they would expand their offerings into professional curricula within established schools of architecture or, in some cases, into new schools.

Somehow, 30 years of realistic planning, zoning, construction, writing, and schooling seemed to make less difference than they should have. Plans of the twenties and thirties got no further, with some exceptions, than had "Boston — 1915." Zoning in 1945 seemed much less a savior than it had in 1915, although communities without zoning ordinances were considered by outsiders to be cultural Possum Trots. Demands for professional recognition had brought more conferences, courses, and textbooks. Whether the apparatus of professionalism was responsible for any results on the ground, or whether it merely served careerism, was a question not objectively answerable. Despite government intervention in two world wars and the New Deal, planners had no more than scratched the surface of dealing with the housing problem.

At the same time, realists succeeded in bringing many grand if specialized projects from the drawing boards. The realists' excellent quantitative showing depended on five related developments that they turned to good account. First, millions of people were willing to pay heavy taxes and suffer many direct and indirect burdens if only they could operate private motorcars wherever they wished. Second, to meet the demands for urban services, governments at all levels began increasing taxes, expanding their taxing and bonding limits, and devising new ways of separating the citizen from his coin. Third, people were ever more willing to assign complex and serious problems, such as water supply, to the experts on special metropolitan district boards or to increasingly powerful municipal governments. Fourth, thoughtful businessmen came to understand that a lot of realistic planning aimed at saving retail and industrial cores that were losing customers to suburban competitors, relatively if not yet absolutely. Fifth, more sophisticated techniques of advertising and propaganda enabled planners and their business allies to convince the public of the need for spending money to realize the plans.

The RPNY committee's careful cultivation of local interests was an example of sophisticated propagandizing. In New York City itself, a group of privately financed "quiet-lovers" organized against noise pollution. They succeeded in making the public aware of the problem through skillful publicity of scientific noise-measurement studies and research on the physiological effects of noise. Antinoise ordinances of 1930 and 1936, little enforced, were the chief legislative victories. Crusaders against the "din of inquiety," like those against dens of iniquity, had to count their gains mostly in growing public understanding. In Philadelphia during the twenties and thirties, parkways, subways, bridges, and many other public improvements were related to downtown and the maintenance of its property values. Outlying centers, the retail lifeblood of many residential areas, received only incidental attention. Such was the stuff of realistic planning in the interwar years.

Many improvements centered on New York City, not because the city was large, but because it was the home of the greatest realist of them all — the brilliant Robert Moses. Moses's accomplishments as city park commissioner included a professional parks and recreation staff; expanded recreation areas; reconstructed zoos; and the construction of the 1939 World's Fair. Had he done only those things he would deserve a high place in New York's history. But he did so much more that he became known in New York and among planners the country over as "the man who gets things done." Any man who gets things done has enemies, but Moses garnered more than his share, largely because of his calculated vituperation against those who deplored his methods and his aims. His pen sometimes cut a wider swath than his parkways.

Moses was born in 1888 at New Haven, Connecticut, where his father was a well-to-do merchant. His background was Jewish although his parents did not practice the traditional faith. His family moved to New York before young Robert was nine, but he fulfilled a boyhood ambition to matriculate at Yale. In 1913 he took an Oxford M.A., and earned a Ph.D. at Columbia University by examination and submission of a manuscript on the British Civil Service. By his midtwenties Moses appeared much as he would in later years: tall and handsome, with a powerful build of a champion swimmer, which he had been at Yale.

Although Moses was diffident about family finances, his father and his mother's family had accumulated enough to relieve him of money worries. He earned good salaries and consulting fees throughout his career, but they were nominal for a man of his ability. His first job, with the New York Bureau of Municipal Research, led to meetings with Alfred E. Smith. Later, as secretary of the private New York State Association, he worked with Governor Smith at various plans for statewide improvements. Moses's interest in athletics led him to concentrate on park and parkway planning, and in 1924 when Smith appointed him chairman of the State Council of Parks, Robert Moses was on his way.

Moses continued to come forward with projects, appropriations bills, bond issues, and shrewd publicity. Smith meanwhile established the pattern for Moses's public career by piling title after title upon him, including the presidency of the Long Island State Park Commission and the chairmanship of the Jones Beach State Parkway Authority. La Guardia continued the practice, naming him to a growing list of jobs, the most important of which (other than Park Commissioner) was the chairmanship of the Triborough Bridge Authority. The authority was an independent government agency selling bonds for public works, supervising the works, and redeeming the bonds through charges on users. The Triborough Bridge Authority for example, constructed, operated, and collected tolls from drivers on its bridges.

It is not possible to give an adequate picture of Moses's great achievements without more visual apparatus than a book allows. Recitals of dollars spent, miles of parkway constructed, and acres of parks laid out do not help much in perception or valuation. What he strove for and in large measure achieved was an integrated park, parkway, and recreational system reciprocating between New York City and the state's lesser cities, and between the cities and the recreational sites themselves. His vast undertakings within New York City tied into the outer network of parkways and parks. Moses's beliefs and methods, as well as his personality, explain his amazing success.

First, Moses believed in dedicated public service as firmly as he believed in anything. Public service involved long hours, hard work, sacrifice, and scrupulous honesty with public funds. Anyone who failed to deliver on any one of those criteria had a brief career with Moses's staff. The same went for everybody in any department under his supervision, including common laborers. He recognized the value of partisan politics; indeed, he ran for the governorship in 1934, only to lose overwhelmingly to Democrat Herbert Lehman. Moses did not, however, see any virtue in patronage appointments. He alienated Franklin D. Roosevelt when he refused to appoint Louis Howe, Roosevelt's confidant, to a sinecure in the state park system. Later, when he was president, F.D.R. unsuccessfully tried to withhold federal funds from the Triborough Bridge Authority until Moses resigned as chairman. Moses also had words with the Works Progress Administration because of his conviction that WPA employees should be workers first and reliefers last.

Second, despite his public service ideals, Moses was at pains to disassociate himself from the old-style efficiency cult represented by the bureaus of municipal research. He was anxious to spend money aplenty if, in his opinion, the public weal justified it. He prided himself on acquiring more than the necessary right-of-way for bridge approaches, then converting the extra land into parks and playgrounds. He was willing to spend money to save money, as in antilitter and antivandalism campaigns. On rare occasions he ordered parkways redesigned to more expensive locations, to escape exhausting haggles over right-of-way acquisition.

Third, Moses acted extralegally (and resourcefully) when his assessment of the situation warranted corner cutting. One example was his overacquisition of bridge approaches. At times he deliberately underestimated costs to make them more palatable to the politicians. He could always return later with requests for supplemental appropriations. He was at the center of the bitter disputes of the twenties over park and parkway construction on Long Island. On one occasion an official attempting to serve papers halting a Moses project was dumped into Long Island Sound, and his papers set adrift. Another time Moses borrowed $20,000 from his mother to see some construction through before a legal deadline. At no time did he profit financially from any of it. The public good was the great end that always justified the means.

Fourth, Moses was well aware that New York and other cities would have to find the wherewithal to finance their survival. He did not express the problem in those terms, but he acted to get the most from the urban dollar. After the New Deal began, he kept Mayor La Guardia's office well supplied with projects eligible for federal funds. He created authorities, with their revenue bonds, to avoid overstraining city budgets and to generate income for still other projects once the bonds were retired.

Fifth, Moses used his various state and city positions to plan and build unitedly. He had held seven major official positions and a scad of minor ones by the late 1940s, although he drew a salary for only one of them, City Park Commissioner. Certainly by the early 1930s, and possibly before, he was using his multifarious jobs to coordinate recreational and highway developments impossible to integrate by any other means. It was not the best method, but Moses, ever the realist, understood how necessary it was. In the early days, at least, no legislature would have granted one man the power that Moses gathered piecemeal but wielded comprehensively.

All this makes Moses out to be a great man, which he was. It scarcely explains why his name was a swear word to many thoughtful planners who might be expected to forgive his tactical ruthlessness and vituperation. The explanation lies in three of Moses's controversial assumptions. They were, first, that New York could be saved by making it more livable for its middle class; second, that meeting its recreational and automotive demands was the way to keep the middle class contented and, third, that regional planning meant the exploitation of the region by the metropolis.

To save New York Moses worked to make it possible for middle-class people to enter the city, move about in it, and leave it in reasonable comfort. As a member of the middle class, though near its upper limits, he best understood its needs and desires. He had no patience with the rich people who often fought the parkways that he built through their estates and preserves and who in any case could take care of themselves. He struggled to break up the clubby atmosphere on the boards of the city's public museums and galleries. Those institutions relied too heavily on the patronage of people who had, or wished to acquire, status. His proposed changes were careful and reasonable, designed to encourage intelligent, aware middle-class people to exploit their cultural opportunities more fully.

When it came to the needs of poor people, Moses was less comprehending. He built recreational areas in Harlem, a decent and humane thing to do, but he refused to designate Harlem as a special area with needs more pressing than those in some other sections of the city. He did not become involved with public housing until the late 1930s, when it was evidently going to run into big money. Then he became involved because housers, in his opinion, were often impractical visionaries who gave inadequate attention to the recreational needs of the residents. Public housing and recreation, he said, had to be planned together from the beginning. Moses's criticism of the housers and his perception of linked housing and recreational needs were apt. He was not, however, so much interested in public housing because poor people needed it as he was concerned about the proper combination, under his direction, of housing and recreation.

Moses shared a narrow, class-oriented view of urban problems with many other public officials. It is as effortless as it is fatuous to criticize a man for being a child of his time, yet his limited conception of the public weal must be called by its right name. Neither New York nor any other city could be saved by a combination of recreation, uplift, and coordination of a few essential construction activities.

When Moses concentrated on recreation and roads for wheeled traffic he planned well but again, too narrowly. Most middle-class people spent most of their time at work, or at home, or commuting, or shopping. As the utopians insisted, it was essential to arrange the whole of life humanely, not merely to plan recreational escape hatches for the middle class. Because New York and all large cities were overcrowded, comprehensive planning should have involved decongestion and increased reliance on mass transit, so much more economical of space than automobiles. Yet Moses piled on the parkways, bridges, and tunnels in a frantic effort to keep wheeled traffic moving into, out of, through, and around New York. By building with such extraordinary vigor, he helped to inculcate the notion that highway construction of epic proportions was a basic solution to the urban crisis. Even before World War II the utopians were predicting an urban arteriosclerosis brought on in part by the insatiable space demands of the private car. Some realists, such as those in Los Angeles, had long since recognized the need for "mixed" transit facilities. Moses, however, was wedded to what was possible, and it was always possible to float more bonds for more highways.

One of the sadder aspects of Moses's commitment to the car was that he spoke more understandingly than he built. That was true, at least, of his pre-World War II career. In an address published in 1939 he depreciated the Manhattan skyline. Skyscrapers, he announced, "symbolize thoroughly bad planning, crazy land values which cannot in the long run be sustained, overcrowding, deprivation of light and air, concentration where there should be decentralization, inhuman transportation and traffic arrangements, and a dozen other monstrosities."[3] Trenchant talk. Yet when he illustrated a 1944 article with photographs of his deeds, he chose projects devoted to recreation and the car: the great Triborough Bridge system with its complex of playgrounds and parks; the West Side Improvement, a park containing the Henry Hudson Parkway; and the Corlears Hook Park with the East River Drive running through.

Moses also raised critics' wrath because he was an urban imperialist. He believed in satisfying New York's transportation and recreational needs by grabbing off huge chunks of land outside the city. Nobody could criticize him for his adroit realization of Jones Beach, dedicated in 1929, and for other far-flung recreational projects. His efforts might have been better directed toward making the city itself more livable, so that its residents would not need his great projects quite so desperately.

Certainly New Yorkers required some extensive beaches and natural environments, no matter how humane their city. But Moses proceeded to engulf rural land with gross disregard for its inhabitants, with arrogance, and with a hypocrisy as unconscious as it was stupefying. To defeat the people who stood between him and land for middle-class city dwellers, he worked unremittingly at condemnations, negotiations, and searches for defective titles. His opponents all were, according to him, unlovely: the idle rich who wanted to keep their rural solitude inviolate; snobs who hated the urban hordes escaping from their confines; greedy descendants of original patentees; and immoral people of various sorts, including an ex-Klansman. Of course, a person arrayed against baddies like that could justify any amount of vicious infighting, and Moses did. But it sounded odd, coming from a man who often waxed sentimental over New York City's hallowed traditions. To ambitious replanners Moses usually replied (in his mellower moments) that the city was rich in history, that New Yorkers loved both the city and its traditions. Only some sort of monster in human shape could entertain serious thought of tearing down whole blocks or neighborhoods of the beloved old town. The New York countryside was another matter. It and its people had no particular history or traditions or ways of life that Robert Moses was bound to respect. City dwellers needed the land, and that was that.

Finally, Moses's vituperative attacks on his critics added a personal dimension to controversies already bitter enough. He commonly indulged in generalized criticisms, such as his reference to "partisans, enthusiasts, crackpots, fanatics, or other horned cattle" in his 1939 address at Duke

University.[4] Rexford G. Tugwell, a prominent New Dealer, felt his verbal shafts. When Tugwell became head of New York's City Planning Commission in 1938, Moses fought the Commission's master planning with every political weapon including the epithet "Planning Reds."

Moses went further in 1944, when he indulged in the wholesale personal vilification that would become part of his theatrical stock-in-trade. The choice in planning, he declared in the *New York Times Magazine,* was between people like himself who worked in the real world and "the subsidized lamas in their remote mountain temples" who subtly influence public opinion in favor of their outrageous schemes. Many of these visionaries were "Beiunskis," foreigners who fled their homelands only to criticize the United States "beiuns" how things were done differently in Europe. He then denounced several great architect-planners, including Eliel Saarinen for advocating municipal land ownership as an aid in defeating overconcentration; Walter Gropius for declaring that new ways of thinking about city problems must precede an attack on urban "anarchy"; and Eric Mendelsohn for wishing to eliminate all wheeled surface traffic from congested areas.

Next Moses took up the utopians' charge that they were strategists, he a mere tactician. Where were the strategists, he asked, when he put through Jones Beach and the Long Island parkway? Nowhere around, for rough-and-tumble was not to the taste of "the Vestal Virgins of long-haired planning." It required too many battles with politicians, with avaricious real estate interests, with uppity owners of sprawling estates. Then he trained his guns on some native planners. He called Frank Lloyd Wright the "brilliant but erratic" inventor of the Broadacre City. Moses summed up his reaction to Wright's plan: "You would get further if you tried an experiment on a reasonable scale, frankly called it an experiment, and refrained from announcing that it was the pattern of all future American living." Tugwell's cooperative ideas came in for criticism, as did Lewis Mumford's six stages of urban growth and decay.[5]

The best that could be said for the article was that it was lively, clever, and funny. But it also revealed a Moses who was impatient with abstract ideas, who tarred a variety of men with the same brush, and who was unforgivably superficial, as when he ripped Mumford's stages of urban development from their context. Finally, Moses took too much license with his "beiunski" characterization of several brilliant exiled Europeans. It was some time before the howls produced by his article died away. Moses, who could damn an opponent by name and then shake hands when the fight was over, never understood why others were offended.

It was Moses's private friend and public critic, Frank Lloyd Wright, who best summed up New York's Park Commissioner. Wright remarked that the city, defined as a pre-World War II retail-commercial node, was dying. But Moses had kept New York alive by his brilliant improvisations. What would be a suitable reward? Wright answered: "New York should be given outright to Robert Moses."[6]

The Utopians

While Moses built, others built less and dreamed more. They dreamed of new and better cities and societies, and for that Moses ridiculed them. Perhaps the plans devolving from their dreams were ridiculous in their own time. Yet it takes but one turn of the wheel for utopians to seem utterly practical and the works of the realists to appear fantastic. Of all the utopians, three have been chosen because they were representative of the larger group while possessing unique qualities themselves. They are Lewis Mumford, Frank Lloyd Wright, and the planners in the Suburban Division of the Resettlement Administration who built the New Deal's greenbelt towns.

The utopians held four ideas in common. They believed that mankind possessed dignity and worth. They believed that the commercial-industrial cities of the twentieth century degraded man, exploiting his worth rather than cultivating it. They believed that urban decentralization and regional settlement were already well advanced and were definitely the living patterns of the future. Existing cities could not be saved in their present form, no matter what the expedients. And they believed that men would have to abandon their individualistic, competitive society for one cooperatively organized before deconcentration could develop in socially constructive ways.

Lewis Mumford, a gifted social critic and brilliant stylist, was born in 1895. His utopianism took shape early. Before he was 20 he had been influenced by the Scottish ecologist and planner Patrick Geddes, and through Geddes, a host of other European thinkers and planners. From Geddes and his other teachers, and from his own spacious intellect, Mumford developed the principles guiding his voluminous writings. By 1945 he had published many articles and a dozen books. Those best known to students of architecture and planning were *Sticks and Stones* (1924), *The Brown Decades* (1931), and the massive *The Culture of Cities* (1938).

Mumford's principles, though not always articulated in every work, permeated each of his books. First, he believed that all civilizations and cultures were organic, retaining some past habits and forms while developing new modes of thinking and acting. Second, because cultures were the sum of their past developments, true scholarship consisted of discovering and presenting the origins and paths of those developments. Of course the study of culture required specialists who hacked culture apart and examined the pieces carefully. In the process the specialists gained manageability and depth but lost essential breadth. It was the business of the generalists, the Mumfords, to reassemble the pieces into broad, interdisciplinary studies.

Third, he believed, cities had two purposes: to collect, reinforce, and develop their cultures; and to provide the good life for their inhabitants. The "good life" was not materialistic in the sense of the technological abundance associated with North American middle- and upper-class lives in the late twentieth century. Mumford argued for material sufficiency, but his emphasis lay elsewhere. Cities could function successfully as reservoirs of culture, he wrote, by freeing their inhabitants to develop their own potentials. Thus individual contributions would reinforce the culture. People lived full lives when they experienced interaction with one another in neighborhoods small enough for them to identify with and to understand entirely.

Fourth, Mumford believed that the commercial-industrial city failed to provide the good life. For one thing, it existed primarily to produce and distribute goods and services for a profit. For another, it robbed its region to produce glitter for the advantaged few at the heart of the metropolis, but impoverishment for the unfortunates who were failures by the canons of a capitalistic society, or who lived "in the sticks" away from the metropolitan core. Fifth, he hoped for a renascence based on the death of the economic and social forms of the imperialistic metropolis, and the rebirth of true regionalism built up from neighborhood units. The renascence would occur when men triumphed over technology and turned it from profit making to humane ends.

Mumford's principles shaped his understanding of urban development in the western world. In the tenth century, he believed, men lived in humane cities. Medieval cities were relatively small, were in close connection with their surroundings, were based on human relationships of neighborhood and craft, and were the cultural centers of their countries. From the twelfth century, capitalistically controlled technology began to disrupt medieval patterns of life and the easy symbiosis between city and region. In destroying the medieval city, technology undermined its sense of community and common purpose. From the eighteenth century cities expressed increasing mechanical refinement, at least whenever mechanical refinement made a profit and, simultaneously, growing social chaos. The process reached its nadir in the "paleotechnic" age, roughly the middle to late Victorian period. Paleotechnic culture submerged humanity and its values in an orgy of filth, overcrowding, clatter and environmental destruction.

Even while most western urban dwellers suffered the horrors of the paleotechnic age, men were perfecting their machines. They were suggesting ways and means for the people who could afford it to escape the city, and inventing all the wondrous contemporary technology that would make it possible. Then came the "neotechnic" megalopolis, that marvel of mechanization, of sprawl, of fantastic skyscraper palaces. But the neotechnic age was fading away in its turn. The "biotechnic" age represented the forseeably final development. Biotechnic society heralded man's victory over technology, or the control of machines for social ends. It would come about when men acted upon their knowledge of what capitalistically controlled machines had done to them.

Although this is the barest sketch of Mumford's assumptions and his historical thinking, it is enough background for judging his ideas and some of the strictures against him. First, there was an uneasy relationship between his evolutionary view of technological culture (plus man's ability to shape that culture) and his conviction that human history reaches some sort of plateau with the biotechnic era. Mumford was careful to write that nothing human was ever final or complete but his references to the biotechnic age — if his words are taken at their plain meaning — wrap the biotechnic in a cloak of finality. Furthermore, Mumford's attack on "capitalism" as an independent force did not quite square with his belief that man was the master of his fate. Men, after all, directed capitalistic development.

Other criticisms of Mumford, in and out of academic circles, were mostly hooey. Some critics, including Robert Moses, ridiculed Mumford's belief in the organic development of cultures and cities. Cities are not organic, so the criticism ran, because men shape them. But men consciously (and unconsciously) shape many organisms, as they do in the selective breeding of domestic animals, the hybridizing of plants, and the spraying of pesticides. The charge that Mumford disliked cities is refuted by his praise of cities in medieval times. Neither was he lost in a romance with the medieval city, for he had little sympathy with its undifferentiated, poorly heated houses, and the consequent restriction on adult lovemaking. Medieval culture's primitive etiology and the massive deaths from plague or other causes were even more appalling to him. That Mumford was in the throes of a cultural revolt against Victorianism there is no doubt. He did, however, appreciate the creative efforts of Henry Hobson Richardson and John W. Root, two nineteenth-century pioneers in architecture. Nor did his revolt against bric-a-brac and overstuffed chairs blind him to the work of the Roeblings in bridge construction, Albert Pinkham Ryder in painting, Frederick Law Olmsted in landscape architecture, and Montgomery Schuyler in architectural criticism. His writing was as subtle and sympathetic as it was intelligent.

Above all, Mumford's attack on contemporary cities and his plea for humane regionalism were uncannily brilliant. His analysis began with the gargantuan commercial-industrial city of the multimillions. Megalopolis, he wrote, was simply too large to be efficiently or economically operated. More and more human intelligence and effort were diverted to keeping the city going, in finding water for its growing population, and in devising expedients for circulating its sluggish traffic. Megalopolis was depersonalizing because it was too huge for the human mind to grasp. The virulent pathology of urban dwellers was alarming but understandable. Wanton violence could be explained as the only possible response to a horrible environment. Because contemporary cities were organized to inflate property values, they put a premium on crowding and still more crowding. So people jammed buildings to the bursting point, wearing them out, discouraging effective maintenance, finally abandoning them. Then there were no more property values, no monetary values, and certainly no human values except when cities condemned the worthless land and converted it into a park.

Junk the present-day city and plan on a true regional basis, Mumford insisted. That was the only hope for salvation. His proposal seemed wildly radical to critics of the Moses persuasion. In truth it would have required a lot of physical reconstruction to carry through his ideas. Whether it would have required much more than the sum of the post-World War II pulling down and putting up is doubtful. His ideas were really quite cautious and conservative. Mumford argued that regions were historical and cultural entities serving human purposes, not financial or capitalistic ones. Although not autonomous, they were sufficiently complex, diverse, and balanced to supply many of man's economic and cultural needs. Thus they were neither metropolitan playthings, nor were they synonymous with arbitrary political boundaries. Because they had grown up as the products of human need and human imagination, they were large-scale environments requiring comprehensive treatment. They could not be planned from a mere metropolitan or state point of view.

This was reasonable enough, but most realists jumped Mumford's ship when they read his basic requirement for a true regional plan: scrap power-seeking politics, and "getting things done" as a means of personal advancement and control over other's lives. Mumford meant all such politics, local, state, national, international, because in seeking power it recognized no interests other than its own. That was more than enough for most realists, but Mumford had only begun to raise the hackles of those who were still reading him. Proper regional development required common land ownership, he maintained. He carefully explained that communal ownership was not an end in itself, but simply a means to controlled, rational land development. Because men yearned for security in their lives, individuals would be secure in their land tenure during their lifetimes. When present politics and landholding systems ceased, so would public developments of the Moses type.

Anyone who thought Mumford a communist, an egalitarian, or a dreamer simply did not follow the meaning of his assaults on Moses's recreational developments. For in Mumford's assessment, Moses erred by opening up all the wilderness to everybody, or, at least, to everybody with a car or the price of a train ticket. In reality, not everyone could properly appreciate or conserve every natural environment. To bid culturally underequipped people to invade nature was to invite the destruction of nature. Mumford was no more a cultural snob than he was a Red, but he did believe that not all people enjoyed the same types of nature in the same ways. Men who had dwelt in narrow urban confines so long that their sensibilities were blunted would have to be carefully introduced to nature.

Mumford's blueprint for regional planning was the Garden City idea as developed by the Englishman Ebenezer Howard and first presented in *Tomorrow: A Peaceful Path to Real Reform* (1898) revised in 1902 as *Garden Cities of Tomorrow*. Howard envisioned compact residential settlements surrounded by a permanent buffer of unsettled land in orchards, farms, and parks. The garden cities included all the services, retail shops, and industry required to support their residents. For major cultural services, industrial requirements, and the like they would draw on somewhat larger central cities. Their transportation arrangements would emphasize intercity rail transit and highways but allow few through streets for heavy traffic within the cities themselves. Their land policies would preclude speculative investment and enrichment. Howard refused to commit himself to absolute population maxima but he suggested 32,000 as a comfortable upper limit.

Mumford, his associates who formed the loosely knit Regional Planning Association of America, and many others were captivated by the vision of this English law court stenographer. Howard's conception inspired the two English garden cities of Letchworth and Welwyn, the greenbelt towns of the New Deal, and many suburban developments, though the greenbelt towns and the suburbs were but truncated renditions of the original idea. For Mumford the virtues of Howard's plan lay, first, in its adaptability to regional planning on a human scale; second, in its controlled growth; and third, in its functional balance between commerce, industry, agriculture, and residence.

The ideal of greenbelt decentralization within a region would be achieved, Mumford believed, in four stages. A thorough survey of the region's total resources was the first step. Next came a "revaluation" of common assumptions and ideas about the region, bringing them into line with newly discovered realities. Third, experts drew up the plan. Finally came implementation and the necessary modifications, necessary because no plan could foresee all circumstances and because people would resist some changes no matter how desirable in the abstract.

Most of all Mumford hoped for regional planning that accomplished two purposes. It would develop a region as a whole, not as the slave of some metropolis. And it would try to anticipate the future. Intelligent planners perceived the future, not as the glorified extension of the dying present, but as the development of forms and trends only emerging. In identifying and encouraging the emergents of a better tomorrow lay the challenge and the danger of Mumford's thought.

Frank Lloyd Wright's Broadacre City scheme generated more controversy than the remarkably similar Mumford-RPAA ideas, in rough proportion to

Wright's calculated outrageousness and his gift for self-publicity. Wright's prose — bitter, ironic, rambling, repetitious, with its cabalistic vocabulary, punctuation, and capitalization — obscured some shallowness as well as some almost incredible profundity.

Broadacre City was a thin slice from the rich creative life of a colossal genius. Had Wright died in 1910, instead of in 1959 when he was almost 90, he would still have been ranked among the greatest of American architects, if not the greatest. To cite but one example of his greatness, his so-called "prairie houses" built in the first decade of the twentieth century were so advanced that 60 years later they appeared contemporary to unpracticed eyes. Nothing Wright did could ever be considered apart from his personality. He made certain of that. He broke up a good marriage for a series of well-publicized, disastrous love affairs. He was sartorially impossible, affecting capes, belted jackets, wide, wide lapels, canes, and porkpie hats over his long white hair. His criticisms of other architects were always scabrous if not always fair. His staggering egotism was a stance he preferred, he said in a typical wisecrack, to "hypocritical humility." All this lodged in some minds the conviction that Wright was unstable and utterly out of touch with the real world.

In truth Wright was an incurable nineteenth-century romantic with deep faith in the goodness of man. Broadacre City, with its acre for each family, was his anodyne for the inhuman cities that were crushing out mankind's essential goodness. His understanding of cities' historical development and present crisis is quickly told. Cities, Wright believed, grew from man's desire for security and for the evident advantage of multiple face-to-face contacts in an era of crude transportation and communication. But now (1932), he argued, the centralizing process of cities was out of control because the system of capitalism was itself out of control. Man lived either to pay capitalism's rent exactions or to coerce other men so that he and they might pay. The exactions were three: land rent, money interest, and most iniquitous of all, profits from machine production and invention. Profits from the machine especially offended because the machine should be used for man, not man for the machine, and because they were mostly the result of "good fortune," of being at the right place at the right time.

Happily the big city was on its way out, first, because man's wanderlust was once again asserting itself over his quest for security and second, because of a rebirth of democracy. These two developments occurred as soon as machine technology radically altered the basis of life. Electronic communications eliminated man's need to bunch up while performing complex tasks and being entertained. In 1932 Wright even referred to the birth of "teletransmission," a development — here came one of those infuriating Wright remarks — as infant as the minds in charge of it. Rail, auto, and air transportation freed man from any one place, and endowed him with amazing mobility. Mechanical heating, refrigeration and lighting placed the pasha's life, potentially at least, within the reach of all. New materials, including steel and stressed concrete, made possible a cheap, light, airy "organic" house architecture, built low to the scale of man and his immediate environment. Mass production, if properly organized, would make both necessities and luxuries available to all. Taken together these developments had lifted the burden of degrading heavy labor from the backs of men.

Since the city was slowly dying from its own poisonous wastes and from suburban decentralization of living and work, why not rejoice and let well enough alone? Wright could not, for he believed that the transition was thoughtless. People, numbed to the good life by urban environments, were misusing the land, violating the proper spatial relationships, and building new but inhumane houses, factories, and stores. The United States had no culture and esthetics comparable to its great political idea of democracy.

Broadacre City was the answer. Although his critics called it everything from insane to plain dull, Wright's purposes were entirely rational and humane. First, he proposed to lower living costs by abolishing rent, interest, and profits. Since the savings would be so great, they would more than compensate for the higher costs of small, decentralized factories and farms. (This was not Wright's argument, at least not directly. He maintained that smallness itself involved overlooked efficiencies.) Second, he wished to reestablish the lost symbiosis between man and nature. He intended to achieve it by allotting one acre in secured tenure to each family for house, garden, and fruit trees. In this blessed environment people would once more learn to nurture and be nurtured by growing plants. Whether there was enough arable land for Wright's purposes is conjectural, but the proposal was not ridiculous given his grudging admission that some people will not wish to fool with nature and must be provided with apartment houses.

Third, Wright wanted to restore citizen awareness of rural primacy. No longer, he wrote, would farmers be despised "hicks" in thrall to the city. Broadacre Cityites would see small farms all about them and would know where their sustenance came from. Fourth, he intended to exploit machines for people by, among other things, building compact, unitized, prefabricated bathrooms and kitchens for every family. Fifth, he hoped to reintegrate living and working. Factory workers would travel but short distances to small, pleasant, pollutionless factories. Shoppers would whisk their cars to decentralized, small-scale shopping centers. Professional people would have offices at home.

Sixth, Wright required a radical deemphasis of government and politics. They, together with capitalism, were responsible for the enormous public and private bureaucracies battening on the people. Seventh, he hoped to make Broadacre City an architectural jewel box. Indeed his perspective drawings of

Broadacre City are beautiful, with examples of his arresting architecture placed in lovely natural landscapes. Factories, apartments, stores, houses, all built according to Wrightian principles, would rebuild popular notions of beauty to the point at which people could for the first time enjoy tasteful luxuries.

Finally and most important, Wright yearned for society's renascence through the contributions of liberated individuals. Broadacres would provide both freedom and stimulation to individual efforts. Individuals would use their talents to enrich the whole, a sublime individualism when compared with "rugged individualism," which was merely self-indulgence.

Such a place might be dull for a few, but Wright understood that most people beyond adolescence are uninterested in much more entertainment than an evening at home with friends or an occasional night on the town. Certainly they are not panting after symphonies, the opera, or poetry readings at sidewalk cafes; electronic communication had done away with the need for most cultural getting-together, anyhow. The unsatisfied few probably could have made their cultural arrangements within the Broadacre City framework. Wright knew from his own experience that anybody with marketable talent, particularly if it carries implications of snobbery, can write his own ticket.

There were gaps in Wright's design for his new order, and the critics delighted in romping through them. Wright was vague about the politics of Broadacres, and about the relationship between government and the non-capitalistic economics of Broadacre City. But these were areas he had always treated with disgust or amused contempt. They were not his strengths. Possibly he understood that detailed political and economic blueprints from a nonspecialist would invite criticism and deflect attention from his main message.

Wright's conception of quasi-governmental "design centers" or "style centers" was less realistic, and more disturbing. In theory at least the design centers were to be decentralized, spirited, and free. Yet Wright projected the style centers' virtual dictatorship over the cultural and esthetic life of Broadacre City. Graduates of the centers would call the shots in industrial design and the arrangement of public works. Supposedly they would be as the technician-beauticians of the new order. Wright never supposed that someone else might have his own ideas. Indeed, he came close to arguing that most problems were not really social or political, but esthetic. Problems would be solved by the expert manipulation of man's environment. The proposition may be true, but it is certainly not democratic by most definitions, Wright's included.

Wright also played fast and loose with the problem of poverty, a rather persistent problem in most human societies. According to Wright, the poor man would earn his house piecemeal by piling up work credits at his neighborhood factory. First would come the prefab bathroom, next the kitchen, then a bedroom or two and an end to camping out. A finished house, fruit trees, and whatever else was required could be earned by work credits, too. Unfortunately the work-credit system was suited only to someone already in touch with the ethic of work and the rudiments of factory labor. Wright had no plan for the mass of acultural people attuned to neither. It is doubtful whether he was even aware of their existence. Wright was really designing for white, middle-class Americans, the people who commissioned his houses, the people whom he understood.

Finally, Wright leaned too heavily on the car for transportation. His greatest error, functionally speaking, was to sneer at railroads as archaic, and to defend his view with a photograph of a crowded freight marshaling yard. His mistake was at least understandable, for Wright was mature when the practical car came along in the first decade of the twentieth century. His generation experienced personal liberation by car as none other ever could. But it was unwise to project his love of cars onto the drawing boards of Broadacre City. Some of Wright's cars were weird tricycles with a tiny steering wheel at the end of a long, sloping snout and a bubble for the driver set high at the back above rear wheels some five feet tall. His superhighways (if one takes his table models seriously) boasted primitive interchanges and pavement lighting that would send any sane highway engineer into shock.

These are serious charges against Broadacre City and its creator, but they scarcely disqualify Broadacre's or Wright's humane ideals from consideration. Robert Moses sometimes ridiculed Wright, a distant cousin by marriage, in their witty if acidulous "Cousin Bob" and "Cousin Frank" exchanges. But Moses understood how desperately society needed visionaries with Wright's dynamic intelligence. Moses once received a medal from the Society of Moles, an organization of construction men. Showing the medal to Wright, he exclaimed, "See, I am a Mole. You are a Skylark."[7]

The planners of the New Deal's famed greenbelt towns came to resent the word "utopian," at least as anti-New Deal ideologues applied it to them and their work. They were utopian nonetheless. Because they were such a diverse lot, it would be rash to declare that all of them believed in the death of the big city. Almost all of them were convinced that America's residential future lay with its suburbs. They were shaping the future, staking out the path of suburban development from their own time forward.

The greenbelt towns enjoyed precedents aplenty. Federal intervention in housing came with World War I and the well-designed war workers' units built under the auspices of the Emergency Fleet Corporation and the United States Housing Corporation. The wartime housing had little if any direct influence, but it was a part of the gigantic federal involvement so inspiring to New Dealers. The lineage from Ebenezer Howard's garden city was more direct, even if filtered through the earnest group of thinkers in the RPAA. Three members of the RPAA had actually realized a segment of the garden city idea on the ground, albeit in the shape of a middle-class housing development. Clarence Stein and Henry Wright designed Radburn, New Jersey with superblocks, interior courts, and bypass traffic streets. The City Housing Corporation of Alexander Bing, who combined wheeler-dealer and visionary in one personality, provided the funds. The first families moved into Radburn in 1929, just in time for the stock market crash and the opening scenes of the Great Depression. Radburn was never completed.

Precedents do not entirely explain the greenbelt towns. Rexford G. Tugwell, the greenbelt's overall administrator, shared the belief that future populations would live in the suburbs. He dismissed as wishful thinking the back-to-the-land movement and the hope of rebuilding slum areas into spacious housing. Both the farmstead and the overcrowded inner city were archaic, and were losing population to the suburbs. "Rex" Tugwell — brilliant, handsome, a natty dresser, and an academic with a burning vision of the future cooperative commonwealth — was an early member of the New Deal "Brain Trust." He convinced President Franklin D. Roosevelt to make the greenbelt experiment part of the New Deal's resettlement program.

Tugwell formally administered the greenbelt project from the inception of his Resettlement Administration in April 1935 to his resignation at the end of 1936. However, the active day-to-day administration was in the hands of John S. Lansill, the head of the RA's Suburban Resettlement Division. Lansill, a wealthy, courtly, engaging Kentucky Republican, smoothed over disputes and coordinated land acquisition, design, and construction. Frederick Bigger, a member of the RPAA, was brought in as chief of planning for the Suburban Division during an organizational crisis in October 1935. Bigger was a first-rate designer in the Radburn tradition as well as a smooth administrator. As Tugwell was responsible for the inception of the greenbelt idea, so were Lansill and Bigger responsible for its execution.

The Suburban Division established a number of location criteria dovetailing with the New Deal's pro-labor bias and with the RA's plan for low-income, garden-type cities. RA researchers studied urban centers to discover those having the steadiest employment and payroll growth, the most enlightened labor policies, the greatest industrial diversity, and a potential greenbelt site on the outskirts. Most selections were made from the list compiled, but a site at Bound Brook, New Jersey was chosen because the distinguished city planner Russell V. Black prevailed on the RA to select it. Since the list was too long for the funds available, many cities had to be dropped: Los Angeles was too far away from Washington, St. Louis officials too quarrelsome, and so on. Finally the list was narrowed to four: Greenbrook at Bound Brook in the New York metropolitan region; Greenhills, just north of Cincinnati; Greendale, on the southwestern fringe of Milwaukee; and, the most important, Greenbelt, Maryland some seven miles northeast of Washington, D.C.

Land acquisition — in the hands of local real estate agents in each area —encountered the usual number of embattled farmers who did not wish to sell their land. Opposition was especially strong in Bound Brook, where family landholdings sometimes dated back to pre-Revolutionary times. To these historic and emotional considerations were added fears of the "scum of the earth" moving into the quiet old area. Two opponents were especially determined and effective. One, a wealthy Republican industrialist, was bitterly anti-New Deal. The other, a local tax assessor, was miffed because the RA would not buy his farm for double its value. The upshot was a federal court injunction against the construction of Greenbrook. The RA abandoned the project rather than risk a Supreme Court ruling against it and the other greenbelt towns as well. Because Greenbrook would have included an industrial park, it was the closest thing to a true garden city planned by the New Deal. Whether Greenbrook, as a working community, would have spawned imitators across the country is purely conjectural. Its sacrifice on the altar of vanity, ill will, and emotionalism was sad indeed.

Meanwhile work went ahead at the other sites. There was a lot of initial confusion that Bigger resolved partly by creating three semiautonomous planning and architectural staffs, one for each community. The first families moved into Greenbelt (near Washington) in September, 1937, into Greenhills (near Cincinnati) in May, 1938 and into Greendale (near Milwaukee) during the following month. What greeted them in each instance was a representation of the Radburn idea, with extra land in superblocks given over to gardens, with play and work spaces in interior courts. Each town had a large number of multiple-unit dwellings to hold down costs, a compact shopping center, and (especially at Greenbelt) severe restrictions on through automobile traffic plus a system of protected pedestrian walkways. Greenbelt was arranged in a giant fishhook curve and sported a large lake. Greenhill's streets followed its rugged topography, many of them ending in cul-de-sacs, while at Greendale the layout was close to that of any conventional farming community.

For a time the new residents shared the eagerness of the builders of their towns. They considered themselves pioneers on a suburban frontier. They were enthusiastic about their new living quarters, were delighted with their children's larger, safer play spaces, and were excited about cooperative ownership of the stores in their shopping centers. The youth of the first residents — the adults averaged a little more than 30 years of age — contributed to the initial interest.

The first blush of enthusiasm faded fairly quickly for reasons internal and external to the projects. The internal reasons were, first, resident selection and income limitations that made for a high turnover. Depending on family size, potential greenbelt residents could earn as little as $800 or as much as $2200. By later standards these salaries seem minuscule, but they were "low to moderate" incomes in the late thirties. The RA early gave up the idea of having really poor people who could not afford even the $21 to $45 per month rent. Incomes at the towns averaged from about $1600 to $1800 in 1938. Whenever a family's income bumped against the ceiling, it had to move. This arrangement lent a temporary aspect to life in the greenbelt towns. They became a warm, friendly place to live, better for the money than anything else available, until one could afford a home of one's own. The air of impermanence remained even though allowable incomes rose under inflationary pressure.

Second, the greenbelt towns were overorganized civically and socially. The pace of meetings was so rapid at first that stay-at-home weeks were declared. Less organized socializing became the rule within a year after residents resolved most of the basic civic issues and turnover had split the towns into "old settlers" and "newcomers." Third, cooperative marketing prospered only at Greenbelt, which held 855 families to Greenhills's 676 and Greendale's 572. In 1941, 1000 units of defense workers' housing at Greenbelt sent co-op sales soaring even though they disrupted the community socially. Finally, international events weighed more heavily on residents' minds after World War II began in September 1939, making local matters seem less important.

External pressures effectively limited the town to three, and to the first units built, except for the added defense housing at Greenbelt. The limits related to a significant shift in the national mood between 1935, when the towns were planned, and 1938, when they were occupied. By the latter year there was little public sympathy for innovation and experiment. Most of the criticisms, from real estate interests and other ideologues, pandered to the new mood. They focused on the socialism involved in government housing, a supposed threat to land values in the neighborhoods of the greenbelt towns, a set of regulations no more severe than those imposed by many private landlords, and costs.

Many criticisms were either emotional, or arguments from first principles, but costs were the project's Achilles heel. The unit costs ranged from about $15,400 at Greenbelt to $16,600 at Greendale, fairly expensive housing by prices then current. Apologists for those figures, then and later, argued for an average unit cost of less than $10,000. They pointed to the expense of relief labor and the unfairness of saddling the units built with the costs of utilities systems, designed for twice as many residences, with the expense of farmland buffer areas, with the cost of furniture and other items. Viewed in either way, however, the greenbelt towns were not inexpensive housing. At 1941 rentals, it would have taken 300 years to pay for Greenbelt, even with interest forgiven. Tugwell boldly admitted needing the subsidy, cited the hidden subsidies involved in slum housing, and declared that the country required 3000, not three greenbelt towns. He was right, probably, but costs were against it.

Another criticism, the esthetic, was borne out by time. Critics attacked the severe, slab-sided, flat-roofed houses at Greenbelt and some of the barracks-like row houses at Greenhills. In truth the styles of the thirties have not worn well. The flat-roofed houses were kin to the International Style, scarcely a fresh approach to housing design by 1935. The architectural *cognoscenti* of the day defended them over the neocolonial designs also used in the greenbelt towns. They forgot that the neocolonial, though derivative, is gracious and adaptable. The flat-roofed houses instead are period pieces, well-designed and functional, but too stark to be attractive.

For all the enthusiasm, the greenbelt towns did not amount to much as demonstrations or indications of the future suburbia. The government sold most of the land, houses, and buildings in 1952, the rest by 1954. The original towns remain the physical expression of a utopian vision. The national mood, the expense, the deepening international crisis all preclude any further development of the greenbelt idea. Nor did the towns indicate how either public or private building might house the poor. The RA excluded blacks without really justifying the policy. RA administrators probably decided that they were taking enough ideological flack without having to deal with racist accusations of a plot to infiltrate blacks into suburbia.

Ironically, the practical utopians of the Suburban Division built the most but inspired the fewest followers. Their real legacy is more general and more enduring than their vision of the future suburbia. For they showed how concrete responses to urban problems could develop within the federal government, sometimes more effectively than within the cities themselves.

NOTES

1. Seymour I. Toll, *Zoned American*, Grossman, New York, 1969, p. 147.

2. *Ibid.*, p. 238.

3. Robert S. Rankin, ed., *A. Century of Social Thought*, Duke University Press, Durham, North Carolina, 1939, p. 137.

4. *Ibid.*, p. 128.

5. "Mr. Moses Dissects the 'Long-Haired Planners,'" *New York Times Magazine*, June 25, 1944, pp. 16-17, 38-39.

6. Jeanne R. Lowe, *Cities in a Race with Time*, Knopf, New York, 1967, p. 52.

7. Cleveland Rodgers, *Robert Moses, Builder for Democracy*, Holt, New York, 1952, p. 250.

7

Radburn and the American Planning Movement

The Persistence of an Idea

Eugenie Ladner Birch

SUMMARY. *Many intellectual streams have contributed to the ideology of the American planning movement. Radburn, a partially built, planned, New Jersey settlement, represents the influence of English garden city theories. Radburn's plan was so well designed and rationally organized that it has become a permanent resource for planners who in every generation examine and sometimes adapt it to solve contemporary problems. As a result, it has survived as testimony to the planners' vision of suburban growth. It also represents, however, a neglected promise unfulfilled because of larger currents in American culture.*

Planned cities have been part of America's heritage for over three hundred years, but a domestic city planning movement did not emerge until early in the twentieth century. Since that time, its leaders have refined techniques and ideas in the effort to make planning a unique profession and a supportable cause. As part of this process planners have developed a literature and an iconography of model plans to act as guides for practitioners.[1]

In accordance with their beliefs, early proponents selected examples illustrative of their definition of rational land use. At first, they drew upon European experience, notably the British garden city projects. With the appearance of American developments, they turned to domestic efforts. One

Reprinted from Eugenie Ladner Birch. 1980. "Radburn and the American Planning Movement: the persistence of an idea," *Journal of the American Planning Association* **46**, 4 (October): 424-439. Copyright© 1980, the American Planning Association. Reprinted by permission.

of the most publicized, long-lived, and influential models was Radburn, the partially built garden city located in northern New Jersey. Despite its failure in contemporary economic terms, the city planning supporters promoted it as a normative pattern for their movement. As such, Radburn represented many of the basic principles of planning theory from the thirties to the sixties. Although planners did not always practice according to the full Radburn ideal in this period, they believed they should aim for its objectives: decentralized, self-contained settlements, organized to promote environmental consider-ations by conserving open space, harnessing the automobile, and promoting community life.

So ingrained in planning thought were these tenets, that by the sixties, with the restructuring of the field to eliminate the emphasis on land and so-called middle-class values, planning theorists discredited Radburn. Nonetheless, by the seventies, they began to reaffirm the uniqueness of the project as an example of the foresight and expertise of the profession. While these later students renewed praise of features recognized by the earlier generations, they also discovered new, equally noteworthy, elements in the plan.

Radburn's history, then, is closely tied to the evolution of the planning movement in the United States. As a continuous element in planning theory, Radburn's story can be used as a case study to trace the development of the profession focusing on its changing aims, its propagation, and its reception in American society. Although there are other examples worthy of investigation, Radburn is unique for its constancy and familiarity in planning literature.

A study of Radburn must take place within the context of the times, rather than by solely focusing on the project itself. For this reason, Radburn will be assessed through an examination of four interrelated topics: first, its timely invention at a critical point in the development of the profession in the late twenties; second, the adaptation of its contributions to the planning process and physical design in the output of publicly financed land development schemes of the New Deal and later eras; third, its condemnation as a symbol of the defects of the field in the sixties; and fourth, its treatment in educational and promotional literature used in spreading the ideas of the movement throughout the period.

The Appearance of Radburn at a Critical Point in the Early Planning Movement

Radburn appeared at a critical juncture in the history of American city planning. While the movement's leaders were still struggling to define the profession, they were soon to be thrust into the forefront of massive New Deal construction projects.

In 1928, the year of Radburn's initial construction, the movement was less than a quarter of a century old. Like the housing and social welfare campaigns, it was the product of progressive reform activities of the late nineteenth century.[2] Planning's formal organizational structure dated only from 1909 when the National Conference on City Planning (NCCP) began to hold annual meetings. By 1917, some NCCP members had created the American City Planning Institute (ACPI), a technical branch designed to "study the science and advance the art of city planning."[3] Other peripheral but important participants were the American Civic Association (a conglomerate of municipal improvement societies), the American Institute of Architects, and the American Society of Civil Engineers.[4] Overlapping memberships among these organizations were common. City planning ideas were as likely to be discussed as at the National Conference on City Planning.

From its beginning, the members of the American City Planning Institute vigorously promoted the development of a theory and process of systematized planning. Although the Institute members represented only a small percentage of the NCCP rolls, and purposely limited its numbers by imposing strict eligibility standards, they soon dictated the movement's concerns and direction.[5] They exchanged ideas at their own annual meetings and the NCCP sessions, in their journal (entitled the *City Planning Quarterly*) and through an informal network based on friendship. All practitioners, they were driven by the need to identify specific professional skills, and develop momentum by capturing mass support. Their deliberations frequently weighed the relationship between theory, practice, and the public input. In 1926, Thomas Adams, head of the Committee on the Regional Plan of New York and its Environs, expressed a typical concern to Institute President and NCCP board member John Nolen:

> No profession is so open as City Planning to the danger of being watered down to dilettante level by groups of amateur civic reformers and untrained exponents of civic improvements. . . There is no danger of pushing out the new in city planning because it is all new and the very fact that it is still a long way from settling down, as a science and an art, means that some group is necessary to give it the right direction and a small degree of solidity.[6]

Throughout the early days, the city planners strove to develop the right direction referred to by Adams. Their varied activities ranged from the designing of war housing to promoting the creation of local planning and zoning boards, the writing of master plans and zoning ordinances for municipal governments, and participating in regional studies. In addition, they kept pace with developments abroad through communication with their counterparts in the International Housing and Town Planning Federation. From these efforts they began to create a body of American planning thought for their followers.

By the late twenties, planners had articulated the basic goals of the profession. In 1927, then NCCP president Nolen's keynote speech before the 19th Conference presented several: relieving traffic congestion and promoting street safety, alleviating crowded living and working conditions, providing city dwellers with more sunlight and air, ensuring "a more favorable city environment for the rising generation," reducing the amount of waste generated by excessively large cities, regulating the size of cities, and combining a new, modern, and appropriate beauty with American ideas of efficiency.[7] He followed by surveying the movement's progress toward meeting these objectives and admitted that "the record is not spectacular."[8] Nolen closed with a challenge to his audience. He bid them to work to develop a broadened city planning science:

> If we are to find real solutions, we must dig still deeper into the subject itself and more especially into a consideration of the related social, economic and governmental conditions which influence and color all that is now being done or attempted.[9]

It was into this environment of expansion and aspiration that Radburn came. It could not have been developed at a more critical time. The embryonic movement needed a symbol — a demonstration of its doctrine and a laboratory for its techniques. Radburn would fulfill many of these needs. In short, it was the right development at the right time.

Radburn and the Planning Process

Radburn was the brainchild of members of the influential Regional Planning Association of America (RPAA), and was constructed under the sponsorship of the City Housing Corporation (CHC), a private, limited-dividend company. The RPAA, founded in 1923 by a group of like-minded architects, engineers, economists, and sociologists, worked in conjunction with the CHC, which had been created in 1924 by a wealthy New York real estate entrepreneur, Alexander Bing.[10] Although the RPAA addressed a variety of planning issues and drew inspiration from European concepts of regionalism, in Radburn it tailored British garden city ideas to the distinct legal and social customs of the United States. The CHC, the economic partner of the RPAA, began Radburn after experiencing financial and architectural success with an earlier, smaller project, Sunnyside Gardens in New York. Although restricting its dividends to 6 percent, lower than the current rate for real estate development but in line with other interest-bearing investments, it sold enough stock to raise sufficient capital for its endeavors.[11]

The RPAA members worked as a team on the Radburn project and in the process they developed the new planning methods Nolen had urged. In addition, the social scientists among them contributed significantly to the physical design. At first, the RPAA meetings were closed and casual, but later they were supplemented by lengthy technical sessions attended by outsiders. Referring to early activities, Clarence Stein reminisced to Catherine Bauer, "Our essential meetings were informal. There is no record except our memories."[12] However, when the group began to work seriously on Radburn, it held formal planning sessions. In October of 1927, it sponsored a weekend seminar at the Hudson Guild Farm in Netcong, New Jersey, to which it invited social scientists and others to study the preliminary plans and comment on important community issues of education, health, governance, and race.[13] The minutes of this meeting list some of the questions discussed. The agenda underscored members' concern for alleviating social tensions with a better planned environment. A sample demonstrates the scope of their concerns: "What should be the policy in relation to the admission of negroes and other people of other races than white?","How many people must there be before there could be a good elementary school?", and "What sort of unified controls are necessary to attain and protect an American garden city's beauty?"[14]

The RPAA continued its meetings in New York City, purposefully seeking information for rationally based decision making. Its members fully realized that they were undertaking pioneering work in planning. Charles Ascher wrote to Edith Elmer Wood in February of 1928, with an explanation of the group's objectives:

> The fundamental problems of planning and policy as you can well imagine are most staggering. We have tried the plan of asking experts in various fields to meet with us to discuss the several problems — not so much initially to answer problems, as to suggest lines of thought and put us in touch with the people and agencies who can help to answer questions.[15]

The plan for Radburn, clearly the effort of the RPAA team, was not created in the traditional architectural manner. It reflected a multidisciplinary synthesis of the most current data and expert advice. Furthermore, decisions were made by a rudimentary form of what evolved into the "planning process."[16] First, the planners formulated goals, then collected data, developed and selected a plan, implemented that plan, and later evaluated it (Plate 7.1).

A by-product of enlarging the participation in the planning meetings was Radburn's rapid acceptance by the general planning movement. The participants were influential propagandists. Not only did the RPAA have vocal members such as Lewis Mumford, Charles Ascher, and Clarence Stein, but

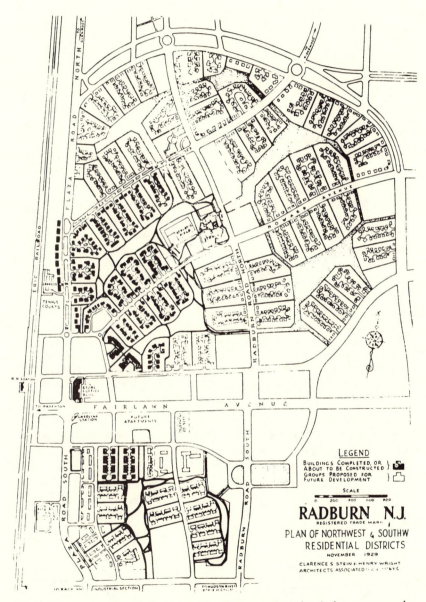

7.1 The final plan for Radburn reveals the hierarchical circulation system and a less rigid land use pattern than preliminary plans.

also the consultants included others of critical importance: Russell Van Nest Black (a long-time power in the American City Planning Institute), Edith Elmer Wood (a highly regarded housing authority), Thomas Adams (the prominent teacher, writer, and practitioner), and Harold Buttenheim (editor of the *American City Magazine*).[17] All were in positions to promote Radburn and the planning process responsible for it.

Radburn's fame spread rapidly. *American City Magazine* had numerous articles (February, November, December, 1928, and November, 1929), the NCCP and the ACPI featured it in their discussions, and the academic and popular press gave attention to the experiment. At that time, the praised elements of the settlement, subtitled by its promoters as a "Town for the Motor Age," included the superblock (the high density clustering of single, double, and multifamily housing around large areas of commonly held parkland), whose demographic dimensions were based on the neighborhood principle so recently articulated by Clarence Perry in the *Plan for New York and its Environs*; the separation of vehicular traffic (with automobile routes designed in a hierarchical fashion to eliminate unnecessary traffic in residential areas); and the development of a community organization, the Radburn Association, to administer the public lands, enforce restrictions, and supply supplemental municipal services such as recreation and day care activities.[18] A few years after the initial construction was completed critical comments extolled the development's quality of life. The *American Architect* made this observation in 1980:

> [Radburn] represents the first scientific effort that has ever been made to establish a community designed exclusively to minimize the danger of automobile accidents. Yet there were other things to consider too. . . It was the desire of the builders to create not only a [safe] community . . . but also one . . . of beauty in appearance and the utmost in modern efficiency.[19]

Ultimately the 1929 national financial collapse would cripple Radburn's sponsor, the City Housing Corporation. CHC's 1933 bankruptcy prevented the full execution of the original plan which had called for a complete town with housing, employment, and commercial facilities for a projected 30,000 population. Although only a small fraction had been executed (housing for about 3,000 and the commercial center), the plan and demonstration would be influential in the coming years.[20]

Radburn and Its Transferal to the American Landscape

The American planning movement experienced a deep change in the thirties. The focus of its activity changed from local to national as New Deal programs undertook slum clearance, new town and public housing construction, mortgage insurance, and national planning. Also, an increased number of planners were employed directly by the public sector rather than indirectly as consultants. Along with these changes, by the end of the decade, the Radburn imprint would be on most federal housing activities. However, because of the nature of the movement's organizational developments, only parts of the Radburn plan, not the totality, would be transferred to the American landscape.

During the Depression, professional and lay supporters of city planning undertook the reorganization of the movement. In 1934, the National Conference on City Planning merged with the American Civic Association to become the American Planning and Civic Association. The American City Planning Institute became an independent professional organization, which later changed its name to the American Institute of Planners. An entirely new group, the American Society of Planning Officials, emerged to supply technical information to the growing number of paid and volunteer government leaders. The movement's leaders had designed a structure which would respond to the changed environment and conditions of planning.[21]

The movement, then, was actually a three-pronged structure. The American Planning and Civic Association channeled citizen support, the American Society of Planning Officials strengthened its public administrators, and the American City Planning Institute would develop professionals. All three organizations had separate offices and publications but they met together annually to exchange ideas about the state of the art.[22]

The Radburn plan was of critical importance to the restructured movement. For lay citizens, it provided a well-publicized and comprehensible image of planning. For government officials, enough of Radburn was built to show how it worked and what elements were successful. For professionals, it was a fertile laboratory experiment. Tracy Augur, planner for the Tennessee Valley Authority, articulated these three functions of Radburn in an article for the *Michigan Municipal Review*:

> Radburn stands out singly not because it is the biggest or most beautiful of cities but because it is the first tangible product of a new urban science . . . that seeks to make the places of man's habitation and industry fit the health requirements of his daily life . . . Radburn is not a theory, it is a demonstration . . . Radburn cannot be a model for all types of city, nor for all cities of the residential type; it stands in recognition of the varying functions cities serve, and in planning to serve one of the more common of them, it points the way to the service of others.[23]

Although many aspects of the Radburn plan were immediately incorporated in new town experiments of the thirties, its regional implications were only partially realized. Since the Tennessee Valley Authority and the Resettlement Administration, two of the key regional agencies, hired planners who either worked on or were aware of Radburn, it is not surprising that

7.2a   Radburn

7.2b   Norris

7.2   Radburn's interior park (a) is copied at Norris (b), becomes a lake at Greenbelt
(c), is considerably smaller at Jonathan (d), and no longer protected from the street at
Columbia (e).

7.2c Greenbelt

7.2d Jonathan

7.2e Columbia

transferable aspects of the plan such as the superblock, transportation system, and park arrangements cropped up repeatedly in designs for federal settlements.[24] Radburn's translation into these efforts, its propagation by the planning associations, its adoption by the British in their work, and its use as a model in graduate curricula, explain why the pattern became associated with later American new town development.[25] Reston, Virginia, Columbia, Maryland, Jonathon, Minnesota, and Irvine, California would repeat the design devices if not the overall concepts.

A brief survey of selected elements illustrates their transfer to the American landscape. Radburn's much noted interior park (Plates 7.2 a,b), designed by RPAA members Clarence Stein and Henry Wright, was adapted by Earle S. Draper in his plan for the Tennessee Valley Authority community of Norris. Draper, who had considerable experience in company town planning, frankly drew upon the Radburn concept but changed it to meet the topographical requirements and residential customs of the southern site.[26] For these reasons, he dropped the superblock cluster housing. At Greenbelt, Maryland, one of the four Resettlement Administration projects, the superblock-interior park constellation appeared along with a new variation, a centrally located lake (Plate 7.2c). In Columbia, Maryland, and Jonathon, Minnesota (later developments undertaken by private entrepreneurs with some federal aid), a faded remembrance of the space is seen in examples unenclosed by housing (Plate 7.2d) and unprotected from the street (Plate 7.2e). Comparisons of the cul-de-sac design, footpath systems (Plate 7.3), and underpass adaptations (Plate 7.4) show similar variations as the developers tailored the devices to meet their needs. Finally, the shopping center became a prototype for the later settlements as well as for others not related to overall residential plans throughout the United States.[27]

Other less-publicized aspects of the Radburn plan became embedded in planning philosophy. For example, Augur, and later the Urbanism Committee of the National Resources Board, praised the town's homogeneous population of young, college-educated, middle-income families, claiming that their common backgrounds and interests promoted a "much fuller enjoyment of social life," "a healthier community" with a more responsive government than could be "had in larger cities, more diverse in scope."[28]

Large-scale development, an integral part of the Radburn idea, carried over in both pre-war and post-war public housing as well as in urban renewal. The redevelopers favored the method for economic and moral reasons. Not only did they argue that large sites had lower infrastructure costs, but they also believed that superblocks stood as safe islands amidst crime ridden slums (Plate 7.5, 7.6).[29]

In 1931, housing professionals argued:

> A reduction of delinquency rates is most likely to result from a program which combines improvements in housing with modifications in other elements in the complex. This combination means at least, the development of improved housing in neighborhood units. . . This neighborhood unit should have a physical plan which would make the neighborhood relatively distinct. . . A physical plan of this nature will tend to produce neighborhood organization and a local social control which are lacking in many parts of the modern city.[30]

The concepts of homogeneity and large-scale development were further extended in the enormously influential work of the Federal Housing Administration (FHA). As with public housing, only parts of the Radburn idea survived. Barriers to its wholesale adoption came from two limitations. First, the FHA structure requires self-sufficiency, which dampened opportunities for experimentation as called for by Radburn. Second, American zoning prohibited clustering and mixed uses. Notwithstanding these strictures, less than ten years after the construction of Radburn, FHA officials promoted many of its principles. For example, the cul-de-sac idea, which Henry Wright had urged in 1928, was doctrine by 1939.[31] Although this dead-end street design had appeared in several earlier developments, such as the British Letchworth, Hempstead Garden Suburb, and Welwyn), its more extensive use as part of a complete street system at Radburn aided in convincing the FHA administrators to call for its use in government-insured subdivisions. Their 1939 manual, *Planning Neighborhoods for Small Houses*, flatly stated:

> Homes located on *cul-de-sacs* . . . offer distinct advantages especially to families with small children. In addition to the reduction of the traffic hazard, the creation of such sites has many other advantages to both the buyer and the developer. The cost of street improvements may be greatly reduced.[32]

In the same manual many illustrations of ideal subdivisions incorporate Radburn ideas, and a section of the actual plan was even included (Plate 7.7).

Finally, the FHA endorsed the restrictive convenant, a tool used extensively by earlier twentieth-century high-priced real estate developments such as Palos Verdes, California, and Shaker Heights, Ohio, and adopted at Radburn. At Radburn, provisions in homeowners' deeds specified architectural controls. Unfortunately, the FHA recommendations suggesting their use as a "protection for residential development" ultimately led to vicious racial and ethnic discrimination.[33]

FHA housing constituted up to 25 percent of all domestic new construction betwen 1934 and 1970.[34] In some features, it did perpetuate—though in a fragmentary manner—a few Radburn notions, namely the hierarchical transportation systems and large scale developments. This transferal bears

7.3a   Radburn

7.3b   Norris

7.3   The footpath at Radburn (a) is copied at Norris (b), crosses at street at Greenbelt (c), goes under an underpass at Jonathan (d), and is placed next to a main street at Columbia (e).

7.3c Greenbelt

7.3d Jonathan

7.3e Columbia

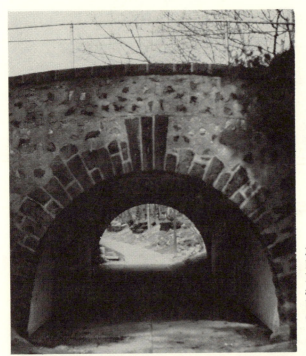

7.4 The underpass at Radburn (a) shows up at Norris (b), Greenbelt (c), and Jonathan (d), and becomes an overpass at Columbia (c).

7.4a Radburn

7.4b Norris

7.4c Greenbelt

7.4d Jonathan

7.4e Columbia

7.5   View of a typical PWA low cost housing project incorporating Radburn principles.

7.6   The interior court of Brooklyn's Williamsburg Houses, also a PWA effort, is safe and serene.

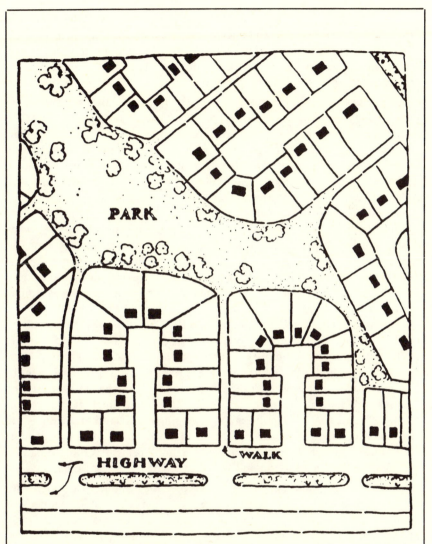

The Radburn plan showing a series of culs-de-sac grouped in a super-block around a central park. The traffic highways border the super-block. The houses face the front yards and parks rather than the streets. The cul-de-sac roadways are service drives and give access to the rear of the houses. Traffic passes by rather than among the houses.

7.7   The 1939 FHA manual reprinted part of the Radburn plan.

testimony to the strength and adaptability of these aspects of the plan; yet the absence of wholesale adoption indicates that the total pattern was still alien to the majority of American land developers. Planners had not convinced them of the plan's desirability. In the main, it remained an ideal, most frequently emulated in public, not private, projects.

With the expansion of public planning programs, the movement—as measured by organizational affiliation—had grown rapidly. However, its actual numbers were small. Furthermore, between the two planning associations, the influence of the government officials' group (ASPO) surpassed that of the professional society (AIP). (Membership figures show ASPO's 450 dues payers in 1934 expanding to 3,600 twenty years later while the AIP 200-member constituency grew to only 1,000.)[35] During this time, ASPO took over the direction of the movement. It did so not by membership growth alone but also by extending essential services to local government. In 1949, when ASPO's original grants from the Spelman Fund ran out, its longtime executive director, Walter Blucher, developed the *Planning Advisory Service* and the *Zoning Digest*. Dependent on selling subscriptions, he marketed them to municipal leaders of the expanding metropolitan areas who sought immediate, tangible, technical advice on how to deal with the postwar onslaught of people and automobiles.[36] By 1954, these widely circulated publications reached 60 percent of all American cities having populations of 50,000 or more, and all the key federal and state agencies.[37] Through these publications, ASPO promoted some Radburn principles—particularly the by now quite acceptable large scale development and hierarchical transportation systems—but it did not fully endorse the clustered superblock. It more readily promoted anti-Radburn policies such as single-lot, large-individual-yard residential zoning.[38] The AIP continued to advance Radburn's garden city ideas, but on the whole, these remained textbook principles too utopian for complete American adoption and undercut by ASPO propaganda.

Thus, while the planning movement accepted the Radburn plan as a model, its few practitioners, frequently operating within a relatively unsympathetic environment, could execute only those aspects which melded easily with pre-existent customs. While suburban property and energy were abundant and low priced, the conservation aspects, particularly the superblock, mixed-density residential units and the regional organization of employment, were not attractive to land developers and municipal officials who favored simpler, cheaper Euclidean-based subdivision arrangements. In contrast, the super-block based on the neighborhood principle was more widely applied in postwar public housing projects but with a new twist. The carefully calculated human scale densities of Radburn were distorted as legislative, economic, and political considerations dictated the construction of high rise buildings in slum cleared areas.

Radburn's Fate in the Sixties

In the sixties, the planning movement continued its geometric growth of the fifties. The number of practitioners more than doubled, the number of planning schools expanded to meet the demand, and the opportunities for employment proliferated as the federal government became increasingly involved in urban progams.[39] For the first part of the period, the profession's intellectual capital remained primarily tied to the ideals articulated in Radburn.

Basically, the official objectives of the movement remained unchanged from the earlier period. Shortly before the beginning of the decade, MIT professor John T. Howard, also a former president of the AIP, articulated the goals in "City Planning as a Social Movement, a Government Function and a Technical Profession," a paper he presented before the Joint Committee on Planning and Urban Development of the Carnegie Institute of Technology and the University of Pittsburgh. Later the influential study group, Resources for the Future, published the remarks. Howard noted:

> The ultimate goals are clearly social although plans themselves are related to physical things and physical places. . . Within this broad framework, I suggest the following: First would be the arrangement of functional parts of the city—residence, commerce and industry, etc.—so each part can perform its functions with minimum costs and conflict. . . Second would be linking of all the parts of the city to each other and to the outside world by an efficient system of circulation. Third, the development of each part of the city according to sensible standards—for lot size, for sunlight, for green space in residential areas, for parking in business areas. Fourth, the provision of housing that is safe, sanitary and comfortable and pleasant —in a variety of dwelling types to meet the varied needs of all kinds and sizes of families. . . Fifth, the provision of recreation and schools and other community services of a high standard of size, location and quality. And sixth, the provision of water supply, sewerage and other utilities and services, adequately and economically.[40]

Radburn's plan of course, continued to act as a model for fulfilling these objectives.

Soon, however, the standard theories came under heavy attack. Leading the critics was *Architectural Forum* author Jane Jacobs, whose 1961 *The Death and Life of Great American Cities* condemned planners' bias toward decentralization as "city destroying ideas" and questioned their indices of blight and deterioration. Her work had been preceded in 1947 by the Goodman brothers' *Communitas*, in which the philosopher-architect team dismissed the highly touted garden city community life with the comment that "rather than live in a Garden City, an intellectual would rather meet a bear in the woods" claiming that such an existence was too lackluster. Following Jacobs in the early sixties, a number of social scientists, including Herbert

Gans, John R. Seeley, and William Moore, Jr., expanded her theses through a series of detailed studies. They concluded that the mindless application of the superblock-neighborhood unit principle in public housing needlessly destroyed the useful social structure of low-income communities. They further charged that projects replacing slums were "badges of social identification and affliction [which] the outside community reacts to as though they were leper colonies and the lives of the residents seem to have neither dimension nor meaning."[41]

Soon others joined, calling for a total reevaluation of the field. For example, in 1964 designer Kevin Lynch condemned the use of stereotypical plans noting that the repetition of the garden city and superblock without reference to purpose demonstrated a glaring "unawareness of the vast range of potential city forms."[42]

Another equally important criticism attacked the profession's traditional reliance on technical expertise coupled with political neutrality. As heirs to the progressive assumption that knowledge of problems would lead to their rapid, scientific solution, planners had long ignored political realities. Hunter College professors Jewel Bellusch and Murray Hausknecht noted this behavior in their 1967 collection, *Urban Renewal: People, Politics and Planning*. They observed that numerous studies, in particular Martin Meyerson and Edward Banfield's documentation of the failure of the Chicago Housing Authority in *Politics, Planning and the Public Interest*, made planners realize that this "naiveté [had to be] abandoned [and] the profession [had to] recognize the intimate relationship of politics and planning."[43] From these thoughts, it was not a very long step to the citizen participation-advocacy planning movement that developed in this period. This effort brought the pluralistic nature of American society to the planners' attention, and called for practitioners to represent the interests of a variety of clients, specifically the powerless lower-income groups.[44]

Ironically, some critics continued to support the broader Radburn ideas, now relabeled new town planning. In 1965, Herbert Gans, intent on his criticism of urban renewal, made the following proposal:

> If the slums are really to be emptied and their residents properly housed elsewhere the rehousing program will have to be extended beyond the city limits, for the simple reason that that is where most of the vacant land is located. This means admitting the low income population to the suburbs; it also means creating new towns—self-contained communities with their own industries.[45]

The decade of the sixties was a turbulent period for planning. Former *AIP Journal* editor Melvin Webber caught the spirit of the times in his landmark essay "Comprehensive Planning and Social Responsibility" when he diagnosed the nature of the changes:

City planning is moving through a period of rapid change; some have called it a revolution, so dramatic is the transformation likely to be. The major sign is a growing sophistication. The main prospect is a large increase in the profession's effectiveness. The chief stimulant has been the injection of a large body of theory and method that has been accumulating in the social and behavioral sciences over the decades and which until recently the profession has been largely immune to.[46]

By the late sixties, the movement had absorbed much of the change. The professional associations amended their objectives to reflect the practitioners' activities, which now included the use of new analytical tools—namely the computer—and also added concerns such as environmental issues, energy conservation, and human resources. Nonetheless, as the Gans proposal reflects, the ideals articulated by the Radburn plan lived on to be adjusted for contemporary needs. Their persistence can be further studied in the following survey of their propagation in planning literature.

Radburn's Treatment in Promotional and Educational Planning Literature

From the outset, Radburn was highly visible. From 1929 to the present, promotional and educational planning literature has consistently pictured

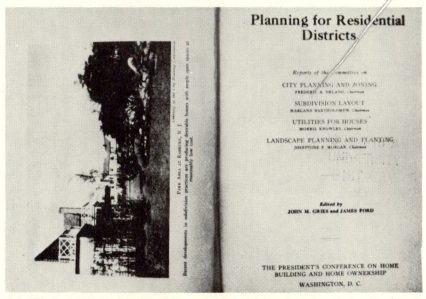

7.8 The report of the Committee on Subdivision Layout of the President's Conference on Home Building and Home Ownership recommended adoption of Radburn principles. (Note the frontispiece.)

and discussed it. Over time, planners have restudied the plan to find new solutions for their own work. Thus, Radburn has been a remarkably resilient model for the movement.

Throughout the thirties, writers looked to Radburn as a major accomplishment. In 1932, the reports of the Conference on Home Building and Homeownership (a meeting called by President Herbert Hoover and attended by three thousand delegates), pictured Radburn in the frontispiece of one, *Planning for Residential Districts*.[47] In 1934, Thomas Adams's *Design of Residential Areas*, part of the multivolume Harvard City Planning Series, also featured Radburn as the frontispiece (Plate 7.8). Even then Adams recognized its fame: "it is unnecessary to describe the features of the ... plan in detail as these are well known."[48] He concluded his critical evaluation of the plan with the judgment that it was a success. Later in the decade, Lewis Mumford's *The Culture of Cities* would promote Radburn, comparing it favorably with similar work by Frank Lloyd Wright and LeCorbusier.[49] At the same time, the Urbanism Committee of the National Resources Board surveyed 154 American planned communities and focused on Radburn as one of the 29 given detailed coverage.[50] In 1939, the Federal Housing Administration publicized it in *Planning for Small Neighborhoods* (Plate 7.9), already discussed; its 1947 manual carried on the tradition.[51] In 1949, the passage of a housing act with comprehensive urban renewal provisions led Coleman Woodbury to compile a basic handbook, *Urban Redevelopment,*

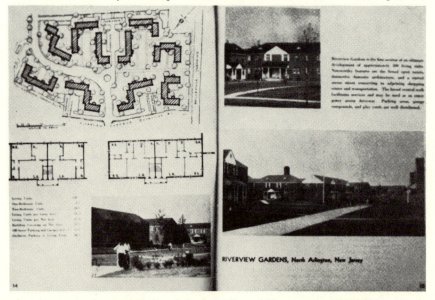

7.9 Illustration in *Neighborhoods Built for Rental Housing,* the 1947 FHA manual, shows the incorporation of some Radburn design elements.

Problems and Practices. In this extensive collection of essays, Charles Ascher contributed "Government by Contract in Radburn, New Jersey," an evaluation of the settlement's use of restrictive covenants, giving attention to the possibilty of their use in urban renewal sites.[52] About the same time, two new textbooks appeared: Arthur B. Gallion's *Urban Pattern* and Christopher Tunnard's *City of Man*. Both praised Radburn. Tunnard challenged his readers with this question: "How much longer can we coast along on the . . . reputation for good-looking civic design achieved by Radburn?"[53] These texts have been used extensively in schools of architecture and planning.

In the sixties, despite the strife created by differing opinions about the ranking of social and physical priorities, a spate of articles appearing at the time often entitled "Radburn Revisited" showed that professionals and lay supporters alike found the settlement still worth studying.[54] In 1964 Anthony Bailey, writing in the *New York Herald Tribune*, observed its enduring quality:

> To Radburn . . . come engineers, architects and planners from all over the world and Mr. Sporn takes them around to see the parks, lanes, paths, pools and the famous Olmsted-type underpass. . . There also come study groups from the Urban Land Institute and the FHA . . . and students from Harvard, Princeton and Cornell who . . . reflect on how relevant Radburn seems. . . [55]

Furthermore, the Radburn visits probably added a vision of the benefits of cluster zoning and planned unit development which municipal governments would begin to accept in this period.[56]

The planners of the seventies have not forgotten Radburn. In 1970, John Lansing of the University of Michigan included Radburn in an important study of six American planned environments, and concluded that Radburn's plan remains a model.[57] He found its design to have important implications for energy conservation, recording that 47 percent of Radburn's residents shopped for groceries on foot while comparable figures were 23 percent for Reston, and only 8 percent for a nearby unplanned community. Other findings, such as low figures for weekend trips and low average numbers of miles traveled by car per resident, bore out this claim.

In September 1978, *Building Magazine* reported on a contemporary extension of the Radburn concepts, the Harmon Cove project built by Hartz Mountain Industries in the newly reclaimed meadowlands area of northern New Jersey. Only a few miles from its prototype, the forty-acre settlement designed by architect Jerome Larson, Land Design Associates of Long Island, and Hartz Mountain planners has approximately six hundred dwellings clustered around centrally located open space laced with separate vehicular and pedestrian systems, including the typical underpass.[58]

Finally, in the spring of 1979, professional and lay interest arose again, probably stimulated by Radburn's fiftieth anniversary. The *New York Times* ran a feature article in April and *Planning Magazine* had one in May.[59] In addition, John Gallery, then Director of Housing and Community Development for the City of Philadelphia, reassessed Radburn in an address before the annual meeting of the Society of Architectural Historians. In this talk he emphasized the plan's lessons for him in his current position, noting that the community's mix of residential uses allowing for a multigenerational population was a particularly important model.[60]

Also, in 1979, revisions of the standby planners' textbook, *The Practice of Local Government Planning,* issued by the International City Management Association, included extensive coverage of Radburn in its sweeping "Planning Portfolio." Seeking to demonstrate the story of planning in the United States in the last generation, its author, Louis B. Schlivek, perpetuated Radburn, labeling it "a pioneering new town." Using photographs and text to highlight the major features, Schlivek concluded that this "most ambitious and durable of planning efforts was and is in many ways even more relevant to our present problems than it was at the time it was conceived."[61]

Conclusion: Radburn's Impact

Radburn has had a significant impact on planning theory and vision in the twentieth century. Not only did it act as an exemplar of the profession's principles but also its design became a steady resource for practitioners. Furthermore, in every generation since the beginning of the movement, planners—always affected by the economic, social, and political environment of their times—have found answers to specific contemporary problems in Radburn. Though the issues change, Radburn, the icon, does not.

The original group of Radburn designers, the members of the Regional Planning Association of America, developed the plan as a team, each contributing his individual skills and seeking additional advice when needed. Their product, a comprehensive, rational, technical plan, demonstrated the benefits of this prototype city planning process. Later planners would emulate these procedures.

They produced a superior plan. Its complex program addressed contemporary needs, primarily the integration of the automobile into residential life. Its failure to anticipate mid-century multiple car ownership and its awkward positioning of dwellings with back doors fronting the streets were notable weaknesses, but they were excused by the originality of Radburn's suggested suburban pattern based on the hierarchical arrangement of streets and large recreational areas. Over time the plan acted as a permanent resource for practitioners' reference. Durable and ingenious, the design suggested seminal solutions to a panoply of new concerns ranging from community organization to energy conservation.

In succeeding years, planners considered Radburn a success, a view based on the plan's intellectual strength, not on its execution. Their stance bolstered their ambitions for promoting a profession claiming expertise in land use matters. In the thirties, planners working with various New Deal projects treated the Radburn design as dogma; but they were only able to propagate parts of it in efforts as diverse as the Resettlement Administration's Greenbelt towns and Federal Housing Administration regulations. In training new generations of planners, practitioners proselytized the Radburn plan—along with other adaptations—with the result that individual design devices became associated with enlightened planning.

However, the New Deal planners failed to convince the majority of land developers, public and private, to adopt the complete Radburn concept. The consequent application of diluted Radburn forms to planning problems, in particular in the postwar public housing and urban renewal programs, set the scene for later attacks on physical planning solutions. (Certainly, in this period Radburn was only one of many examples of designs for large-scale neighborhood unit development, but it was well known and lingered on in the literature as a normative pattern.)

By the sixties, critics discredited Radburn and all that it had come to represent. They attacked the planners' assumption that designs based on middle-class values could promote social progress. They indicted the technically based procedures producing physical plans for their failure to include citizens in the planning process. Ironically, they called for holistic solutions, such as the original Radburn planners had suggested. Even in these turbulent times, then, the Radburn idea persisted but in a new form.

Planners have based their positive reevaluation of Radburn in the seventies on a new application of the plan's design and on its seeming proof of the field's accomplishments. As professionals seek to reassert themselves as technically competent, Radburn provides useful evidence of this expertise.

Finally, this brief case study of Radburn demonstrates a chronic issue in the planning field: the divergence of theory from practice. Postwar suburban developments clearly did not follow the Radburn pattern, even though planners participating in this radical transformation of the American landscape held the Radburn plan as an ideal. The profession was too weak, its practitioners too few, and its existence too market-oriented for practicing planners to overcome deeply ingrained political, economic, and social traditions with the rational but radical goals expressed by the Radburn concept.

Unquestionably, Radburn has been an important influence in the intellectual tradition of the American planning movement. It has served as a testimonial of the profession's potential. It has acted as a permanent reference for generations of planners, and it persists as a respectable icon in the field's literature. However, as an applied pattern, it has failed to be a determining force.

NOTES

1. John Reps in *The Making of Urban America* (Princeton: Princeton University Press, 1965) gives an ample survey of American town planning from the colonial period to the modern era. Mel Scott in *American City Planning Since 1890* (University of California Press, Berkeley, 1969) covers the growth of contemporary efforts. John L. Hancock has written two excellent studies of the early planning movement: "Planning in the Changing American City, 1900-1940," *Journal of the American Institute of Planners* (Sept. 1967) and "John Nolen, The Background of a Pioneer Planner," *Journal of the American Institute of Planners* (November, 1960).

2. The growth of the housing movement can be found in Roy Lubove, *The Progressives and the Slums* (Pittsburgh: University of Pittsburgh Press, 1962) and E. L. Birch, "Woman-Made America: The Case of Early Public Housing Policy," *Journal of the American Institute of Planners* (April, 1978). The emergence of the social welfare movement is covered by Allan F. Davis, *Spearheads for Reform* (New York: Oxford University Press, 1967) and Robert Bremner, *From the Depths, The Discovery of Poverty in the United States* (New York: New York University Press, 1964).

3. This statement of purpose comes from the Constitution of the American City Planning Institute, June 1925.

4. Scott in *American City Planning* discussed the American Civic Association and its development. Early planners such as Nelson P. Lewis, Henry V. Hubbard, and John Nolen were extremely active in the professional organizations pertaining to their respective areas of interest, engineering and landscape architecture.

5. Correspondence among the early officers reveals their concern with membership standards. See, for example, George Ford to John Nolen, letters through 1927 in the John Nolen Papers, City Planning Collection, Cornell University, Ithaca, New York. Among the requirements for membership were eight years of practical high level experience and personal endorsements from sponsors.

6. Thomas Adams to John Nolen, October 17, 1926, John Nolen Papers.

7. John Nolen, "Twenty Years of City Planning Progress in the United States," in *Planning Problems of Town, City and Region*. Papers and Discussions at the 19th Conference on City Planning (Washington, D.C.: National Conference on City Planning, 1927), p. 19.

8. *Ibid.*

9. *Ibid.*, p. 20.

10. Roy Lubove, *Community Planning in the 1920's: The Contributions of the Regional Planning Association of America* (Pittsburgh: University of Pittsburgh Press, 1962). Clarence Stein, *Towards New Towns for America* (Cambridge: MIT Press, 1973).

11. *Ibid.*, pp. 68-72.

12. Clarence Stein to Catherine Bauer, September 27, 1961, Clarence Stein Papers, City Planning Collection, Cornell University.

13. "Summary of Discussions of Problems Connected with a Garden City at a Series of Conferences of the Regional Planning Association of America," Oct. 8 and 9, 1927, Clarence Stein Papers.

14. "Problems Connected with a New City," Clarence Stein Papers.

15. Charles Ascher to Edith Elmer Wood, February 6, 1928, Edith Elmer Wood Collection, Avery Library, Columbia University.

16. Actual codification of the planning process did not appear until much later. See, for example, Alan Altshuler, *The City Planning Process* (New York: Cornell University Press, 1968).

17. See, for example, Louis Brownlow, "Some Problems in New Planning," in *Proceedings of the National Conference on City Planning* (Philadelphia, 1929); "Economy, Charm and Safety of the Cul de Sac Street," *American City Magazine* (November, 1928); Henry M. Propper, "Radburn's Unique Plan Shows Results," *American City Magazine* (November, 1929); and "New York's First Satellite Town, An Interview with Mr. Alexander M. Bing," *National Municipal Review* (March, 1928).

18. Louis Brownlow, "Radburn: A New Town Planned for the Motor Age," *International Housing and Town Planning Bulletin* (February, 1930); Committee on Regional Plan of New York and its Environs, *Regional Plan of New York and its Environs*, Vol. VII (New York: Russell Sage Foundation, 1929); Stein, *Towards New Towns*, pp. 37-73.

19. "Radburn, A Town Planned for Safety," *The American Architect* 137 (January 1930): 42.

20. Frank So, Israel Stollman, Frank Beal, and David Arnold, *The Practice of Local Government Planning* (Washington, D.C.: International City Management Association, 1979), p. 447.

21. "Report of the Committee on Re-organization of the National Conference on City Planning," Spring, 1934, Russell Van Nest Black Papers, City Planning Collection, Cornell University.

22. For further discussion of these changes see Donald A. Krueckeberg, "The Story of the Planner's Journal, 1915-1980" and E. L. Birch, "Advancing the Art and Science of Planning; Planners and their Organizations, 1909-1980," *Journal of the American Planning Association* (January 1980).

23. Augur, "Radburn—The Challenge of a New Town," *Michigan Municipal Review* (February 1931): 40.

24. For details see Aelred J. Gray, "The Maturing of a Planned New Town, Norris, Tennessee," *The Tennessee Planner* (xerox sent to the author by the TVA Library, Knoxville, Tennessee); Tracy B. Augur, "The Planning of the Town of Norris," *American Architect* (April, 1936); Joseph L. Arnold, *The New Deal in the Suburbs* (Athens: Ohio University Press, 1971); and Clarence Stein, *Towards New Towns*.

25. British new town administrators used Radburn principles. By the sixties Radburn had become common parlance for them. See for example, A. E. J. Morris, "Private Sector Housing: The Radburn Dilemma," *Official Architecture and Planning* 33 (May 1970); Michael Fagence, "The Radburn Idea," *Built Environment* 2 (August, 1973).

26. Scott, *American City Planning*, p. 312.

27. John T. Howard to E. L. Birch, Sept. 5, 1979; Clarence Stein and Catherine Bauer, "Store Buildings and Neighborhood Shopping Centers," *Architectural Record* (February 1934).

28. National Resources Committee, *Urban Planning and Land Policies* (Washington, D.C.: U.S. Government Printing Office, 1939); Augur, "Radburn," p. 40.

29. Housing literature of the period promoted this view. See, for example, Catherine Bauer, *Modern Housing* (Boston: Houghton Mifflin Company, 1934); Louis Pink, *A New Day in Housing* (New York: John Day Company, Inc., 1928); Kenneth K. Stowell (ed.) "Housing and the Emergency," *Architectural Forum* (March 1932).

30. This is only one of many such statements of this and later periods. President's Conference on Home Building and Home Ownership, *Housing and the Community* (Washington, D.C.: U.S. Government Printing Office, 1932), pp. 47-48.

31. Wright struggled to convince his followers in an article appearing in *American City* (December 1928). He wrote:

> In order to appreciate the economics of the plan it is necessary to examine an individual lane. This lane contains 16 house lots averaging 43 feet wide or 680 feet of frontage. The lots are served by 1/2 of 230 linear feet of utilities on the main street and 300 lineal feet from the

center of this street to the end of the lane, a total of 415 lineal feet of utilities or 26 feet per lot. However, let us suppose the street end of the land containing the first 10 lots to be doubled on axis A, forming a normal block 400 feet long continuing 20 lots, averaging 45 feet. This would require twice 1/2 of 230 lineal feet of utilities on the two end streets, and 4 feet of utilities from center to center of the main streets, total of 710 lineal feet for 20 lots or 35.5 lineal feet of utilities per lot, an increase of 36 percent in utilities required by the Radburn plan. . . Admitting the obvious problems brought up by this or any other new method of planning, it would seem worth an experiment to save from 25 to 30 percent of the utilities now required in residential neighborhoods.

Federal Housing Administration, *Planning Neighborhoods for Small Houses* (Washington, .D.C.: U.S. Government Printing Office, 1939).

32. *Ibid.*, p. 31.

33. *Ibid.*, p. 64.

34. Henry J. Aaron, *Shelter and Subsidies* (Washington, D.C.: The Brookings Institution, 1972), p. 15.

35. American Society of Planning Officials, *Newsletter* 20, 9 (September 1954): 6; Perry Norton, Interview, Leonia, New Jersey, January 29, 1979; "Kit for Board of Governors," 1952, APA Archives, Washington, D.C.

36. For further discussion, see Birch, "Advancing the Art and Science."

37. *ASPO Newsletter* (September 15, 1954): 7.

38. A survey of the *ASPO Newsletter*, the list of *Planning Advisory Service* topics, and the *Zoning Digest* reveals these tendencies.

39. Birch, "Advancing," p. 34.

40. John T. Howard, "City Planning as a Social Movement, A Governmental Function and a Technical Profession," in Harvey S. Perloff (ed.) *Planning and the Urban Community* (Pittsburgh: University of Pittsburgh Press, 1961, pp. 153-154.

41. Jane Jacobs, *The Death and Life of Great American Cities* (New York: Vintage Books, 1961), p. 18; Paul and Percival Goodman, *Communitas* (New York: Vintage Books, 1947), p. 35; Herbert Gans, *The Urban Villagers* (Glencoe: The Free Press, 1962); John R. Seeley, "The Slum: Its Nature, Use and Users," *Journal of the American Institute of Planners* (February 1959); William Moore, Jr., *The Vertical Ghetto* (New York: Random House, 1969), p. 214.

42. Kevin Lynch, "Quality in Design" in Lawrence B. Holland (ed.) *Who Designs America?* (New York: Doubleday, 1966), p. 123. He went on to decry the lack of innovation among designers, contemptuously observing: "We notice that the plan for a new port city in Africa looks suspiciously like a student scheme for an American 'new town.'" The Goodmans also questioned some aesthetic assumptions of elements of the Radburn plan; "Urban beauty does not require trees and parks. . . And when finally . . . the aim is to make a city in the park, a Garden City, one has despaired of city life altogether." In all fairness, the Goodmans did approve of greenbelts, an integral part of garden cities which actually did not appear at Radburn because of the CHC's objections to their expense. In *Communitas* they were working toward a clearer definition of urban space (*Communitas*, p. 50).

43. Jewel Bellusch and Murray Hausknecht, *Urban Renewal: People, Politics and Planning* (New York: Doubleday, 1967), p. 214.

44. For a discussion of advocacy planning see Paul Davidoff, "Advocacy and Pluralism in Planning," *Journal of the American Institute of Planners* (November, 1965); Lisa R. Peattie, "Reflections on Advocacy Planning" and Richard S. Bolan, "Emerging Views of Planning" in *The Comprehensive Planning Process: Several Views* (Washington, D.C.: AIP, 1977), 45.

45. Herbert Gans, "The Failure of Urban Renewal, A Critique and Some Proposals," *Commentary* (April 1965): 35.

46. Melvin M. Webber, "Comprehensive Planning and Social Responsibility," *Journal of the American Institute of Planners* (November 1963): 237, or reprinted in *The Comprehensive Planning Process.*

47. President's Conference on Home Building and Homeownership, *Planning Residential Districts* (Washington, D.C.: U.S. Government Printing Office, 1932).

48. Thomas Adams, *Design of Residential Areas* (Cambridge: Harvard University Press, 1934), p. 237.

49. Lewis Mumford, *The Culture of Cities* (New York: Harcourt Brace Jovanovich, Inc., 1938), p. 437.

50. National Resources Committee, *Urban Planning and Land Policies.*

51. Federal Housing Administration, *Neighborhoods Built for Rental Housing* (Washington, D.C.: U.S. Government Printing Office, 1947).

52. Coleman Woodbury, ed., *Urban Redevelopment Problems and Policies* (Chicago: University of Chicago Press, 1953),pp. 278-93.

53. Arthur B. Gallion, *The Urban Pattern* (New York: D. VanNostrand Co., 1950). This book has had four printings, the latest in 1980. Christopher Tunnard, *City of Man* (New York: Scribner, 1953), p. 343. This book was also reissued recently. In addition, Tunnard and Henry Hope Reed's *American Skyline* (New York: Houghton Mifflin, 1953) dealt extensively with Radburn.

54. See for example, Henry M. Wright, "Radburn Revisited," *Ekistics* 199 (March 1972), a reprint of an earlier article; Alden Christie, "Radburn Reconsidered," *Connection* 7, 1964. The latter piece was critical of the settlement as its author's views reflected the unrest of the times.

55. Anthony Bailey, "Radburn Revisited," *New York Herald Tribune*, reprinted in *The Regional Plan News* (December 1964).

56. The political leaders were aided by several publications, including Frederick H. Bair Jr.'s "How to Regulate Planned Unit Development for Housing"(Chicago: ASPO, 1965) and the U.S. Federal Housing Administration's *Planned Unit Development with a Homes Association* (Washington, D.C.: U.S. Government Printing Office, 1964).

57. John B. Lansing and Robert W. Marans, *Planned Residential Environments* (Ann Arbor: University of Michigan, 1970), p. 213.

58. Michael B. McNally, Vice President of planning and engineering, Hartz Mountain Industries, Interview, June 25, 1980; Hale Cole, partner, Land Design Associates, Interview, June 27, 1980; "The Meadowland Tweet Smell of Success," *Building Magazine*, September 1978 (reprint).

59. Paul Goldberger, *New York Times* April 19, 1979; Mildred Jailer, "Model Community Little Changed at 50," *Planning Magazine* (May 1979).

60. John Gallery, "Radburn, 1929-1979," Annual Meeting, Society of Architectural Historians, April, 1979; John Gallery, Interview, Savannah, Georgia, April 5, 1979; January 13, 1979.

61. International City Management Association, *The Practice of Local Government Planning* (Washington, D.C.: 1979).

8

City Planning in World War II

The Experience of the
National Resources Planning Board

Philip J. Funigiello

From its inception in the depression-haunted thirties the National Resources Planning Board (NBRPB) was inextricably caught up in the problems
of the American city.[1] It is, perhaps, less well known that the NRPB continued
to extend its activities in the area of neighborhood conservation and
rehabilitation planning during the period of defense preparations in 1940-
1941, and that it experimented with new programs for urban redevelopment
during the war itself.[2]

The NRPB and Postwar Urban Planning

Between 1941 and its demise in 1943, the NRPB proceeded along four
parallel but complementary paths. These were: *(1)* the canvassing of informed
opinion about the federal role in the postwar reconstruction of American
cities; *(2)* establishing liaisons with other federal agencies, planning bodies,
and private institutions committed to reform of the urban environment;
(3) sponsoring studies bearing on specific aspects of the urban problems, such
as metropolitan consolidation, new sources of revenue, and recreation; and
(4) drafting a progressive urban planning procedure as a model for cities to
emulate. An in-depth analysis of the last-mentioned item is fruitful, because it
subsumed the first three and thereby affords some insight into the Roosevelt
administration's policy toward the urban communities.[4]

Reprinted from Philip J. Funigiello. 1972. "City Planning in World War II: The Experience of the
National Resources Planning Board," *Social Science Quarterly* **53**, 1 (June): 91-104. Copyright
© 1972. The University of Texas Press. Reprinted by permission.

One year prior to America's entry into World War II, President Roosevelt instructed the NRPB to undertake a study of what then was termed "post-defense planning."[5] Two urgent questions confronted the Board's directors: first, how far should the NRPB go in seeking the assistance of urban experts, private voluntary groups, and public agencies on specific problems; and second, should the planning confine itself to the immediate demobilization period or extend over a longer span of time. After considerable discussion, the directors agreed to make planning literature available to private parties but not especially to stimulate them to plan—a decision they eventually reversed.[6]

The directors also decided to conduct urban planning along two lines, for the transitional period following cessation of hostilities (when returning veterans would be seeking employment) and for the decade after reconversion.[7] To this end they established an Urban Section, instructing it to take full advantage of the work of other governmental and private agencies in the field of urban rehabilitation and to think as boldly as the skilled and disciplined imagination of its personnel allowed.[8] For the directors recognized that the government could permit neither a sharp break nor a temporary lag to occur between the civilian defense program and the postwar reconstruction of cities.

The war, declared Louis Wirth, professor of sociology at the University of Chicago, in an influential position paper prepared for the Urban unit, offered a better opportunity than had existed before for each city to mold the quality of life within its boundaries more nearly in accord with its resources and aspirations.[9] It would be an exaggeration to say that Wirth, a pioneer in the field of urban ecology, was the intellectual godfather of the NRPB's urban policies, but there is no question that his writings shaped its thinking.[10]

Origins of the Urban Section's Interest
in Progressive Planning

The most notable expression of Wirth's influence was the joint proposal of Charles S. Ascher and Frank W. Herring, both staff members, requesting the Board to authorize six demonstration experiments to test a markedly new approach to urban planning. With an initial allocation of $50,000, their objective was to evolve "a progressive planning procedure that can serve as a base for long-term programming and for post-defense deployment of men and materials in city rebuilding."[11] They hoped to attain a new level of sophistication in urban planning by treating the city not simply as an artifact but by integrating social, economic, and cultural factors into the planning process. When woven into a continuously revised long-term capital program, they expected to demonstrate that planning was "a continuous process, not a one-time undertaking that results in a 'master plan' to be put in a pigeon-hole."[12]

The experimental projects were to serve, in the first instance, as the yardstick for critically appraising other neighborhood redevelopment programs seeking federal assistance and as a catalyst for generating an integrated series of local projects. The first stage, which would last only a few months, was to culminate in an outline plan for overall development. Before and during the physical planning, and as a basis thereof, the planners expected to target the goals of economic, social, and cultural development and to produce a practical blueprint to attain them. The plan itself would remain in skeletal form, being changed from time to time as required by changing objectives or local conditions.[13]

The emphasis throughout was put upon local action and responsibility, with a corresponding deemphasis on strong central direction from Washington. This was intended as in the case of other New Deal programs, to reverse the concentration of control in the federal government and minimize opposition. The decision was predicated on the realistic assumption that private citizens, private organizations, and local public officials possessed the knowledge, good judgment, and experience to manage some segments of the planning better than outside technicians. Federal agencies would supply what data they had and the technicians would offer expert assistance, but the initiative and personnel to conduct the day-to-day planning had to originate in the local community.[14]

Prior to submitting the proposal to the Board's directors, Ascher and Herring systematically cultivated the support of other federal officials, planners, and professional organizations. Walter H. Blucher, executive director of the American Society of Planning Officials, Hugh Pomeroy, of the Virginia State Planning Board and future director of the Urban Land Institute, Frederick S. Bigger, the forward-looking head of the Pittsburgh City Planning Commission, and Dean Arthur Comey of the Harvard University School of Architecture endorsed the idea of demonstration projects.[15]

A few professional planners privately had doubts about the projects' feasibility, but these were recorded in confidential letters to Board members and passed largely unnoticed by the general public. Alfred Bettman and Ladislas Segoe of Cincinnati worried that popular participation in each stage of the planning process would dilute the quality of the plan and thus erode respect for the profession.[16] Bettman, especially, feared that so-called "progressive" urban planning was no more than a fad which, if mismanaged, would set back the cause of city planning in the United States.[17]

Despite the criticisms, Herring and Ascher were optimistic that the Urban unit could produce a progressive planning manual (based upon the successful demonstration projects) that would be used by hundreds of localities across the United States. Nor did they minimize the obstacles confronting them; the latter included a dearth of experienced personnel relative to the demands of post-defense city rebuilding; the absence of institutionalized planning commissions in most cities; the choice of project cities; the degree to which local officials were willing to cooperate with federal agencies and the NRPB's agents; the writing of a manual that would enlighten city officials ignorant of planning concepts; and the ability to persuade urban leaders that the principles laid out in the handbook worked in practice. They were confident, however, that the Urban Section, under the direction of Robert B. Mitchell, author of the Woodlawn and Waverly neighborhood conservation and redevelopment plans for the Federal Home Loan Bank Board, could surmount these barriers.[18]

Toward the close of 1941 the Board agreed to permit the Urban Section to conduct the demonstrations. Speed was all-important, for the directors wanted the project to commence in February 1942—a deadline that proved impossible to meet given the fledgling condition of the Urban unit.[19]

It was not until the spring of 1942 that the Urban Section began the spadework to insure a successful demonstration experiment. Ascher drafted a confidential memorandum to guide the staff. The document rested upon three assumptions: that urban conservation and development constituted the "fourth dimension" in the Board's work; that the fact of the city should be recognized in all matters pertaining to national planning; and that, since urban considerations permeated all the Board's general approaches to planning, "the Urban unit must be free to champion the cause of cities throughout a wide range of subjects."[20] The progressive urban planning procedure was clearly intended to attain these objectives.

With the directors' permission, the Urban unit also had begun to examine, as a part of its process of self-definition, the obstacles to post-war urban redevelopment and their elimination. In line with its "total approach" to urban planning, it assembled an interdisciplinary team of specialists and encouraged them to break new ground. Thus, Ralph Temple, a lawyer, began drafting a new definition of the traditional sovereign power of the state (with respect to eminent domain, taxation, and the police power) for the social control of urban land use; Dr. Edwin H. Spengler, a Brooklyn College economist, investigated alternative sources for financing local units besides the property tax; Alvin H. Hansen and Guy Greer, economists, studied the implications of urban land acquisition and the funding of urban development for a full-employment economy; and V.O. Key, Jr., the Johns Hopkins political scientist, the problems of readjusting urban governmental machinery to facilitate planning and land acquisition control.[21]

Supervising their efforts was Mitchell, who refined the procedure the Urban unit ultimately followed.[22] He instructed the field agents to capitalize on the existing data in federal, state, and local files, and to organize local resources for particular segments of the experiment. "We are really proceeding on the assumption that 'planning is a continuous process' and that no plan will or should be considered final. If we can get the local people into the habit of thinking of their plans in this way, I believe we can increase the chances of planning being integrated into the municipal function as a living process," he observed.[23]

Mitchell expected each agent to remain in a given community the length of time required to complete the comprehensive planning outline and to organize the local planning function, "so that it will continue as a permanent process of the community."[24] He also invited their suggestions for cities to be designated demonstration experiments.

Selecting the Demonstration Cities

After Congress severely reduced the Board's appropriation for fiscal 1942, the Urban Section scaled down the original calculation of nine experimental projects to three and designated the remainder as "area studies," wherein the federal government offered formal recognition and only token assistance to local groups wanting to conduct their own intensive planning. Thus Mitchell was placed in the position of having to select only cities in which the project was likely to succeed—and quickly. Under these circumstances, the Urban unit drew up a new set of criteria, more exacting than the directors had sketched. The guidelines rested on two fundamental premises: (1) which cities could utilize the funds most efficiently to yield the quickest results; and (2) since the preponderance of urban development had occurred in the East and Midwest, the distribution of projects ought to be weighted there.[25]

There were other criteria governing the choice of sites. The staff agreed, for example, to give priority to communities whose demographic, economic, social, and cultural data was current and readily accessible and to cities having regional problems in economic layout or political administration.[26] The negative criteria were more rigorous. Population was a controlling factor—no city below 10,000 or above 150,000 was eligible; the Urban unit might conduct experiments in declining communities, but "not more than one in places such as Scranton, Pennsylvania, which seem to have a pretty hopeless future as they now are," nor in more than one satellite part of a metropolitan region. Certain categories of communities were excluded altogether—cities artifically boomed or revived by the defense program; those in which local leadership was antagonistic to federal planning and the New Deal; and communities already blessed with efficient and productive planning organizations.[27]

It is regrettable in retrospect that the budget reduction, Congressional pressure, and the failure to adhere strictly to the guidelines compromised the total impact of the planning procedure as a tool for other cities to utilize. The selection of Buffalo, New York, as the demonstration project in Region 2, and its later reduction to area studies status, elucidates this point. Under the criteria set forth above, New York, Philadelphia, and Baltimore—cities that experienced urban blight *in extremis* —were excluded from consideration because they were too large and their problems too complex to yield the swift results desired. For similar reasons the war-swollen urban complex of Norfolk, Newport News, Hampton, and Portsmouth, in Virginia, was ineligible.[28]

Given the guidelines, Albert C. Schweizer, a technician, pointed out that the logical site in Region 2 was Wilmington, Delaware, which had a population of 112,000 and a tentative master plan. He wrote up a convincing brief in support of his choice and played as his trump cards Wilmington's proximity to the District of Columbia, which made it possible for the Urban unit to monitor closely the progress of the procedure, and the presence of John Hyde, who knew the city's needs and was eager to direct the experiment. Violating its own criteria, the Urban unit instead selected Buffalo. Later, because of the unfavorable local conditions there, it had to reduce its commitment and redesignate it an area study.[29]

Progressive Planning in Action

Mitchell, acting for the Board, ultimately settled on Corpus Christi, Salt Lake City, and Tacoma as the most promising communities to test the progressive planning procedure. At its best—in Corpus Christi, Texas, a community that had achieved big city status through a succession of booms in shipping, chemicals, oil, and war industry—the demonstration or experiment embodied the principles of coordinated, continuous and, in the eyes of the Board, democratic planning.[30]

As with other cities once the nation went to war, Corpus Christi had had to defer its normal public works construction, its building of streets, sewers, utilites, its new city hall, library, and school.[31] With the assistance of the Urban Section, however, city officials attempted to carry this Texas coastal community beyond the "city beautiful" and "city engineering" stages into a comprehensive design for work, play, and decent living. By planning for the orderly development of its public works and studying proper location and design, they hoped to foster what had always been lacking in the daily struggle to catch up with the rapid growth of the city.[32]

Members of the chamber of commerce, city councilmen, planning commissioners and *The Caller-Times* wanted a plan that would provide direction to economic and industrial development and a pattern for the quality of urban living they deemed desirable. "For the first time," commented the chairman of the city planning commission, "Corpus Christi was consciously designing its own future. For the first time, planning was based on a true coordination of plans—economic, social, physical."[33] Complying with their request, the Urban Section dispatched Sam B. Zisman, one of its best technicians, to work with the local people in organizing the program and lending technical assistance. Zisman at no time attempted to draw up the plans for the city; rather, he aided Corpus Christi to do its own planning.[34]

The first step in the procedure was to organize the entire community. Mayor A. C. McCaughan directed all municipal departments to contribute up-to-date data; the school board, housing authority, library, and real estate boards resolved to collaborate with the planning commission in developing programs and providing clerical assistance. The Industrial Committee of the Chamber of Commerce provided leadership in working out the plan for economic and industrial development. Over the months, its members met regularly, drawing in business, financial, and labor interests, marking out the problems to be tackled, surveying the resources of the city and its surrounding region, and defining long-range goals. It professed to give high priority to training programs that would eventuate in full-employment opportunities for minority groups, and to housing, adequate consumer income, and regional economic development. Thus the pattern of individual and economic development became as much a part of the plan as did street paving or slum elimination.[35]

Local service and citizens groups also joined in analyzing needs and proposing programs. The school board, for example, instituted studies of new schools and recommended improvements in the existing plant. It also worked closely with the recreation people, coordinating plans for schools with those for parks and playgrounds. The director of the housing authority, the real estate board, and private agencies grappled with the thorny question of a city-wide public housing program. They gave strong emphasis to the redevelopment of slums and blighted areas that cut through the heart of the city. Complementing their work were committees on health, welfare, and institutions organized under the supervision of the Council of Community Agencies. The engineering department brought its plans for streets into the picture, and the police department drafted blueprints for a badly needed modern safety center.[36]

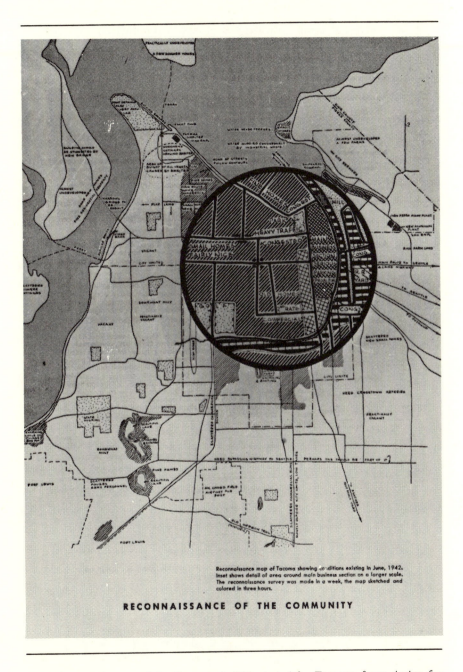

RECONNAISSANCE OF THE COMMUNITY

8.1 "Reconnaissance of the Community" illustrated for Tacoma, from *Action for Cities*, p. 9.

At each stage of the procedure, the planning commission attempted to employ to good advantage the resources of neighboring educational institutions and government agencies. The University of Texas conducted demographic studies; the department of architecture at Texas A&M analyzed waterfront patterns, and the Texas College of Arts and Industries initiated faculty studies of agricultural and industrial problems. The highway study required cooperative planning between the local and county engineering departments, the State Highway Department, and the Public Roads Administration. And the design for a major new airport spurred collaborative efforts on the part of local officials and the Civil Aeronautics Authority. The whole program was thus to be a demonstration of cooperation between private enterprise, private institutions, and public agencies.[37]

Toward the close of the demonstration in March 1943, over 30 agencies and 600 citizens were meeting, exchanging information, exploring problems and

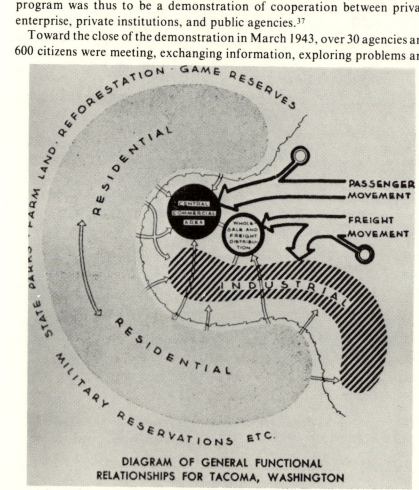

DIAGRAM OF GENERAL FUNCTIONAL
RELATIONSHIPS FOR TACOMA, WASHINGTON

8.2   A diagram from *Action for Cities*, p. 57, to "help dramatize in 'graphic language' the essential relationships of areas and uses."

projecting plans. At the center was the planning commission, coordinating the separate programs and driving toward the development of a comprehensive plan. The experience had significance beyond this appreciation of a coordinated plan. Zisman afterwards claimed that the project had enlisted a wide democratic participation; that political difficulties and old prejudices had a hard time elbowing into the work; and that the citizens of Corpus Christi retained a hard-headed realism about how much they had accomplished and how far they still had to go.[38] This observation was correct insofar as it went, but Zisman neglected to give the complete picture.

The experiment at its worst failed conspicuously in Tacoma, Washington, a nineteenth-century railroad community to which the war had given new impetus. In entering Tacoma, the Urban unit violated some of its own criteria, ignored others, and neglected to do its homework. It clearly understood very poorly the leadership problem in the community. The mayor was the most dynamic and enthusiastic local booster of the project, but his interest in improving the community was constantly frustrated by subordinate commissioners who either disapproved of his methods and specific proposals or feared he would set a city manager above them. The commissioner of public works, who appointed members to the planning commission, retaliated by refusing to cooperate with Art McVoy, the NRPB's field agent, or to call a meeting of the planning commission.[39]

For his part, the mayor weakened his hand by insisting that planning be done on the quiet so that afterwards he could spring it on the people. This tactic made it impossible for McVoy to identify his backers, to explain what he hoped to accomplish, or to bring local groups into the planning process. Understandably, he wrote to Mitchell: "I think if I had it to do over again, I would attempt to find out all the complexities of local politics before attempting to start applying the program."[40]

The record elsewhere in the case of the experimental projects and the area studies was mixed, as the Urban unit modified its approach in accordance with particular geographical settings or in response to different emphases in a number of problems. In Denver and Buffalo, for example, the staff confronted fundamentally large metropolitan complexes and had to engage in planning for the metropolitan region.[41] In these urbanized areas the land use plan was primarily urban land use in which the plan for industry focused upon decentralization rather then dispersion. The situation was quite the reverse on the Wasatch Front, which embraced Salt Lake City and its environs, where the Board had to contemplate the requirements of both the urban core and the more rural hinterland.[42]

The Wasatch Front required a regional plan in which rural, mining, and urban land uses were interlocked. The industrial plan, for example, had to accommodate not merely population density, housing and urban size, but also the reconversion of war plants to civilian uses, the development of local processing industries, the agricultural program, the mining of metallic and non-metallic resources, trade, the availability of public services, and transportation (as transfer and service points for the national highway and air systems). At each stage of the planning, the Urban unit also had to take cognizance of the integrating force of the Mormon Church in the social and cultural development of urban life.[43]

Buffalo: The Failure of Local Initiative

After the initial delay, the Salt Lake City demonstration progressed smoothly, unlike the Buffalo area study that was plagued by foot-dragging and other obstacles. Albert C. Schweizer summed up the New York situation for Mitchell, following extensive conferences in September 1942, with NRPB representatives. He concluded that the Board should not sink its resources into the area study, because of the unfavorable atmosphere within the city.[44] Buffalo, unlike the demonstration experiments and most area studies projects, had experienced a mass in-migration of Blacks seeking war-created jobs and opportunities. The rapid growth of the Black population from 17,694 to 30,000 between 1940 and 1944 exacerbated tensions with the older, White ethnic (mainly Polish) communities. Sterling Albert, regional director for the National Housing Agency, informed Schweizer that local real estate interests and some Catholic Church leaders motivated either selfishly or from a lack of sympathy with the New Deal's social objectives, had organized to block the public housing program.[45]

The volatile element of racism had received almost no consideration when the Urban unit first broached the question of progressive planning in Buffalo. Worse still, there was a very real doubt that local officials in the Buffalo-Niagara Frontier area were interested in planning.[46] The city's transportation system, moreover, was chaotic. The New York Central Railroad, headquartered in Philadelphia, acted as an absentee landlord. From what Schweizer could discern, the railroad evinced absolutely no interest in transportation planning and looked upon Buffalo as "just a way station between more important cities."[47]

Not all the difficulties originated with the local officials, however. John D. Spaeth, Jr., the NRPB's Technical Director, had instituted studies of three substandard neighborhoods, implanting some doubt in Schweizer's mind as to whether "he was willing to abandon his own tactics in favor of the procedure advocated by the Urban unit." Thus, by the winter of 1942, the NRPB's participation in the Buffalo-Niagara Frontier area project was in complete disarray, and Mitchell was disgusted.[48]

Buffalo, unfortunately, procrastinated well into 1943 before establishing an active planning body. The Committee on Post War Problems was established to parallel the county's Niagara Frontier Post War Planning Commission. The relationship between the two agencies was described best in a bulletin of the Municipal Research Bureau, dated March 1943: "It is important to the Buffalo taxpayer that he is not charged with what is of no real benefit to the city, whatever the benefit to the Frontier or other portions thereof." Adding insult to injury, the Common Council appropriated a niggardly sum to conduct planning—an amount so small that the Buffalo planning body experienced a real hardship in hiring a full-time director.[49]

Progressive Urban Planning: An Evaluation

If the Board's city-planning experiments and area studies were not wholly the success their enthusiasts proclaimed, neither were they the failures New Deal critics were eager to believe. The progressive planning procedure had accepted the functional interdependency of city and suburb, acknowledging that the basic problems of the core area originated in large measure in the flight of the productive middle class to the fringe and the expensive fragmentation of governmental and social services within an uncoordinated metropolitan region.[50] It spurred the communities to act to stem the flight of industry by seeking alternative sources of revenue to the real property tax.

Also, the thrust of the neighborhood conservation and urban rehabilitation program brought the NRPB into close contact with other agencies, such as the Urban Land Institute, property owners' and taxpayers' associations, aggressively interested in housing and planning projects. As Abrams, Scott, and other scholars have observed, it was in the developing programs of government, organized realtors, and their allies that the tentative outlines of the urban redevelopment statutes of the several states in the 1940s and the salient features of Title I of the Housing Act of 1949 were located.[51]

The final product of the Urban unit's action was the compilation of the progressive planning manual, written in simple nontechnical language. *Action for Cities: A Guide for Community Planning* was intended to offer the kind of help interested and intelligent citizens and officials needed to develop planned programs for their communities. Its value as an instrument for coping with the postwar redevelopment problems of even small and medium-sized cities was questionable, however, because the principles enunciated therein were not closely adhered to in practice. The incomplete development of the economic study for Corpus Christi, the city in which the Urban Section claimed its greatest success, is illustrative. Zisman reported in 1943 that the manual had not been followed "to any appreciable extent," for, "it was not

SUMMARY OF THE GUIDE

I. THE PLANNING PROCEDURE outlined in this guide is based on:

1. Development of a sketch plan

a. Within a relatively short period—in months rather than years.

b. To be progressively refined from the first quick reconnaissance survey and the first drafts through later detailed drafts.

c. Making use of existing data and knowledge—not involving extensive programs of new research.

d. Through democratic collaboration—participation of informed citizens and outside consultants when needed, cooperation between public and private groups, and between local, state, and federal agencies.

2. Comprehensive planning

a. In recognizing the interrelatedness of problems of population, economic activities, social patterns, physical arrangements, and planning action—giving new emphasis to the economic and social base so that physical arrangements will be planned to meet the requirements of the kind of economic activities and community life desired by the people.

b. In relating the community to the region of which it is a part, and to the nation as a whole, so that the community will receive its full share from and will in turn contribute its full share to regional and national development.

II. THE PLANNING METHOD in each stage of the procedure is based on the following steps:

1. Determination of goals—what do the people of the planning area *want* their area to become in the light of:

a. Its possibilities—what *could* the area become if proper use were made of its resources—physical, human, economic, social, cultural?

b. Feasible paths of development—what *should* the area become in the best judgment of those who have made a special study of community problems?

2. Determination of needs—what must be provided in order to reach goals, measuring:

a. Existing conditions and facilities.

b. Shortages of physical facilities and arrangements, and of programs of services.

3. Programs of meeting needs—how can the necessary changes, facilities, and services be provided in terms of:

a. Time schedules—what order of projects and programs should be followed.

b. Physical changes—new development, redevelopment of existing arrangements.

c. Legislative, administrative, and financial means.

d. Community organization and public opinion.

III. THE PLANS to be developed include:

1. A statement of community objectives answering such questions as:

a. Size—smaller, larger, or stationary population?

b. Economic base—the same or broader or narrower base? What existing activities should be retained, expanded, contracted, converted, abandoned? What new activities should be introduced? What relocations should be encouraged?

c. Community living—what improvements are needed? in the way of facilities, programs of services, kinds of community organizations?

d. Physical arrangements—what arrangements in land use, central facilities, neighborhood designs? What areas changed, expanded, conserved?

2. Reports, charts, maps presenting what is to be done, when, by whom, and by what means, covering:

a. Population estimates—size, characteristics and distribution.

b. Program for economic development—steps to achieve maximum employment, with special attention to problems of demobilization; high levels of production; employment stabilization, high standard of living, and economic security; programs relating to the labor force; recruitment, training, counselling, placement; capital, entrepreneurial, and managerial requirements; policies for industrialists, businessmen, investors, organized labor groups to follow; programs for private and public development.

c. Program for community services in housing, education and cultural activities, recreation, health, welfare, community organization, and institutional development.

d. Programs for physical development—land use, transportation, and density plans; public work, and housing programs; designs for neighborhood units, central business, and other areas.

e. Programs of planning action—programs of public and private action; legislative, administrative, financial tools; official and citizen organization.

8.3 "Summary of the Guide" from *Action for Cities: A Guide for Community Planning*, 1943, published by the Public Administration Service, reflecting the working programs of the NRPB demonstration projects.

satisfactorily organized, was over-detailed in many places. It was not really tested by the industrial technician who preferred to follow his own lines of thinking and approach."[52]

Despite its limitations, *Action for Cities* forced planners to look beyond the exclusively physical dimension of urban planning. Urban unit officials, for example, categorized American cities according to socioeconomic and cultural status, age of residents, mobility, health, and other services. It would be an exaggeration to say that they were acquainted with the modern tools of the social scientist for analyzing specific urban problems (e.g., multiple regression analysis or determinants studies), or that their plans adhered strictly to economies of scale, but they had gained experience and compiled raw data to make future analyses a distinct possibility. In this sense, the war years were a seedtime in which city planners, government officials, and social scientists approached the city as a functional organism whose ills were eradicable given the application of certain procedures.[53]

The NRPB, moreover, had expanded upon the depression experience to provide new models for federal aid to the cities in the form of human, technical, and financial resources. Mitchell believed the experiments had introduced, however rudimentarily, the democratic concept of community participation in the planning process. If one equates the "community" with the local civic-business-realty leaders then the observation is accurate. For Mitchell had secured the endorsement of the city's political, economic and social establishment in Corpus Christi and elsewhere well in advance of the selection of the site. Thus, in the Texas community, the mayor, the president of the largest bank, the head of the Southern Alkali Corporation, representatives of the extractive industries (oil, gas, and fishing), the real estate board and Junior Assistance Club, who were interested in redeveloping the central part and preserving land values, each pledged the support of his particular constitutency. The NRPB's agents in turn, were sensitive to the interests of those whom it relied upon for assistance.[54]

On the other hand, the needs of other segments of the community (i.e., Chicanos, Blacks, the unorganized and inarticulate) seem to have been ignored with relative impunity. The largely WASP elite, for example, slighted the "Mexican" chamber of commerce and Black civic groups. Insensitive to their wishes, the power structure transmitted its decisions through Dr. Segrest, the Commissioner of Water and Gas, and "Professor" Sampson, principal of the all-Black high school. The result in Corpus Christi was to institute the now familiar practice of demolishing inner city ghettos, uprooting ethnic minorities, and replacing them with high-rent commercial and residential dwellings occupied by well-to-do Whites.[55]

Further weakening the "democratic" aspect of community participation was the fact that, once the city fathers and boosters made their bid to have

Corpus Christi selected as the demonstration site, there was no meaningful avenue for vocalizing dissatisfaction with the planning process. George Kunkel, for example, threw the editorial support of *The Caller-Times*, the city's largest newspaper (circulation 49,000), behind the project and, with Zisman, prepared a carefully orchestrated public relations program to counteract adverse publicity.[56]

If there was opposition to planning, it was thoroughly muted. War-induced regimentation, a housing shortage, lack of local funds, and the opportunity to be among the first to tap the federal treasury for urban redevelopment funds (which, in turn, promised to create new jobs for returning veterans) stilled dissent. This, too, contributed to a pattern that was to become familiar after the war, i.e., the use of federal funds to expand housing for the middle and upper classes with proportionately fewer funds to finance public housing for the lower classes which needed it most urgently. Again the evidence from Corpus Christi is illuminating. Finley Vinson, the director of the local housing authority, in his final report did not touch upon the problems of financing postwar public housing or the role of the Federal Public Housing Authority.[57]

Conclusion

How much postwar urban planning was stimulated as a direct consequence of the NRPB-sponsored experiments is uncertain. The answer appears to be not very much during the war years, or at least no more than would have occurred in any event. Here, too, the experience of the Board's field agents in Corpus Christi is instructive. Zisman reported in April 1943, shortly before terminating the project for lack of funds, that many of the studies (including the surveys of social and cultural problems, school, medical, and housing needs) still were incomplete. He attributed the delay to the fact that various groups "still had not completely captured the concept of planning as something more than survey and analysis," and to their "reluctance to set sights high, a tendency to think only of immediate and existing shortages."[58]

Elsewhere, the NRPB paid casual attention to independent, privately financed urban planning projects, as in the example of *Fortune* magazine's sponsorship of the Syracuse plan, and cooperated indirectly with the Federal Housing Administration's Tri-Cities project in Tennessee and Virginia. But a series of polls conducted between 1942 and 1944 by *The American City* indicated that, while most cities in all size categories said they were thinking about postwar planning, a relatively large percentage conceded that they had no professional body, or even plans to establish one. Nor were they laying aside reserves to finance postwar improvements, although the fiscal position of the cities was probably better than at any time since 1929. Moreover, a disturbingly large number of cities admitted that they were waiting for, or anticipated, a federal hand-out, despite the mounting hostility to federal postwar expenditures in Congress and the nation.[59]

The promising work of the Board, particularly its initiative as the leader in postwar urban redevelopment and neighborhood conservation, was short-lived. Congressional critics of planning and the New Deal, fiscal conservatives, rural Democrats and Republicans, and interest groups such as the National Association of Real Estate Boards, seized upon the comprehensive plan of social security which the NRPB had submitted to vote in two previous annual reports in 1943 not simply to phase out the Board but to obliterate its activities.[60] These foes had, over the years, come to resent the efforts of the NRPB, a public agency, to operate as though it were a private advocate of a public policy.[61] Thus, the nation forfeited a sterling opportunity to undertake the physical, social, economic, and spiritual reconstruction of American cities, and left the problems of the thirties and forties to persist more stubbornly into the present.

NOTES

1. See the Urbanism Committee's landmark report, *Our Cities—Their Role in the National Economy* (Washington, D.C.: Government Printing Office, 1937), and its supplementary statements on municipal government, planning, land use policies, housing, public works, and transportation.

2. The study of urban problems was a parallel but secondary development to the emphasis on the river basins and rural land planning which had President Roosevelt's strong support. Frederic A. Delano, a director of the NRPB and advocate of regional planning, had worked with both the Chicago Plan and the Russell Sage Foundation's study of New York City and its environs. See David Cushman Coyle, "Frederic A. Delano: Catalyst," *Survey Graphic*, 35 (July, 1946), pp. 252-254.

3. As of January 1937, there were 1,073 town or city planning boards in the United States, 933 of which were official and 84 unofficial. There were 128 zoning boards and 515 cities without planning or zoning boards but which had adopted some kind of zoning ordinance. See National Resources Committee, *Status of City and County Planning in the United States* (Washington, D.C.: Government Printing Office, 1937), pp. 4-6, 10-13.

4. The NRPB immediately narrowed the focus of its inquiry because of dwindling funds, Congressional hostility to planning, and the hope of achieving quick dramatic results. It built upon rather than duplicated the work of other agencies.

5. The Board's authority to function in this sphere flowed from the Federal Employment Stabilization Act of 1931. See Samuel I. Rosenman, comp., *The Public Papers and Addresses of Franklin D. Roosevelt* (14 vols., New York: Random House, 1938), 3, pp. 335-338.

6. See Louis Wirth, "Functions of the Urban Section" (Oct. 16, 1942), Urban Section Files, National Resources Planning Board Records, Record Group 187, National Archives. (Cited hereafter as Urban Section Files, NRPB.)

7. Cf. "Post War Agenda" (Feb. 3, 1942); Luther Gulick to Charles Eliot (Dec. 5, 1941), in *ibid.*; and NRPB, *After Defense—What? After the War—Full Employment;* and *Better Cities* (Washington, D.C.: Government Printing Office, 1941-1942).

8. Cf. Louis Wirth, "The Background and Organization of the Urban Section" (Aug. 19, 1942), Urban Section Files, NRPB.

9. *Ibid.*

10. See "Notes on National Resources Planning Board Urban Planning Committee," n.d., in *ibid.*

11. "A Proposal for Progressive Urban Planning" (Nov. 7, 1947), in *ibid.*

12. *Ibid.*

13. See the typewritten memo, "Urban Planning Procedure," n.d. in *ibid.*

14. *Ibid.* Also, Robert B. Mitchell to Staff (Aug. 17, 1943), in *ibid.*

15. *Ibid.*

16. Cf. Mitchell to Ascher (March 26, 1942), in *ibid.*

17. Alfred Bettman to Eliot (Feb. 12, 1942), in *ibid.*

18. The applicability of Mitchell's experience, particularly in Waverly, to the extreme manifestations of urban decay in cities like New York, St. Louis, or Philadelphia was open to question. For, as the report of the Federal Home Loan Bank indicated, the predominantly residential district of Baltimore, located 2½ miles north of the central business district, was not a slum—nor were the homes substandard but in need of minor repairs and painting. More seriously, the report revealed the class-cultural bias of the participants, describing Waverly as being occupied by "a wholly white population of moderate means and substantial character, predominantly American born, which in general gives definite evidence of social and civic pride . . . " Elsewhere, the report warned of the danger to Waverly from "infiltration by undesirable (i.e., Black and poor) families having more limited earning capacity and lower living and civic standards." Clearly, Waverly was not even a microcosm of a small American city as the report claimed; the experiment was valid only for other neighborhoods of identical composition and problems. See Ascher, "Recommendations for the Urban Program "(June 12, 1942), in *ibid.*; and Federal Home Loan Bank Board, *Waverly, A Study in Neighborhood Conservation* (Washington, D.C.: Government Printing Office, 1940), esp. pp. 8, 11, 16,30, 53-55, 67.

19. Eliot to Regional Chairmen and Counselors (Jan. 2, 1942), in Urban Section Files, NRPB.

20. Ascher, "Proposed Program for Urban Conservation and Development, 1942-1943" n.d., in *ibid.*

21. See Mitchell to Eliot (Nov. 2, 1942), and the accompanying memoranda of Spengler, Hanse, and Key in *ibid.*

22. Mitchell to Ladislas Segoe (March 7, 1942), in *ibid.*

23. *Ibid.*

24. *Ibid.*

25. Cf. Mitchell to Carl Feiss (July 16, 1942), in *ibid.*

26. "Criteria for Choosing Cities for Demonstration Projects," (1942), *ibid.*

27. *Ibid.*

28. See United States Department of Labor, *The Impact of War on the Hampton Roads Areas* (Washington, D.C.: Government Printing Office, 1944), chaps. i, v, vi.

29. Albert C. Schweizer to Mitchell (July 17, 1942), Urban Section Files, NRPB. On Buffalo, see NRPB, Region 2, *Preliminary Report: Niagara Frontier Area: War and Post-War Planning* (Unpub. report, June 1941), pp. 1-61, in *ibid.*

30. For the origins of the Corpus Christi project see Sam Zisman to Mitchell (Aug. 1942), in *ibid.*

31. Corpus Christi had been established from the plan of 1930 prepared by Major E.A. Wood, city planning engineer of Dallas. It was fairly typical for its time—heavily loaded on the zoning side and was the basis for the city's original zoning ordinance. Although an improvement over the old, it fell far short of being a comprehensive city plan. At the same time, the city rejected various sections of the Washington-Arneson Master Highway Plan of 1939. See "Corpus Christi Reconnaissance Report" (Oct. 3, 1942), in *ibid.*

32. *The* [Corpus Christi] *Caller-Times*, June 2; Aug. 25; Nov. 15, 1942.

33. Quoted in Sam Zisman, "Cities in Action," *Survey Graphic*, 32 (Oct., 1943), p. 412.

34. Mitchell to Eliot (Sept. 10, 1942), Urban Section Files, NRPB.

35. "The Corpus Christi Planning Demonstration" (May 12, 1943), in *ibid.*

36. *The Caller-Times*, Oct. 12,; Dec. 2, 7, 15, 1942.

37. *Ibid.*

38. Zisman, "Cities in Action," p. 412.

39. Mitchell to John D. Spaeth, Jr. (Sept. 18, 1942), Urban Section Files, Area Studies Division, NRPB.

40. Art McVoy to Mitchell (June 29, 1942), Urban Section Files, NRPB.

41. See NRPB, *National Resources Development Report for 1943*, House Doc. 128, Pt. 2, 78 Cong., 1 Sess. (Washington, D.C.: Government Printing Office, 1943), pp. 74-75; Mitchell to Eliot (Nov. 9, 1942), Urban Section Files, NRPB.

42. Zisman to Mitchell (Sept. 3, 1942), in *ibid.*

43. *Ibid.*

44. Schweizer to Mitchell (Sept. 25, 1942), in *ibid.*

45. *Ibid.* Also, *Just a Moment*, Bulletin 678 (Buffalo, New York: Municipal Research Bureau, Jan. 27, 1944), n.p.

46. *Ibid.; Buffalo Evening News*, Nov. 14, 1943.

47. Schweizer to Mitchell (Sept. 25, 1942), Urban Section Files, NRPB.

48. See, for example, Mitchell to John Miller (Nov. 2, 1942), in *ibid.*

49. *Just a Moment*, Bulletin 631 (March 4, 1943).

50. Cf. "The Concept of a Planning Region—The Evolution of an Idea in the United States," in John Friedmann and William Alonso, eds., *Regional Development and Planning* (Cambridge: M.I.T. Press, 1964), pp. 500-501.

51. Charles Abrams, *The City is the Frontier* (New York: Harper & Row, 1965), pp. 74-79, 257-258; Mel Scott, *American City Planning Since 1890* (Berkeley and Los Angeles: University of California Press, 1969), p. 365.

52. *Action for Cities: A Guide for Community Planning* (Chicago: Public Administration Service, 1943), Div. 520; Zisman, "Corpus Christi Project—The Development of the Economic Study," n.d., Urban Section Files, Area Studies Division, NRPB.

53. For the application of such tools see Roy W. Bahl, *Metropolitan City Expenditures* (Lexington: University of Kentucky Press, 1969).

54. See Mitchell to Eliot (Aug. 27, 1942), Urban Section Files, Area Studies Division, NRPB.

55. Cf. Zisman to Ervin K. Zingler (Jan. 14, 1943), in *ibid.*

56. See "Report on Publicity and Public Relations—Corpus Christi"(Dec. 31, 1942), in *ibid.*

57. Cf. "Progress Report No. 1"(Sept. 28, 1942), and Bernard J. Smith to Jacob Crane (March 16, 1943), in *ibid.*

58. Zisman, "Corpus Christi Project, Progress Report No. 12" (April 19, 1943), in Urban Section Files, Area Studies Division, NRPB.

59. Cf. "Syracuse Tackles Its Future," *Fortune*, 26 (May, 1943), pp. 120-123, and "How Cities are Planning for Post-War Municipal Improvements," in *The American City* beginning with volume 57 (Nov. 1942), pp. 35-37.

60. The reports in question were *Toward Full Employment* and *Security, Work and Relief* (Washington, D.C.: Government Printing Office, 1942).

61. For criticisms of the NRPB see *Congressional Record* (Washington, D.C.: Government Printing Office, 1942), 77 Cong., 2 Sess., LXXXVIII, Pt. 9 (May 19, 28, 1942), A1827-1829, A1970; and Robert A. Walker, *The Planning Function in Urban Government* (2nd ed.; Chicago: University of Chicago Press, 1950), pp. 364-365.

9

Visions of a Post-War City

A Perspective on Urban Planning in Philadelphia and the Nation, 1942-1945

John F. Bauman

World War II instilled in American city planners and housing reformers a renewed dedication to revitalize the metropolis. Charles Ascher, a staff member of the National Resources Planning Board (NRPB) saw the war giving "a new intensity to our thinking about the future of cities." Planners, observed Ascher, were "determined that the (urban) community of the future must be a nobler embodiment of the democratic responsibility for the worth of the individual, if our war effort is to be justified." Urban planning could redeem "dying city districts, . . . create better home conditions in both cities and suburbs, banish apple selling and leafraking in the days to come [and] . . . underwrite a sounder prosperity than America has ever known."[1]

Although in 1942 Ernest Goodrich of the American Institute of Planners placed first priority on organizing the nation's resources for war and favored urban planning as "a sort of after regular hours occupation," by 1943 planners projected "vast changes . . . for post-war society." After the imminence of victory in Europe and Asia was no longer questioned, the blighted city, more than Hitler or Tojo, posed the ultimate challenge for planners and housing reformers (called "housers").[2]

Reprinted from John F. Bauman, 1980-81. *Urbanism Past and Present* 6 (Winter-Spring): 1-11. An *in gratis* reprint of John F. Bauman's article has been granted by *Urbanism Past & Present* of the University of Wisconsin-Milwaukee, Board of Regents of the University of Wisconsin System, 1982.

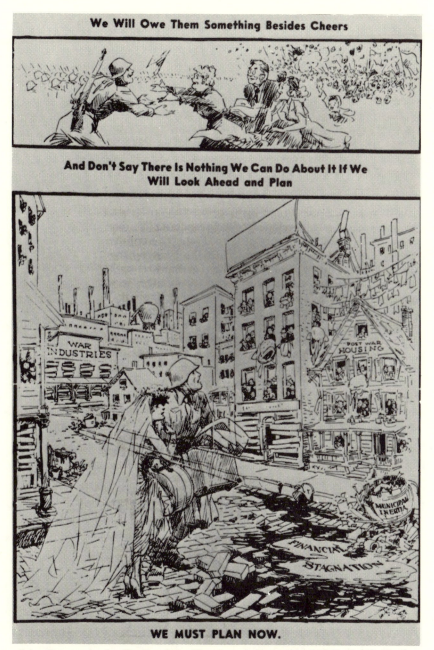

9.1 Cartoon by Jay Darling from *Tomorrow's Town,* April 1943, Vol. 1, No. 1, a publication of the National Committee on the Housing Emergency, Inc. Courtesy of the Temple University Urban Archives.

The present study looks at the housing and planning ideas which abounded in Philadelphia and the nation during World War II. It bears on the propensity of wartime housers and planners to spawn visions about the future of the post-war city. Phillip J. Funigiello's study *The Challenge to Urban Liberalism: Federal-City Relations during World War II* suggests that, ends aside, wartime planners differed mainly on suitable means; some planners emphasized comprehensive planning; others settled for quickly executed public works projects. Then, too, certain planners envisaged federal aid, while more individualistic planners like New York's Robert Moses shunned the centralizing tendencies inherent in federal intervention. This study, however, concerns the ends and narrows the focus to the two broad visions of the post-war city which emerged by 1943; one emphasizing the rehousing of urban slum dwellers and the other stressing the reconstruction or redevelopment of the downtown. It suggests that for cities like Philadelphia the ideological conflict embedded in these competing views postulated a major dilemma for the shaping of post-war urban policy.

The War and Philadelphia

Wartime considerations of the future of cities like Philadelphia focused on two major fears: the possibility of a post-war economic depression, and the social, economic, and physical deterioration of the historic downtown. Most policymakers regarded post-war unemployment as the greatest threat. A 1943 Bureau of Labor Statistics report forecast a post-war national jobless population of between 7,000,000 and 12,000,000 people, of which Philadelphia would account for from 200,000 to 350,000. Writing in the *Philadelphia Record,* reporter Leeds Moberley warned that the city "faces the danger within six months after the end of the war of an unemployment problem comparable to the worst in the Depression." Even optimists calculated Philadelphia's post-war jobless toll at 100,000 to 200,000.[3]

Along with this grim spectre of post-war urban unemployment was the fact of urban physical decay. Although defense and war mobilization drew 50,000 new workers into the Philadelphia region, officials in the City of Brotherly Love like their counterparts in New York and Boston continued to register alarm at the 1940 census data showing a decadal decline in population. For real estate magnates such as Philadelphia's Albert M. Greenfield the census findings confirmed fears that decentralization was eroding the vitality of the city's downtown. Year after year advancing slums, abandoned businesses and higher crime rates deepened the malaise. Downtown real estate values plummeted while assessors propped up the city's precarious financial structure by preserving fanciful valuations on the tax rolls. Greenfield angrily charged that this artifice only drove stable businesses and tax ratables out of the city. Meanwhile, Philadelphia's already notoriously poor water, sewer and lighting services worsened. Wartime housing shortages not only halted the city's fledgling slum clearance operations, but also created a heavy demand for substandard housing units; by 1944 the Philadelphia Housing Association branded 80,000 of the city's estimated 550,000 occupied residential units as "substandard," and asserted that 1,040 city families lived in quarters without indoor plumbing.[4]

Not surprisingly, planners and housers promoted a massive and professionally guided public works program for the redemption of the city. As early as 1941 Philadelphia civic leaders such as Thomas Gates, president of the University of Pennsylvania, and Walter P. Phillips, a civic-minded lawyer, urged the city council to replace its figurehead planning committee with a "working" commission charged to halt the gnawing decay of the city's core. To that end Gates and Phillips founded the Citizens Council on City Planning (CCCP); in 1943 the City Council created and funded a Planning Commission chaired by Edward Hopkinson, Jr., a senior partner in Drexel and Company. For executive director the Commission appointed Robert B. Mitchell, a well-known planner who had recently headed the Urban Section of the National Resources Planning Board (NRPB), and who was the much-touted author of the neighborhood conservation projects in the Waverly section of Baltimore and the Woodlawn section of Chicago. Raymond F. Leonard was selected by the Commission as comprehensive planning director, and Harold M. Mayer headed the Division of Planning Analysis. According to Leeds Moberley, the City charged the Commission to halt urban decentralization, revitalize the downtown, and simultaneously "create employment to cushion the changeover from war production to peacetime living."[5]

By 1943, old cities like Philadelphia, caked with industrial grime, and fiscally impoverished, suddenly displayed considerable planning energy. Long unsolved city problems moved prominently into the foreground of discussions. Described as "filtered filth," "a bluish-black liquid stinking with chlorine, puckery with alum," Philadelphia's scandalously bad water forced both candidates in the 1943 mayoralty campaign, incumbent Republican, Bernard Samuel, and Democratic challenger, William Bullitt, to make planning and public works a central political issue. At town meetings such as the one sponsored by the CCCP, Bullitt and Samuel debate subway expansion, housing, a proposed $60,000,000 sewerage and waterworks project, new expressways, and even the dismantling of the city's famous eyesore, the Chinese Wall, the huge stone fortifications which sealed off commercial Market street west of City Hall from the downtown switching yards of the Pennsylvania Railroad.[6]

Philadelphia houser-planners such as Edmund Bacon, the executive director of the Philadelphia Housing Association (who viewed post-war housing "and well thought out public works as part of . . . a new scientific city") reflected in part planning ideas germinating at the federal level. Guy Greer and Alvin Hansen, both economists for the recently terminated in 1943 Urban Section of the NRPB, incorporated their ideas on federal aid for urban land acquisition into two proposed federal laws introduced into Congress between 1943 and 1945. Both the stillborn Federal Urban Redevelopment Act of 1943 (the Thomas Bill, S.953) and the Wagner, Ellender, Taft legislation, which languished in Congress four years before passage in 1949, called for local planning and federal monies to write down the high cost of redeveloping downtown land; the Wagner legislation linked urban development closely

TEMPLE UNIVERSITY URBAN ARCHIVES

9.2 Edmund Bacon, Executive Secretary of the Philadelphia Housing Association, circa 1942. Courtesy of the Temple University Urban Archives.

with slum clearance and the improvement of housing. Once law, the 1949 Wagner-Ellender-Taft Housing Act established the pattern for future housing and urban redevelopment in America.[7]

The grandiloquent if not conflicting outpourings of the World War II housers and redevelopers found less sublime expression when translated into physical urban redevelopment after 1949. This study suggests that the critical shortcomings of America's post-war housing and redevelopment can be traced to these conflicting visions. Even among the visionaries emphasizing rehousing, housers favoring a "regionalist" perspective offered a different view of the post-war city from those described herein as "houser-redevelopers," who limited their purview to the downtown. As for the second group, the planner-redevelopers, they abjured social experimentation, and regarded rehousing merely as the handmaiden of downtown renewal.

The Regionalists and the Housers

By 1943 the coalition of communitarian and progressive housers, social workers, and union officials, which had pushed through Congress the housing legislation of 1937, disintegrated. Nonetheless, housers such as Catherine Bauer, Ira Robbins, Ernest Bohn, John Ihlder and Carol Aronovici continued to press the cause of decent, low-income housing through organizations such as the National Public Housing Conference, the National Committee on the Housing Emergency, the National Committee on Housing, the National Association of Housing Officials, and local bodies such as the Philadelphia Housing Association. Undoubtedly, housers in the early 1940s lacked the communitarian verve and reformist zeal of the early 1930s; still they believed fervently in the social desirability of federally funded low-income housing programs and in planning which incorporated public housing into the comprehensive redevelopment schemes. Despite this broad and significant area of consensus housers in 1943 broke into two camps: (*1*) regionalists —committed to an expansive, urbanistic view, who welcomed the trend toward the deconcentration of the old industrial city, while entreating planners to manage the process through vigilant control over land use, zoning and utilities extension;(*2*) houser-redevelopers — people fearful of the erosive effect of decentralization who espoused federal housing and redevelopment to contain and restore life to the expiring central city.[8]

Regionalist-oriented housers included not only old communitarians such as Catherine Bauer, the vice-president of the National Public Housing Conference, but also fresh enlistees in the housing army such as Dorothy Rosenman, wife of presidential advisor, Samuel I. Rosenman, and president of the National Committee on the Housing Emergency, and R. J. Thomas, president of the United Auto Workers and chairman of the UAW-CIO Postwar

Planning Commission. In Dorothy Rosenman's book, *A Million Homes a Year,* and in the National Committee on the Housing Emergency's monthly, *Tomorrow's Town,* regionalists propounded their vision of the post-war city. While decrying the planlessness of the emerging decentralized city, regionalists trumpeted the expected virtues of spatial decongestion. Regionalists observed that the advent of modern automobile, truck and air transportation, as well as new highway and parkway construction, favored a continuation of the pre-war suburban trend. In fact wartime population shifts of between 15,000,000 and 20,000,000 people, and the relocation of defense plants beyond the urban built-up areas encouraged suburbanization in the post-war era. However, Bauer and Thomas were convinced that if planned and controlled this deconcentration promised a "new era for rather than the death of the city," and they rejoiced that "cities can afford to remake themselves in a spacious manner."[9]

Regionalists envisioned a new urban configuration marked by plentiful open space, light, playgrounds, and parks. Inspired by the challenge of post-war regional planning, labor spokesmen such as Thomas demanded an end to the artless and pernicious "business as usual psychology" which abetted the urban deterioration of the pre-war age. Thomas was captivated by the Office of Production Management director Donald Nelson's observation in 1943 that "while the profit motive continues to exist, it is no longer the mainspring."[10]

As a housing theoretician with a keen awareness of the social consequences of modernization, and as the founder in 1934 of the Labor Housing Conference, Catherine Bauer helped design the labor position. In Bauer's view World War II had unleashed a massive social and technological upheaval which could easily transform the old definition of an "adequate urban living environment." Looking toward the future, Bauer beheld "decency based upon national housing norms replacing vague and arbitrary minimal [housing] standards," as the national goal for low-income housing. In Bauer's words America "must achieve for every family a home where children can be reared in decency and health, where they may develop the mental-moral vigor and pride in community that will make them first class citizens . . . . This means better housing and not merely 'minimal standards' that sacrifice space and privacy to better plumbing, a private garden for every family that wants one and not at the expense of hours of travel." Bauer accepted the dichotomy between city and country. "City is city, and country is country," she pleaded, and "planners should articulate a careful spatial harmony to preserve the vital features of both." In Bauer's conceptualization, the ideal post-war city would have a strong regional mooring, "with center, sub-center and open areas permanently differentiated for varied functions." However, Bauer feared that the post-war building boom in not-planned "cities will look as if intentionally bombed . . . surrounded by a huge gray amorphous blob of suburbs without community integration, without adequate breathing space between home and work place."[11]

According to regionalists, planned orderly decentralization involved both community development and public housing. Public housing, asserted Rosenman, "has been the greatest spur to private achievement, providing more and more low-cost housing." However, regionalists objected to massive low-cost housing projects that, in Rosenman's words, constituted "distinguishable islands and many too many families to an acre." Like Bauer, Rosenman believed that "the drab can no longer exist side by side with the good." Low-income families must be decently housed in well-planned neighborhoods. Although Rosenman vehemently disagreed with Bauer's seemingly radical notion — shared by the NRPB — that "having government provide housing for all income groups might necessitate freeing public housing from the present limitations upon the incomes of those whom they may serve," she, like Bauer, saw private and public enterprise teaming to provide decent housing for all in well-planned communities.[12]

Rosenman warned against confusing public housing with redevelopment. The two must be distinct. To regionalists, redevelopment mainly sought the orderly replanning and development of the old urban core to relieve congestion, promote healthful open space and provide a more aesthetically pleasing city. Regionalists were intrigued by the 1942 British *Report on Compensation and Betterment* written for Parliament by Mr. Justice Augustus Uthwatt. Since 1941 the British had recognized the vital necessity of post-war planning and centered their efforts on establishing tight controls on land use affecting the urban periphery as well as on the processes of producing and utilizing parcels of renewable inner city land. In addition to creating a central planning authority Uthwatt's report called for the rapid dispersal of industries and congested populations from blighted urban areas. The Uthwatt report formed one of the important bases for the Town and Country Act, which put all British land under the control of a central authority.[13]

As the backbone for an effective post-war American housing and planning policy Bauer proposed that government purchase and own land, not only in blighted areas, but also in outlying "greenbelt" sites. Like other regionalists, Bauer argued that government should not be frustrated in its efforts to serve the commonwealth by the excessive and artificial values of inner city land. The "acquisition of such property will have to be gradual and judicial. . . .", surmised Bauer, and "if new standards of density and housing quality are firmly adhered to, and obsolete buildings gradually outlawed . . . , exhorbitant prices will come down by themselves." As the keystone of their entire post-war program regionalists called for a federal Department of Urbanism which would monitor and assist the activities of strong local planning and housing commissions which were empowered by law to prepare master plans, purchase and own land.[14]

While Bauer, Rosenman and Thomas shared the communitarian penchant for a social-psychological interpretation of housing, increasingly the old corps of professional housers viewed housing in the post-war city more as an adjunct of urban redevelopment. These houser-redevelopers traced their roots to Lawrence Veiller and the movement for progressive housing legislation of the early 20th century. Since 1937 their numbers were significantly augmented by the growth of a public housing bureaucracy. People such as Philadelphia's Edmund Bacon, Cincinnati's Bleeker Marquette, Bryn J. Hovde, head of the Pittsburgh Housing Authority and president of the National Public Housing Conference, and John Ihlder of the Washington, D.C. Alley Dwelling Authority, equated good housing with stable neighborhoods. Houser-redevelopers balanced their interest in carefully planned neighborhoods with an acute concern for post-war housing and the redevelopment of the blighted central city where a decade of economic depression followed by the heavy wartime in-migration of workers had rotted the urban core, socially, economically, and physically. To combat the crisis Philadelphia's Bacon, like Cincinnati's Marquette, prescribed comprehensive planning, strong public controls over land use, and urban redevelopment.[15]

The Philadelphia Housing Association's (PHA) "Post War Program" (ca. 1943) accurately mirrored the outlook of the houser-redevelopers, especially where it emphasized the utilization of public power to redevelop the inner city. PHA anchored its three-tiered program on comprehensive metropolitan planning, including the creation of a city-wide master plan, the strict enforcement of zoning ordinances, the municipal acquisition of land and the administration of its development, and an aggressive campaign for "neighborhood conservation." At the second level PHA urged a residential construction program, including modernized building codes and privately built housing underwritten by low-interest Federal Housing Administration (FHA) mortgages. PHA advised that "the amortization period could be lengthened for well planned and solidly built houses in well planned and permanently protected neighborhood developments." While the PHA extolled home-ownership, it maintained that in addition to enlarging the stock of public housing, the government should expand the supply of existing housing, not only by requiring credit to private rental housing and federally insuring the "yield" (or profits) to investors in low-income rental housing. Finally, PHA proposed to preserve the supply of existing housing, not only by requiring occupation permits in every dwelling unit, and the strict enforcement of housing and building codes, but also by empowering municipal agencies to clear and redevelop "blighted areas determined by the City Planning

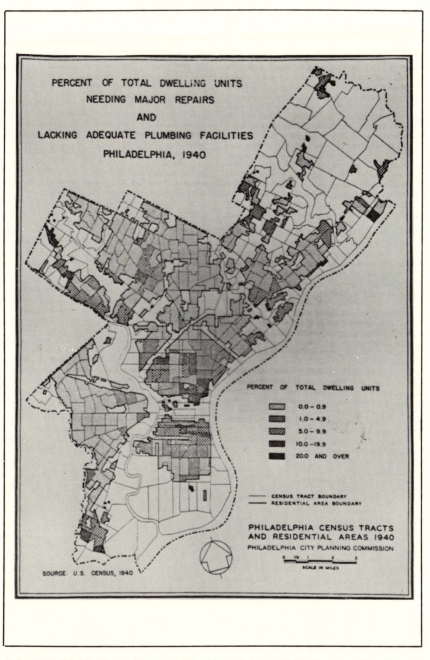

9.3   Philadelphia Census Tracts and Residential Areas, 1940. Courtesy of the Temple
University Archives.

Commission and extending credit to the municipalities for the acquisition of areas suitable for such schemes."

In 1943 the PHA saw little risk that urban development might make thousands of families homeless or burden redevelopment agencies with inflated prices for slum properties. According to the PHA a large-scale rehousing program solved both problems by housing displaced families and nullifying the demand for substandard dwelling units.[16]

Despite their concern for urban reconstruction, houser-redevelopers such as the members of the National Association of Housing Officials (NAHO) stressed the critical importance of the post-war housing problems. To meet the nation's housing needs NAHO calculated that America would need half a million houses in the decade and a half following the war. Housing officials united solidly behind Bleeker Marquette's demand that Congress make "decent, hygienic housing" a post-war priority. Testifying in 1945 before a Senate subcommittee on Housing and Urban Redevelopment, Marquette asserted that the "public temper . . . will no longer accept a situation in which the health of nine million children is sapped by slum living or saying to millions of soldiers go back to the slums or . . . crowd up with some other family."[17]

While most houser-redevelopers acknowledged the preference of Americans for "quaint New England architecture," and while some fantasized with Buckminster Fuller about the potential of prefabricted geodesic domes, soya bean derived igloos, or modernistic group housing, they all concurred that taste and technology notwithstanding, millions of Americans, many Black, lacked the income to buy shelter even at the lowest rung of the rental or homeownership ladder. For families unable to afford an "economic rent" only public housing provided safe and sanitary accommodations. Marquette vigorously denied the widespread allegation that public housing attracted "undesirables." A study of public housing in his Cincinnati found only 5% of the project tenants fit the description "they call undesirable — they're rowdy, . . . they don't pay the rent, or they are destructive; the indigent, the pauper, and the laggard."[18]

Obviously, houser-redevelopers regarded public housing as a key ingredient in their revitalization formula for the city. The Committee on Postwar Housing of the National Association of Housing Officials (NAHO) saw government housing as "a balance wheel for the [private] homebuilding industry. If the slums are to be cleared and the needs of low-income families met, the local authority will need a plan and a program for the part of the job it needs to do, subject to modification as private enterprise succeeds in reaching down the income scale in the provision of housing. While the public housing program will need to be a continuing one, it can be contracted when private building is at a high level and accelerated when the situation is reversed."

Rather than competing, houser-redevelopers believed public housing helped the movement of tenants into the private market. Well-trained management "encouraged among its tenants habits of prompt rent payment, good housekeeping, and care of property. As the incomes in public housing facilities increase these families will be passed on to private enterprise housing — as better tenants than they were before."

Therefore, for the houser-redevelopers the post-war offered an "unparalleled opportunity to build better homes, better neighborhoods, and better communities. . ." However, there was a caveat. Without professional city planning, code enforcement, and federal assistance, "these crucial [post-war] years may bring an avalanche of bad building and create more of the conditions that blight our cities."[19]

Thus, as during the 1930s, a schism divided the ranks of the propublic housers. Housing progressives who in 1943 manned posts in city housing associations and housing authorities extolled central city redevelopment not merely as a matter of city efficiency, but in the name of urban survival itself. These houser-redevelopers viewed low-income housing as a key element in any city plan. On the other hand, regionalists demonstrated a deeper concern for housing as an environment for living. Unlike their houser-redeveloper cousins, regionalists accepted the American norm for more spacious single-family housing on the so-called "crabgrass frontier," and asserted that the trend toward urban deconcentration promised a post-war city graced with open spaces and attractive low-density neighborhoods.[20]

Whether centralists or decentralists, housers exhorted Washington to increase the total supply of low and moderately priced housing in the post-war era. They urged urban policymakers to mobilize the nation's post-war technology, manpower and fiscal resources to produce less costly dwellings and to harness state police powers to secure better land use planning in the public interest. Finally, both groups implored the federal government to build more subsidized housing for young veterans, poor Blacks and all families excluded by low income from living in good private housing.

The Origins of Urban Renewal

In *American City Planning*, Mel Scott groups together housers and redevelopers, regionalists and centralists, park and highway experts as part of a monolithic planning tradition rooted in the late 19th century. However, during World War II a separate school of urban redevelopment emerged, distinct from the houser-redeveloper clique, and possessing a unique vision of the post-war city. While the American planning tradition always embodied the concept of urban redevelopment, the war years gave birth to a fully articulated program which reached maturity in the early 1950s.[21]

During the war the vision of large-scale urban redevelopment titillated economically and politically conservative downtown businessmen as much as it did planning professionals. Corporate executives with downtown head-quarters, center city merchants, as well as planner-architects, all yearned for a deslummed, beautiful — *qua* efficient — city. In Philadelphia redevelopment was championed by, among others, civic leaders such as Walter Phillips and Thomas Gates, who in 1941 with Dean Holmes Perkins of the University of Pennsylvania School of Fine Arts, founded the Citizens Council on City Planning. Full of enthusiasm, business leaders, particularly realtors Albert M. Greenfield and Roland Randall, the latter an officer of the Philadelphia Real Estate Board and also chairman of the Philadelphia Housing Authority, touted urban redevelopment through the Greater Philadelphia Movement.[22]

Like houser-redevelopers, urban redevelopers lamented the deterioration of the inner city. In their view the old city, the historic downtown, to be more exact, comprised the heart of urban America. According to the popular etiology of urban disease, the cancer of blight originated in lax planning, unenforced housing and building codes, pernicious tax policies, and corrupt politics. Blight and decay depressed property values and the unadjusted tax assessment burden, compounded by rising inner city crime rates and the influx of "undesirable neighbors," drove stable businesses and middle class families outside the city.[23]

Planner-redevelopers especially inveighed against the trend toward urban decentralization. Rampant wartime plant expansion on the urban periphery persuaded Greenfield that the war was accelerating the pace of decentraliza-tion, making it imperative that the city rebuild its core in order to restore appeal. Speaking before the Philadelphia Engineer's Club, planner Allen G. Mitchell of the CCCP enumerated millions of dollars of post-war projects for subway expansion waterworks and housing, and warned that without the expenditure "Philadelphia will lose business and fall far behind other cities."[24]

Mark Gelfand, in *A Nation of Cities*, observed that in the 1940s the dual crisis of war abroad and urban malaise at home transformed business attitudes in favor of a federal-urban partnership. By 1943 business-redevelop-ers openly solicited federal assistance in the urban revitalization process. However, business-affiliated research groups such as the Twentieth Century Fund and the National Association of Real Estate Board's (NAREB) Urban Land Institute advocated a limited cooperative and information-disseminat-ing role for government; they rebuffed any suggestion of federal control over projects or planning. In fact, at the same time that organizations like NAREB described a role for federal participation in urban redevelopment they reaffirmed their belief in the wisdom of local control over planning. NAREB spokesmen at the Congressional hearings on the General Housing Act of 1945 testified that federal assistance to the cities should be in the form of outright

9.4 An example of Philadelphia's notorious "bandbox" tenements, 1943, cleared in the redevelopment following the 1949 Housing Act. Courtesy of the Temple University Urban Archives.

9.5 A group of all-Black slums along Warnock Street, located only a few blocks from the Richard Allen Homes, one of Philadelphia's first USHA projects built for 95% Black occupancy. These houses were also cleared in the redevelopment following the 1949 Housing Act. Courtesy of the Temple University Urban Archives.

grants with no conditions. Blighted areas should be redeveloped for "the use most suitable for them and should include commercial buildings, industrial development, public buildings, park and recreation space . . . as well as housing."[25]

Vice President of NAREB Herbert U. Nelson's ideas foreshadowed the final form of the 1949 housing and redevelopment legislation. Nelson envisioned local redevelopment authorities armed with broad powers of eminent domain acquiring "perhaps whole square miles of blighted area," and preparing these great swaths for rebuilding "mainly by private developers." To write down the enormously inflated purchase price of these tracts (values which Nelson believed owners should rightfully recoup since for years they had paid taxes on these high values) Nelson proclaimed "incentive taxation," a system whereby the federal government allowed persons to deduct from their income tax the purchase price of 99-year redevelopment bonds.[26]

Redevelopers ordinarily opposed public housing, especially the 1944 Wagner bill, which subordinated redevelopment to housing objectives. Urban redevelopment, declared Seward Mott of the Urban Land Institute, "should not be a disguised housing program." To increase low-cost housing supply, redevelopers favored federal tax policy which would lure timid investors into the low-income housing field "preferably in redevelopment areas as part of a general diversified neighborhood." NAREB pronounced public housing "a failure. . . . It has not taken care of the people it should have, it is building political constituencies founded on shelter, it puts a premium on dependency. . . . We don't believe in it . . . and we challenge it as a social policy."[27]

Roots of HUD

Through the NRPB's Urban Section and after 1943 through the National Housing Administration, the federal government kept fully informed about all post-war city planning. Moreover, the NRPB and the NHA indulged in their own urban visionmaking. In fact during the war the federal-urban connection loomed as such a vital force shaping the urban future that many urban experts such as Bauer, Bacon and Rosenman urged the creation of a separate Department of Urbanism.[28]

While Congress delayed the arrival of an urban department until the Housing and Urban Development Act of 1965, the department had some predecessors. In 1941 President Franklin Roosevelt asked the NRPB to undertake the study of "post-defense planning." To this end the NRPB established the Urban Section, headed by Robert Mitchell and staffed by such people as Charles Ascher, Frank Herring, and economists Guy Greer and Alvin Hansen. Early in 1942 the Urban Section conducted a six-city demonstration project which historian Phillip Funigiello sees as a forerunner of the 1966 Model Cities program. For its demonstrations the Urban Section chose cities such as Tacoma, Washington and Salt Lake City, Utah, deliberately bypassing cities like New York and Philadelphia as "too large and too problem ridden to yield swift results." Billed by Hansen and Greer as an experiment with "continuous planning," to promote neighborhood conservation, combat metropolitan fragmentation and stem the "flight of the productive middle class to the fringes," the demonstration projects along with the Urban Section expired in 1943 when Congress terminated the NRPB for being "tainted with socialism."[29]

Meanwhile in 1942 the National Housing Agency spawned a Division of Urban Studies (DUS), described by the agency's second administrator, Jacob Crane, as a "rather obscure name for a staff unit in the administrator's office which functions to . . . advise the administrator on all matters relative to urban development and city building." Crane, a well-known professional houser-planner, aspired to transform this "obscure" division into a central clearing house for post-war urban plans. To this end he staffed the division with professionals and enlisted distinguished consultants such as Ernest Bohn, Frederick Adams, Frederick Law Olmstead, Jr., and Lewis Mumford. Yet Crane nurtured few illusions concerning the possibilities of post-war urban planning. Writing in 1943 to Mumford about the "transition and post-war period from the point of view of housing and city-building," Crane confessed that he had anticipated great changes during the war as a result of the Revolution of the common man. However, he had concluded that the changes were slower in coming than he had first thought. Thus, he observed,

> If the war ends in two or three years, we will find in 1945 that the idea and the institutions of private ownership and private profit in urban land will still be fully entrenched; that the idea and the lure of home-ownership will still be strong, and that this creates a huge market for the speculative builder of shoddy homes for sale in the suburban fringe; that metropolitan government will not have advanced very far; that taxation will still be a muddle; that opposition to participation by government and to governmental debt will still be powerful; that public comprehension of the problems and potentialities will be meager; that the legislators and the Congress will reflect old misconceptions and taboos.[30]

Subsequent action by Congress and the federal bureaucracy vindicated Crane's remarks. The NHA adorned its literature on post-war planning with praise of capitalism and local initiative. National Housing Administrator, Robert Blandford balanced America's concern for a post-war housing shortage "with the permanent question of making our economy function in the post-war period." This latter concern led him to see housing as "predominately a job for private enterprise and a local responsibility." . . . Government, asserted the nation's chief houser, "should do what cannot be done otherwise. It should help private enterprise to serve the largest possible portion of the nation's housing needs." Blandford asked Philip Klutznik, NHA's Public Housing Commissioner, to more clearly delineate the federal housing role. In response Klutznik pledged that public housing would never compete with private capital in the housing marketplace. In 1945 NHA plighted troth with private enterprise by carving out of the marketplace a "no man's land," a rent pricing void of 15% and 20% between the lowest income population serviced by new public housing.[31]

The Emerging Postwar City

Clearly, between 1943 and 1945 key federal planning agencies such as NHA joined with housers and planners and redevelopers in fashioning visions of a post-war city; however, in addition to producing a bevy of plans and ideas, including the roots of the 1949 housing and redevelopment legislation, the war-time visionmaking bared the dilemma confronting post-war city planners. Although by 1943 businessmen, housers, and planners alike bemoaned the chaos of planless urban growth, still most questioned even the slightest federal competition with private enterprise. Even planners professing a sense of commonweal eschewed tight government restrictions on the reuse of redeveloped land. Despite forecasts of a post-war housing shortage, and in the face of uncontrolled slumification, only Catherine Bauer prescribed any alternative to the "filter system" whereby the middle class conveyed used housing to the less affluent through the operation of conventional market processes. Most offered nothing more radical than tax-incentive programs, streamlined homebuilding methods, prefabrication, and expanded Federal Housing Administration mortgage guarantees.[32]

In conclusion, for urban planners, housers, redevelopers and businessmen alike, World War II afforded an attractive model of large-scale federal-business cooperation. However, this study suggests that the participants in homefront urban planning posited conflicting interpretations of the urban crisis and its resolution. The housers — Bauer, Rosenman and Thomas — perceived the crisis as primarily a housing problem: poor people lived in unsafe, unsanitary housing. Because World War II intensified urban decentralization these housers perceived the opportunity to design spacious cities replete with well-planned and well-housed neighborhoods.

Other World War II urban visionaries, however, regarded urban blight and slum formation as the main target for post-war urban strategies. Planners like Philadelphia's Bacon pronounced blight and decentralization as cancerous lesions to be excised by redevelopment. Enthralled by this wartime vision of redevelopment, planners subordinated the housing crisis to their desire for a restored downtown. Considerations of housing quality, ideal structure types, and neighborhood quality paled beside the lure of blight prevention, tax incentives, yield insurance, eminent domain, and land use controls.

Yet, Bauer and the heady visionaries at the DUS excepted, few appreciated the degree to which the urban redevelopment goals conflicted with rehousing; few understood that only by confiscating the artificially high urban property values and using the increment to reduce the cost of decent shelter could housing and redevelopment authorities provide residences for "all" families without regard to race, ethnicity or income.

However, not even Bauer realized the degree to which the vision of a revitalized post-war city would be obscured in the wake of subsequent developments. America's post-war suburban boom demolished traditional housing reform arguments by draining the city of its middle class and decently rehousing the majority of the hardworking, submerged middle class. Housers in the post-war world found their arsenal of rhetoric and baggage of housing remedies increasingly powerless in confronting the dilemma of the post-war ill-housed: segregated Blacks, the aged, the unskilled, the so-called "other America." With the passage of the landmark 1949 housing act, housers of all persuasions lost the verve which fueled the wartime vision-making. While redevelopers cleared the way for modern downtown hotels, civic centers and skyscraper offices, a skeletal and intellectually enfeebled housing movement wearily groped for elusive answers to the "housing problem."[33]

NOTES

1. Although this paper argues that housing and planning represented a major theme in wartime America, the theme has been absent from the agenda for historical research. It was ignored in Jim F. Heath's, "Domestic America during World War II: Research Opportunities for Historians," *The Journal of American History*, LVII, 2 (September 1971), 384-414. While the major historical studies of planning have examined war-time housing and urban planning they do not assign the movement particular significance; see Mel Scott, *American City Planing Since 1890* (Berkeley: University of California Press, 1969); Mark Gelfand, *A Nation of Cities: The Federal Government and Urban America, 1933-1965* (New York: Oxford University Press, 1975). Only two monographs afford proper emphasis, Phillip J. Funigiello, *The Challenge to Urban Liberalism: Federal-City Relations During World War II* (Knoxville: University of Tennessee Press, 1978); Martin J. Schiesl, "War-time Planning in Los Angeles, 1941-1945," a paper read to the meeting of the Organization of American Historians, April 1977, unpublished. For the Ascher quotation, see Gelfand, *A Nation of Cities*, p. 125.

2. *New York Times*, June 28, 1942; Mel Scott, *American City Planning*, pp. 308, 397-403; Funigiello, *Challenge to Urban Liberalism*, pp. 187-188.

3. Philadelphia *Record*, March 3, 1944 and August 27, 1943; Philadelphia *Daily News*, November 19, 1943; Mel Scott, *American City Planning*, p. 398; Funigiello, *Challenge to Urban Liberalism*, p. 217.

4. Scott, *American City Planning* p. 380; Philadelphia *Record*, February 18, 1944. Philadelphia *Inquirer*, March 27, 1944.

5. Kirk R. Petchek, *The Challenge of Urban Reform: Politics and Progress in Philadelphia* (Philadelphia: Temple University Press, 1973); Philadelphia *Record*, August 23, 1942; Philadelphia *Inquirer*, April 17, 1942; George Whitewell to Edmund Bacon, November 4, 1943; in Box 32, Papers of the Housing Association of Delaware Valley (HADV), in Temple Urban Archives, Temple University, Philadelphia.

6. On "Filtered filth," see John F. Bauman, "The City, the Depression and Relief: The Philadelphia Experience, 1929-1941," unpublished Ph.D. dissertation, Rutgers University, 1969, 327; Philadelphia *Record* October 19, 1943.

7. For Bacon's views, Philadelphia *Record,* August 24, 1943, Schiesl, "Wartime Planning in Los Angeles," pp. 9-10; Scott, *American City Planning,* pp. 382-383; Alvin Hansen, "Urban Redevelopment," *Survey Graphic,* 33 (April 1944), 204.

8. Lee F. Johnson, Executive Vice President of the National Public Housing Conference, to Robert Blandford, Director of the National Housing Agency, February 29, 1944, in Record Group (RG) 207, Key Officials File, National Archives, Washington, D.C. (NA); "Statement by the National Public Housing Conference to the Senate Subcommittee on Post-War Housing," in Box 47, HADV.

9. Dorothy Rosenman, *A Million Homes a Year* (New York: Harcourt, Brace, 1945); see *Tomorrow's Town,* a magazine publication of the National Committee on the Housing Emergency (later simply National Committee on Housing). The Committee was headed by Mrs. Samuel I. Rosenman (Dorothy) and emphasized federal cooperation with cities; an assortment of magazine copies is found in RG 207, NA. Catherine Bauer, "Cities in Flux," *American Scholar,* XIII (Winter 1943-1944), 70-84; "Memorandum on Post-War Housing," n.d., probably written by Catherine Bauer, RG 207, Key Officials File, Blandford, NA.

10. "Memorandum on Post-War Housing."

11. Bauer, "Cities in Flux," 75, 78.

12. Rosenman, *Million Homes a Year,* 11, 14, 214-215. Dorothy Rosenman, "A Truce Upon Your Housing," *Survey Graphic,* 33 (June 1944), 22; Bauer quoted the National Resources Planning Board study *Better Cities* in "Fundamentals for Post-War Housing," mimeographed, n.d. RG 207, Key Officials File, Blandford, NA.

13. Rosenman, "A Truce Upon Your Housing," 21-22; Symposium on "Can We Adopt England's Uthwatt's Report on a Proposed Land Program from Britain to a Program of Rebuilding American Cities," in *Tomorrow's Town* (April 1943); Funigiello, *Challenge to Urban Liberalism,* pp. 187-216; Those who participated in the symposium in *Tomorrow's Town* were Harold S. Buttenheim, Miles Colean, Homer Hoyt, and Alfred Bettmen.

14. Bauer, "Fundamentals for Post-War Planning;" "Memorandum on Post-War Housing." Gelfand, *A Nation of Cities.*

15. Edmund Bacon, "Defense Problems and Housing Situation," February 9, 1942, mimeographed, in Box 41, HADV; B. J. Hovde, "How Public Housing Works," *Survey Graphic* (April 1944), 205-206; Testimony of Bleeker Marquette, *Hearings* Before the Subcommittee on Post-War Economic Policy and Planning, U.S. Senate, 79th Congress, 1st sess. (Washington, D.C., 1945), p. 427.

16. Philadelphia Housing Association, "Preliminary Statement on Housing and Urban Development," August 24, 1944, HADV.

17. Marquette testimony, *Hearings* on Post-War Economic Policy, January 16, 1945; National Association of Housing Officials, *Housing for the U.S. After the War* (Washington, D.C.: NAHO, 1944).

18. The cartoon on soya bean housing appeared in *Tomorrow's Town* (January 1943); Marquette testimony, *Hearings* on Post-War Economic Policy, January 16, 1945.

19. NAHO, *Housing for the U.S. After the War,* esp. pp. 21, 57.

20. Catherine Bauer and Jacob Crane, "What Every Family Should Have," *Survey Graphic* (February 1940), 63-65; Ira Robbins, "Slums are Like Treadmills," *Survey Graphic,* 33 (April 1944).

21. Scott, *American City Planning,* passim.

22. On Walter, Phillips and the CCCP, see Petchek, *The Challenge of Urban Reform;* Philadelphia *Record,* February 4, 1945.

23. Victor Gruen, *The Heart of Our Cities: The Urban Crisis, Diagnosis and Cure* (New York: Simon and Schuster, 1964); Joseph R. Fink, "Reform in Philadelphia 1946-1951," unpublished Ph.D. dissertation, Rutgers University, 1971; Petchek, *Challenge of Urban Reform.*

24. Philadelphia *Record*, March 28, 1940, January 14 and November 18, 1944.

25. Gelfand, *A Nation of Cities*, pp. 126-127; Scott, *American City Planning*, pp. 385, 417; see Testimony of M. Henry, *Hearings on General Housing Act of 1945*, November 27, 1945, before Committee on Banking and Commerce, U.S. Senate, 79th Congress, 1st sess. (Washington, D.C., 1945).

26. Herbert U. Nelson, "Incentive Taxation (Espoused)," *Survey Graphic*, 33 (April 1944), 210; on eminent domain, see Scott, *American City Planning*, pp. 417, 425; and *Philadelphia Bulletin*, May 5, 1944.

27. Statement of Seward H. Mott of the Urban Land Institute, *Hearings Before the Subcommittee on Housing and Urban Redevelopment, Special Committee on Post-War Economic Policy and Planning*, U.S. Senate, 79th Congress, 1st sess. (Washington, D.C., 1945), p. 1603; Nelson, "Incentive Taxation," 310.

28. NAHO, *Housing for the U.S. After the War*; Bauer, "Fundamentals of Post-War Housing."

29. Gelfand, *A Nation of Cities*, p. 100; Funigiello, *Challenge to Urban Liberalism*, p. 217-245; Funigiello, "City Planning in World War II: The Experience of the National Resources Planning Board," *Social Science Quarterly*, 53, 1 (June 1972), 91-104.

30. Jacob Crane to Rexford Tugwell, Governor of Puerto Rico, November 17, 1942 and Crane to Staff of Urban Studies Division, March 2, 1943, Summary of Remarks of Jacob Crane, National Housing Agency, at North Central Conference of Housing Officials, Chicago, January 12, 1943, RG 207, Subject File, Housing-Urban Housing, NA.

31. John F. Blandford, "National Housing Agency — What it is and What it Can Mean," *Proceedings of the National Association of Housing Officials*, 1942 (Washington, D.C., 1942), p. 65; Blandford, "Housing Principles for America," *Survey Graphic*, 33 (April 1944), 213; "Post-War Housing," July 8, 1944, mimeographed, RG 207, Key Officials File; Commissioner's Meetings, NA. Phillip M. Klutznick, "Public Housing Charts its Course," *Survey Graphic*, 34 (January 1945), 15.

32. Bauer, "Fundamentals for Post-War Housing."

33. On suburbanization and ghettoization, see Charles Abrams, *The City is the Frontier* (New York: Harper and Row, 1965) passim; Herbert J. Gans, *People and Plans: Essays on Urban Problems and Solutions* (New York: Basic Books, 1968); on Philadelphia in particular, see William Cutler, "The Persistent Dualism: Centralization and Decentralization in Philadelphia, 1854-1975," in William Cutler and Howard Gillette, eds., *The Divided Metropolis: The Social and Spatial Dimensions of Philadelphia, 1820-1940* (Westport: Greenwood Press, 1980).

10

The Intercity Freeway

Alan A. Altshuler

Introduction

Most laymen tend to think of city planners as proposers, but in fact only a small portion of the time of any planning agency is devoted to developing independent planning proposals. Each specialized public agency generally develops its own project proposals. In virtually every city the total public expenditure on projects initiated by city planners is insignificant. No one would contend, however, that this fact establishes the insignificance of city planning. City planners themselves reject such a conclusion by stressing their role as evaluators of other people's projects. They claim to be the people best suited to formulate goals for project planning, to point out relationships between the ideas of different specialists, and therefore to criticize the projects proposed.

If ever there was a public works project worthy of careful evaluation, that project was the Interstate Freeway. Its sections in and around St. Paul constituted the largest public works project that the city was likely to witness for decades. Its influence on the city's future development would probably be monumental. Although the project was not initiated within St. Paul and the city would not bear any part of its cost or administrative responsibility for its execution, no action involving the freeway could be taken inside the city without the municipal government's approval. The city planners of St. Paul

Reprinted from Alan A. Altshuler: *The City Planning Process: A Political Analysis*. Copyright © 1965 by Cornell University. Used by permission of the publisher, Cornell University Press. A shorter version of this chapter appeared as *Locating the Intercity Freeway*, ICP Case Series, No. 88 (Bobbs-Merrill, 1965). *Copyright*© 1965 by the Inter-University Case Program, Inc.; reprinted with permission.

therefore had, and publicly acknowledged, a responsibility to evaluate the freeway project from a comprehensive point of view.

They knew that no highway could serve traffic needs without having innumerable other repercussions, often less obvious to the casual eye than its intended purposes. They also recognized that some of these repercussions would probably disturb the public if there were full and open public discussion. This was the source of much proposer-evaluator conflict: comprehensive and careful study tended to turn issues from black and white to gray, thereby sapping public conviction and enthusiasm, and undermining the chances for approval of projects. In other words, the public relations requisites of any project proposal, needed to give it political momentum, conflicted with the prime characteristics of comprehensive evaluation: detached, systematic curiosity about the pros and cons of every alternative. Therefore, the planner who conscientiously subjected a popular proposal to searching criticism risked his own, his agency's, and his profession's standing in the community.

Of the three sets of actors whose approaches to St. Paul's freeway program will be described — highway engineers, organized private interests, and professional city planners — only the first had technical procedures for predicting the precise benefits to be derived by building on the basis of any particular design. Only they and the private interest spokesmen had explicit notions of what they hoped to achieve. Only the planners lacked both a clear notion of what values their efforts should serve and procedures for discovering what values any specific proposal would serve.

Consequently, the planners' work with regard to the freeway should not be evaluated according to some abstract criterion of "rationality." The emphasis of this case study is rather on how well the planners of St. Paul articulated key questions about the relations of problems and proposals to community values, brought together available knowledge bearing on these questions, formulated arguments supporting the various sides of each question, and tried to bring these arguments before responsible officials for their consideration.

Genesis of the Interstate Freeway

As metropolitan area populations grew after World War II, the nation's rising level of personal income permitted massive switches by metropolitan area dwellers from bus (and in the largest cities, rail) transportation to the more comfortable — but also far more expensive and space-consuming — automobile. To move a given number of people, even on roads of the highest quality, automobiles had to use at least four times the space required by buses and up to twenty times that required by rail transit. Even aside from the public costs imposed by automobile habits and the fixed costs borne by automobile owners (whether they drove or not), the expense of driving (figuring one person to a car) often ran several times higher than travel by public conveyance. However, commuters throughout the country (who caused most peak-hour congestion) remembered the waiting out-of-doors, the crowding, the delays, the stale air, and the general discomfort of public transportation. In ever-increasing numbers they chose to pay the price of automobile travel.

Their choice both encouraged, and was encouraged by, changes in the physical layout and spatial relations of urban areas following World War II. The movement known familiarly as urban sprawl greatly reduced the number of people living near public transportation routes while greatly increasing the number of, and distances between, their desired destinations. With an ever-declining number of people to patronize public transit on any route, transit companies were forced to reduce frequency of service, to eliminate some routes altogether, to raise prices, and to neglect maintenance. The cycle of declining patronage and service turned steadily, while the future of self-sustaining — not to say profit-making — urban public transportation was seriously challenged.

In cities throughout the country, increased traffic volume was channeled into street systems that had been laid out before the invention of the automobile. Until the end of World War II, amelioration of congestion had seemed feasible in most cases through piecemeal efforts to raise the traffic capacity of existing streets. Bottlenecks had been eliminated, sidewalks had been narrowed to permit street widening, and various traffic-control techniques had been employed — staggered traffic lights, prohibitions against parking, restricted left turns, and experimentation in the use of one-way streets.

After the war there was a gradual exhaustion of the available techniques for solving the problems of traffic congestion. Where sidewalks had been narrowed, for example, the only way to widen existing streets was to tear down the structures that lined them. The buildings that lined the major streets of a city were generally the most expensive. Even if city governments wanted to purchase the properties and demolish these structures, the very act of doing so would reduce the need for street widening at the point concerned, while increasing the need elsewhere. Crowded traffic arteries were caused not by people driving randomly through the city, but by trips designed to accomplish particular purposes. The concentration of economic, social, or other facilities on a particular street or at a particular corner was the factor that generated the congestion.

Most trips were, from the driver's point of view, economic in purpose. The 1949 Twin Cities Traffic Survey revealed, for example, that three-fifths of all passenger-car trips were for work, business, or shopping. Assuming that all truck traffic was economic in intent, the proportion of all traffic undertaken for economic reasons was more than 75 percent. Economically generated traffic tended to concentrate at places of employment and at retail centers, which together occupied only one-eighth of the area of the Twin Cities proper and a much smaller proportion of the metropolitan area. Highway engineers called such places, where people habitually congregated in large numbers, "major traffic generators." The efforts to widen streets by tearing down adjacent buildings had the effect of destroying these generators to provide room for street widening — which was like tossing out all the merchandise in a store to make room for a maximum number of customers.

The first clamor from automobile owners throughout the nation for massive highway improvements had been cut short by the depression of the 1930's. During that decade federal aid for highway construction had risen, but not sufficiently to offset the decline of state and local expenditures. Highway funds frequently had been used to provide jobs with little regard for the enduring value of the projects undertaken. Then came the war. During the period of hostilities, no new highways were built and the decline in highway maintenance that had begun in the 1930s continued. At the war's end street networks in many cities were in worse condition than they had been in 1929.

Cities in Minnesota, as elsewhere, lacked the resources to meet their transportation crises. All local needs had been neglected during the previous fifteen years. Voter resistance to tax increases had stiffened in response to the unprecedented level of federal taxation. Local tax revenues, based primarily on the property tax, tended to lag behind inflation, which had halved the value of each tax dollar. The rising of property assessments was no less sensitive politically than the raising of tax rates, and few assessors tried to keep pace with the cost of living. The cost of building new high-quality thoroughfares was enormous. Even in the Twin Cities, one of the least densely built-up of the nation's large urban complexes, the estimated cost of construction ran in some instances to $10 million a mile. There were not, of course, any $10 million miles built prior to 1956. Politicians who raised a city's taxes sufficiently to finance a new system of highways or a thorough revamping of public transportation facilities would have run the twin risks of overwhelming defeat in ensuing elections and of having numerous taxable activities flee the city.

Nevertheless, the mass conversion to auto travel seemed to be relentless. Auto registrations in the Twin Cities area increased by 58 percent in the years 1947-1950 alone (twenty times the rate of increase during the previous two decades). The number of miles traveled by the average car also increased rapidly.

Highway engineers, who had refined their techniques dramatically since 1929, promised that they could give lasting relief if the money to build new highways were found. They had discovered that gently curving limited-access highways could carry twice as much traffic per lane — at higher speeds and with greater safety — as the best streets built previously. The immediate cost of building these highways was great, but they seemed certain to repay it by reducing tax payers' expenditures on vehicle operation and insurance. For those who cared, there were bonuses — intangible benefits of time saved, injuries avoided, and greater driving pleasure.

The key concept in the new approach was "limited access." A limited-access highway was one that permitted vehicles to enter and exit only at designated points — interchanges — and then only at angles gentle enough to eliminate the need for other vehicles to slow down. Cross traffic was eliminated by providing bridges over and tunnels under the highway. Commercial development was forbidden along limited-access highways, so that there was no reason for vehicles ever to slow down suddenly or to turn off at sharp angles.

Highway engineers coined new names for the new highways: "turnpike," "tollway," "thruway," or "freeway." The engineers urged that tolls not be charged on the new highways, to avoid the danger of discouraging use, and that they be built in urban as well as rural areas, despite their great expense and the dislocation they would cause. This was conceived not as mere street widening, but rather as the creation of wholly new highways on new rights-of-way. The engineers confidently acknowledged that it was bold surgery. State and local officials liked the idea but were unable to finance it.

The Federal Aid Highway Act of 1956 offered a solution. It provided for construction of a 40,000 mile national system of freeways, 90 percent of whose cost would be borne by the federal government and 10 percent by the states. The excise taxes levied to pay for its construction would fall evenly on automobile and truck users throughout the country; no one could escape by changing his residence. The freeways would cut through, around, and between the nation's cities, serving local as well as intercity traffic. Many people compared the importance of this ambitious highway program with that of building the railroads in the nineteenth century. (For estimates of its total cost, see note 11.)

The highway program evolved from more than a decade of planning at all levels of government. Highway engineers expected the freeways to be paramount traffic carriers for at least fifty years. Their impact on national development and patterns of living would presumably reverberate long afterward. During the decades of construction a million people would be forced from their homes to provide land needed for rights-of-way, and countless businesses would be compelled to move or would find the values of their locations affected by the new pattern of vehicular transportation. Soon after passage of the Highway Act, the federal Bureau of Public Roads decided that the rights-of-way in cities should be 400 feet wide. Most street rights-of-way in St. Paul were 60 feet wide, although the widest street had a 200-foot right-of-way. The bureau wanted to ensure that it would never have to purchase additional right-of-way for freeway widening, or to eliminate the strips of greenery on either side and in the center of the freeway. The center strip was a safety factor; that on the sides was a health factor (designed to keep nearby residents from the worst concentrations of noise and exhaust fumes); and both were aesthetic factors.

The concept of a federally financed superhighway network first had arisen in response to the perceived needs of military security in World War.I. The Roosevelt Administration had revived it as a potential public works project when, in 1939, the Bureau of Public Roads had recommended a 26,700-mile highway system. During World War II the idea had received further study; and in 1943 a presidential commission had recommended a 40,000-mile system offering two major reasons: (*1*) to provide a system for the rapid movement of men and equipment in time of war, and (*2*) to provide jobs during the expected postwar depression. The relief of peacetime traffic congestion had been offered as a desirable, but distinctly secondary, purpose. The possible indirect repercussions of such a program had attracted little attention. Here, it had seemed, was a public works project meant to serve useful purposes, not merely to create jobs. In 1944 Congress had authorized the Bureau of Public Roads to supervise the planning of the proposed highway system. The bureau, in turn, had prescribed standards for state highway departments to use and had then delegated to them the task of actually selecting the routes.[1]

Two points characterized the original planning of the interstate system. First, engineers did the planning. In Minnesota, which was typical, their conception of the function of the highway system was highly specific: the solution of traffic problems. They frankly declared that they did not have time to concern themselves with other aspects of the program. Second, the engineers of the federal bureau and the state highway departments had hitherto worked primarily on rural roads. The cities had built their own streets, laying them out in most cases before buildings and other structures blocked the way. In Minnesota, the state Highway Department had had, beginning in 1933, some experience improving urban routes, but it had had virtually none locating new roads in urban areas. Nonetheless, its engineers now had to work quickly. The war was rapidly nearing an end, and they wanted to be prepared to move quickly once the expected economic depression developed. There seemed to be no time to theorize about subtle differences between urban and rural planning problems.

Selection of the Freeway Routes

The men who had cut dirt trails and roads in the early days of St. Paul's history had not been able to alter the landscape significantly; they had simply

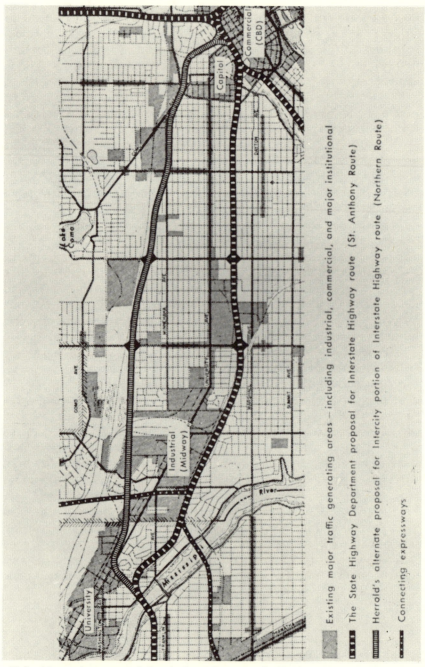

10.1 Alternative proposals for the intercity route, St. Paul.

had to go around major natural barriers while trying to create routes as straight as possible between major centers of activity. As of the late 1950s the main routes into and out of St. Paul were still located on the same land. Some of them, such as Route 61 — the main artery stretching north from the St. Paul business district — twisted and turned. Others, on flat land, were straight throughout their length.[2]

Facilities for work, shopping, and entertainment concentrated along the few early roads. Although they were the best roads in the city, in time they became some of the most congested. They served well, however, and outside the central business district peak-hour traffic on the city's major routes still averaged twenty miles an hour in 1949, according to the state Highway Department. Within the central business district, however, traffic frequently moved more slowly than a man could walk.

At an early date St. Paul's street planners had decided that entirely new highways, close to the existing major routes and located on the more heavily traveled side of them, would provide more lasting relief than piecemeal improvement. On this basis the city engineer in 1920 had proposed routes for a new radial highway system, with four routes projecting from the center of the city. He had supplemented this radial principle with two subordinate principles: (*1*) right-of-way costs should be minimized and (*2*) severe natural barriers should be avoided.

He had reasoned, for example, that a route parallel to University Avenue —the main artery between the central business districts of Minneapolis and St. Paul — should be built. A concentration of industry and railroad tracks blocked any route directly to the north of University Avenue. (See Plate 10.1) Bridging it would be difficult and expensive. Farther north, residential development was sparse. A highway in this area would clearly be so far from any heavily traveled routes that it would attract virtually no traffic away from them. Eight blocks south of University Avenue, on the other hand, was Marshall Avenue, heavily traveled itself, carrying a trunk highway and connecting with one of the major east-west streets of Minneapolis.

St. Anthony Avenue was almost precisely centered between University and Marshall Avenues. When University Avenue curved northwest toward the Minneapolis central business district, which was one and one-half miles north and eight miles west of St. Paul's central business district, St. Anthony, but not Marshall, followed it. Of all the streets between University and Marshall, St. Anthony alone was platted through to Minneapolis. Moreover, it connected with a major thoroughfare in Minneapolis. St. Anthony Avenue, therefore, was proposed as the western radial of the system.

Highway engineers had begun to make traffic counts in the 1920s; methods for articulating the data developed later. A traffic count merely showed the number of vehicles passing a given point during a particular period of time. It did not, however, indicate the pattern of traffic on routes approaching the point; therefore, it was of very limited use in explaining why traffic volumes reached a certain rate at a particular point. During the 1930s the interpretation of traffic count data had been greatly facilitated by the development of traffic-flow mapping techniques. A traffic-flow map was a pictorial summary of many traffic counts; it showed the number of vehicles passing each point on the map during a given period of time. Assuming that the day or hour represented was an "average" one and that traffic patterns hewed closely to the same average, day after day, one map could show a city's whole existing traffic pattern accurately and clearly. Trouble spots, and the extent of the remedy required to relieve them, could be clearly revealed, if the design capacity of existing streets was known.

Traffic-flow information was, however, better suited to piecemeal remedies than to comprehensive ones. It did not fully explain why drivers used some streets rather than others, nor what location would enable a new highway to attract the most traffic from existing congested streets. It did not indicate how traffic patterns would change during the projected life of the new highway, let alone explain the manner in which it would be desirable for traffic patterns to change. In short, a traffic-flow map was simply a pictorial representation of a large number of traffic counts, making the information easy to read but not necessarily easy to interpret.

After World War II highway engineers developed a new tool — the desire-line map. This map was the product of interviews rather than traffic counts. It showed not the routes that people were currently using but rather the straight-line routes from their origins to their destinations, which they presumably would take if they could. A desire-line map purported to show whether people used existing heavily traveled streets because they were the shortest possible routes, or the shortest available, or the shortest high-quality routes available. Assuming that most people took the route that minimized their travel time, and that it was desirable for the new highway to attract the maximum possible amount of traffic to it, the desire-line map showed the technician who performed certain calculations where the "ideal" route should lie in order to serve current desire lines.

When the highway engineers first chose the freeway routes in 1945-1946, desire-line techniques were new. The routes were chosen partly on the basis of "control points," which were ascertained by means of a very partial origin-destination survey. For the rest, the "art" of highway location — the common sense approach — still prevailed. The method employed by the Minnesota Highway Department in selecting the route from downtown St. Paul to downtown Minneapolis was typical and can be compared with the city engineer's method of plotting the same route in 1920.

The first question dealt with in 1945 was where the Mississippi River should be crossed. The new bridge bearing the freeway was going to be expensive, and it was intended to be very efficient as a traffic carrier. Since the purpose of the bridge was to relieve existing bridges as much as possible, the proper location for it was where it would attract the maximum traffic. Motorists crossing the river on the existing bridges were interviewed; their origins and destinations were plotted on maps. In the center of the greatest desire-line concentration was placed the freeway "control point."

Interviewers then moved to three of St. Paul's leading north-south streets: Prior Avenue, Snelling Avenue, and Lexington Parkway. Motorists crossing them in an east-west or west-east direction at any point were interviewed, and their origins and destinations plotted. At Snelling and Lexington the center of desire-line gravity was slightly to the south of University Avenue; traffic was somewhat heavier south of the center of gravity than north of it. At Prior Avenue the emphasis was farther north, but to build the freeway through the desire-line center on Prior would require expensive overpassing of the wide railroad track and industrial complex described earlier. Four control points were then known, and the long-projected St. Anthony Avenue route suited three of them quite well.[3] Its single defect, from a traffic point of view, was that it was slightly south of the center of desire-line gravity.

As noted previously, St. Anthony Avenue was the only street between University and Marshall that extended from St. Paul's business district to the Minneapolis city line. It was the only east-west street in the city continuing to parallel University Avenue as it angled northwest toward the Minneapolis central business district. St. Anthony Avenue ran directly south of the University of Minnesota and the Midway Industrial District, the third and fourth greatest traffic generators in the Twin Cities area after the two central business districts. Although it ran for one and one-half miles through the center of St. Paul's Negro district, it cut through no other neighborhoods. For more than half its length, it passed to the north of residential sections and to the south of trucking terminals and railroad tracks. This latter portion would require demolition of some homes — St. Anthony Avenue was too narrow for a freeway — but thereafter it would serve as a convenient buffer between the residential and industrial land uses.

St. Anthony Avenue connected with Arthur Avenue S.E. in Minneapolis. The freeway could continue adjacent to a railroad spur line until it curved west for a river-crossing slightly to the south of the University of Minnesota. However, the section from the Minneapolis city line to the river-crossing cut through a pleasant residential neighborhood (already cut by the railroad spur), inhabited largely by university employees. Nonetheless, analysis of the driver interviews had demonstrated that the river-crossing "had to be" slightly to the south of the university. A crossing farther south, sparing the residential neighborhood, would not serve traffic to and from the university very efficiently.

The St. Anthony route proposed in 1920 would have connected in Minneapolis with Arthur Avenue S.E. and the Franklin Avenue Bridge. By 1945 the Franklin Avenue Bridge was itself overworked, so a new bridge was proposed for a location one-third of a mile north of Franklin Avenue and just south of the university. Otherwise, the Highway Department proposal was identical with that made by the city engineer twenty-five years earlier.[4]

An Old City Planner's Approach

George Herrold had been chief planning engineer of St. Paul for a quarter of a century by 1945. He had drafted highway improvement proposals many times during his tenure and was one of the officials who in 1920 had helped to develop the plan for a major thoroughfare on St. Anthony Avenue. A still-existent drawing depicted what he had envisioned: a four-lane divided parkway, landscaped and tree-lined. Limited access highways, of course, had not been conceived in 1920.

A graduate in civil engineering, class of 1896, Herrold was a product of the "reform" and "nonpartisan" periods of Minnesota history. He thought rather little of politicians; and in turn he had never been popular with local political leaders, many of whom considered him impractical and unbending in his idealism. Consequently, Herrold had never had much influence in City Hall. On the other hand, he had good relations with many of St. Paul's older business leaders, and for many years he had enjoyed a measure of public renown as St. Paul's "founder of city planning."

The Planning Board had published dozens of reports during Herrold's tenure. All of them had reflected some research and had been highly competent pieces of work by the standards of Herrold's generation. The City Council had never granted him funds for professional staff, but at times during the 1930s he had had several hundred WPA employees gathering data under his direction. The research conducted had almost always been of an inventory nature, but it had provided Herrold with a considerable store of information on which to base his general views concerning community land-use problems and needs.

The fact was, nonetheless, that in the late 1940s St. Paul had a chief planning engineer in his eighties, working with virtually no professional assistance. Largely for this reason, the city planning tradition in St. Paul did not stress intensive research or general planning. Issues were dealt with in an informed intuitive fashion as they arose. Herrold cited planning literature and data published by other agencies with larger staffs. He believed that he could make a substantial contribution even working under these handicaps. His work, he felt, was primarily thought and recommendation based on long experience with the city's problems. He said that he did not see how planners newly brought to a city could plan well; even the best of men required many years to understand and feel the needs of a city.

Herrold had little faith in his political superiors and conceived his role as independent advisor to the community as well as to them. He saw that engineers and other specialists who planned public works generally prevailed within City Hall, and he doubted that they would ever take account of planning needs except under public pressure. He felt certain, therefore, that city planners were most effective when they kept the general public informed of their views. Planners usually would be defeated in public controversies of course, but no more ignominiously than they lost any other kind of political controversy. At least public disputes might have educative value.

Herrold did not believe that the automobile should dominate cities, and he preferred to keep new highway construction out of built-up areas. He knew that the freeway routes had been chosen before any elaborate traffic studies had been done, and this led him to doubt the impartiality of all Highway Department traffic analyses that came out in the late 1940s and 1950s — especially since none challenged the original route choices.

Herrold's interest in St. Anthony Avenue dated back to his work on the 1920 city engineer's report which had recommended improvement of the avenue as a surface highway. In 1938 he and others had proposed a trunk highway on St. Anthony Avenue. In 1942, at the request of the chairman of the City Planning Board's Street and Highway Committee, he had prepared a report on highway approaches to the city and on needed street improvements. In the report he again had recommended the improvement on St. Anthony Avenue. Nonetheless, when Herrold discovered that St. Anthony Avenue was being proposed as part of the interstate system, with a block-wide right-of-way, he was very surprised. Parkways with intersections at every corner, he declared, lined and divided by well-kept grass and majestic trees, with truck traffic excluded from them, would grace a neighborhood. To provide room on St. Anthony Avenue for a parkway, a 200-foot right-of-way would suffice —half of that prescribed for the interstate system. A freeway might carry more vehicles more quickly, but in Herrold's opinion it would also be a gigantic, unshaded, unsightly, noisy ditch and an unwelcome concentrator of exhaust fumes. He believed it was foolish to concentrate traffic so heavily on one artery; the city streets near the freeway's exit points were sure to be swamped, and the cycle of piecemeal improvements would begin again.

Herrold was basically opposed to any freeways in the city: urban freeway mileage was very expensive; it divided neighborhoods; and it encouraged vehicles to enter the city. He believed that a belt-line freeway encouraging through traffic to bypass the city would alleviate traffic congestion adequately. A parkway on St. Anthony, from which trucks should be excluded, would eliminate completely the problem of serious congestion between the two central business districts. The parkway needed to be only four lanes wide; at peak hours three lanes could be used in one direction; left turns and parking could be forbidden.

In arguing against the freeways, Herrold occasionally referred to consideration of mass transit, the economic position of downtown, and urban sprawl; but his primary objections to the freeway were social, and he expressed them frankly. He wrote, for example, that "the freeway idea . . . requires the moving of thousands of people, who must give up their homes, churches, schools, neighbors and valued social contacts, who lose the institutions they have built for their pleasure and profit." When considering the intercity freeway, he typically emphasized that five-sixths of the Negro population of St. Paul lived in an area two miles long and one-half mile wide. St. Anthony Avenue ran the length of this area, precisely through its center. The prescribed right-of-way would take about one-seventh of the area. A comparable proportion of its structures would be destroyed and its population forced from their homes. Either of two results was likely: (1) displaced Negroes might try to move into other neighborhoods, public reaction would be extremely unpleasant, and Negroes would find it virtually impossible to buy or rent homes in the neighborhoods to which they aspired; or (2) the Negroes might remain within their ghetto — reduced in size, more crowded, more completely Negro in composition. Herrold did not presume to be a social reformer. He had no wish for dispersion of the Negro population throughout the city, but he believed that Negroes should be protected from encroachments upon their traditional community in St. Paul.

In reaching his conclusions about the proposed freeway route, Herrold did no original research and held no hearings. He analyzed the data that were available, however, and he wrote numerous memoranda setting forth his views. He contended that long experience and a disciplined mind could give a man familiarity with the "heart" of a city and enable him to make some wise judgments even if he did lack staff for conducting intensive research. Thus, whenever the opportunity arose he reiterated his arguments that no freeway should run on St. Anthony Avenue.

The engineers of the state Highway Department disagreed vigorously with Herrold's views. They believed that their task was to build highways, not ruminate about the general needs of cities. Their method was research that yielded quantitative conclusions; art, they reasoned, was needed only to fill in the gaps. Their commodity was expertness, not wisdom. They and Herrold shared the belief that the public could not contribute much to their thinking; the groups that approached them, they believed, were self-seeking. The vast driving and taxpaying public had no interest group spokesmen; the department should stand firm and "build the best damn highways possible." The public should be won over, however, not alienated.

The engineers admitted the importance of circumferential routes but said such routes would not significantly alter traffic volumes within the cities. After 1949 they pointed to their desire-line maps for "proof." Driver interviews had revealed that through traffic was only a minute proportion of traffic on city streets. Most trips within the city were no more than several miles in length. It would not pay drivers to go out of their way to use the belt-line freeway for such short trips. The largest proportion of traffic, particularly at peak hours, was generated by the central business districts, the Midway Industrial District, and the University of Minnesota. All were along a line bisecting a circle that would be formed by the circumferential route; few drivers to and from these areas would find the circumferential route of any use. Only routes through the cities would substantially relieve urban congestion. The engineers estimated that by 1975 the intercity freeway would be compelled to carry 5,000 vehicles an hour at peak hours, and that six lanes of parkway in the peak-hour direction alone would be required to carry an equivalent load. The cost of an adequate parkway would equal that of the four-lane freeway. A parkway would move traffic more slowly; furthermore, it would divide neighborhoods more seriously than the freeway, because freeway overpass and underpass crossings were safer to traverse than busy surface streets.

Herrold's attitude toward the freeway remained unchanged. State and U.S. trunk highways that were well-located in St. Paul, he believed, were being abandoned unnecessarily in favor of the freeway idea. After 1949 he pointed to a section of the origin-destination survey report showing that a vehicle starting from the center of St. Paul's central business district, except during the peak hour, could travel far past the city limits in any direction within fifteen minutes. The peak hour was defined as the four consecutive fifteen-minute periods during the day when traffic was heaviest. Generally, a morning and an afternoon peak hour were measured. During the peak hour, traffic moving north, south, southeast, and southwest could travel as far as the city limits in fifteen minutes. Traffic moving east, west, northwest, and northeast could travel two-thirds of the same distance in fifteen minutes. Congestion was no problem beyond the fifteen-minute zone, and Herrold did not object to building freeways beyond it. He believed it was a question of value whether so much money should be spent and so many people dislocated to save drivers a few minutes within the fifteen-minute zone.[5]

Herrold lamented the freeway's foreseeable impact on land use in St. Paul. Twenty-two railroad lines passed through the city. Most of the city's growth in the late nineteenth century had been due to its position as the railroad center of the Upper Midwest. The railroads, however, together with the city's main thoroughfares, divided the city into "islands," often too small and irregular to permit the establishment of attractive neighborhoods. The freeway would be likely to increase the number and decrease the size of these islands, unless it were built adjacent to railroad lines or existing main streets. The cost of land next to main streets prohibited construction next to them, but development was light in the immediate vicinity of most of the rail lines. If freeways had to enter the city, Herrold reasoned, they should be put next to railroad lines. Dislocation of people and commerce would be minimized. The city's minority-group housing problem would not be intensified.

Moreover, if the freeway route did not follow present desire-line patterns precisely, its construction would encourage deconcentration and the development of new lands within the city; both were desirable and over the years would tend to decrease congestion. Although this approach to highway location would fail to maximize the use of the freeway in its first years, drivers would travel farther out of their way to use it when congestion increased on city streets in the future — if it increased. It was better, Herrold said, to cause drivers to go out of their way and to get less than maximal traffic relief than to destroy neighborhoods and exacerbate racial tensions.

Applying this approach, Herrold developed an alternative to the St. Anthony route proposal. He concentrated his fire on the St. Anthony route because he thought it would do the greatest amount of social harm. He hoped that if his views prevailed in this instance, city officials might listen when he spoke about other freeway sections. He viewed his alternative as a compromise between the Highway Department's proposal and his own belief that the freeway should be kept outside of the city. It became known as the "Northern Route" because it ranged from three-quarters of a mile to one and one-quarter miles north of the St. Anthony Avenue route. At one point it was almost a mile to the north of University Avenue. It ran adjacent to railroad tracks most of the way between downtown St. Paul and the city line. Herrold proposed to cross the Mississippi River at the same place proposed by the Highway Department, but he wanted to approach the river from a different direction, thereby eliminating most of the freeway section through the Prospect Park neighborhood in Minneapolis. The most important virtues of his alternative route were its avoidance of the Negro neighborhood of St. Paul and its minimal passage through the Prospect Park area. He also claimed, however, that the northerly growth of suburban communities eventually would justify the Northern Route in traffic terms.

Highway Department officials, on the other hand, argued against the Northern Route. It bordered the Midway Industrial District only at the district's northwest corner, whereas the St. Anthony route ran along the entire southern boundary. The St. Anthony location was a direct route between downtown St. Paul and the Midway District. The Northern Route was indirect; following it from the Midway District to the downtown area, one would have to travel north and then southwest. The time saved by using the freeway would not justify its use for other short trips either, although it was satisfactory for trips from the central business district of St. Paul to the University or to the Minneapolis central business district. Yet most trips were shorter than five miles. The freeway would not be certain to relieve existing streets substantially unless it hewed within one-quarter to one-half mile of the major desire-line concentrations. Moreover, the Northern Route would pass through extensive railroad and industrial property at the western edge of St. Paul. Any savings in right-of-way cost vis-a-vis the St. Anthony route would be offset by the cost of elevating this section of the freeway.

Herrold wrote a ten-page report analyzing the probable social and economic costs of building on the Northern Route as compared with the St. Anthony route, but he had no funds for collecting traffic data and thus could not estimate the amount of traffic that would be diverted from existing streets to his proposed freeway. Nor could he demonstrate with figures that a four-lane parkway would suffice for thirty to forty years. The Highway Department had estimated that twelve lanes — the equivalent of a freeway —would be needed. Department personnel reminded the city that if fewer vehicles used the freeway, more would use the city streets, thus increasing the city's maintenance bill. (The federal and state governments were to maintain the interstate system as well as build it). They reminded the driving public that it would forego some of the benefits of freeway use if the freeway were inconvenient for more people than it had to be. Moreover, they declared flatly that the cost of a freeway on the Northern Route could not be justified to the Bureau of Public Roads, in view of the route's limited traffic-service potential.

City leaders, who had to approve Highway Department plans for work within the city, considered still another objection to Herrold's plan. The parkway would have to be built with local tax revenues; the freeway would cost the city nothing. Trucking interests in the Midway area were very conscious of the mileage and travel time — equivalent to money — that they would save each year if the freeway route followed the St. Anthony route. Midway retailers had noted that the St. Anthony route passed one-third as far from them as the Northern Route. Commuters from the western part of St. Paul, most of whom lived south of University Avenue, knew that a Northern Route freeway would not save them time. Minneapolis officials were pleased that the St. Anthony route connected conveniently to a projected river-crossing and to a locally financed expressway in south Minneapolis.

The Highway Engineers Proceed

For a number of years prior to passage of the Highway Act in 1956 there had been public discussion of the proposed freeway in St. Paul. Beginning in 1942, a number of civic organizations had engaged in a study of postwar public works needs. Mayor McDonough, with the approval of the City Council and the Ramsey County Board, had appointed an Improvement Coordinating Committee, a civic group authorized to coordinate and activate long-range plans for the improvement of the metropolitan area. The St. Paul City Planning Board, the St. Paul Chamber of Commerce, the Midway Civic Club, and other organizations had contributed to the work of the committee. There had been public meetings and press publicity, but little or no controversy appears to have been generated. In 1947, despite Herrold's counterarguments, the city had approved the Highway Department's proposed route locations with little public dispute. After losing his fight in the early postwar years, Herrold returned to do battle again after 1956. At the age of ninety, he took to writing long letters-to-the-editor defending his position. He stirred some controversy, but public officials ignored him.

As early as 1946 and 1947 the city engineer had begun informally to discourage new construction along the proposed freeway routes. His purpose had been to hold down the eventual right-of-way cost. He had not had any legal authority to prevent new construction, but he had found that few people were anxious to build after he informed them of their property's uncertain future. Of course, they might have gambled on being reimbursed adequately when the Highway Department took their land, but no one had been certain what government appraisers and the courts would think fair. Moreover, government agencies had seldom compensated people for the mental strains and personal inconveniences of moving.

In 1949, Congress had authorized federal financing of urban redevelopment projects. Mayor Delaney had been enthusiastic and had seen to it that St. Paul was the first city in the country to win a project approval. To secure federal approval for its projects, the city had been required to demonstrate that a market demand for the land was likely to exist after it was cleared. The procedure was for the Housing Authority to purchase the property, exercising eminent domain to force the hands of reluctant owners. The land was then cleared and made available to private purchasers. The Housing Authority might, and often did, sell land for less than it had paid if it believed that the public interest would benefit from such a transaction. The developer who purchased land from the Housing Authority was spared the pain of bargaining with large numbers of property owners, and he was assured of newly developed surroundings within the project area.

The Housing Authority located St. Paul's renewal projects adjacent to the proposed freeway routes. Its officials said that investors would clamor for land so close to the freeway, especially as the freeway would provide a buffer between the blighted areas proposed for renewal and those not so designated. The Highway Department assured local officials that Congress would eventually finance the freeway's construction. After work began on the renewal projects, the city's commitment to the 1947 route locations⁵ was deepened. Had local officials subsequently chosen to request that sections of the freeway be relocated, they would have embarrassed their colleagues who had to deal with the federal Urban Renewal Administration.

As the urban renewal program got under way, city engineer Shepard used his powers of persuasion more vigorously to discourage construction along the proposed freeway route. At his urging, the voters ratified a $200,000 bond issue in 1953 authorizing him to purchase property on the freeway right-of-way when the moratorium on construction imposed extreme hardship on specific owners. Still, most landowners who found themselves unable to sell or improve their property continued to suffer — not "extremely" in the city engineer's opinion — without compensation.

Meanwhile, the freeway program was making headway in Washington. It was also being altered somewhat in concept, if not in procedure. Although fear of depression had waned in the country and the national administration was trying to reduce defense expenditures,[6] urban traffic had burgeoned, and with it had increased political pressures on Congress to finance the interstate system.[7] The President's Advisory Committee on a National Highway Program, chaired by General Lucius Clay (ret.), reported in January 1955 that the total construction needs of the nation's highways required a $101-billion, ten-year crash program.[8] The interstate system accounted for $27 billion of this total.

The federal share of the proposed program was thirty times greater than the 1943-1953 rate of federal highway aid. The proposed rate of expenditure on streets and highways for all levels of government combined was four times greater than the 1947 combined rate, and twice the 1953 rate. The committee indicated, however, that the project would repay its cost with ease. It reported that "agriculture, industry, and our defense planning [are] closely geared to motor transportation" and noted a presidential statement that "an adequate highway system is vital to continued expansion of the economy. . . . The relationship is of course reciprocal; an adequate highway network will facilitate the expansion of the economy which, in turn, will facilitate the raising of revenues to finance the construction of highways."[9] As if this were not conclusive, the committee added that "the improvement of our highway systems as recommended herein would reduce transportation costs to the public through reductions in vehicle operating costs currently estimated to average as much as a penny a mile. Based on present rates of travel, this saving alone would support the total cost of the accelerated program."[10]

Although some city planners felt misgivings about the dislocation of people and economic activity that would accompany building freeways in cities, the hard political reality was that urban area residents constituted a national majority. They were the most conscious of traffic congestion. If the crash program were to be supported by a general gasoline tax, as the President's committee proposed, they would bear the brunt of it. The committee had recommended financing by tax rather than user tolls because it believed that only 8,500 miles of the system could possibly pay for themselves in tolls; 5,000 of these miles had already been built or were under construction by the states. Therefore, the crash program had very little to do with this mileage.

After two sessions of debate, Congress voted in 1956 to authorize a crash program limited to the 40,000-mile interstate system, now officially christened the "National System of Interstate *and Defense* Highways" (emphasis added). The system was to be built over a period of thirteen years. No effort was to be made to relate the program to the business cycle. The long lead time between commitment to contractors and construction, it was now recognized, severely limited the usefulness of the program for economic stabilization purposes. Commitments made in time of economic recession might take effect in time of boom, and vice versa.[11]

As soon as the Federal Aid Highway Act became law, the Bureau of Public Roads asked the state highway departments to submit cost estimates for their freeway mileage within one year. The Minnesota Highway Department organized for the monumental task in four months; eight months remained until the deadline.

To make cost estimates, the state highway engineers had to know in detail the land over which the state's freeways would run. Of course, they used the routes approved a decade earlier. There was no time to argue with local officials; only the governments of the largest cities were kept informed of the decisions being made. Even they were told that if they wished to protest, they might do so after the deadline passed. Local protest was not, however, to be easy at any time. The state Highway Department had authority to determine the order in which sections of the freeway system were to be constructed. Right-of-way acquisition for each section had to begin eighteen months or two years before construction. If agreement with the officials of one city was not reached in time, the department could (and made clear that it would) simply shift its order of priorities. A section scheduled originally for 1960 might be delayed five or ten years.

The cost estimates submitted to the Bureau of Public Roads in 1957 had official status. The bureau's position was that future upward revisions should be made only in response to inflation, engineering improvements, or new traffic data. The Highway Department might propose changes for other compelling reasons, but the bureau did not intend to be very flexible. Inflation was already adding to highway costs.

The Highway Department had its own reasons for appearing inflexible. Traffic and cost data were recognized as authoritative and impartial by all parties. Such data could be collectd without time-consuming political consultation. Secrecy could be maintained until the proper time for public announcement, thereby minimizing real estate speculation. At the stage of public discussion, inflexibility tended to hold down the level of controversy. Highway personnel noted that when the department acceded to the demands of one group of interested citizens, other groups were encouraged to make demands. If one group succeeded in having a freeway section removed from its neighborhood, residents near the proposed new location were extremely likely to protest. Every neighborhood and every property owner threatened in fact or fancy by the freeway had to be assumed to be watching closely to determine the potential rewards of complaint. Highway officials concluded that if they were flexible, it was unlikely that total public satisfaction from the freeways would be greater in the end. Every change would probably make the freeways more expensive and less efficient as carriers of traffic. There was no consensus about the extent to which other values ought to be served. If freeway plans were not completed on schedule, years of benefits to road users might be lost. Congress might unexpectedly cancel the program, in which case the state would never retrieve its loss.

City officials could not single-mindedly support displeased citizens because important pressure groups within the city wanted the freeways to be constructed quickly. Downtown businessmen and property owners wanted the task of driving downtown to be more inviting, and they wanted to arrest the flight of investment and consumer dollars to the suburbs. Truckers believed they lost money every moment that freeway construction was delayed. St. Paul's Midway District was the third largest trucking center in the United States, and the truck owners were a force to be reckoned with when their interests were threatened. They knew much more precisely than private motorists how many dollars the freeways would save them. Labor was interested in the great number of jobs for construction workers that the freeway program would provide. Taxpayer groups noted that although the freeway would remove much land from the tax rolls, it was expected to encourage commercial development downtown and along its own right-of-way. By diverting traffic from city streets, it would reduce the cost of street maintenance. It promised an end to the cycle of widening old thoroughfares and constructing new ones. By carrying several times as many cars per lane as surface streets, the freeway might save land for the tax rolls in the long run. Booster groups emphasized that delay would sacrifice St. Paul's lead of several years over Minneapolis. Habits of shopping and working in St. Paul, if once developed, might persist after the Minneapolis freeways came into operation. The reverse might occur if Minneapolis took the lead.

The city's own engineers said freeways were needed desperately. The Highway Department had fine engineers on its staff. Only a fool would delay construction, it seemed, to satisfy specially interested voters who knew nothing about highway construction. St. Paul's elected office holders, therefore, answered evasively the questions of citizens who complained, often implying that the Highway Department made all decisions without consulting the city. Every so often they quietly approved Highway Department plans at some new level of specificity.

A Young City Planner's Approach

Let us return for a moment to the period of the late 1940s, when members of the St. Paul Planning Board began to believe that the city needed more vigorous and politically acceptable planning. As a result of the Planning Board's dissatisfaction with the existing state of affairs, two young city planners were hired successively in 1947 and 1948 to assist Herrold. Both resigned after short periods.

In April 1950 C. David Loeks, recently graduated from Massachusetts Institute of Technology, became the third to try his hand. Herrold's first assignment for Loeks was to study alternative routes for the intercity freeway. Loeks, unwilling to be impaled between Herrold and the rest of St. Paul officialdom, wrote a report urging further study. He soon found that city officials expected to talk to him rather than to Herrold when they entered the planning office. He said he felt sad to see them hurting Herrold in this way, but Herrold came to see him as a very ambitious young man. After a year of discomfort, Loeks prepared to follow his predecessors. The federal Housing and Redevelopment Act had been passed in 1949, however, and Mayor Delaney cared deeply about urban renewal. He believed that one prerequisite of a good renewal program was comprehensive planning, and he refused to accept Loeks' resignation. Instead, he created the post of Planning and Zoning Consultant and induced Herrold to accept the position.

In 1952, while still in his twenties, Loeks became St. Paul's planning director. He was almost sixty years younger than Herrold, and an entirely different kind of city planner. He was uncertain who, in theory, the planner was supposed to serve; but he was sure that in practice ineffective planning was worthless. The planner, he knew, operated in a political environment. He must gain the confidence of important community leaders, primarily within but also outside of government. He should never speak hastily. He should not only consider the validity of his statements but also the effect of making them in the form he did. If he alienated too many people, he would see his recommendations ignored, and make the task of his successors more difficult. The example of Herrold was before him.

Loeks chose to study as much as resources permitted and to confine his recommendations to matters on which he had highly persuasive evidence. He hoped to build a reputation for speaking only when he knew what he was talking about, even if this stand prevented him — with a total annual (1952) budget of $25,000 — from making recommendations on all important subjects in the first years of his tenure. As far as his role within City Hall was concerned, he intended to be as deferential as possible without compromising his professional integrity. Although he realized that after study he might come to disagree with veteran city officials and political leaders on specific matters, his basic feeling was respect for their judgment. The avoidance of forceful opposition to their views seemed appropriate to Loeks, except in situations where he was certain the facts supported him.

Loeks did not question the concept of the freeway. He agreed with the engineers that because the automobile had inevitably come to stay, freeway construction was desirable. The route locations were, of course, another matter; but several factors dissuaded him from examining them seriously. First, he was confronted by the fact that the Highway Department and the City Council had approved the routes years earlier. Second, they neither asked nor expected him to evaluate these decisions anew. Finally, he believed that worthwhile route evaluations could only be made on the basis of intensive research. Given the governmental environment and his budget, this appeared to be an impossible condition to satisfy.

Loeks, an introspective man, later admitted that he might have considered the problem more thoroughly had he been City Planning Director when the Highway Department first presented its plan in 1946, and had the planning function in St. Paul been more secure at that time. Coming on the scene when and as he did, he deemed such a course unwise, especially since the decisions appeared to have been made intelligently on the basis of all available facts. He recalled that no drastic change in circumstance had ever made him feel that a comprehensive reevaluation of this position was necessary; therefore, in dealing with the Highway Department, he had focused his energies on particular matters of design rather than on general questions of freeway desirability or location.

Herrold remained as Director *de jure*, if not *de facto*, through 1952; and during the next two years, Loeks as Planning Director still had no planning staff. Moreover, during these years the attention of city officials was on urban renewal and public housing. Loeks worked closely with the Housing and Redevelopment Authority to provide an adequate community planning framework for the two major redevelopment project applications that were being prepared in this period. He also had to spend a substantial amount of time on zoning matters. At the request of the City Council he studied such problems as the possibility of a one-way street system for downtown, channeling traffic at downtown intersections, billboard control, junkyard regulation, and civil defense. Some of his recommendations in these areas proved quite controversial, but he stood by them because he felt that he had done enough research to support firm professional judgments. On one occasion, as members of the City Council pressed him to withdraw on a controversial point, he explained that he would not appeal to the public over their heads but that he thought his usefulness would end if he became known as one whose professional recommendations were manipulable.

None of the studies he did in this period involved comprehensive planning, of course, but Loeks believed that it was necessary to demonstrate the utility of the planning approach by working on those matters that the community's leadership felt needed attention. If he won the leaders' confidence by serving them well, he hoped that in time he would be able to educate them to desire comprehensive planning. Throughout the period to 1957, when he left the St. Paul Planning Board to become director of the new Twin Cities Metropolitan Planning Commission, Loeks brought out about half a dozen publications intended for the general public rather than local leaders. None of these formal publications contained controversial recommendations. All were presentations of census data on the city or of already approved recommendations that had been conceived primarily by other agencies, namely the Highway Department and the Housing Authority. Shortly before he left St. Paul, however, Loeks acquired financial support for master planning, and he directed the first stages of work on St. Paul's comprehensive plan.

We have moved ahead of the story to set out Loeks's general strategy. There is a bit more to be said about his official environment on highway matters, however. The predominant figure in that environment was George Shepard, city engineer of St. Paul since 1922. Because the Planning Bureau had been part of the Public Works Department until 1947, Shepard had been Herrold's nominal superior until then. (Actually, the Planning Board, whose staff the Planning Bureau was supposed to be, was an independent body whose members enjoyed fixed terms of office.) While Herrold tended to be rather uncompromising and acid in his personal relations, Shepard got along well with nearly everyone. Since, in addition, his high professional competence was very widely acknowledged, Shepard's advice carried immense weight in City Hall. Herrold had tended to look on Shepard as something of an antagonist and to blame him in part for the Planning Bureau's shortages of funds and staff, and for lack of political support on policy issues.

Shepard's concept of planning led him to agree with the Highway Department that freeways were worthwhile and that engineers alone should determine freeway routes. In an address to a businessmen's conference on urban renewal in 1947, for example, he had described what he believed the planning function, operating independently of other functions, should embrace.

> Planning Commissions or Boards should devote the greater part of their time and energy [to broader matters of policy for guiding the future growth and arrangement or rearrangement of our cities]. . . It is assumed, of course, that operating agencies, such as the Department of Public Works, City Engineers's Office, park and other similar departments are adequately staffed with trained professional personnel for the preparation of detailed plans and specification of approved projects and for supervision of such work when it gets underway

He acknowledged the need for long-range planning, but emphasized that planners should not become involved in the "details of administration."

Shepard resigned as city engineer to become city highway coordinator in 1957. His job was to help handle the increasing burden of work in the city and to act as liaison officer between the Highway Department and all city agencies. All official contacts with the Highway Department were to go through him. He had, of course, been the city's chief evaluator of highway plans for many years before this, but his new position seemed to ensure that no challenge to the highway program by the planners could succeed without his approval.

From the start of his tenure as planning director, Loeks sought to maintain good relations with Shepard. He respected Shepard's official responsibilities and professional judgments. In addition, he felt strongly that planning was futile if ignored. His own future and that of city planning in St. Paul, he later pointed out, depended on overcoming the legacy of hostility toward Herrold. One of the most important ways to do this was to minimize conflict and seek to enlarge areas of agreement. The fact that Shepard was an engineer and tended to feel rapport with the approach of Highway Department engineers suggested to Loeks that he should also strive to avoid conflict with the department engineers.

Loeks tried to keep informed about the Highway Department's intentions, and he frequently was asked to comment on new design proposals.[12] He maintained good relations with the personnel of the department and won some concessions by following three rules-of-thumb (outlined later to the writer): (*1*) never criticize the department publicly; (*2*) never claim authorship of a change accepted by the department; (*3*) rely on negotiations as much as possible and force showdowns as rarely as possible.

In practice, Loeks later noted, no dramatic showdowns ever seemed necessary. The Highway Department seemed to make reasonable decisions, and it never presented firm plans at meetings with city officials. All plans were presented as tentative, and all meetings with city personnel were primarily to elicit ideas for further study. (Loeks later jokingly described the decision process as it appeared from his vantage point as "creeping *fait accomplism*.") If Loeks didn't approve of some detail, he usually would draft a map suggesting an alternative. Six months later, at the next meeting with Highway Department personnel, his alternative might or might not appear on the new set of tentative plans. Neither side ever intimated to the other that Loeks's suggestion had affected the new design. During the years that followed, this pattern of relationships between Loeks and the Highway Department endured.

Loeks published nothing on the freeways until June 1957, when he brought out a booklet entitled *The Proposed Freeways for St. Paul.* Despite its late date, this was the first effort made by any agency of the city government to explain the implications of the freeways for St. Paul in general terms. It was a rather sophisticated though simply presented functional analysis, and even years later Loeks was proud of it. In accord with his policy of not taking official disagreements to the public, Loeks did not include anything in the booklet that might give offense to other agencies. It was cleared with the Department of Public Works in its successive drafts and was approved by the City Council without controversy in July 1957. In one sense the booklet was a public relations effort because its whole thrust was to justify official policies rather than to call any into doubt. Loeks later commented that from his standpoint it had appeared to be a statement of planning conclusions that happened (largely as the outcome of a continous process of discussion) to coincide with and reinforce the conclusions of the Highway and Public Works departments. He further believed that justifying the freeways publicly in *planning* terms was likely to have a beneficial effect on future public discussions of highway proposals.

The Negro Community Reacts

Negro leaders first became aware that the city and state had approved the St. Anthony route as part of the proposed freeway system in 1953. In that year the school board recommended rehabilitation of an old elementary school in the Negro district. Residents of the district, led by Reverend Floyd Massey, Jr., of the Pilgrim Baptist Church, mounted a campaign aimed at persuading the board to build a new school instead. Massey learned from city engineer Shepard that the old school lay on the path of the proposed freeway route, and that therefore investment in it was likely to be wasted. His group used this argument to bolster its position, and it did achieve its objective. Negro leaders apparently thought little more about the freeway until 1955, when it became apparent that massive federal aid for freeway construction would soon become available.

Toward the end of 1955 Reverend Massey became aware that the City Planning Board, of which he was a member, would soon be asked to express itself again on the freeway proposals. He thought that the most effective way for the Negro community to impress its views on the Planning Board would be through a single organization. He therefore urged the members of his congregation to take the lead in organizing, and a number of them followed his advice. In January 1956 they established the Rondo-St. Anthony Improvement Association, the first property owners' group to appear in connection with the proposed Twin Cities' freeway routes.

The association, which soon included nearly 100 percent of the threatened property owners and quite a few others as well, selected Timothy Howard as its president. Howard was a member of Massey's congregation and a middle-aged bachelor with many contacts in the White community. He had long been active in Negro community affairs and was a vehement though seldom bitter critic of racial discrimination. He earned his living as a barber, but he seemed to have virtually unlimited amounts of time and energy to devote to causes that interested him.

Most of the members of the association viewed it as a mechanism for fighting the freeway right down the line. Howard and Massey, however, along with other Negro leaders whom they consulted, perceived the choice of objectives as a very difficult one.

On the one hand, it was possible to oppose construction on the St. Anthony route, pointing out that a St. Anthony freeway would split the Negro district and force one-seventh of its residents to leave their homes. Federally aided urban redevelopment projects had already displaced many of the district's residents since 1953. Although the residents had been able to find homes in other neighborhoods, it seemed likely that those displaced by the freeway would similarly contribute to overcrowding within the district.[13]

On the other hand, it was possible to emphasize the opportunities created by the freeway program. It would replace some of the most dilapidated structures in the district with a modern landscaped highway. By increasing pressure on the housing supply available to St. Paul's Negroes, it might provide the impetus for some of them to buy homes in other neighborhoods. If they were prevented from doing so, even after being forced from their homes to make way for a public project, they could righteously demand passage of an open occupancy ordinance (i.e., a law making discrimination in the sale and rental of private housing illegal). Political leaders might recognize the moral justification of the Negro cause and appreciate the fact that Negro leaders had not tried to obstruct progress.

Either of these two strategies might fail. The latter seemed more enlightened, however, and if it succeeded it might produce a significant victory for the cause of racial integration in St. Paul. This strategy also seemed more likely to succeed than its alternative. The few Negro leaders who had visited the Highway Department had come away convinced that the traffic data were conclusive; they had informed their colleagues that any effort to have the location changed would almost surely prove fruitless.

The leaders inclined to think, therefore, that they should accept the route line and focus on means of influencing its repercussions. They believed that their most feasible objectives were the following: to help the displaced Negroes find decent housing, to publicize their hardship as part of a continuing campaign for an open-occupancy ordinance, and to minimize the harmful effects that the freeway might have on the rest of the neighborhood. Massey and Howard accepted this evaluation, but most of Howard's "constituents" were primarily interested in saving their homes. He felt duty-bound to represent them. In addition, he believed that it would not hurt any other causes to make a fuss about the route line itself initially. If the Negro community began by opposing the route line, it would have a chance to air all its grievances and to dramatize the making of later concessions.

Howard did therefore protest the location of the freeway itself on every possible occasion, but he focused most of his attention on more limited objectives. Massey focused on the lesser objectives almost exclusively.

The first two of these objectives, helping the displaced Negroes and using their plight to advance the cause of open occupancy, were closely related. During the early months of 1956 all the city's major Negro organizations stepped up their continuing campaign for an open-occupancy ordinance. At the same time, Massey and Howard urged Mayor Dillon to request a City Council appropriation for the purpose of supporting relocation services for those displaced by the freeway. When the Planning Board took up the St. Anthony route proposal in May and June, Massey argued that the displacement of Negroes by urban redevelopment and the freeway made the passage of an open occupancy ordinance and the establishment of a relocation agency imperative.

None of these efforts bore immediate fruit at the local level. The City Council showed no disposition to pass an open occupancy ordinance. Moreover, some officials professed to believe that Negro leaders were exploiting the relocation issue as just one more way of obtaining publicity for the cause of open occupancy. Mayor Dillon refused to ask the City Council for relocation funds, but after Massey and Howard reiterated their concern on several occasions he did agree to appoint a committee to consider what might be done to help those displaced. The committee never became active, however. The Mayor later explained that he had been unable to find a chairman. The Planning Board heard Massey sympathetically, but suggested only that the Negro leaders prepare a formal letter explaining in more detail what they thought the serious problems were. The board then adjourned for the summer.

Considering themselves rebuffed at the local level, Massey, Howard and several other Negro leaders secured a meeting with Governor Orville Freeman and top Highway Department officials in the summer of 1956. The Negro leaders urged the Governor to assign responsibility for relocation to a state agency with legal authority and funds to act. The Governor said that he would refer the problem to the state Commission on Human Rights. The commission had no legal power of any kind and no budget.

The Negro leaders expressed their discontent vigorously in the last months of 1956 at hearings held by the Highway Department, the St. Paul City Council, and the State Senate's Public Highways Committee. Early in 1957 Governor Freeman created a subcommittee within the Human Rights Commission — the Committee on Housing and Relocation. It consisted of twenty-two members, most of whom were from St. Paul. Reverend Massey (a regular member of the Human Rights Commission), Howard, and a number of other Negro leaders were included. The committee held several meetings in its first months of existence, and decided that its first requirement was a census of the St. Paul families to be displaced by the freeway program in the next couple of years. The St. Paul Housing Authority, which already provided relocation assistance to families displaced by urban renewal projects, was anxious to make the survey but it had no funds available. The federal Bureau of Public Roads, which had estimated that a million people would be displaced nationally by the freeway program,[14] had a policy of contributing 90 per cent of the cost of relocation programs if the state contributed 10 per cent. The Highway Department reported, however, that no state agency had legal authority to contribute funds for this purpose. The next biennial legislative session was not scheduled until 1959, after most of the Negro families were scheduled to be displaced.

Finally, as the Highway Department began to file awards, the Housing Authority agreed to finance the census itself. It reported early in 1958 that right-of-way acquisition during 1958 and 1959 would displace 2,319 St. Paul families, and other public actions would displace another 592 families, for a total of 2,911. There were 399 Negro families in the total, with all but a handful scheduled to be displaced by the freeway during a period of several months early in 1959. Another 168 families had been displaced by urban renewal during the preceding five years. The total was well over one-fifth of the small Negro population of St. Paul.[15] The majority of the families—Negro and White—that would have to relocate were poor. Half had annual incomes of less than $3,500; more than five-sixths had incomes of less than $5,000. The Housing Authority offered to provide relocation assistance through 1959 for families displaced by the freeway program if the city or the Highway Department would pay it $30,000 to cover expenses. No money was found.[16]

During 1958 and 1959 the Housing Authority's Relocation Office did unofficially advise those threatened with displacement by the freeway who came in, but it could not actively seek homes for them. In addition, Timothy Howard informally sought them out. Aware that the lump sum payments were the largest amounts of money that many of the home owners had ever seen at once, he warned them of the ways in which they might be cheated if they bought homes in panic. When he heard of vacant dwelling units he passed the word along. He tried to ascertain which real estate men in the city could be expected to deal fairly with Negroes. Howard also maintained continuous contact with Highway Department officials. One of his objects was to persuade them that because of overcrowding within the Negro community and discrimination outside it, any given house represented a greater investment when owned by a Negro than it would when owned by a White man. It was imperative, Howard contended, for the department to use appraisers in the Negro community who were sympathetic to the Negro plight and who would let it affect their awards.

Looking back in 1960, Howard and most other Negro leaders agreed that the relocation had proceeded smoothly and with less inconvenience than anyone had expected. They believed that the department had used sympathetic appraisers and that its awards, for whatever reasons, had been generous. It had also declared a policy of permitting residents a full year in their homes, rent free, after awards were filed in court. The Negro leaders' original hopes, however, on which they had based their strategy, had not borne fruit. The great majority of those displaced had found it impossible to buy or rent outside the boundaries of the Negro district.[17] The city government had failed to provide official assistance for those displaced. It had also ignored the Negro community's pleas for an open-occupancy ordinance until 1959. Then, with the Negro leaders conducting an extremely vehement campaign, the St. Paul city attorney had written an opinion contending that the state constitution precluded local action on open occupancy. He had insisted that his opinion was devoid of political motivation and was offered as advisory only. Negro leaders had urged the City Council to pass an ordinance and let the courts decide, but they had been firmly (though politely) rebuffed. The Council had refused even to discuss the issue.

Massey's and Howard's third objective, after relocation and open occupancy, was to control the impact of the design of the freeway on the Negro district. Their primary concern in this regard was that the freeway might be elevated as it passed through part of the district. The Highway Department's preliminary profile as of early 1956 showed the freeway elevated over Lexington Parkway and Victoria Street, the two major north-south streets in the western half of the Negro neighborhood. Department personnel claimed that economic considerations might make at least this amount of elevation unavoidable. The land was low-lying, and drainage would be expensive if the freeway were built below existing sewers. Moreover, it was normal procedure in building roads to balance cut and fill between depressed and elevated sections. It cost money otherwise to haul away the unneeded earth. The cost of depressing the section shown as elevated in the profile might be as much as $1 million.

Massey, Howard, and their associates envisioned a raised freeway as a massive ugly barrier running through their neighborhood. They thought that rubbish would collect under it and that hoodlums would terrorize citizens who had to traverse the underpasses at night. They noted that the grass slopes next to a depressed freeway might muffle the noise and channel the fumes skyward to some extent, but that an elevated freeway would not. They pictured vehicles in accidents on an elevated freeway as occasionally escaping onto adjoining streets. The blighting effect of an elevated freeway on residential property, they said, would surely extend several blocks on either side, and the Negro district itself extended no further than that.

As noted earlier, the City Planning Board took up the St. Anthony route proposal in May and June of 1956. Massey acted as the Negro spokesman. After demanding passage of an open-occupancy ordinance and establishment of a relocation agency, he expressed the view that an elevated highway in particular would ruin what remained of the Negro neighborhood. Loeks reminded the board that he had previously mentioned the possibility that depression might be desirable. He believed, however, that city engineer Shepard might be inclined to favor elevation if the Highway Department found that engineering considerations made it necessary.[18] The board confined itself to asking Massey for a formal letter stating all the positions of the Negro community in detail. The Negro leaders did prepare a letter, which the board considered at its October meeting. The board did not take a position on the relocation and open-occupancy issues, but it authorized Loeks to send a letter in its name recommending depression of the freeway in the Negro district to the extent feasible in engineering terms.

The Negro leaders, fearing that the Highway Department might not give the Planning Board recommendation sufficient weight, continued to press for some stronger official commitment by the city. They demanded and secured a hearing before the full City Council in the fall of 1956. At this meeting, Commissioner Marzitelli of the Department of the Public Works — St. Paul had a commission form of government; each commissioner both sat on the City Council and headed an executive department — proposed that the matter be referred to a special committee representing the Department of Public Works, the Planning Board, and the Traffic Engineering Office, with their report to constitute the city's official position upon approval by the City Council. This proposal was adopted.

Before the committee had a chance to formulate its views, the Highway Department's first public hearing on the St. Anthony freeway occurred in December 1956. The department's spokesman noted that they still had only a preliminary profile to discuss, because engineering consultants to prepare a detailed design of the St. Anthony freeway had not yet been appointed. Massey argued, as he had previously, that if the freeway had to run on St. Anthony Avenue it should certainly be depressed through the whole Negro district so as to protect adjacent properties. The Rondo-St. Anthony Association as a whole went on record as opposed to the St. Anthony route but as very anxious to have the freeway depressed if the route were adopted over its objections.

Two weeks after the Highway Department hearing, City Engineer Shepard advised former Chief Engineer Kipp of the department, who was now a consultant to the department, that he thought depression would be desirable if it could be afforded. (Shepard later recalled that this did not represent a change of position for him, only a slight shift of emphasis.) When the department selected its engineering consultants for the St. Anthony freeway in March, Shepard wrote in a similar vein to Chief Engineer Zimmerman of the department.

Meanwhile, Timothy Howard had independently continued his campaign for depression at the Highway Department. He had been told, he said, that the Bureau of Public Roads would be very unlikely to sanction a million-dollar expenditure for depressing the freeway. Hearing one day that a high bureau official was in St. Paul, Howard cornered him and was told that the bureau probably would not object to the expenditure if the Highway Department recommended it. Howard told Shepard of this, and Shepard agreed to investigate the matter more intensively by writing his friend, the city engineer of Detroit, to ask about that city's experience with elevated highways. His letter, dated March 13, 1957, said in part:

> In connection with the planning and construction of the Interstate Highway system in St. Paul, we are confronted with a problem of whether or not the highway shall be depressed or raised. In some locations physical conditions definitely determine the issue; in others, the matter of complete depression has been weighed by the Highway Department as against a balancing of cut and fill. In the particular instance which I have in mind: namely, the intersection of the Interstate system on St. Anthony Avenue with Lexington Parkway, depression, which I believe to be preferable, will require the wasting of nearly a million cubic yards of dirt.
>
> I am advised that over the years in which your Detroit expressways have been planned, a general policy of depression has been adopted. Will you kindly advise as to the principal reasons for the adoption of such a policy and also as to whether or not any particular problems were involved in the wasting of dirt.

The response, received early in April, noted that elevated highways in Detroit had created serious noise, fume, and crime problems. This answer apparently helped to convince Shepard that the matter was important. He decided to make this one of the few issues on which to recommend that the city stand firm. The Highway Department thereafter raised no serious questions about the desirability of depression, though it delayed making a firm decision (on the ground that economic questions still remained) for some time.

Finally, with Shepard clearly in favor of depression and the Highway Department agreeing that depression was desirable in principle, the doctrine that freeways in residential areas should be depressed received formal public expression in June 1957 with the appearance of the Planning Board booklet, *The Proposed Freeways for St. Paul.* In it Loeks wrote that although it was regrettable when freeways passed through residential neighborhoods, such routing was sometimes unavoidable. There was, however, no need for alarm in these cases; if the freeway were depressed and frequent bridges built over it, "the divisive effect on the neighborhood can be less than that of a moderately heavily traveled city street." The effect on property values of a depressed freeway with gradually landscaped slopes alongside it was "not too different from a narrow park strip; in view of the well-known beneficial effect of park areas on residential values it appears the net result of such a highway design would be reasonably favorable."

Thus, some social consequences of running freeways through residential neighborhoods did receive consideration, although not until late in the planning process. The task of dealing with these consequences fell primarily to engineers rather than to politicians or planners. Perhaps for this reason, they were articulated essentially as aesthetic rather than social problems. The Negro leaders found it discouraging that their only important victory had been on the issue of depression, and they attributed the decision to depress almost solely to the continous pressure they had brought to bear. Loeks agreed that they had done well on the depression issue. He noted, however, that he had joined them before any other public official, that he had spoken favorably of depression to other officials at every opportunity, and that the Planning Board had been the first city agency to go on record in favor of depression. He felt that it was impossible to know whether the final decisions would have been any different if pressures had never been exerted, if he had never used his persuasive powers, and if the Planning Board had not blazed the trail for other city agencies at the level of public expression. He did feel certain that his "non-antagonistic" mode of operation had constituted an intelligent and sensible approach to a highly complex and potentially explosive situation. City Highway Coordinator Shepard contended that the pressures exerted had had virtually no effect and that he had expressed himself officially in favor of depression almost as early as Loeks. He had always hoped that the depression would be feasible, he said, and his decisions throughout had been based on engineering and aesthetic, not political, considerations.

Other Reactions

The St. Paul Negro community was not the only group to react unfavorably to aspects of the intercity (St. Anthony) freeway in 1956 and the years immediately thereafter, and several other controversies arose.

One had to do with the impact of the freeway on related streets in western St. Paul. Snelling Avenue was three-fifths of the way from downtown St. Paul to the western city limit. From Snelling to the city line, the freeway would run along the northern edge of St. Paul's greatest concentration of middle- and upper-class neighborhoods. Home-owners' associations in several of these neighborhoods became vocal in 1957 and 1958 when they realized that two freeway interchanges were planned between Snelling Avenue and the city line. Two streets, previously moderate traffic carriers, were suddenly to become major arteries. The increased traffic and any street widenings that became necessary threatened considerable annoyance and perhaps eventual dislocation to property owners along these streets. Parents of children who had to cross either of these streets on their way to school were concerned about safety aspects. Highway Department officials contended that the neighborhood as a whole would benefit, because total north-south traffic in western St. Paul would remain constant and it would now be concentrated on two streets whereas it had previously been dispersed over many. Local residents were not mollified, however, because they believed that the freeway would generate enough new traffic to cancel this benefit quickly. In support of their position, they cited the Planning Board's 1957 booklet, which had observed that

> freeways will generate traffic which previously did not exist. When a new high-speed, congested-free route is opened, many people will find they can drive to their destinations in shorter time and with greater ease and comfort than before, and with the result that more people will be induced to drive.[19]

Highway personnel assigned to deal with the residents vigorously rejected this view. Along with supporters of highway construction throughout the nation, they insisted that highways themselves were not traffic generators. They inclined to feel that the whole controversy was essentially a public relations problem. The city officials immediately concerned with highway matters agreed. In truth, however, the department was not in a position to do much for the distressed residents even if it had accepted their forecast. The traffic engineering need for the two interchanges was undeniable. Snelling Avenue was already congested. If all the freeway traffic destined for parts of St. Paul west of Snelling were dumped on it, the resulting congestion would be intolerable. Moreover, vehicles coming from west of the city line would be forced out of their way.

A second controversy had to do with the impact of a section of the intercity freeway on the Prospect Park neighborhood in Minneapolis. Residents of the neighborhood asked simply that the freeway be placed *on* a right-of-way currently used as a railroad spur line, rather than adjacent to it. They contended that their proposal would save several hundred fine homes and would thereby serve some important social objectives.

Prospect Park was the only family neighborhood within walking distance of the University of Minnesota. Many of its residents were faculty members. Another portion of them were occupants of a public housing project, the only one ever built in Minneapolis outside the Negro section. The residents had deliberately permitted the project to be placed in their neighborhood — their alderman could have prevented it — hoping to set an example for others in the city. They now maintained, contemplating the projected freeway, that the Highway Department's plan would leave the neighborhood 50 per cent middle class and 50 percent project residents. It could not long survive as an "integrated" community with that ratio, they said. Middle-class residents would move out, leaving a predominantly lower-class and Negro neighborhood behind them. Not only would a noble experiment have failed, but another of the nation's big city universities would be plunged into a "neighborhood problem." The consequences in terms of the university's attractiveness to students and faculty and of its evening activities would be difficult to calculate. The consequences for the city's tax base would also be noticeable, as its supply of attractive middle-class homes would be diminished by several hundred units.

The Governor of Minnesota, Orville Freeman, was a former resident of Prospect Park. He took a personal interest in the threat to the neighborhood posed by the freeway, but he knew that railroads had the right of condemnation in Minnesota and would merely condemn a new right-of-way if the spur were taken. If any efforts were made to prevent them from doing so, the result would be prolonged legal suits and intense lobbying by the railroads at the State Capital. Freeman therefore did not believe that it would be feasible to build at ground level or below on the railroad property. He wrote the state highway commissioner a confidential note, however, asking whether the freeway could be elevated above the spur line. The commissioner replied that building over the tracks would bring about "benefits desirable and real for the community," but that such an approach would be "economically unsound from the standpoint of funds available for trunk highway improvements." In other words, the highway budget was tight, and its purpose was to improve traffic service, not to conserve middle-class neighborhoods. The exchange between the governor and the commissioner was never made public.

The department maintained in its dealings with the residents of Prospect Park simply that sound engineering principles had dictated its original recommendation. It apparently persuaded a good many of the residents. The controversy gradually died without any concessions having been made by the department.

A third controversy had to do with the impact of the intercity freeway on business in downtown St. Paul. Until 1957, St. Paul's downtown retailers and property owners were ardent proponents of the freeway program. They reasoned that traffic congestion was a major cause of downtown decline and that improved access was the key to revival, or even survival. They overlooked, or preferred to ignore, the possiblity that the most important consequences of the freeway might be to accentuate the trends toward urban sprawl and downtown decline.[20] Between the 1948 and 1954 censuses of business, as "sprawl" had become the dominant pattern of Twin Cities development even without the aid of new freeways, retail sales in the St. Paul central business district had — whether coincidentally or not — declined by 15 per cent (in constant dollars).

Most students of urbanism believed that highway improvements encouraged urban sprawl by making possible commuting from greater distances in any given travel time. Suburban residents tended to drive to work and to shop, in part because frequent and inexpensive transit services were impossible to sustain in low-density residental areas. Transit services had traditionally converged on downtown, making radial travel far easier than circumferential travel for most urban residents. For the driver, however, free parking at his destination tended to be more significant than central location, or even distance. Consequently, shopping services and employment tended to follow residents to the suburbs, seeking cheap land near major highways. Moreover, as residential sprawl continued, a larger and larger proportion of central area employees and shoppers would rely on their automobiles to bring them downtown. A survey published by the City Planning Board in 1958 would show that the number of *persons* entering the central business district each morning had increased by only about 25 per cent since 1944, but the number of *vehicles* had increased by 150 per cent. The city's traffic planning in the late 1950s was based on an estimate that traffic converging on downtown would increase by only 50 per cent more to 1980. If the rise were much greater, highly expensive street improvement and peripheral parking ramp projects were expected to become necessary. No money for them was in sight.

Consequently, there was reason to believe that unless great investment could be generated to make the central business district more attractive and less congested, the impact of the freeway on balance would be to harm downtown. No state or local agency encouraged businessmen to think seriously about this prospect, however, until 1958. The Highway Department emphasized the importance of access to downtown and denied that highway construction bore any relationship to such phenomena as urban sprawl and the decline of public transportation, except that all reflected popular preferences. The city's engineers agreed with this position. The city's planners did not, but they kept their views on this subject within the official family. In their 1957 booklet on the freeways, they devoted almost a page to the question: "How can public transit make best use of the freeways?" They did not mention the possibility that the two might be in conflict. In view of the fact that the freeways were definitely on the way, they explained privately, it seemed reasonable to focus on the opportunities they created rather than on their unfortunate and unavoidable side-effects. The planners did not turn their attention to the general outlook for downtown until 1958. Then they maintained in a published survey and economic analysis[21] that great investment was needed to improve the attractiveness of the downtown area. They noted, however, that such action would, if successful, bring about an "unprecedented traffic demand in the core area." Downtown businessmen received the report antagonistically because it publicized a number of unfavorable economic trends. Ironically, therefore, even it failed to spur much serious thought about the future requirements of downtown economic health.

An event had already occurred in 1957, however, which, although it had not involved sprawl beyond the city limits, had significantly reduced the enthusiasm of downtown businessmen for the freeways. For some years St. Paul's largest department store had been Montgomery Ward's, situated on University Avenue midway between the central business districts of St. Paul and Minneapolis. It had a vast parking lot surrounding it. The freeway was destined to pass a quarter of a mile from the store, making it more than ever accessible from all parts of the metropolitan area. In 1957 the St. Paul Housing and Redevelopment Authority sold a 24-acre tract in its Western Redevelopment Area to Sears Roebuck for construction of a retail complex comparable to Ward's. The freeway was scheduled to pass adjacent to the tract, which was itself adjacent to the major state government office buildings but not within easy walking distance of competing downtown stores. Government employees had long provided a large part of downtown retail trade.

When downtown businessmen learned of Sears's plans, they were outraged. One group of them brought an unsuccessful legal suit challenging the basic principle of urban redevelopment — acquisition of land by government for resale to private developers, often at noncompetitive prices. They simultaneously hired planning consultant Victor Gruen to propose an alternative freeway route line. Gruen came up with a proposed route line that cut across the planned Sears parking lot. It was received unfavorably, however, by both the Highway Department and the city's own engineers. They noted that it would serve traffic bound for downtown less adequately than the original route line, and that it would require substantially larger collateral expenditures by the city.

The reaction of downtown businessmen came too late, and although their legal suit brought urban renewal work in St. Paul to a halt for two years, they obtained no concessions. When it became apparent that further protest could only postpone freeway construction, not alter the route, many downtown businessmen gloomily urged an end to obstructionism. If there must be a freeway in the present location, they said, let us at least have it before Minneapolis has its freeway.[22]

The groups that had occasion, for one reason or another, to oppose some aspect of the intercity freeway never joined forces. The Negro community, the Prospect Park community in Minneapolis, the neighborhoods concerned about the interchanges in western St. Paul, George Herrold, and the downtown businessmen opposed to the Sears Roebuck store all sought objectives that not only did not conflict, but that might have been coordinated to form the basis of a single intercity route proposal. Herrold supported the businessmen, recognizing that the Gruen proposal fit in better than the Highway Department's plan with his own northern route proposal; but his interest in potential allies appears to have been unique. The Highway Department managed to deal with each irate group individually, and to focus attention primarily on traffic data and approved techniques of route location. It apparently convinced many of those who attended its meetings that even though they might be inconvenienced by the freeway plan, the traffic data left no doubt as to the interest of the entire public. The department's success in this endeavor could not help but sap the will to battle of the groups concerned. Moreover, each irate group was interested in a different section of the freeway. People who rejected the Highway Department's arguments concerning their own source of dissatisfaction were likely to accept easily its arguments concerning someone else's.

Finally, the Highway Department's carefully cultivated image of rocklike strength plus amiability seemed to have persuaded many otherwise intractable opponents that pleading would prove more effective than fighting. The strategy of pleading assumed that the department could not be *forced* to do anything; therefore it was incompatible with the formation of alliances. In reality, neither the strategy of pleading nor the strategy of fighting (when indulged in by particular groups, such as downtown businessmen in St. Paul or Prospect Park residents in Minneapolis) ever induced the department to move a route line or relocate an interchange.[23] The Negro leadership's persistent pleading may have been responsible for the official decision to depress the freeway as it passed through their neighborhood. The plans still provided, however, for elevation of the freeway as it passed through other neighborhoods whose residents had abjured organized action altogether. The Negro leadership could also claim that it had induced the department to give displaced Negro residents generous prices for their homes, plus a year of rent-free occcupancy. The department found these financial inducements to peaceful acceptance of its plans so useful, however, that they were soon extended to all Minnesota residents threatened with displacement.[24]

Conclusion: Standards and Political Influence

The relative influence of engineering and city planning considerations on decisions concerning the intercity freeway illustrated a fairly simple point: clarity of standards and strength of conviction were extremely important political variables. When standards were clear, and a profession felt confident that they were right or "the best available," conscientious men could look to them for guidance and take on from them the energy that flowed from unclouded conviction. If those who proposed a project were perceived as moral and realistic men, their passionate conviction as technicians was likely to persuade doubting laymen to support their project. The formula was not perfect, of course. The project might seem too expensive, or it might threaten important vested interests or sacred beliefs. Some other group of technicians might testify passionately against it. But observers of politics had long recognized that, other things being equal, the political value of having a clear sense of direction and honest conviction was substantial.

It was a crucial advantage of the highway engineers in freeway disputes that they possessed and believed implicitly in a set of clear normative propositions, applicable to the most important of their problems and convincing to the vast majority of the people with whom they had to deal. The most important of these propositions, in their general order of priority, were the following:

(*1*) Highway improvements were desirable. Although a saturation point was conceivable, St. Paul was so far from it that one could say with confidence that the cost of foregoing new highways was almost always higher than the cost of building them.

(*2*) The location of highway routes should be determined according to engineering criteria, of which by far the most important were traffic service and cost.

(*3*) The articulate public should never be confused with the entire public. The former should be won over to the department's point of view, if possible, but not at the cost of traffic inefficiency, excessive expense, or undue delay.

(*4*) It was preferable, engineering considerations being equal, not to build a highway through a residential neighborhood or very far from existing investment, since the highway would tend to stabilize existing investment if built near it, while it might bring about costly shifts of economic patterns if built elsewhere. Engineering considerations were, however, seldom equal. Since centers of heavy investment were generally major traffic generators, there was seldom any question of building far from them. As there were usually no vacant corridors of land near such centers, it was sometimes necessary — more candidly, less expensive — to go through the residential neighborhoods that surrounded them. In such cases, it was reasonable to show the utmost consideration for those inconvenienced: e.g., by landscaping the road as attractively as possible, by giving displaced home-owners fair and prompt conpensation for their property, by allowing them more than ample time to find new homes, and by building pedestrian overpasses and underpasses at locations chosen by the neighborhood's own leaders.

Highway Department engineers later explained that they had seen no reason to lament the side-effects of progress. They admitted that change inevitably hurt some people but maintained that great nations had never been built by foregoing progress to pamper people. Those hurt by any project should be treated fairly and kindly, they explained, but should never be allowed to obstruct projects designed to benefit everyone.

The engineers did not have to worry about the allocation of all public resources or the abstract meaning of progress. They had only to ask themselves whether highway building was a significant contribution to progress, and they responded affirmatively and unhesitatingly. Of all the groups involved in this narrative, the engineers were the least susceptible to political pressure. Their pride in their techniques permitted them to scoff publicly at irate interest groups, and they pointed out that any change in plans to satisfy self-interested groups would cost taxpayers and drivers unnecessary millions of dollars. So long as the owners of property along the freeway right-of-way received fair compensation, they could only be protesting to safeguard their own convenience or, as in the case of the slum speculators, their immoral profits. In the first case, the property owners' convenience should not be allowed to outweigh the convenience of millions of drivers for years to come; in the second, society had no moral obligation to satisfy their demands.

Highway engineers emphasized that traffic and cost data were quantitative and impartial. They believed they were able, therefore, to prove that they had selected the highway routes without favoritism toward any group or interest. The department enjoyed an additional advantage, although one it did not boast about — traffic and cost data could be compiled without time-consuming consultation with the public. Such data were conclusive, while public consultation was seldom so. One could never be sure which interests had failed to appear at the hearings, nor which might appear if a new proposal were made. The only thing one could be sure of was that the general public had been inadequately represented.

The Highway Department was not completely unbending, but it had to guard itself against the appearance of weakness. So many people were going to be inconvenienced by the freeway that the first sign of "softness" by department officials would open the floodgates. The department had to deal more candidly, however, with the governing bodies of the state's large cities, which had their own disinterested engineers. Consequently, the department made its concessions only to those interest groups that were championed by their own local governments.

Department officials knew, of course, that the local mayors and councilmen were themselves in an embarrassing position. Virtually any change in plans intended to appease one set of constituents would antagonize some other set. Local officials had no desire to alienate any group, and therefore they tended to deny that they had any voice in freeway planning. When any group approached the Highway Department, it received courteous but firm treatment. Occasionally, when some group became particularly adamant, the department induced local officials to defend the engineers' position.

To department officials, this method of handling complaints was not only the most practical but also the most ethical possible. If every pressure group were granted the concessions most desired by it, they said, public satisfaction would probably be no greater, while public officials would constantly be accused of favoritism. In short, Highway Department engineers who reflected on their position generally concluded that ethics and engineering, in most cases, simply happened to coincide.

Next in certainty that his position was righteous was George Herrold. In some ways he was even more certain than the engineers, but his assurance was less convincing to others. In part, his inability to persuade others was due to the situation and his own personality. It was also due to the nature of his standards.

Herrold was fighting what he perceived as a federal-state offer to spend $400 million in the Twin Cities area and well over $100 million in St. Paul alone, in return for nothing but freedom to do so in accord with "sound engineering principles." Had the federal and state governments offered the city the same sum of money and told the city to spend it "rationally," the question of whether to spend any portion thereof on highways would have been approached in quite different fashion. As it was, local officials had the choice of taking the whole sum for freeways or taking nothing. Furthermore, highway congestion was a problem about which many voters had strong feelings.

Herrold had no standards that he could say he *always* applied to highway proposals. Because he also had virtually no resources for acquiring statistics to bolster his recommendations, he was generally limited to examining data made available by others and pointing out implications that they had ignored or de-emphasized. When he discussed possible repercussions not clearly pointed to by Highway Department traffic and cost analyses, he generally had no means of proving that they would occur; in many cases highway officials denied that they would. When highway officials admitted that certain repercussions *would* occur, Herrold had no general standards to cite in support of his judgment about their importance. He could only assert his opinion and let the engineers assert theirs. Without some invocation of general standards, the public could not understand the dispute.

The Highway Department could set plausible specific standards for the amount of traffic service needed to justify each unit of expenditure. Herrold, on the other hand, wanted to bring in any other values whenever he believed they were important. Although he recognized that his beliefs did not add up to a tight theoretical system and that some critics thought his policy views stemmed from nostalgia for the horse-and-buggy age, his conviction did not waver. The components of decency, he felt, did not change overnight; they did not have to be systematized to acquire validity and technical computations should not be allowed to obscure them. An engineer himself by training, Herrold was not awed by engineers or engineering competence. The automobile was merely a gadget of convenience, he believed, and tens of thousands of people should not be put out of their homes simply to save drivers minutes and pennies. His experience told him that many sets of road improvements in the past had been treated as "final solutions" — and that each had brought more unpleasant and costly congestion to the city. The whole approach, he thought, was a cruel distortion of the meaning of progress.

Herrold's standards could not be analyzed as a "system," but he believed in them and insisted that he was more capable of expressing the public interest than were local politicians. In pursuit of his mission, he rather disdained political caution. To his successors, however, Herrold's career proved that "those who speak too frequently and dogmatically, and who ignore the requirements of political prudence, cannot accomplish anything as planners."

C. David Loeks lacked Herrold's generalized sense of righteousness. There appeared to be three major reasons why this was so. First, Loeks felt a need to justify his recommendations in terms of systematic and well-articulated normative theories, but his profession had not made much progress in developing such theories since Herrold's day. Second, Loeks's standards of empirical theory and research required to support strong policy views were as high as those of the engineers, but his financial and manpower resources were hardly less limited than Herrold's had been. And third, Loeks felt a more compelling obligation than Herrold had to nurture the planning function's store of good will in the community. Each of these factors tended to sap Loeks's sense of conviction on most issues.

Loeks fully appreciated the paradox that although his profession enjoined him to plan comprehensively, it did not provide him with a comprehensive set of criteria for making value choices. He attributed the lack of systematic planning theory to the diffuseness of planning objectives. This was not very helpful, however. He understood that he needed such criteria before he could successfully argue against specialists' recommendations in their own fields. It was necessary to present alternatives and demonstrate their superiority, not merely to argue abstractly that many values should be considered. Yet Loeks had scarcely more resources than Herrold had had for conceiving independent alternatives. His standards of theory and research prevented him from taking his own capacities seriously in this area. One might add that the whole planning profession seemed to have been similarly inhibited in developing a distinct viewpoint on highway matters. It rather tended to accept the basic highway engineering viewpoint and to argue, if at all, about occasional and highly marginal (though important to the individuals affected by them) design details.

The depression controversy may be taken as illustrative. Loeks felt that the Highway Department's original proposal to elevate part of the freeway in the Negro neighborhood was a rather clear-cut instance of insensitivity to social values. It aroused him to opposition more than any other issue involving the freeways that arose during his tenure as St. Paul planning director. To the Highway Department the issue of elevation or depression was extremely marginal, however. More to the point, it was marginal from the standpoint of land-use planning: that is, in the context of the overall impact on land use of the whole St. Paul freeway program.

Loeks did not consider himself obligated to assert jurisdiction over subjects simply because their significance for planning objectives was great. He did feel obligated, however, to tell the unvarnished truth when his opinion was asked and to mention courteously to the officials directly responsible when it occurred to him that obvious injustice was likely to flow from one of their projects. Loeks tried to keep his unsolicited references to injustive at the level of quiet suggestion. He said that he believed his capacity to do good would increase proportionately with his willingness to let others get the credit. This was reasonable, but it was also true that Loeks had no theoretical basis for *arguing* with officials who might maintain that the obvious injustices to which he called attention were unavoidable — that the expense of avoiding it was justifiable — he had no professional standard to help him in determining what his political obligations were. Thus, even on the fairly simple issue of depression, the Planning Board qualified its recommendation by noting that it might not be feasible in engineering (a euphemism for "economic") terms.

This is not to say that Loeks or the staff he was gradually building up lacked ideas about how cities should be laid out. Their profession did provide them with such ideas, but not with standards for determining when and how to strive for their effectuation. Planners recognized that many important aspects of life had no price because they could not be bought or sold. They seemed to have made progress, however, in defining these aspects, discovering how they were affected in specific situations, or evaluating their importance. Consequently, planners in St. Paul were more or less forced to accept on faith the Highway Department's assumption that other effects of the freeway besides those involving traffic would somehow "balance off" or prove beneficial on balance. Lacking conviction that another plausible viewpoint was available, they accepted the engineering point of view — except on a few matters of detail — as their own.

It was possible, of course, to contend that planners and highway engineers independently agreed on all except matters of detail. Loeks himself believed that he had brought a distinct point of view to the discussions of detail in which he had engaged. He also thought that he had probably had some influence on the highway engineers' thinking. He pointed out that one does not leave a public record — may not even leave a record in men's minds —when he exercises influence by subtle and continuous suggestion. Perhaps Loeks had served the cause of comprehensiveness better than a case writer could know.

NOTES

1. In practice, the Bureau of Public Roads almost never adopted standards except on the recommendation of the American Association of State Highway Officials. Approval and promulgation by the bureau, however, was necessary to give them binding status and thus to ensure uniformity throughout the nation.

2. Some exceptions to this pattern were the sections of Routes 12 and 61 that had been planned during the 1930s and constructed at the close of World War II. The Mississippi Street development, later incorporated as part of the interstate system, had been planned initially in the 1930s.

3. Data gathered in the St. Paul Central Business District Traffic Survey, published in 1946, had also supported the St. Anthony route.

4. At this point in the original version of this chapter a section appeared entitled "Development and Application of Traffic Forecasting Techniques," approximately twelve pages in length. It was noted as optional reading then and is omitted now in the interest of brevity.

5. A decade after completion of the 1949 survey, the city engineer of St. Paul told this writer that he thought traffic could still move about the same distances in the same time. He added that the freeway would reduce the commuting time to the city limits by only a few minutes because drivers would still have to make their way to its entrances on city streets.

6. The national administration was also pressing a policy of "no new starts" in the domestic public works field, but economic stabilization and defense had been the ostensible main purposes of the superhighway program according to official statements over the years.

7. For a lively and useful, if highly critical, account of the political pressures in favor of the highway program, see Daniel P. Moynihan, "New Roads and Urban Chaos," *The Reporter*, XXII, No. 8 (April 14, 1960), 13-20.

8. U.S. Congress, House, *Message From the President of the United States Relative to a National Highway Program*, 84th Cong., lst sess., 1955, House Doc. 93.

9. *Ibid.*, pp., 4, 7.

10. *Ibid.*, p. 7. The committee carried the profit calculation a step further citing the President's statement as follows: "'A simple dollar standard will not measure the "savings" that might be secured if our highways were designed to promote maximum safety . . . But whatever the potential saving in life and limb may be, it lends special urgency to the designing and construction of an improved highway network.'" The fact that automobile travel on the most modern superhighways involved accident rates many times higher than the national average for bus, train, and air travel was not mentioned.

11. Parenthetically, it may be noted that the Clay Committee's rough estimate of $27 billion as the total cost of the interstate program was revised to $41 billion by the Bureau of Public Roads in 1959. Early in 1965, the estimate was revised officially again, this time to $46.8 billion.

12. The distinction between design and location should be kept clearly in mind. The latter had been settled for all practical purposes in 1945 and 1946.

13. The Housing Authority published data on a much larger area which included the Negro district in mid-1959. The area contained a 2.8 percent of the city's land, 10 percent of its population, and 19 percent of its substandard dwelling units.

14. These people were expected to be disproportionately poor, because highway engineers sought low cost rights-of-way and public officials generally liked to see dilapidated buildings go.

15. About 2 percent of St. Paul's residents were Negro.

16. In its next regularly scheduled session, the legislature did authorize Minnesota cities to levy a one-tenth mill tax — worth about $25,000 annually in St. Paul — to support relocation services for people dislocated by public action. The St. Paul City Council enacted the tax rate in 1959 and designated the Housing Authority to provide the service.

17. The district had experienced some contiguous expansion, however.

18. On reading this, Loeks commented that he had believed that "necessary" was a relative term, the applications of which depended on judgments of priorities. He had thought that engineering and planning priorities might legitimately differ — even when the relevant "facts" were established — leading to differences of opinion between engineers and planners about what was "necessary." The author would add that, in the rhetoric of public life, the term "necessary" tends to be used to indicate that grounds for legitimate controversy are lacking.

19. Walter Blucher, then Executive Director of the American Society of Planning Officials, had made the point even more strongly as early as 1953: "Is there any instance in this country where a new expressway or highway or elevated street hasn't invited so much additional traffic as to almost immediately create congestion?" (*Problems of Decentralization in Metropolitan Areas*, Proceedings of the First Annual University of California Conference on City and Regional Planning, 1953 [Berkeley: Department of City and Regional Planning, University of California, 1954], p. 12.)

20. Blucher had written: "I am convinced that the expressways leading to the centers of our cities will be one of the most important instruments we have created toward the cities' decentralization. I marvel that downtown merchants are usually in the van in urging their construction" (*ibid.*, p. 13).

21. *St. Paul's Central Business District*, Community Plan Report 7, December 1958. This report was completed and published under the direction of Loeks's successor as planning director, Herbert Wieland.

22. It was expected that the freeway would be completed several years earlier in St. Paul than in Minneapolis, partly because no central Minneapolis plan existed. St. Paul did not have a

downtown plan either, of course, but the downtown was smaller and its problems were less complex. Also, Minneapolis planners were considering construction of ramp garages adjacent to the downtown freeway interchanges.

23. For a case study of an instance in which another state highway department was induced to move a route line, by a strategy of fighting, see Polly Praeger, "Extinction by Thruway: The Fight to Save a Town," *Harpers*, No. 1303 (December 1958), pp. 61-71.

24. While it was difficult to prove that the state was following a policy of paying generous prices, there was widespread agreement among local officials and the homeowners involved that the department's awards were higher than the properties taken would have brought on the open market. The law authorized payment only of "fair" prices, but appraising was not a precise skill.

11

1968: Getting Going, Staffing Up, Responding to Issues

Allen B. Jacobs

Nationally, 1968 was not a particularly good year for the United States. The light at the end of the Viet Nam tunnel went out with the *Tet* offensive, and President Johnson withdrew as a candidate amidst increasing discontent with the war. Martin Luther King and Robert Kennedy were murdered. Continued attempts to solve long-standing social problems through civil rights and social equity legislation and massive funding programs were often overshadowed by the violent nature of the times. The Kerner Commission report blamed racism for the riots that continued throughout the year in cities like Cleveland, Seattle, Gary, and Peoria. Most notable and noticed were the confrontations at the Democratic National Convention in Chicago. As the year drew to an end, Richard Nixon was elected President after an end-the-war-with-honor and law-and-order campaign.

The mood in San Francisco was both reflective of and distinctly different from the national mood. As in other places, antiwar demonstrations were commonplace. And the militancy of the nation's poor, especially the Blacks, who were demanding their fair share of rights, privileges, and wealth was mirrored in San Francisco. But unlike other major cities, San Francisco had three big minority groups: Blacks, Chicanos, and Chinese. Whether this meant that San Francisco was three times or one-third as militant as other cities is hard to tell. It made no difference to the poor that San Francisco's slums were not as bad as Detroit's or Pittsburgh's. They wanted jobs, they

Reprinted with permission from *Making City Planning Work*, by Allan B. Jacobs. Copyright © 1978 by the American Planning Association.

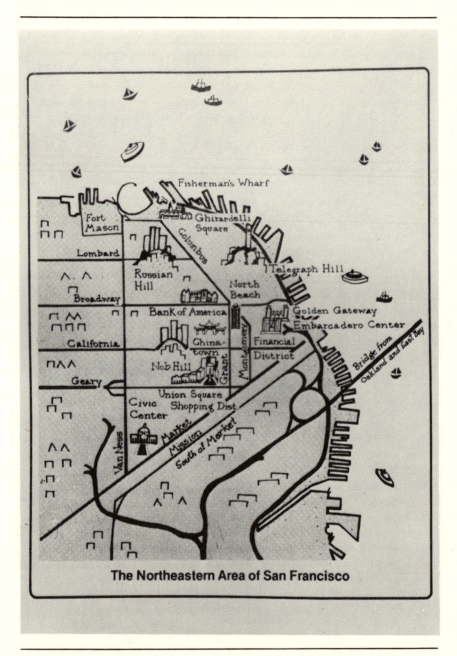

The Northeastern Area of San Francisco

11.1   The Northeastern Area of San Francisco (map designed by Jack Sidener and drawn by Heather Trossman).

wanted good housing they could afford, and they were tired of being pushed out of their homes for public works and redevelopment projects. They expressed their anger at every turn. One had merely to appear in public to be called a racist or bigot.

At the same time, however, this was the era in San Francisco of the hippies, the flower children, and love. It was a period of serious, youthful questioning of old values and life styles and of experimenting with new ways. It was a time for "drop-outs," bare feet, and parents searching for missing children in the Haight-Ashbury district. It was a period of antifashion fashions that soon became fashionable, a time when people were nice to look at. On Sunday, thousands went to "be-ins" at the Speedway Meadows in Golden Gate Park to eat, drink, look at each other, dance to rock bands under a low haze of pot smoke, and be watched by city police, who stood leisurely at the edges of the crowd. The flower children, it seemed, were a San Francisco invention, perhaps by way of Berkeley. Their love existed side by side with anger about social inequities and the war. San Franciscans tolerated, even nurtured them all.

However bad the problems were, the mood in San Francisco in 1968 was hopeful. One had a sense that the city was not nearly as bad off as its eastern and midwestern counterparts, that here problems could and would be solved. And no one was more optimistic or exuded as strong a "can do," "will do," and "things are not so bad" aura as the new mayor, Joseph Alioto. A bright, energetic, eminently successful lawyer and New Deal-type Democrat with strong labor backing, who could and would talk with enthusiasm, passion, and compassion on just about any subject, Alioto was accessible to everyone. He listened and seemed to understand the problems, and he gave promise of solutions. He had access to the Johnson administration and he was admired by local liberals, who appeared to have his ear. His deep roots in the Italian community stood him in good stead with most ethnic groups. His enthusiasm was contagious. San Francisco might have problems but they could be solved. There was no better place to be.

For reasons that I will never fully understand, I seemed to have had it "made" with the mayor from the beginning. Perhaps he and his staff had been advised, although I'm not sure by whom, that his city planner was one of the better department heads around and that he had a sense of the important issues in the city. Or it might have been because the planning department was quick to produce a list of 40 possible sites for mini-parks when he needed the information in a hurry. When the mayor asked for my professional opinions, I gave them to him without mincing words. When I first met him, I had the opportunity to recommend a new planning commissioner. I had not known that Mortimer Fleishhacker had supported the mayor's opponent, and I cannot even be certain that my strong recommendation had anything to do with his appointment, but Alioto did appoint him. Maybe we got along in those early days because we were both learning and because my lack of concern with what he might want to hear was matched by this own desire to hear and learn as much as possible. In any case, I was considered to be "one of the team" or "one of the inner circle," as a mayor's aide put it. I liked it. To be sure, I was not kidding myself about Alioto's being a planner's mayor. He was not. My initial sense was that he was highly development-oriented, even when development might be ill placed, and that he would not be terribly concerned with long-range views. His early addresses, in which he talked about his "Darwinian theory of urban development," confirmed my fears. But then, how many mayors are planners' mayors? One could wait for a long time for that happy situation.

In the meantime, it was personally pleasant and professionally important to be in the mayor's good graces. There were things to be done. This would be a year of responding to immediate issues while establishing a solid professional base in the community; of attracting high-quality staff; of establishing good working relationships with the Board of Supervisors and with the planning commission; of citizen involvement in citywide and neighborhood planning; of looking for opportunities to make planning more relevant, effective, and responsive; and of starting to roll on long-range programs. It would be much easier to get things done if the relationship with the mayor and his office were friendly rather than hostile or neutral.

In large measure, 1968 was a year of responding to immediate issues in a "best as can" way while simultaneously staffing up and initiating policies that might provide a better basis for day-to-day decisions and programs. We were still inadequately staffed, although we had added some people in 1967, and the quality of existing plans was, to my taste, less than adequate. So we "winged it" a lot in 1968, although not as much as in the previous year. We looked for opportunities to address the issues we had identified, to make city planning more relevant. And there were plenty of immediate issues.

During the year about 100 zoning cases came before the planning commission. Each one required a staff recommendation. They included proposals to change the zoning on a hilltop to prevent apartment house development and to convert the basement and garage of a home in a residential area to medical offices.[1] Although some cases were more important to the whole city than others, each one was critical to the applicants and the contestants and had to be responded to in that light.

By far the most significant zoning matter was one that had been previously decided by both the staff and the commission: the proposed major changes to the city's zoning ordinance, which would affect the downtown and adjacent areas. The proposal had been lodged in the planning committee of the Board of Supervisors since July 1967 and would finally be acted on in May 1968. The man who chaired the committee in 1967 was known as a proponent of increased downtown development. He was hard to contact and seemed uninterested. In 1968, the chairman was Ronald Pelosi, who was sympathetic to the ordinance and to city planning in general, but he was the minority member of the committee. We met with him whenever possible to bring him up to date and to convince him of the rightness of our course, hoping that he would persuade other new supervisors. On the whole, though, I was not confident. What I feared was that the supervisors and the city planners would become involved in a game, spending years shuttling amendments and changes back and forth. Meanwhile the passage of time would make the proposals meaningless and the staff would be debilitated. If that were to happen, all of my worst fears about zoning would be confirmed.

By chance, one or two developments that would be permitted under the proposed ordinance were not permitted under the existing zoning code. The sponsors of the new developments wanted some kind of action and helped persuade the committee to bring the matter before the full board for a debate and a vote.

The breakthrough came when the committee recommendations finally came out on May 10. The majority (two to one) proposals were in the form of a series of amendments to the new ordinance that would make it less in keeping with good planning than the old. I suspected the fine hand of the chamber of commerce had been at work.

Our views did receive public attention. On a totally separate matter I had called the chief editorial writer of the *Chronicle* to express my disagreement with the paper's position, but also to express my appreciation for the fairness and accuracy with which the paper had reported the views of the planning department. The writer, unaccustomed to such calls, thanked me and asked what I thought of the committee's proposed changes to our ordinance. I blurted out that I thought they were so bad I'd rather not have any ordinance at all. Both the editorial and the news story ("High Density Plan Hit by Alioto, Planning Chief") that appeared in the paper borrowed heavily from a memo we immediately sent to explain our position.

Mayor Alioto, although never briefed by me as to the details of our proposal, endorsed it rather than the committee's version after I explained to him that I thought it was reasonable. Personal conversations with supervisors indicated we might have a chance, especially if at a later date we would agree to include two or three of the small changes suggested by the committee. When the measure came to the floor of the Board of Supervisors, the most critical first vote was six-to-five against postponing action. This was followed by a string of six-to-five or seven-to-four votes against weakening amendments and finally by a six-to-five vote for the ordinance.[2] It was a major city planning victory, one that for the first time established a strong liberal bloc on the board. It was also the first time I had ever been in the position of strongly advocating a planning proposal that I had not prepared personally in the first place.

The biggest conflict of the year erupted over a proposal for development in the northern waterfront area at the foot of Telegraph Hill, the so-called International Market Center. The initial proposal was for a complex of buildings that would cover eight blocks and approximately 17 acres. It would include a wholesale home furnishings and apparel market center and a hotel that would be as tall as the nearby Coit Tower, a San Francisco landmark. Building the complex would require the closing and public vacation of some unused or unimproved streets. I was concerned that such an overall massive development was unsympathetic to the character of that part of the city. Together with our northern waterfront consultants, I also was concerned that new development not block historic views from or to Telegraph Hill, and further, that it allow room for a waterfront roadway we were contemplating. We advised the developers and their architects that we would oppose any street vacations unless they would comply with what we called "urban design terms of reference" for the site. They didn't take us too seriously. One well-known architect gave me a lecture on what was best for San Francisco, to which I replied that as long as he had a client in tow I was not interested in his views, since his interests were those of his client, not the city. He had trouble speaking to me again for six months.

The development proposal was announced with hoopla. I immediately denounced it and soon found myself in a meeting with both the developers and the mayor. The mayor, who was sympathetic to my concerns about views and about Coit Tower, advised the developers to pay attention to me. After that it was downhill. The developers agreed to most of our conditions, and we built them into a strong legal document that would govern all street vacations. Except for some residents of Telegraph Hill, everyone was happy. In a 12-hour public hearing that didn't end until two in the morning, the Board of Supervisors approved the projects subject to all of our proposed conditions.[3] The irony is that the project was never built. A lawsuit by Telegraph Hill opponents held up the project, and, by the time the suit was settled, changes in the financial climate made the project impossible. In any case, it had been a nice fight, and it provided yet another lesson about the nature of San Francisco.

By no means were all of our positions negative. As I noted earlier, I was a member of the Market Street Transit Task Force, which was involved in planning for the two-mile stretch of Market Street that would have to be reconstructed after the new subway was in place. The design proposed by the task force, with considerable aid from its consultants, included widening the sidewalks. But the public works people valiantly fought almost any proposal that would in any way hinder the automobile. They lost, though, and a $24 million Market Street bond issue—Proposition A—placed before the voters in the June election passed by almost 70 percent of the vote (146,657 in favor and 65,158 opposed). I wondered whether the people in any other city would vote, by that margin, to spend that kind of money to beautify two miles of street.

In 1968 the federal government declared Alcatraz Island to be surplus property. The rapidity with which public officials became public entrepreneurs was wondrous to behold. The city was supposed to be given first chance to buy at a cheaper price if it wanted the land for public purposes. But the feds, all in favor of selling to the highest bidder for a commercial venture, semed to discount the possibility that the city might be interested. I tried to impresss upon the mayor that it was the Board of Supervisors, not he, that was responsible for setting the kind of policy that would determine use of the island, and I also reminded the federal folk that the city, not they, would determine its ultimate use (and thereby influence its price). Although it was a practical impossibility, I remarked to one federal employee that we could zone the island for single-family housing, which would of course have a devastating effect on its value. He seemed to get my point.

Once the matter was in the hands of the supervisors they had to be convinced that it was proper to refer it to the planning department for a recommendation. They and the mayor preferred to deal directly with developers, one of whom, Lamar Hunt, wanted to build a space museum complete with an observation tower in the form of a space capsule. We got proposals from any number of would-be developers, and we had to hear them all. There were many trips to the island amidst proposals for a western Statue of Liberty, hotels, colleges, housing, and the inevitable gambling casino. An ex-guard who was working on the island as a custodian and guide thought it would make a good prison.

Our report, prepared with our consultants, called for retention of much of the open space and preservation of the older structures underlying the newer prison buildings. It also included a number of commercial recreational uses of the sort usually associated with tourism.[4] I had some personal misgivings about this part of the proposal and was angry with myself for not thinking of the idea that planning commissioners Kearney and Fleishhacker came up with: they favored just letting it be. The other commissioners agreed with them (and passed Resolution 6425 to that effect on September 12, 1969). But the mayor and the Board of Supervisors were running hard to find a use that would make the city lots of money. As the controversy continued into 1969, a local dress manufacturer, Alvin Duskin, placed a full-page announcement in the local newspapers opposing any commercial development of the island. His campaign was very successful; the public response forced the federal officials to take a go-slow attitude. Ultimately, Alcatraz was invaded by Indians and the government took it off the market.[5]

Another policy matter for the Board of Supervisors came up in 1968. Agents of the federal government planned to release three old fort sites: Forts Mason, Miley, and Funston. In part, it was intended by them that the property be used to solve local housing problems, although not necessarily for low-income people only. But it was hard to convince the mayor and his staff that this was indeed a policy matter. In fact, one of the mayor's aides, Jack Tolan, was negotiating directly with possible developers. In the meantime, the planning department was studying the best uses for the sites. Our report, *Forts Mason, Miley, and Funston*, proposed a combination of open space, housing for low-income and moderate-income people as well as market-rate housing, preservation of historic structures on the sites, and a major public educational use for one of the sites.[6] When the matter finally did get to a board committee, its members were furious that they had been by-passed and that a mayor's aide was negotiating directly with a developer. They voted to keep all of the sites as open space. Committee chairman Pelosi advised me, in an aside, that any proposal for development would have been rejected on principle. It was one of the first defeats by the board of a proposal by Mayor Alioto. Since our mixed-use proposals had been turned down, and since some socially oriented housing would not get built, I did not view it as a victory for city planning.

There were many other immediate issues to be dealt with in 1968. We were not lacking for things to do.

About a dozen of the professional staff members who were on hand when I arrived were proving to be as competent city planners as anyone might hope to meet anywhere. A few, such as Peter Svirsky, Bob Passmore, Peter Groat, Jim Paul, Jim White, Phoebe Brown, Tom Malloy, and Lynn Pio, were a lot more than competent. But overall, the staff was still not up to the caliber I wanted: there were too few people trained as city planners or as specialists in the areas of expertise that city planning required and too many people who looked at planning differently than I. Our staff did not have the technical skills to hold its own with other bureaucrats, especially those in the Department of Public Works, and we were not nearly as sharp as the staff of the Redevelopment Agency. Public presentations by staff members were too often weak and unsure, and we lacked experienced leadership and managerial skills. If we were going to establish a solid professional base in the community and get on with our work, we needed to attract good people to fill unstaffed positions as soon as possible.

There were two parts to attracting and hiring good city planners: finding them and persuading them that San Francisco would be a productive place in which to work, and getting them on the staff despite the civil service system.

That system was to prove a much more formidable hurdle than attracting good people in the first place.

San Francisco's civil service system was and is incredibly cumbersome and time consuming. It is not geared to attracting top people. The process of agreeing on qualifications; getting out announcements; preparing, administering, and grading written and oral exams (with appeals permitted and common at every step along the way) took forever. Exam questions, to be "fair" and "objective," were either of the factual or multiple choice variety. Questions like, "In what direction does the Seine River flow through Paris?" became famous. It was extremely difficult for anyone living outside the Bay Area to take exams. Employees' unions even protested required minimum

11.2 Drawing by Jack Sidener, reproduced with the permission of the San Francisco Department of City Planning.

qualifications for entry level positions on the grounds that those standards might later be used to prejudice minimum standards for promotive positions. If they passed the exams, existing employees almost always had priority over outside candidates when higher level openings occurred. The time between the announcement of an opening and the appearance of a list of those who passed the exam often was more than a year. In the interval, the most qualified people had long since taken other positions. I concluded that the good people who were already on the staff were there despite, not because of, the system.

Once a list of passing candidates was established, I had no choice in hiring, a policy that made it difficult to seek out and hire minority employees. That law has since been changed so that now a director may choose from the top three scorers, but back then the top scorer got the job. It was only during the six-month probation period that every employee served that I had the authority to fire anyone.

All of this was taking place during a period when jobs in city planning were plentiful, and the best applicants could pick and choose. For opening positions, the salary structure in San Francisco was anywhere from $1,000 to $3,000 less than was being offered by other big cities.

Although our approach to overcoming hiring barriers was by no means original (sometimes a system includes mechanisms, however dreary and time-consuming, to overcome its own excesses), our doggedness and perseverance may have been noteworthy. We hired people on what was called as "limited tenure" basis. This meant hiring, with Civil Service permission, on a temporary basis to fill vacant positions for which examinations were not yet in progress. We tried to get exams delayed so that people already hired would be better prepared to take them. Some exams would be postponed for years. We also tried to change the emphasis from written to oral exams. When exams were announced for positions that were already filled with top-notch but temporary professionals, we tried to influence the Civil Service staff to make the filing periods as brief as possible. I tried to create specialty positions to get the people I wanted.

Representatives of the employees' unions watched us carefully, and our moves were countered by their moves—appeals, attempts to do away with limited tenure hiring and the like. I had shouting matches with them in front of the Civil Service Commission, most of whose members I felt were overly sympathetic to the unions. At one Civil Service Commission meeting, attorneys for an employees' union accused me of cheating and lying. During one short period I made arrangements to have a lawyer—my personal attorney from a prestigious office—represent me. He would stand next to me and silently pass his card around. His presence seemed to inspire the Civil Service Commission to treat me more gently.

On one or two occasions we requested and received Mayor Alioto's assistance in influencing the staff of the Civil Service Commission to do things our way. One of these times involved an exam for my administrative assistant. The administrative assistant position was a professional position created at my behest. Bruce Anderson was filling it magnificently on a limited tenure basis, and he more than met the criteria that were important to me: compatibility, trust, and the ability to attend to the myriad details that are associated with the job of director. Ultimately, however, Anderson had to take an examination, and he feared that he had failed the written part because the questions were unrelated to the position (which was often the case on such exams). But I was not about to have anyone in that position who was not totally acceptable to me professionally and personally, and I told the mayor as much. Although Anderson's fear later proved ill-founded, I requested that the passing score be lowered by five to ten points. It took the mayor's influence on the head of Civil Service to do that, and it took more influence to get an oral examination board that was likely to listen to my admonition not to pass anyone who was unlikely to be personally acceptable to me.

The battles with Civil Service over testing, hiring, firing, promoting, setting qualifications, and determining proper salaries were continual and enervating. The rules always seemed to change, but they almost never became more flexible. I knew even then that hassles with Civil Service would be one of the reasons for ultimately quitting.

During this period, I went to an evening meeting of a supervisors' committee dealing with salary standardization to argue for higher pay for my staff. The chambers were jammed with city employees and their union representatives. I was the only department head present. At one point my ear tuned in on a union official making a case for the same pay for category X-1234 (or some such number) "Laundry Marker" as for Y-5678 "Laundry Packer" (or some such title). My mind skipped around; I wondered what a laundry marker looked like and whether he thought of himself as such. It occurred to me that in 1968 San Francisco was in the final stages of fixing a caste system not too dissimilar to the one that had dominated India for thousands of years. And the results might turn out to be the same. It was a depressing evening.

The immediate job was to attract bright, eager, challenging city planners. If a sense of purpose could be communicated to prospective employees, the Civil Service barriers could be overcome. Pat Cusick, my boss in Pittsburgh, had taught me years earlier never to promise or imply anything you can't deliver. And because I was dealing with other people's lives, I tried to be extremely cautious, even negative, in explaining the terms and conditions, and the pitfalls, of employment with the department. I suspect that people figured that things couldn't be as bad as I had pictured them, so they decided to take a chance. I must have given my speech about what brought me to San Francisco a hundred times: to have a chance to address real people's problems in a direct way, to try to make city planning more relevant than it had been in the operations of the city, and to build a high-quality staff. The promise of being given responsibilities equal to their talents was influential in attracting good people, as was the prospect of working on housing, neighborhood planning, and urban design issues—areas of concern to many city planning graduates at the time. The fact that we made little differentiation between long-range and immediate planning concerns, that people would be working on both together, was also attractive.

A lot of fine young people responded. Most of them were very inexperienced, and I had to keep reminding myself that at their age I had been inexperienced too, and that I still was, as far as being a planning director was concerned. I met and interviewed applicants at conferences; they came with recommendations from friends; and they walked in off the street, attracted by the prospect of living and working in a city that was something of a mecca for young people in the sixties. In 1968 I think I personally interviewed every job applicant.

Coincidence and good fortune played a role in the makeup of the staff. During the summer, two just-graduated city planners from the University of Pennsylvania, former students of mine, were in my office asking about jobs. One didn't interview Trixie Farrar and Dennis Ryan so much as they interviewed you. They were bright, questioning, suspicious, and frustrating. They also seemed to have zillions of other job offers. In response to a question, put in the form of a demand actually, about what we were doing in the areas of neighborhood and minority planning, and tiring before their barrage of unanswerable queries, I suggested that they come to a meeting that night in the largely Black South Bayshore area to see for themselves. We were to present alternative plans for the shoreline area and review the adequacy of local shopping facilities. The meeting was going well and was reasonably tranquil until one young man, in front of the crowd of 50 or so people, tried to take over. I sensed that if we were to be respected and effective in the community, I had better not back down. Shouts led to screams as we got closer to each other. Stupidly, I returned his threat of violence with a challenge, and the man left the room, to do what I'll never know. We may have "made it" in the community that night. I suspect that Trixie's call the next day, saying that she and Dennis would like to have jobs if they were available, was related to the previous night's theatrics. (Years later, in January 1977, Adam Rogers, the young man involved, was murdered in South Bayshore.)

Attracting a new assistant director proved to be more difficult. Both the Civil Service Commission and the Board of Supervisors had to be convinced to raise the status of the position, and its salary as well, and to postpone the exam for two years. The money to pay moving expenses would have to come from private sources, and two planning commissioners agreed to help out. Of course, finding the right person was the big job. It had to be an experienced big-city planner who was well-grounded professionally, especially in comprehensive and project planning, and who could operate knowingly among other high-level city hall technicians. Above all, I needed someone who could lead, inspire, and manage people, since almost half the staff would be under his, or her, direction on a day-to-day basis. Finding such a person took about a year. Finally, after turning the job down once, Dean Macris, with 10 years of experience in Chicago, where he was then assistant commissioner of development and planning, agreed to move to San Francisco.

Establishing and maintaining working relationships with the Board of Supervisors and the planning commission, as well as with the mayor and his people, ranked in importance with the development of the professional staff. They, along with the people of San Francisco, represent clients, and I looked at them in that way. They make decisions; they endorse policies and programs; in the short run, they are the keys to the effectiveness of city planning (the people as a whole being the keys in the long run). They can give and they can take away; and it was good to remember that the planning commission, figuratively, signed my pay check. It was important for the people who made up the board and the commission, and who held key positions in the mayor's office, to know the planners, to value us, to respect us, and to like us if that was possible. It would be beneficial too, if they sensed that we could help them.

I had no special program for endearing myself with the city's major policy makers. Our approach was simply to respond quickly and thoroughly to their requests and to say what we had to say regarding the physical planning of San Francisco in a clear, straightforward, and forceful manner. Our job was not only to present decision makers with thoughtful and clear alternative courses of action, based on as much research and data as we could put our hands on, including assessments of the consequences of the alternatives, but also to advocate, as strongly as necessary, what we thought was good city planning. If we had an ax to grind, it was for city planning. That meant that I was going to give my professional opinion often, regardless of the political ramifications. I assumed that was what my clients—the policymakers and the people— wanted. Besides, I was also a client to be satisfied. I did not want rotten decisions to come back to haunt me, especially if I knew they were politically rather than professionally inspired. It was important to be able to sleep well at night. I felt that a city planner should say what he had to say and have his bags packed in case his client didn't like the advice.

My wife and I did invite individual supervisors to small social gatherings. It seemed reasonable to get to know them and for them to get to know us. But if this was a strategy to gain influence, it wasn't a very good one. I never got around to inviting the supervisors I didn't like, and I didn't need influence with those we saw. The dinners did help form some lasting friendships, as did social evenings with the planning commissioners.

Another exception to my "professionalism" stemmed from the fact that many of the decisions, judgments, and recommendations that we were called upon to make were of marginal significance for city planning or physical development. A permit to use a vacant lot for a fair, the expansion of a grocery store in a residential area, the conversion of an unused church, surrounded by houses, to a small, neighborhood-oriented dance center, or even minor changes in zoning are a few of many examples. My rule was not to compromise on issues where an important planning idea or principle was involved. But I was not opposed to deciding marginal or insignificant items in a manner that would gain for the planning department the most currency—by which I might mean support, stature, friends, future influence, or good will. There was any number of groups or individuals with whom to gain currency, and at any one time one might be more important than another. These would include individual property owners, neighborhood groups, elected officials, planning commissioners, fellow bureaucrats, design professionals, and others. The trick was not to fool yourself into concluding that something of importance was really of no significance.

Our approach seemed to work with the supervisors. Their meetings, in committee and at the full Monday afternoon sessions, were relatively open, and individual supervisors continued to be accessible. So long as we presented our material forcefully and clearly distinguished between fact and opinion, they were prepared to listen. Neither did they respond negatively to our taking strong advocacy positions. One or two supervisors were noted for their propensity to berate, insult, interrupt, and otherwise publicly abuse repre- sentatives of various departments. I found that it was not necessary to take that abuse and that it was acceptable behavior to match insults and false assertions with interruptions, denials, and assertions of one's own. As long as one was not discourteous to start, the board seemed to enjoy a scrap. Sometimes the scrapping was humorous. Supervisor William Blake took every opportunity to remind his fellows, and the public, that the board had paid my moving expenses, something unheard of, and that it would do well to pay my expenses back East. I told him that I expected him to come up with the money on the day after he got the planning commission to fire me.

Contacts with members of the mayor's staff were more than cordial. They were approachable and helpful. It was a straight and uncomplicated relationship. They assumed that I knew my field, and they sought my counsel on matters that were related to city planning. The most significant element in the relationship may have been the fact that most of the mayor's staffers were newer to city hall and knew even less about how things worked than I. I helped them learn as I was still learning, answering their questions about the city's government, the people, and the issues that were important to the community. They were as amazed as I at the difficulty of getting things done. The only clash that I recall, and that was only a momentary one, was with the mayor's deputy for development, Jack Tolan, who seemed to be suggesting, one day, that there were better ways to run my office—in particular, ways that would give him more direct access to my staff. I recall walking around my desk, taking a seat next to him, and suggesting that if he wanted to fill the now vacant seat of planning director, fine, but if not, then he should stop telling me how to run the office.

My views about the planning commission began to change. During the first year, I had tended to view the commission as a cumbersome layer between the professionals on the one hand, and the people, the mayor, and the Board of Supervisors on the other, a carryover from the days when city planning was an elitist activity of high-minded do-gooders who believed that the long-range view and the development of the city had to be independent of both politics and day-to-day decisions. Julia Porter, one of the commissioners, had me sized up correctly when she said that I secretly wished I could do away with the commissioners and be free to do as I wished. The commissioners were not necessarily nonpolitical in their decisions about the future of the city, and they were often out of tune with what was going on in certain areas. For no good reason, their meetings, especially the zoning hearings, were lengthy, and preparing for and sitting through them took inordinate amounts of staff and personal time. Commissioners often gave greater weight to the views of other department heads than to those of their own director and too often represented a potential hurdle for the staff.

Nonetheless, the commission did serve positive functions as well. Some members had knowledge of the city and its people that the staff did not have. Commissioners sometimes acted as a buffer between the staff and the public, taking a lot of heat off the staff. They advocated for the staff, especially before the board and with individual supervisors. One or two commissioners, like Fleishhacker and Walter Newman, took the devil's advocate role before issues came to a hearing, thereby allowing the staff to focus its research and sharpen its recommendations. Commissioners could provide easy entry to certain segments of the community, and their judgment was usually sound and therefore to be respected, especially when no political issue was involved. Perhaps most important, they were quite supportive during this period, and one felt that they would be helpful on most matters.

As we had promised, in 1968 we increased our efforts in the area of neighborhood planning and encouraged more citizen involvement. We still had no preset formula for neighborhood planning. We just went out and did it, understanding that it was both desirable and necessary to involve residents.

Our efforts in South Bayshore increased significantly. Three people were assigned full time to the project. They were all White, and their leader, Phoebe Brown, was a brahmin type who lived in a most exclusive part of town. In retrospect, it is anyone's guess as to why the neighborhood had anything to do with any of us, including me, or why people came to the community meetings we called. But they did come. Perhaps they sensed, as I soon did, that Phoebe Brown was a plain-speaking, no-nonsense professional, who worked tirelessly and would meet with any group, was clear about our abilities and limitations, and radiated dignity and a desire for a better community.

Following the pattern started in 1967, we would call occasional community meetings to present our work and to discuss topics of areawide concern. We didn't produce much in the way of written reports, mostly because the talents of the junior staff did not lie in that direction, but following our hostile reception in 1967, we began to communicate better and, over time, we fought and shouted less and saw and heard more. We learned among other things, that the South Bayshore community was in no way a slum, that there was no inherent reason for it to be any less pleasant a place to live than any other San Francisco neighborhood, that it was isolated from the rest of the city and therefore ignored, that it had a bad image, and that there was any number of opportunities to improve the neighborhood. One of the things we could do was to tell other city departments about problems that residents relayed to us. And so, on occasion, I would call the Public Works director or a high-up police official to relay a complaint about street cleaning or public protection. In time, we became known; there were no more confrontations like the one in early summer. It helped that we could produce, by means of reimbursements from the urban beautification program, about $100,000 for a long-promised recreation center. For me, the real turning point came the morning I was called upon by the community to help mediate a disagreement between the Housing Authority and the Redevelopment Agency. I began then to feel that we were accepted in South Bayshore.

Chinatown was another matter. I knew I didn't know anything about the area, and I suspected that most staff members didn't either. One heard all kinds of stories about "The Real Chinatown" — stories of extreme crowding in terrible housing, sweat shops, gang wars, illegal immigrants, and of the influence of the Chinese Six Companies and the family associations. One also heard that the Chinese bought buildings with cash.

J.K. Choy, elderly banker and activist, called Chinatown a slum and said the height limits should come off. He regularly said something to the effect that if I couldn't stand the heat I should get out of the kitchen, and he called for a plan. Alice Barkley, quite Chinese despite her name, swore at just about everyone in wonderful four-letter words while working incredibly hard to solve housing problems, open space problems, public service problems, and the social and economic problems of the elderly and Chinese. She too, wanted a plan.

Jim Paul was assigned to spend about a month walking around Chinatown, getting a sense of the place, and then to suggest what we ought to do. Our conclusion was that assigning a full-time planner, committed to the area for an extended period and charged with solving immediate problems and developing programs and projects, would be more useful than doing a plan. Late in the year, we presented the alternatives to a lively, everyone-is-welcome meeting in Chinatown. The community wanted both!

In November, our Northern Waterfront consultants produced a plan.[7] It was the culmination of what had been a frustrating experience from the start. The planning had begun before I was hired and at first I had no good understanding of the reasons for making a plan to begin with or of what it was to accomplish, the kind of understanding that comes from living with a problem for a while before attempting to solve it. Moreover, I was uncomfortable in the role of official overseer of a planning contract; I would rather have been doing the planning than trying to relate to the consultants and to the major interests that constituted the client. For the first time, I was exposed to some of San Francisco's more feisty urban conservation advocates, like those who purported to represent Telegraph and Russian hills. Their intransigence was matched by the development-oriented port commission, our own highway-centered Department of Public Works, the waterfront landowners, and the commercial developers. No matter whom we met with— and we had regular meetings to test our proposals —we seemed to be missing some group, or else a new group sprang from nowhere. It was not just that we couldn't please everyone. Rather, I got the sense that we could please no one.

In other parts of the city, we were becoming more involved in the Federally Assisted Code Enforcement program (FACE). The program was already in effect in four areas where residents were beginning to take part in detailed planning of public improvements. In 1968 we worked actively to get three more areas to a point of start-up. We still had to convince many people that FACE made sense, that subsidized rehabilitation of homes combined with a public improvements program was a natural for San Francisco, where most housing was basically sound. Also FACE associated us with a positive action program that could be used to carry out plans. It was positive in that it didn't take away property or demolish buildings or dislocate people (or at least not many) but provided public improvements and subsidized loans instead.

I learned a lot about the federal government, the local redevelopment program, and the Bureau of Building Inspection through FACE. Federal representatives wanted two of the three new areas we were considering to be renewal projects under the auspices of the Redevelopment Agency. I came to realize just how committed the feds were to a bulldozer approach to city problems. Their propensity to question the judgment of local officials on what was or was not appropriate in San Francisco was also more than a little disconcerting.

I learned, also, just how fearful people were of redevelopment. At first, we had to convince them that we were not the Redevelopment Agency and that we were not proposing a renewal program. But later, the residents of a block where there was a real possibility of significant displacement of people— because of elimination of illegal units and rent increases—nevertheless asked that it be included in the FACE program. They reasoned that FACE was better than the alternative of doing nothing, since doing nothing was in fact an invitation to more redevelopment operations.

Before I came to San Francisco, I had never had much use for building inspection operations. In most cities that I knew of, the housing codes were

11.3   Drawing by Jack Sidener reproduced with the permission of the San Francisco Department of City Planning.

rarely enforced in any serious way, and one frequently heard rumors of payoffs. Nor were building inspection departments noted for having the brightest employees in the world. San Francisco was different. Not only did the guys in the Bureau of Building Inspection know their business, but they knew what the laws said and didn't say, and they knew how to organize and run a program. The inspectors involved with the FACE program were serious, straight people, and they were terribly competent pros. Their curt, uncompromising manner before neighborhood groups and elected officials did leave something to be desired, but when they told you something, you knew you had been told. Al Goldberg, the head man, came on as the epitome of a nasty know-it-all who would send his mother to jail over a leaky faucet, but he and his top staff seemed honest beyond any question. And they made the FACE program work. The staff of the bureau was to be an ally in the years ahead.

This was a busy time. One day's calendar, such as the one for January 30, 1968, might include a meeting with the mayor's deputy for development on the Model Cities program, a meeting with staff and would-be developers over use of the shoreline in the South Bayshore area, 40 minutes of paper work and telephone calls, a meeting with the mayor regarding the Embarcadero Center renewal project, and 20 more minutes of private work time before a lunch meeting with local architects to discuss a comprehensive urban design plan. Lunch might be followed by a two-hour meeting with key staff on salaries, job classifications, and recruiting, a review of the proposal for the International Market Center; and a meeting on northern waterfront planning. Miscellaneous telephone calls and one-minute consultations were sandwiched in somewhere. At 6:30 I would go home for dinner. If there was no evening meeting, I would spend a couple of hours reviewing the material that had piled up on my desk during the day. I could have named at least half a dozen other people who were just as active.

The primary responsibility of the planning department is to prepare and maintain the master plan. The existing master plan, completed in 1945, had been amended many times since. It was a small mimeographed document that might have served well for its time but was now out-of-date. Some local planning buffs considered it a kind of embarrassment. However, I was not all that anxious to redo the plan, I had had disheartening experiences with comprehensive, master plans both in the Pittsburgh area and in Calcutta, and the volatile times seemed to call for immediate solutions to crisis conditions. I succumbed to the academic criticisms of comprehensive physical planning that were then widespread: irrelevant, elitist, anti-social equity, and God knows what else. Further, a major revision of the master plan would cost a fortune, and there was no new money for that purpose. The planning commission was not interested and the department did not have the staff on hand for preparing a new plan. But despite all the negatives, a course of action did evolve from our research and information-gathering activities, from our work on the issues that we had identified as being of critical importance to the community, and from the interests and expertise of the staff.

The San Francisco simulation model of the housing market was one of those back-burner activities that was, unfortunately, visible, and it was important to decide what to do with it. Both the model and the Community Renewal Program that it came from were in bad repute around city hall. Although the model had been declared operational by someone, no one was operating it in public. Requests for new positions or for funds to undertake new studies were met with, "Are you nuts? So you can build another model?" Peter Groat, who was in charge of the model, had spent hours on end explaining it to me—how it was supposed to test the effects of various public policy programs upon the city's supply of housing, what went into it, how it worked, its status, and the like. They were painful hours for him. There were a lot of things wrong with the model, including very questionable accuracy, difficulty in interpreting its output, the high cost of operation, and its ability to answer only questions no one was asking. A new terminology had to be invented to deal with computer limitations (a "fract"). In September, we published a report that described the model, its potential and its shortcomings, and put it to bed.[8]

More positively, we produced the first of our *Changes in the San Francisco Housing Inventory* reports in 1968. If housing was an issue, then knowing the amounts, locations, types, sizes, and costs of the housing that was being added and subtracted from the overall stock of the city would help to develop policies and programs to address the issues.

Because housing issues were so significant in the late sixties, because housing is by far the biggest user of land and in large measure its nature and quality determine the character of the city as a whole, and because new and unassigned staff had expertise in the subject, we elected to prepare a comprehensive plan for residence. In making that decision we were really committing ourselves to an element-by-element preparation of a new comprehensive plan for San Francisco. To the challenge that this was not a comprehensive way to prepare a comprehensive plan and that we could not be sure that this or any element would relate properly to another, we responded that we didn't have funds to do the whole job at once, that we were attacking the most important issues first, that in San Francisco it was probably more important for other issues to relate to housing than vice versa, and that later we would make adjustments to completed work if that proved necessary. I might have added that, for me, any plan for San Francisco that I had a hand in was likely to be oriented toward protecting and maintaining the basic character of the city. We would build upon the city as it was. In any case, we had started to roll on long-range, citywide plans.

We also began an urban design study in 1968. After almost a year of preparing study outlines and work programs, estimating costs and personnel needs, tracking down funds, and getting necessary approvals, we started on a plan that was primarily directed to the appearance of the city, to the way San Francisco should look. It would be a major undertaking.

It had been a busy year. There had been more winners than losers. I think we were establishing, or strengthening, a respected professional base in the community. We seemed to be doing relevent work, and we were doing long- and short-range city planning, which is supposedly what we were paid to do. If there was a loser of the kind that stays in one's mind for a long time, and causes a twinge whenever he sees it, it was the pedestrian bridge from Portsmouth Square over Kearny Street to the so-called Chinese Cultural Center, which was really an arbitrarily shaped Holiday Inn. Although I am convinced that I could not have stopped that pompous, shadow-producing, space-reducing bridge—the Redevelopment Agency had managed to convince every public agency that was involved that the others were for it and that there was no turning back—I could have and should have said "No" in the loudest voice possible. Instead, I gave some kind of a wishy-washy, Mickey-Mouse, "only-if" type of recommendation that did nothing to hinder the abomination. In truth, I was a little intimidated in those days by the Redevelopment Agency and its director, Justin Herman. I didn't like him. I knew he had little use for city planning, thought he was devious, and didn't know how to beat him. I felt that way about no one else in San Francisco, an open, free, no-holds-barred, welcoming city that would give all sorts of new people and new ideas a chance and an audience.

Feeling as I did about San Francisco, it seems inconsistent that I would support a study that was aimed at simplifying the existing charter and centralizing power and responsibility with the mayor. The good-government types, especially the liberals, were unhappy with San Francisco's cumbersome, inefficient, slow-to-respond, no-power-to-anyone form of government. The government did not appear to have a very rational structure, if getting things done was a major criterion. The only thing that could be said for it was that it was relatively honest, but that might mean spending $100 to be sure no one could steal $5.

The drafters of the new charter wanted to take power from the entrenched bureaucrats—who ever heard of a chief administrative officer with a lifetime appointment?—and make government more flexible, efficient, and responsible by placing that power in the hands of a strong mayor. City planning would be directly under the mayor, and the planning commission would become merely advisory to the staff. It seemed to be an arrangement that would help city planning increase its effectiveness and its relevance. It would put it closer to the driver's seat. It made sense to me. It was the way things were being done in the smart, eastern cities that I still held as models. Besides, I liked Mayor Alioto and foresaw no problems with being closer to his office, although I did say at the time that if a much-expanded planning operation were to move to the mayor's office, I would resign. My reason, however, was not related to the location of city planning within government. Rather it was the nature of the job that bothered me; it would be much broader than planning and guiding the physical development of the city and more concerned with the planning and coordination of social and economic policies and programs — general purpose governmental planning and coordinating. It would also be less fun and less interesting for me. I did not see at the time the relationship between San Francisco's existing governmental structure and the growing effectiveness of city planning. So I encouraged the efficiency-responsiveness-centrality directions of the Charter Revision Committee in 1968. Their deliberations continued through 1969. In the meantime there was plenty to do.

Whether or not we saw or grasped all the available opportunities to be effective is hard to say. We tried.

It was important to understand the significance of the small day-to-day matters that came to the commission regularly—each with a direct effect on only a few people. In sum, they would prove to be a measure of our effectiveness and relevance. Each of those small zoning and referral cases deserved a well-thought-out and reasonable recommendation. I don't think I understood that very well when I first came to San Francisco, but I was learning.

We viewed the subsidized code enforcement-rehabilitation program, coupled with modest public improvements, as an opportunity to be immediately effective. We also gained points for the department through the federally sponsored urban beautification program, which seemed equally important at the time. We had put the program together in the first place and had considerable influence over its use. Although the amounts of money involved were relatively small compared with other programs, their use helped to raise the visibility and effectiveness of the department. The simple ability to offer something tangible, however small, was enough to suggest to people that planning and "those planners" might hold some immediate pay-offs for them. Much of the money was spent in less-advantaged neighborhoods. That summer we developed an employment program, putting 300 young people to work rehabilitating an almost forgotten area of Golden Gate Park.

The mini-park program was another program that increased our visibility. The planning department staff found sites for the parks on extremely short notice. That meant that we were directly associated with providing things that people wanted in their neighborhoods. On the other hand, the speed with which we had to select the sites was not always consistent with good citizen participation practices. In one South of Market area, especially, people were furious that we had selected sites without talking to them. They let me know with a vengeance that the sites we had chosen were too small, too few, and too poorly located. Their anger was compounded by the fact that they were being dislocated by the Yerba Buena redevelopment project. During two of the most raucous meetings I ever attended—meetings where I was held responsible for the death of a child, the Viet Nam War, and just about everything else, meetings that had no order beyond the opening sentence, meetings that were full of crying kids and adults screaming filthy language and threats of physical violence, meetings that were nothing but nastiness, meetings where I learned to give as well as I got—during those meetings we somehow hit upon an approach that resulted in the building of two mini-parks in the South of Market area. Somehow, through all the shouting and anger, we must have shared a common purpose and common objectives.

NOTES

1. The hilltop zoning case was reported by Maitland Zane in "Supervisors Reject Pleas of Mt. Olympus Residents," *San Francisco Chronicle*, July 17, 1968. An example of a case involving a

residential conversion appears in the minutes of the San Francisco City Planning Commission for November 7, 1968, Case CU 68.27.

2. The supervisors lined up the same way in all of the six-to-five votes, including the vote against a delay and the final vote of approval for the Department of City Planning proposal. Voting aye were Pelosi, Boas, Francois, McCarthy, Mendelsohn. Voting nay were Von Beroldingen, Tamaras, Blake, Ertola, and Maillard. On the seven-to-four votes against certain amendments, Maillard switched his vote to aye.

3. Ron Moskowitz, "Supervisors OK Market Centers," *San Francisco Chronicle*, July 15, 1968.

4. Actually, the San Francisco Department of City Planning produced two reports: "Draft Report—Alcatraz Island," August 22, 1968, and *Development Criteria and Policies for Alcatraz Island*, September 12, 1969. The consultants were Sedway/Cooke, Urban and Environmental Planners and Designers.

5. "As Big a Steal as Manhattan Island," *San Francisco Chronicle*, October 3, 1969; "Alcatraz Not for Sale—U.S." *San Francisco Examiner*, December 3, 1969.

6. San Francisco Department of City Planning, *Forts Mason, Miley, and Funston*, November 1968.

7. John S. Bolles Associates, *Northern Waterfront Plan*, 1968.

8. San Francisco Department of City Planning, *Status of the San Francisco Simulation Model*, September 1968.

12

A Retrospective View of Equity Planning

Cleveland 1969-1979

Norman Krumholz

Summary. From 1969 to 1979, under three administrations which could not have been more different, the Cleveland City Planning Commission worked in a highly visible way to achieve equity objectives. During this period, advocacy planning became less of a hortatory theory than a tangible effort undertaken within the system and directed toward, and achieving, real ends. On given issues, the Cleveland planners publicly challenged some of our favorite urban nostrums, and they not only survived, but prospered.

This article discusses and estimates the impact that the work of the Cleveland planners had on various issues and on the mayors they served. Its conclusions may be useful for planners and others interested in applying their own models of responsible planning and redistributive justice.

In 1969, I came to Cleveland, Ohio as Director of the Cleveland City Planning Commission to serve under Carl B. Stokes, the first black mayor of any American city with over 500,000 people. It is hard for me to express how deeply I felt about the importance of this assignment. I had always been involved in liberal issues; I had hoped for a racially integrated society, and was strongly sympathetic to the civil rights movement. I was deeply devoted to our country but did not believe that America as a nation had solved all its problems or achieved all its objectives. Stokes's election had been of huge importance to large segments of the Black and liberal communities, and I jumped at the chance to work in his administration. I served under Stokes for two years. Later, I continued my work under Republican Ralph J. Perk for six years, and resigned in the waning days of Dennis J. Kucinich's two-year term. During the ten years, my staff and I served in turn a liberal Black Democrat, a

Reprinted from Norman Krumholz, 1982. "A Retrospective View of Equity Planning: Cleveland 1969-1979," *Journal of the American Planning Association* **48,** 2 (Spring): 163-174, by permission.

conservative White ethnic Republican, and a self-styled urban populist. I also watched (and some say contributed to) Cleveland becoming the first American city since the Great Depression to default on its fiscal obligations. The purpose of this article is to describe and evaluate that experience, and to update some of the case studies and findings discussed in an earlier *Journal* article (Krumholz 1975; Gans 1975; Piven 1975; Long 1975; Davidoff 1975).

Regardless of who was mayor, the staff of the Cleveland City Planning Commission consistently operated in a way that was activist and interventionist in style and redistributive in objective. Our overriding goal, articulated in the *Cleveland Policy Planning Report* published in 1975, was "to provide a wider range of choices for those Cleveland residents who have few, if any, choices" (Cleveland City Planning Commission 1975). The approach has been called "advocacy" or "equity" planning by many in the planning profession; it has also been called "cut-back planning" by Professor Herbert Gans and "opportunity planning" by Anthony Downs. It has received considerable scholarly attention, perhaps as a polar example of the application of local planning efforts to issues of social equity.

Why would this particular group of city planners act in a way that was highly visible and frequently politically risky? My thoughts on strategy and tactics of operating a planning department developed jointly with several outstanding co-workers (initially Ernest R. Bonner, Janice M. Cogger, John H. Linner, and Douglas G. Wright) in the following four related lines: (*1*) the urgent reality of conditions in Cleveland, (*2*) the inherent unfairness and exploitative nature of our urban development process, (*3*) the inability of local politics to address these problems, (*4*) our conception of the ethics of professional planning practice.

Conditions in Cleveland

Consider Cleveland's problems — the city's population had fallen rapidly. It dropped 39,000 in the 1950s; 125,000 in the 1960s; and 180,000 in the 1970s. Over that period, the proportion of Blacks in the city's population rose from 16 to 44 percent; and in Cleveland, the poor were more often than not Black, the Black were more often than not poor.[1]

A rising share of the city's population was economically dependent and its income was falling in relative terms. About 20 percent of Cleveland's families received Aid to Families with Dependent Children and one sixth had incomes below $2,000 a year.[2] More affluent families had been departing for decades; in the 1960s the city lost 25 percent of its families with incomes over the median for the Standard Metropolitan Statistical Area.[3]

The city had a high and rising crime rate. Crime was seen as the number one problem by 73 percent of all residents (Cleveland City Planning Commission

1972). In 1975, the rate of violent crimes against persons was 1,730 per 100,000. That was 16 percent over the 1970 rate and 164 percent over the 1965 rate (Cleveland Police Department 1974).

The city had a declining assessed value base—it fell 5 percent from 1969 to 1974 while the Consumer Price Index rose 34.5 percent. Local general fund operating revenues declined 37 percent in constant dollars during that same period.[4]

These depressing central city phenomena were not shared by the Cleveland region. In 1973, per capita income in the region, excluding the city, was $6,750 or 14 percent above the national average. In the city, per capita income was $3,160 or 37 percent less than the U.S. average.

The region continued to expand its employment base with almost 25,000 new jobs added to the regional economy between 1972 and 1976. Between 1958 and 1977 the region gained 210,000 jobs; the city lost 130,000 jobs over the same period.[5]

The Cleveland region's unemployment rate (5.9 percent in 1977) was usually lower than the U.S. average (7.0 percent in 1977). However, the city suffered higher unemployment rates than the U.S. average (11.5 percent in 1977), and among young Blacks the unemployment rate (38.8 percent in 1977) represented a tragic waste of enormous proportions.[6]

Not surprisingly, the fiscal and economic disparities between central city and region were wider in Cleveland than in almost any other place in the U.S.

12.1   The Glenville area of Cleveland, Ohio, 1975 (photo by Susan C. Kaeser).

Unemployment, poverty, crime, inadequate education, rotting housing, and the other elements of the urban crisis were concentrated in the city, and particularly in the city's low income neighborhoods.

Exploitative Development Process

Perceiving these city-suburban disparities, we were profoundly disturbed —even outraged. We saw them as not the result of simple coincidence or of market forces, but as partially the result of an urban development process which was inherently exploitative of the poor and especially of the minority poor. The same customs and institutional arrangements that produced safe neighborhoods, satisfactory schools, and viable public institutions for the middle class also concentrated the poor into neighborhoods where the very business of day-to-day living was extremely difficult. The minority poor were excluded from many suburbs, not by market forces but by zoning codes that maintained unreasonably large building parcels, by restrictive covenants on the sale of land, by building and housing codes that insured ever-rising home prices, by informal customs, and by legal cooperation agreements that sharply limited the location of new public housing to the central city and its worst neighborhoods. We felt these arrangements were not the result of any deliberate malevolent conspiracy but that they were exploitative and contrary to American notions of justice and fairness and so should be resisted by city planners and others.

Inadequacy of Local Politics

Why didn't the local political structure deal with these problems? Because, we thought, the problems were based at their roots on poverty and racial prejudice and were national in origin. Unless there was broad concern over these issues expressed in national legislation and enforcement there was very little that local politics could or would do.

There was also the relative lack of influence of Cleveland's resident population. Influence, like wealth, was unevenly distributed in the population. When goals conflicted, groups with wealth and influence were likely to win every time, although it was hard to see how such winning contributed either to democracy or to the public good. The result was that public facilities rotted without attention in low income neighborhoods while public and philanthropic resources were lavished on public spaces and old buildings downtown. Within the context of this contending but unequal power and influence, placing priority attention on the needs of the poor would tend to provide them with countervailing power and, like universal suffrage and majority rule, would help strengthen democracy.

Professional Ethics

Finally, the planners recognized that this was an ethical issue, not just for us as individuals, but for the profession of city planning. The Code of Ethics of the American Institute of Planners did, in a way, justify our actions, and we quoted it in our work:

12.2 Abandonment and demolition in the Hough area, 1976 (photo by Susan C. Kaeser).

A planner shall seek to expand choice and opportunity for all persons, recognizing a specia responsiblity to plan for the needs of disadvantaged groups and persons, and shall urge the alteration of policies, institutions and decisions which militate against such objectives.

With these views as a guide, we deemphasized many of our concerns with zoning, land use, and urban design. We altered the planner's traditional posture as an apolitical technician serving a unitary public interest. Instead, we devoted ourselves to "providing more choices to those who have few, if any choices."

As a result, our work did not map out an ideal future in terms of land use, public facilities, and transportation routes. Rather it was made up of studies, proposals, and recommendations which seemed likely to resolve or ameliorate the worst problems of Cleveland and its residents. In some respects our work could be criticized as having been "short-term"; in other respects, it was most visionary since it was seeking a society which was fundamentally different from the present, a society where justice and equity were at least as important as efficiency.

Our equity activities in Cleveland covered almost ten years. After my departure in 1979, all the staff members I hired left the planning agency for other positions at city hall, and many left the city entirely. New leadership was introduced to the planning commission which now appears to view its planning responsibilities in a more traditional vein. For the present, at least, the equity planning experiment in Cleveland is over. How much difference did it make?

To try to answer that question, I will try to assess the impact of our work on some of the major issues in which we were involved, on the mayors we served, on other practicing city planning professionals, and on the teaching of city planning.

The CTS-RTA Negotiations

Our greatest success had to do with the negotiations that led in 1975 to the transfer of the Cleveland Transit System (CTS) to the Greater Cleveland Regional Transit Authority (RTA).

Transportation problems are usually defined in terms of rush hour congestion, auto access, or the need for more off-street parking. However, our goal led us to define Cleveland's most significant transportation problem in a different way: the need to improve the mobility of Cleveland's transit-dependent population, those families who lacked automobiles and who depended entirely on public transit.

As we saw it, Cleveland was part of an automotive society which provided unprecedented mobility for those who had been able to take advantage of it.

12.3   The RTA increased transportation options.

In the course of choosing this automotive civilization, however, we had chosen to ignore the problems created for those without access to an automobile. As cars proliferated and new development was scattered at low densities across the region, ridership on transit declined, service was cut, and fares increased. For the transit-dependent rider, most of whom were poor, elderly, or physically handicapped, there were fewer and fewer destinations that could be reached at ever higher fares after longer waiting periods.

This might be a trivial problem except that the transit-dependent population made up a sizable portion of Cleveland's population. About one-third of all Cleveland families had no car; among families over age sixty-five or earning less than $6,000 a year, about one-half had no car.

It seemed clear to us that Cleveland's highest transportation priority should be to ensure a decent level of mobility to those transit-dependent persons who were prevented by extreme poverty or a combination of low income and physical disability (including old age) from moving around our metropolitan area.

We first became involved in the transit issue through the Cleveland area's Five-County Transit Study which began in 1970. The city-owned CTS, at the time the largest system in the world to be operating exclusively from fare-box revenues, was rapidly approaching financial disaster. The five-county planning process was seen locally as providing the impetus and framework for a regional transit system.

We represented Mayor Stokes and later Mayor Perk on the transit study's executive committee. In that capacity, we argued that expanded mobility for the transit-dependent population should be acknowledged as the study's highest priority objective; that staff and consultants should be selected who were sensitive to the needs of the transit-dependent population; and that adequate funding should be provided for the transit-dependent element of the study. We won on each of these points, but they were fleeting victories. The project's staff quickly identified its interests in terms of responding to and even anticipating political pressures, and a wide gap developed between the goals stated in the study and the final recommendations.

The study's final recommendations placed major emphasis on the expenditure of more than one billion dollars for expanded rail facilities. Based upon a careful review of the analysis supporting this recommendation, my staff and I concluded that such a rail system was likely to provide few benefits to anyone except those involved in its management, construction, and financing. Moreover, it threatened to draw resources away from those service improvements offering the greatest potential benefits to the transit-dependent. In the eighteen-month interim between the publication of the study's "Ten Year Transit Development Program" report and the initiation of negotiations over formation of a regional transit authority, we worked to discredit the rail expansion plan at the local, regional, and federal levels.

By the end of 1974, CTS was in crisis, and Cleveland decision makers began the serious business of forming the Greater Cleveland Regional Transit Authority (RTA). With our four years of experience and prepared position papers, we soon began to function as the administration spokesperson.

The negotiations centered around one issue — what the city would receive in return for transferring CTS to a new regional authority. Initially, the city's political leaders simply demanded a majority of the appointments to the RTA Board. We felt that this was insufficient and were convinced that the city should be bargaining for fare reductions and service improvements for the city's transit-dependent population. We took elements of the Five-County Transit Study, translated them into terms which local decision makers could understand, and presented them to the mayor and city council. When the city's political leaders realized that abstract concepts such as "route-spacing guides," "loading coefficients," and "service headways" meant tangible improvements for their constitutents, they shifted the focus of their demands.

Throughout these negotiations, James B. Davis, the city's law director, and I argued for fare and service guarantees while our opposition county officials, suburban mayors, representatives of the business community, and the city's own CTS management argued for "flexibility" for RTA. It was clear that when the transit operators and downtown boosters spoke in terms of "flexibility" for RTA, the billion-dollar plus rail expansion plan was on their minds. Thus, while our opposition fought to keep the guarantees to the city as meaningless as possible, the planners, aided by the law director and a young councilman named Dennis J. Kucinich, fought to insure that RTA would be legally committed to reducing fares and improving service for Cleveland residents. During the protracted negotiations we were forced to make a number of concessions, but when agreement was finally reached, it was clear that we had made substantial progress toward insuring that RTA would be responsive to the needs of the transit-dependent population. In the final agreement the city was guaranteed the following:

1. A twenty-five cent fare would be maintained for at least three years.

2. Senior citizens and the handicapped would ride free during nonpeak periods (twenty hours daily) and pay only half fare during the four peak hours.

3. Service frequencies and route coverage within the city would be improved.

4. RTA would be prohibited from spending funds on planning or developing a downtown subway or elevated system for at least five years.

5. Community Responsive Transit (CRT), a door-to-door, dial-a-ride service, would be initiated.

The best service and fare guarantees we could get were only three and five years long. They have now expired, and RTA's management has begun the dreary cycle of raising fares and cutting services while programming and making heavy expenditures on maintaining and expanding Cleveland's rail system.

RTA's capital expenditures in its first six years were indicative of the system's priorities. Of its first $120 million capital improvement program, $100 million was spent upgrading the entire Shaker Rapid line, a line which carries less than 4 percent of the system's ridership, albeit the most wealthy, influential, and vocal 4 percent. Fifty-one percent of Shaker Rapid riders have two or more cars; only 8 percent have none. So much for the emphasis on the transit-dependent rider! RTA is also planning a $50 million extension of one of the Shaker lines as well as a $.5 billion, four-mile downtown subway. The agency has budgeted $694 million for various rail improvements in its 1982-1987 planning, and has spent over $234 million, or 72 percent, of all capital grants received from 1975 to 1981 on rail. Meanwhile, over 87 percent of RTA's ridership takes the bus.

However, the CRT program we pressed on RTA over management's objections has been under way for five years. CRT now has an organized constituency which understands, uses, and supports the service, so CRT will probably continue even though it is programmed at only about 2 percent of the system's $117 million annual budget. Similarly, the sharply discounted fares for the elderly and handicapped were left untouched by the two RTA fare hikes in 1981. So some elements of our package will outlast the guarantees we were able to negotiate. Even if they all expired on schedule the three to five years of service and fare benefit were more than our transit-dependent clients would have gotten if we were not ready with clear objectives and the will to fight for them.

Tower City

A second major issue in which we were involved had to do with public subsidies to a private downtown development.

In the winter of 1974, a local real estate developer approached the city with plans to construct a major downtown commercial complex called Tower City. The developer claimed that the total value of planned construction would reach $350 million. The media, the business community, and the city's political leadership hailed the proposal as a bold step toward revitalizing downtown Cleveland.

The planning commission staff reviewed the legislation and found several disturbing aspects. The city was asked both to waive rights it held to the development site and to agree to repair some railroad bridges on the site. Our probing revealed that other entities, not the city, were responsible for the bridge repairs, and that the estimated cost of the repairs was an open-ended one which could exceed $15 million. Further, it appeared that the developer would request property tax abatement for twenty years.

We concluded that the city had little to gain from Tower City. The bridge repairs would be expensive and our responsibility for them was unclear; the city might be forced to give away any new property tax revenue; the promise of new income tax revenue was not bright since our studies showed the market for downtown office space was not growing but simply shifting from one location to another; and the developer was not offering any permanent new jobs for the city's unemployed.

We were not opposed to new development per se. We realized new development might keep firms in downtown that otherwise might have left the city completely; that development provides short-term construction jobs; and that it adds to the tax base (unless new tax revenues are abated). We wanted new development which was of benefit to the city and its people.

Following the staff's recommendation, the planning commission refused to approve the legislation unless several amendments were made in which the developer would guarantee a number of new jobs to city residents, agree to forego tax abatement and to pay full property taxes on the project. These conditions were not acceptable to the developer.

Very quickly, our position came under fire from city council and the newspapers. We were accused of obstructing progress and being anti-development. Our rebuttal that the health and vitality of a city did not depend on the construction of new office buildings and hotels in downtown but rather on how well the city helped provide jobs, opportunities, and services to its residents did not convince anyone.

Attacks on the planners grew stronger and more personal throughout the city council committee hearings. Council President George Forbes then, as now, the ringmaster of city hall, called the commission "a bunch of baboons" and on television demanded my resignation. Eventually, council overrode the planning commission's disapproval 32-1 and passed the legislation.

On this particular issue we lost badly, but we succeeded in placing some important issues on the public agenda. We pointed out that the money to subsidize this project would come at the expense of high-priority capital improvements in the city's working-class and poor neighborhoods. We asked to what extent the city should go to underwrite the risk of private development. Also, we tried to make clear that the city's scarce resources should be applied to facilitating private development only if that development provided permanent, productive jobs for the city's people and net increases in tax revenues for the city's coffers. In short, we proposed the doctrine that the city spend its money and power in "businesslike" ways.

Tower City has not been built for reasons unrelated to our opposition, but the idea that the city should expect some return on any public investments it makes in support of private development now seems to be understood. Our position, which was an isolated one at the time, may have been part of a chain of events which later led the Ohio Public Interest Campaign and the Commission on Catholic Community Action to vigorously oppose tax abatements. For whatever reason, no property tax abatements have been granted to any development in Cleveland since 1977, although downtown continues to enjoy a boom in new construction.

Public Versus Private Power

Perhaps the most important issue in which we were involved is still to be resolved, the issue of public versus private electric power. Cleveland is served by two electrical systems — the Cleveland Electric Illuminating Company (CEI), an investor-owned regional utility company that serves about 80 percent of the accounts in Cleveland, and the city's own Municipal Electric Light Plant (Muny Light). In 1971, a series of power blackouts caused us to examine Muny Light's physical needs as a routine part of our preparation of the city's annual capital improvement program. As the analysis unfolded, however, it became apparent that the issue was more complex than Muny's need for a few pipes and boilers.

The planners found that CEI has been interested in purchasing Muny for decades, presumably to eliminate competition. We also found that, apparently to injure Muny's competitive position, CEI has steadfastly refused to allow Muny to tie in to other power sources. Therein lay Muny's problem. Nearly all electric power companies have tie-ins to other power systems so that they can continue service should their own facilities need repair or fail. Because it had no such tie-in, Muny was plagued with power failures. This led to numerous complaints about Muny's service, and several councilmen proposed to sell the facility to CEI.

We concluded that this might solve the blackout problem, but it would also mean that Muny's customers would experience an immediate rate hike and that the city would no longer have an effective brake on future rate increases. Thus, the issue appeared to have serious economic implications for the city's poor. Because electricity is a relatively fixed item of household consumption, any change in rates would have a definite effect upon the real incomes of city residents. Moreover, a significant change in rates might influence the location of firms within the Cleveland region and, thus, the access of city residents to jobs.

The planners analyzed the fiscal and legal aspects of this question and the history of CEI's apparent long-term attempt to subvert and destroy Muny, and proposed something quite different than the sale of Muny to CEI. We proposed that Muny Light use state law to condemn and purchase CEI's transmission and generating capacity in the city. This would expand the small municipal power system into a citywide network, eliminate blackouts, and also provide electricity at a much lower cost to city residents.

Needless to say, this proposal was greeted with derision by the news media, and did not result in the condemnation of CEI. However, it may have helped to forestall the sale of Muny Light and to prevent rate increases. It also served to remind local decision makers of the rationale for Muny Light's establishment. Beyond this, our study may have played a role in the events that followed.

In 1975, under Mayor Ralph Perk, the city filed a $327 million antitrust suit against CEI and four allied power companies for anticompetitive practices. A year later, the U.S. Justice Department filed a brief in support of the city, and the Atomic Safety and Licensing Board of the U.S. Nuclear Regulatory Commission (NRC) handed down a decision that elaborated on the planner's findings of four years earlier, one which confirmed that CEI had a history of acting "individually and collectively to eliminate one or more electric entities and to preclude competition."

In the years that followed, Mayor Perk reversed his long-standing support for Muny and proposed to sell the system to CEI. One of the terms of the sale provided that the city would drop its antitrust suit. However, the sale was never consummated; Dennis Kucinich used the issue as a rallying point in his 1977 drive to the mayor's office and killed it. The present administration of Mayor George V. Voinovich has pursued the suit vigorously, and it is now before the federal court.

Did the work of Cleveland's city planners in publishing their 1972 report, in making depositions in the city's suit, and in publicizing the CEI-Muny Light issue have anything to do with Muny's present affection in the hearts of the city's leadership? Perhaps, but for most of us, it is enough to know that we used our skills in data gathering and analysis for the useful purpose of exposing CEI's stratagems in trying to destroy a municipal asset.

Other Issues

Having recounted three of the most significant issues in which we were involved, a few additional points should be made about the less heroic activities of the planning staff.

First, most planning issues which came before the staff lacked high drama and visibility and had little to do with "providing more choices for those who have few." However, we did this work diligently, no matter how routine, and it served to maintain and elaborate the planning agency's reputation for competence.

Second, although the three issues described above in detail involve conflicting values or political views, many of the issues in which my staff and I were involved were successfully concluded through the building of a broad consensus, not through conflict.

In one such issue, we headed a committee which successfully drafted and saw passed a new state law which shortened and simplified the foreclosure procedure for tax-delinquent and abandoned property. The new law has also allowed the city to land-bank these foreclosed parcels as trustee for the other two taxing bodies, Cuyahoga County and the Cleveland Board of Education. The development of this issue over a three-year period represents a virtually perfect textbook model of effective planning practice where the planners identify a local problem; study its cause; recommend a likely solution to the planning commission, the mayor, and council; develop broad support across the state for the proposed solution; seek and get foundation help to draft a new state law; and lobby the law through the general assembly and governor's office. We even wrote an article and a book about the case (Olson and Lachman 1976)! Such activities can hardly be undertaken, let alone brought to a successful conclusion, without the building of broad, supportive coalitions.

Similar consensus building was essential to our efforts in other issues. In 1977, the city's once elegant lakefront parks were virtually open dumps and Mayor Perk realized both his political vulnerability on the issue and his inability, because of fiscal inadequacies, to reverse the downward trend. He established and asked me to chair a Mayor's Task Force on Lakefront Development which, within a year, had established a new state park in Cleveland using as the core of the park the lakefront parks the city could no longer afford to maintain. In agreeing to set up this park, the Ohio Department of Natural Resources reversed its historic policy of building state parks only in rural areas. Agreement on this issue required political consensus among the mayor and city council, the governor's office, and the general assembly, as well as support from local foundations, the media, and "good government" groups.

Did our reputation as advocates willing to accept conflict in certain situations hinder our efforts to establish cooperative coalitions in other situations? Not so far as we could tell. I believe we were regarded by the other players as competent professionals who might frequently disagree with their views, but who were willing to join others (and anxious for others to join us) when our objectives coincided.

Professionalism, quiet agreement, close communication, and shared confidence were essential as the city planners attempted to improve city services by providing advice and technical assistance to other operating departments. In one such successful example, members of the planning staff worked within the city's Waste Collection and Disposal Division for five years in order to help improve its management capacity. During that time, the planners helped reorganize collection routes, recommended manpower reassignments, and helped direct the division's capital expenditures toward cost-saving equipment. In the process, the division was able to save several million dollars a year. When we were invited to begin working with the division it had no internal planning capabilities whatever. The division knew it was in trouble, but it didn't know how to analytically address its problems. Our work was quiet, completely behind the scenes, and long-term. The division's willingness to accept our advice was based on the trust that our advice was worthy, that we would stay with them over the long pull and that we would take some of the political heat as they sought to implement our recommendations. By the time we ended our work with them, the division's commissioner (a former garbageman) was a frequent speaker at national solid waste conferences where he would talk of picking up garbage "heuristically."

It should be noted that many of our studies and proposals had little discernible impact on the issues we addressed. We drilled a lot of dry holes. For example, one of our first large-scale planning efforts was a 1970 proposal for a new town on some 850 acres of city-owned, largely vacant land located seven miles from downtown Cleveland in a nearby unincorporated township. The proposal was innovative and detailed and interested the HUD new-town desk, the Office of Economic Opportunity, and the Harvard Graduate School of Education. However, city council was not very interested, and the people in surrounding municipalities were actively hostile. When Ralph Perk replaced Stokes as mayor in 1971, the new-town idea was axed and the land remains undeveloped to this day.

A similar fate awaited our proposal to decontrol city council's grip over entry into the taxi business and the setting of taxi fares. We made the proposal so that the city's poor — who use taxis to a disproportionate degree — could take advantage of the lower fares, better service, and job opportunities which deregulation seemed to offer. To no avail; we could find no one with the necessary political power willing to adopt and pursue the idea.

Impact on The Mayors

What was the impact of our work on the mayors we served, Stokes, Perk, and Kucinich?

Stokes enjoyed our studies and analyses of various issues and he supported most of them. He also appreciated the stream of speeches and articles that flowed from his planners and which he used for a variety of local and national purposes. In company with many other mayors, Stokes was not particularly interested in the day to day administrative responsibilities of his office. He provided broad policy direction. Within these broad guidelines, his directors had wide latitude to establish their own policies and programs. If and when they got into trouble, the mayor usually stood by them.

This relatively loose structure gave us great freedom to innovate. As part of our work in the first year we helped block the Clark Freeway (I-290), which would have displaced 1,400 families on the city's east side; proposed a much less damaging alternative route for the highway; published our new-town proposal; set in motion the events that would decertify the Northeast Ohio Areawide Coordinating Agency (the regional planning group) and ultimately quadruple city representation on its board; and proposed a "fair share" plan for public housing in Cuyahoga County. Stokes supported all these efforts. They fit well with his objectives and strengthened the links between the mayor and his constituency. Yet, in the larger sense, we did not have much impact on the mayor's program, and he gave us little public recognition either at the time or in his political autobiography *Promises of Power* (Stokes 1973).

Stokes's major objectives had to do with building Black political power locally and nationally, reforming the police department, and trying to keep the city fiscally solvent in the face of a hostile council. Although his planners had important things to say on each of these issues, we were not the key players. Most of us would agree, however, that recognition by the mayor was considerably less important than the unique experience of working in the Stokes administration.

Ralph Perk, who succeeded Stokes as mayor in 1971, seemed at first to offer his planners no entry into policy making. None of us had met the new mayor prior to his election and we were concerned with many of the conservative views he articulated in the campaign. To our surprise, he was as supportive of most of our proposals as Stokes had been, and against the background of a mayor less charismatic and less liberal than Stokes, our own role as advocate became more prominent.

Perk had built a successful political career as a city councilman, county auditor, and mayor by articulating the grievances of his largely ethnic, Democratic, and working class constituency rather than by being a loyal Republican party functionary. His appointments and his city politics tended to be bipartisan. With some important exceptions, Perk's appointments reflected more concern for patronage than professionalism or technical capacity. His planners, well-trained and seasoned, quickly shouldered into a number of issues with analytical policy papers and bargaining positions that set out how the interests of city residents (and Perk's own political fortunes) might be affected by this or that choice.

As mayor, Perk ran a casual and unstructured operation, presenting an ideal opportunity for planners with specific objectives in mind to become involved in significant matters ordinarily outside their traditional responsibilities. Ironically, although Perk's personal political philosophy was far to the political right of our views, he supported us in important work and we helped each other achieve our most significant successes. In a way, as "house liberals" and advocates for Cleveland's have-nots, we may have played a supportive role for Perk in neutralizing opposition to his administration from minority groups.

Later in his administration Perk began to see himself as a potential governor or U.S. senator, with a broader constituency and funding needs than those represented only by his city supporters. As Mayor Perk moved away from his city base in search of this broader constituency, our influence with the mayor's office waned.

Dennis J. Kucinich, who took office as mayor in November 1977, was a close student of Cleveland's city planning operation. He had a strong sense of the planning staff's political philosophy and technical ability since he had asked for our help on a number of issues during his six years in Cleveland City Council. Kucinich was one of the first councilmen to provide consistent support for our position in the RTA transit negotiation. We looked forward to a close association, and assumed that we would be heavily and continually involved in policy making at the mayoral level. For a period of ten months, Kucinich even gave me increased responsibility as head of his Community Development Department, the agency that spends Cleveland's $35 million plus block grant.

Regrettably, our relationship with the mayor began to deteriorate almost immediately. We agreed on virtually all policy issues: saving Muny Light, ending tax giveaways, and the need to concentrate the resources of the community on its residents and neighborhoods. We also agreed on the ultimate heresy: that elected officials should have more to say about running Cleveland than the leadership of the city's law firms, banks, or utility companies. However, the mayor and his key lieutenants insisted on an approach that was confrontationist in style and unnecessarily brutal, one that many feared would be destructive to the objectives we all sought and to the mayor's very ability to govern. Attempts to point out quietly effective ways to accomplish a given objective were rejected in favor of the bugle call, a fusillade of pejoratives, and a frontal assault. It gave the mayor more trouble than he needed.

After his first tumultuous year in office, during which he came into conflict with virtually every formal institution in Cleveland (mostly justified in my view) and survived a bitter recall election by 236 votes, Kucinich came in conflict with his own political base. He began by demanding loyalty and political support from Cleveland's neighborhood organizations as the price of city support for their projects. The groups, which were issue-oriented and had built their bases on protest tactics and strict political independence, refused to comply. Then, at an annual meeting of neighborhood organizations, his lieutenants threw down the gauntlet — either the groups would accept his decisions and requests without complaint, or they would be entirely cut off by city hall. Before the meeting was over, chairs were flying through the air, several people were wrestling for control of the microphone, and the stage was set for the open political warfare with the neighborhoods which was to sweep Kucinich out of city hall a year later.

Impact on Practicing Planners

How did our work in Cleveland affect the work of other practicing city planners? Probably not to any great degree, so far as I could tell. Our model, after all, asked city planners to be what few public administrators are: activist, risk-taking in style, and redistributive in objectives. As I got around to other cities, I began to perceive that most planners were not so inclined. Despite an ideological mystique which stresses a liberal point of view and selfless service to a broad public interest, planning practice actually is cautious and conservative.

12.4 Community involvement — the Buckeye Road festival, 1975, in Cleveland (photo by Susan C. Kaeser).

Most planners, I began to think, were ordinary bureaucrats seeking a secure career, some status, and regular increases in salary. They rarely took unpopular public positions since these might prejudice their chances to achieve these modest objectives. The average planner came out of a middle-class background and was not likely to be upset with social conditions or matters bearing on who-gets-what issues in society to the point where substantial, radical change would seem a legitimate objective. Many planners absorbed the values and philosophy of business which have helped their status, income, and security.

One of the goals of city planning was comprehensive but most planners were more at home with incremental decisions. They would agree that they were properly involved in locating and laying out a subdivision of low-income housing, but they would rarely seek to explore possible changes in the distribution of income and power that might lessen the need for such housing. Many planning agencies devoted themselves to operating within the narrowest limits of their charters, even if much of their work was repetitive or completely inapplicable. Tried and true techniques might not provide powerful insights into an issue, but at least they were safe. For all these reasons it was not surprising that the Cleveland model has little known application by practicing planning professionals in other cities.

At the same time, practicing planners in other cities will have to note that our brand of equity planning in Cleveland did not lead to disaster, in spite of its having generated conflict from time to time with powerful individuals and institutions having a vested interest in the status quo. Our experience may suggest to other planners that in the right setting an advocacy planning agency not only can survive, it can grow and prosper.

Impact on Teaching of Planning

If our work made little impact with practicing planners, it apparently affected the teaching of planning to some degree. Almost all of the five hundred copies of the *Cleveland Policy Planning Report* which we originally printed were sent to professors of city planning at various universities around the country. It seems likely that our materials were used in seminars on planning administration to present an alternative model of real agency operations. Over the years, various members of the staff and I were invited to talk to dozens of city planning classes in many universities about our program in Cleveland. I also received a good deal of supportive mail on our approach from planning students. Perhaps in this respect our impact on the planners who will be practicing in the future is wider than we can know.

Conclusion

What else do our activities suggest that might be of interest or use to planners or the general public? There are some lessons.

(*1*) Advocacy or equity planning is a way of addressing poverty and racial segregation, the root causes of crisis in many American cities. Unless there is a concentrated attack on these problems, it is difficult to see how many cities can overcome the drift toward the status of being a "sandbox" (where the kids are parked while the rest of us proceed with the important matters at hand) or an "Indian reservation" (an island of dependency). The activities of traditional planning agencies may succeed in slightly altering the physical environment, but they are largely irrelevant to the needs of the people in cities such as Cleveland where the problems are largely economic, social, and political.

(*2*) As a profession planning has been too timid. This criticism is pointed less toward the rank-and-file staff of most agencies than at their directors. They are the individuals confronted with the challenge and opportunity to create an activist role for their organizations, and they have the freedom to do so because there is much "slack" in local government and because planning practice is not uniform by law or tradition. Beyond the narrow powers and responsibilities mandated to planners by their city charters, the scope and content of the planning function in most cities waits to be defined by the planners themselves, by their planning commissions, and by their mayors. However, mayors and planning commissioners will rarely provide leadership, especially toward equity objectives. This means that the planners themselves must seize the initiative and define their own roles relative to the real needs of the city and its people. This course of action involves some political risks, but as our experience in Cleveland indicates, the risks are manageable. As an imperialist for the planning profession, I believe that planners can do much more than they are now doing. We will never know how much more we can do until we try.

(3) The essential step toward developing an activist role lies in the adoption of a clearly defined goal. Without such a goal, planners have had difficulty answering the question of how best to allocate limited agency resources. Our goal in Cleveland of providing more choices for those who have few provided us with a convenient framework for day-to-day practice and a direction for broader, longer-range studies.

(4) Pursuit of equity objectives requires that planners focus on the decision-making process, and focus on it not with rhetoric but with hard, relevant information. In the decision-making process those who have better information and know what outcomes they want to achieve have a great advantage over the other participants. The presentation of policies and programs to mayors, councilmen, and key political and business figures requires basic critical skills and abilities. Among these are the ability to deal with voluminous statistical information, familiarity with public and private financial procedures and techniques, a working knowledge of law, an appreciation of the workings of bureaucracies, and the ability to write and express ideas simply and clearly. Frequently, the successful advocacy of a desirable program or legislative change will rely entirely on the quality of staff work and the ability to present verbal or written recommendations clearly and quickly, remembering always that most politicians do not read much and have short attention spans. The only legitimate power the planner can count on in such matters is the power of information, analysis, and insight, but that power is considerable when harnessed to an authentic conceptualization of the public need.

(5) To be an effective part of the decision-making process, planners must participate in an issue for a relatively long period of time. The transit case evolved over a period of five years, our help to the solid waste division lasted five years, and the public versus private power issue has been in the mill for ten years and is still unresolved. To influence the outcomes of such issues,

planners must be seen by the other participants as serious long-term players who are ready to give the participation necessary to help shape outcomes.

(6) The planner who is interested in affecting outcomes must take his recommendations beyond his planning commission. This is difficult for many planners to understand because they feel the commission is their boss. Ordinarily, a planner will take his study and findings to his commission, present his recommendations as persuasively as he can, and stop. He stops because he feels the presentation to the commission represents the end of his legitimacy and the dangers of politics lie beyond. However, planning commissioners rarely decide the important issues; politicians, business leaders, and important bureaucrats decide them. If a planner's work is to be used, he must take it beyond the commission into the political arena, and take his share of risks while arguing on many fronts for the implementation of his recommendations.

This should not be construed as an argument for the abolition of the planning commission. The commission provides its staff with some protection against the vagaries of politics. It is possible that Mayor Perk, who removed almost all of Stokes's directors on taking office, would have removed Stokes's planners as well except for the buffering presence of the planning commission. The commission also provides a regular, institutionalized forum which its staff can use to place issues, opinions, and analyses on the public agenda.

(7) A planning agency that offers its staff an activist, user-oriented, problem-solving program will never lack for outstanding recruits. In my ten years in Cleveland, the planning agency hired more than thirty planners from all over the country. These recruits were not interested in coming to Cleveland for its sunshine, surf, or other amenities; they came to work seriously on problems related to poverty, unemployment, neighborhood development, and racial discrimination. Most of these young planners left after a few years in Cleveland for more attractive jobs, but several have remained in Cleveland city hall and now occupy important posts in other city departments where they continue contributing their high-quality work. In some respects, I think my most significant accomplishment may have been bringing these dedicated people into Cleveland government.

(8) Finally, the planner must have hope that change in the direction of more equity is possible and that his work may contribute to that change. This observation is not based on some misguided notion of intrinsic moral or political power of the planner. On the contrary, the planning agency is a weak platform from which to call for reform. Nevertheless, if planners consistently place before their political superiors analyses, policies, and recommendations which lead to greater equity, and if they are willing to publicly join in the fight for the adoption of these recommendations, some of them will be adopted

when the time is ripe. It is this process, conducted with verve, imagination, and above all with persistence, that offers the planner challenging and rewarding work and a better life for others.

NOTES

1. See United States Department of Commerce, Census of Population for 1950, 1960, 1970, 1980.
2. These figures are from the ADC caseload figures and from the Cleveland Federation of Community Planning.
3. See United States Censuses of Population and Housing for 1960 and 1970.
4. Figures from the reports of the Cuyahoga County Auditor.
5. Figures from The United States Department of Labor, Bureau of Labor Statistics, *Employment and Earnings*(1977), and the Ohio Bureau of Employment Services.
6. Figures from the Ohio Bureau of Employment Services and the Cleveland Department of Human Resources and Economic Development.

REFERENCES

Cleveland City Planning Commission. 1975. *Cleveland Policy Report*. Cleveland: the Commission.

Cleveland City Planning Commission. 1972. *Two percent household survey: results of all questions*. Cleveland: the Commission.

Cleveland Police Department. 1974. *Census tract distribution of uniform crime report offenses*. Cleveland: the Department.

Davidoff, Paul. 1975. Working toward redistributive justice. *Journal of the American Institute of Planners* **41**, 5: 317-318.

Gans, Herbert J. 1975. Planning for declining and poor cities. *Journal of the American Institute of Planners* **41**, 5: 305-307.

Krumholz, Norman, et al. 1975. The Cleveland policy planning report. *Journal of the American Institute ofPlanners* **41**, 5: 298-304.

Long, Norton E. 1975. Another view of responsible planning. *Journal of the American Institute of Planners* **41**, 5: 311-316.

Olson, S., and Lachman, M.L. 1976. *Tax delinquency in the inner city*. Toronto: D.C. Heath and Company.

Piven, Frances Fox. 1975. Planning and class interests. *Journal of the American Institute of Planners* **41**, 5: 308-310.

Stokes, Carl B. 1973. *Promise of Power*. New York: Simon and Schuster.

Bibliography of Planning History in the United States

Donald A. Krueckeberg

This bibliography is offered as a selective, classified guide to further reading. It contains mainly works on planning history in the United States since 1800. It also includes a section of general works in the broader field of United States urban history and a scattering of works that relate planning history in the United States to the rest of the world. Primary documents have been almost entirely excluded, in the interest of brevity.

The items of the bibliography are arranged in the following classification scheme.

1. Planning history in the United States: general works
2. Planning in the 19th century, before 1890
3. Planning in the progressive era, 1890-1914
4. Planning between the wars, 1914-1945
5. Planning since World War II
6. Special topics in planning history

    A. Planning and housing
    B. Utopias, new towns, and garden suburbs
    C. Zoning
    D. The New Deal
    E. Planning education
    F. Documentary collections
    G. Bibliographies

7. United States urban history: general works

1. Planning History in the United States: General Works

Adams, Thomas. 1932. *Recent Advances in Town Planning*. New York: The Macmillan Company.

Adams, Thomas. 1935. *Outline of Town and City Planning: A Review of Past Efforts and Modern Aims*. New York: Russell Sage Foundation.

Arnold, Joseph L. 1973. City planning in America. In *The Urban Experience: Themes in American History*, edited by R. A. Mohl and James F. Richardson, pages 14-43. Belmont: Wadsworth Publishing Company.

Birch, Eugenie Ladner. 1980. Advancing the art and science of planning: planners and their organizations. *Journal of the American Planning Association* 46, 1, January: 22-49.

Birch, Eugenie Ladner. 1982. From civic worker to city planner: women and planning, 1890-1980. In *The American Planner*, edited by Donald A. Krueckeberg. New York: Methuen, Inc.

Black, Russell Van Nest. 1967. *Planning and the Planning Profession: The Past Fifty Years, 1917-1967*. Washington, D.C.: American Institute of Planners.

Churchill, Henry S. 1945. *The City vs the People*. New York: Harcourt Brace and World.

Ciucci, Giorgio, et al. 1979. *The American City: From the Civil War to the New Deal*. Cambridge: The MIT Press.

Clawson, Marion and Peter Hall. 1973. *Planning and Urban Growth: an Anglo-American Comparison*. Baltimore: Johns Hopkins University Press.

Eskew, Garnett Laidlaw. 1959. *Of Land and Men: The Birth and Growth of an Idea*. Washington: Urban Land Institute.

Ford, George B., ed. 1917. *City Planning Progress in the United States, 1917*. Washington, D.C.: The Journal of the American Institute of Architects.

Gans, Herbert J. 1968. City planning in America: a sociological analysis. In *People and Plans: Essays on Urban Problems and Solutions*. New York: Basic Books.

Gerckens, Laurence C. 1979. Historical development of American city planning. In *The Practice of Local Government Planning*, edited by Frank S. So et al., pages 21-60. Washington, D.C.: International City Management Association.

Gerckens, Laurence C. 1982. Bettman of Cincinnati. In *The American Planner*, edited by Donald A. Krueckeberg. New York: Methuen, Inc.

Goist, Park Dixon. 1977. *From Main Street to State Street: Town, City, and Community in America*. Port Washington: Kennikat Press.

Gutheim, Frederick. 1977. *Worthy of the Nation: The History of Planning for the National Capital*. Washington, D.C.: Smithsonian Institution Press.

Hancock, John L. 1967. Planners in the changing American city, 1900-1940. *Journal of the American Institute of Planners* 33, 5, September: 290-303.

Hancock, John L. 1972. History and the American planning profession. *Journal of the American Institute of Planners* 38, 5, September: 274-5.

Hegemann, Werner. 1936-38. *City Planning, Housing.* 3 Volumes. New York: Architectural Book Publishing Company.

Hubbard, Theodora Kimball, and Hubbard, Henry Vincent. 1929. *Our Cities Today and Tomorrow: A Survey of Planning and Zoning Progress in the United States.* Cambridge: Harvard University Press.

Hughes, Michael, ed. 1972. *The Letters of Lewis Mumford and Frederick J. Osborn: A Transatlantic Dialogue, 1938-1970.* New York: Praeger.

Hugo-Brunt, Michael. 1972. *History of City Planning.* Montreal: Harvest House.

Johnston, Norman J. 1965. A preface to the institute. *Journal of the American Institute of Planners* 31, 3, August: 198-209.

Kent, T.J., Jr. 1964. *The Urban General Plan.* San Francisco: Chandler Publishing Company.

Krueckeberg, Donald A. 1980. The story of the planner's journal, 1915-1980. *Journal of the American Planning Association* 46, 1, January: 5-21.

Krueckeberg, Donald A. 1982. Introduction to The American Planner. In *The American Planner*, edited by Donald A. Krueckeberg. New York: Methuen.

Mumford, Lewis. 1938. *The Culture of Cities.* New York: Harcourt, Brace and Company.

Mumford, Lewis. 1961. *The City in History: Its Origins, Its Transformation, and Its Prospects.* New York: Harcourt, Brace and World.

Newton, Norman T. 1971. *Design on the Land: The Development of Landscape Architecture.* Cambridge: Harvard University Press.

Popenoe, David. 1977. *The Suburban Environment: Sweden and the United States.* Chicago: University of Chicago Press.

Preston, Howard Lawrence. 1979. *Automobile Age Atlanta: The Making of a Southern Metropolis, 1900-1935.* Athens: University of Georgia Press.

Smallwood, J. B. 1980. An American way to conservation: comment on federal river basin development. In *Planning for Conservation: An International Perspective*, ed. Roger Kain, pp. 159-76. London: Mansell.

Scott, Mel. 1971. *American City Planning Since 1890.* Berkeley: University of California Press.

Tunnard, Christopher. 1953. *The City of Man.* New York: Charles Scribner.

Walker, Robert A. 1950. *The Planning Function in Urban Government*, Second Edition. Chicago: University of Chicago Press.

Ward, John William. 1965. The politics of design. In *Who Designs America?*, edited by Lawrence B. Holland, pp. 51-85. Garden City: Anchor Books.

Zukowsky, John, ed. 1979. *The Plan of Chicago: 1909-1979*. Chicago: Art Institute of Chicago.

2. Planning in the 19th Century, before 1890

Bender, Thomas. 1975. *Toward an Urban Vision: Ideas and Institutions in Nineteenth-Century America*. Lexington: University Press of Kentucky.

Blodgett, Geoffrey. 1976. Frederick Law Olmsted: landscape architecture as conservative reform. *Journal of American History* 62: 869-89.

Bloomfield, Anne. 1978. The real estate associates: a land and housing developer of the 1870s in San Francisco. *Journal of the Society of Architectural Historians* 37, 1, March: 13-33.

Choay, Francoise. 1969. *The Modern City: Planning in the 19th Century*. New York: George Braziller.

Collins, George R. and Collins, Christiane Crasemann, 1965. *Camillo Sitte and the Birth of Modern City Planning*. New York: Random House.

Crouch, Dora P. and Mundigo, Axel I. City planning ordinances of the laws of the Indies revisited, I, II. *Town Planning Review* 48:247-268, 433-454.

Goldfield, David R. 1980. Planning for urban growth in the Old South. In *The Rise of Modern Urban Planning*, ed. Anthony Sutcliffe, pp. 11-30. London: Mansell.

Hegemann, Werner and Peets, Elbert. 1922. *The American Vitruvius: An Architect's Handbook of Civic Art*. New York: Architectural Book Publishing Company.

Jennings, J.L. Sibley, Jr. 1979. Artistry as design, L'Enfant's extraordinary city. *Quarterly Journal of the Library of Congress* 36:225-278.

Kaplan, Barry J. 1979. Andrew H. Green and the creation of a planning rationale: the formation of greater New York City, 1865-1890. *Urbanism Past and Present*, No. 8, summer: 32-41.

Lubove, Roy. 1964. I.N. Phelps Stokes: tenement architect, economist, planner. *Journal of the Society of Architectural Historians* 23, 2, May: 89-100.

Mumford, Lewis. 1959. Frederick Law Olmsted's contribution. *Roots of Contemporary American Architecture: A Series of Thirty-Seven Essays. . . .* New York: Grove Press.

Peterson, Jon A. 1979. The impact of sanitary reform upon American urban planning, 1840-1890. *Journal of Social History* 13, 1, fall: 83-103.

Reps, John W. 1965. *The Making of Urban America: A History of City Planning in the United States*. Princeton: Princeton University Press.

Reps, John W. 1967. *Monumental Washington: The Planning and Development of the Capital Center*. Princeton: Princeton University Press.

Reps, John W. 1973. Public land, urban development policy, and the American planning tradition. In *Modernizing Urban Land Policy*, edited by Marion Clawson. Baltimore: Johns Hopkins University Press.

Reps, John W. 1979. *Cities of the American West: A History of Frontier Urban Planning*. Princeton: Princeton University Press.

Roper, Laura Wood. 1973. *FLO: A Biography of Frederick Law Olmsted*. Baltimore: Johns Hopkins University Press.

Schultz, Stanley K. and McShane, Clay. 1978. To engineer the metropolis: sewers, sanitation and city planning in late nineteenth century America. *Journal of American History* 65, 2: 389-411.

Simutis, Leonard J. 1972. Frederick Law Olmsted, Sr.: a reassessment. *Journal of the American Institute of Planners* 38, 5, September: 276-84.

Spreiregen, Paul D., ed. 1968. *On the Art of Designing Cities: Selected Essays of Elbert Peets*. Cambridge: The MIT Press.

Sutcliffe, Anthony. 1980. Introduction: the debate on nineteenth-century planning. In *The Rise of Modern Urban Planning: 1800-1914*, ed. Anthony Sutcliffe, pp. 1-10. London: Mansell.

3. Planning in the Progressive Era: 1890-1914

Buder, Stanley. 1967. *Pullman: An Experiment in Industrial Order and Community Planning, 1880-1930*. New York: Oxford University Press.

Burg, David F. 1976. *Chicago's White City of 1893*. Lexington: University Press of Kentucky.

Condit, Carl W. 1973. *Chicago, 1910-1929: Building, Planning, and Urban Technology*. Chicago: University of Chicago Press.

Davis, Allen F. 1967. *Spearheads for Reform: the Social Settlements and the Progressive Movement, 1890-1914*. New York: Oxford University Press.

Ebner, Michael H. and Tobin, Eugene M., editors, 1977. *The Age of Urban Reform: New Perspectives on the Progressive Era*. Port Washington: Kennikat Press.

Hines, Thomas S. 1974. *Burnham of Chicago: Architect and Planner*. New York: Oxford University Press.

Kahn, Judd. 1979. *Imperial San Francisco: Politics and Planning in an American City 1897-1906*. Lincoln: University of Nebraska Press.

Kantor, Harvey A. 1973. The city beautiful in New York. *The New York Historical Society Quarterly* 57: 149-171.

Lane, James B. 1974. *Jacob A. Riis and the American City*. Port Washington: Kennikat Press.

Lubove, Roy. 1977. Frederick C. Howe and the quest for community in America. *The Historian* 39, 2, February: 270-291.

McCarthy, Michael P. 1970. Chicago businessmen and the Burnham plan. *Journal of the Illinois State Historical Society* 63, autumn: 228-256.

McCarthy, Michael P. 1972. Politics and the parks: Chicago businessmen and the recreation movement. *Journal of the Illinois State Historical Society* 65, summer: 158-172.

Mohl, Raymond and Betten, Neil. 1972. The failure of industrial city planning: Gary, Indiana, 1906-1910. *Journal of the American Institute of Planners* 38, 4, July: 203-215.

Moore, Charles. 1921. *Daniel H. Burnham*. 2 volumes. Boston: Houghton-Mifflin Company.

Mullin, John Robert. 1976-77. American perceptions of German city planning at the turn of the century. *Urbanism Past and Present* No. 3, winter: 5-15.

Peterson, Jon A. 1976. The city beautiful movement: forgotten origins and lost meanings. *Journal of Urban History* 2, 4, August: 415-434.

Schlereth, Thomas J. 1981. Burnham's plan and Moody's manual: city planning as progressive reform. *Journal of the American Planning Association* 47, 1, January: 70-85.

Tunnard, Christopher. 1950. A city called beautiful. *Journal of the Society of Architectural Historians* 9, 1-2, March and May: 31-36.

Wilson, William H. 1964 *The City Beautiful Movement in Kansas City*. Columbia: University of Missouri Press.

Wilson, William H. 1975. More almost than the men: Mira Lloyd Dock and the beautification of Harrisburg. *Pennsylvania Magazine of History and Biography* 99, October: 490-499.

Wilson, William H. 1980. Harrisburg's successful city beautiful movement, 1900-1915. *Pennsylvania History* 47, July: 213-233.

Wilson, William H. 1980. The ideology, aesthetics and politics of the city beautiful movement. In *The Rise of Modern Urban Planning 1800-1914*, edited by Anthony Sutcliffe, pp. 71-98. New York: St. Martin's Press.

Wilson, William H. 1981. J. Horace McFarland and the city beautiful movement. *Journal of Urban History* 7, 3. May: 315-334.

Wrigley, Robert L. 1960. The plan of Chicago: its fiftieth anniversary. *Journal of the American Institute of Planners* 26, 1, February: 31-38.

4. Planning between the Wars: 1914-1945

Abbott, Carl. 1980-81. Portland in the Pacific war: planning from 1940 to 1945. *Urbanism Past and Present* 6, No. ll, winter-spring: 12-24.

Baines, Peter. 1974. Back-door socialism: reflections on T.V.A. *Working Papers for a New Society*, fall: 26-35.

Bauman, John F. 1980-81. Visions of a post-war city: a perspective on urban planning in Philadelphia and the nation, 1942-1945. *Urbanism Past and Present* 6, No. 11, winter-spring: 1-11.

Brownell, Blaine A. 1980. Urban planning, the planning profession, and the motor vehicle in early twentieth- century America. In *Shaping an Urban World*, edited by Gordon E. Cherry, pp. 59-78. New York: St. Martin's Press.

Caro, Robert A. 1975. *The Power Broker: Robert Moses and The Fall of New York*. New York: Vintage Books.

Churchill, Henry. 1960. Henry Wright: 1878-1936. *Journal of the American Institute of Planners* 26, 4, November: 293-301.

Foster, Mark. 1979. City planners and urban transportation, the American response, 1900-1940. *Journal of Urban History* 5, 3, May: 365-396.

Friedmann, John and Weaver, Clyde. 1980. *Territory and Function: The Evolution of Regional Planning*. Berkeley: University of California Press.

Funigiello, Phillip J. 1978. *The Challenge to Urban Liberalism: Federal-City Relations during World War II*. Knoxville: The University of Tennessee Press.

Goist, Park Dixon. 1969. Lewis Mumford and anti-urbanism. *Journal of the American Institute of Planners* 35, 5, September: 340-41.

Goist, Park Dixon. 1972. Seeing things whole: a consideration of Lewis Mumford. *Journal of the American Institute of Planners* 38, 6, November: 379-91.

Guttenberg, Albert Z. 1978. City encounter and desert encounter: two sources of American regional planning thought. *Journal of the American Institute of Planners* 44, 4, October: 399-411.

Hancock, John. 1960. John Nolen: the background of a pioneer planner. *Journal of the American Institute of Planners* 26, 4, November: 302-12.

Hays, Forbes B. 1965. *Community Leadership: the Regional Plan Association of New York*. New York: Columbia University Press.

Kantor, Harvey. 1973. Charles Dyer Norton and the origins of the regional plan of New York. *Journal of the American Institute of Planners* 39, January: 39-42.

Kantor, Harvey, 1973. Howard W. Odum: the implications of folk planning and regionalism. *American Journal of Sociology* 79, 2, September: 278-292.

Krueckeberg, Donald A. 1982. Between the housers and the planners: the recollections of Coleman Woodbury. In *The American Planner*, edited by Donald A. Krueckeberg. New York: Methuen, Inc.

Krueckeberg, Donald A. and Williams, Sydney H. 1982. Recollections of Ladislas Segoe. In *The American Planner*, edited by Donald A. Krueckeberg. New York: Methuen, Inc.

Lubove, Roy. 1963. *Community Planning in the 1920s: The Contribution of the Regional Planning Association of America*. Pittsburgh: University of Pittsburgh Press.

Morgan, Arthur E. 1974. *The Making of the TVA*. Buffalo: Prometheus Books. Ross, John R. 1975. Benton MacKaye: the Appalachian trail. *Journal of the American Institute of Planners* 41, 2, March: 110-114.

Simpson, Michael. 1981. Thomas Adams: 1871-1940. In *Pioneers in British Planning*, edited by Gordon E. Cherry, pp. 19-45. London: The Architectural Press, Ltd.

Sussman, Carl, ed. 1976. *Planning the Fourth Migration: The Neglected Vision of the Regional Planning Associations of America*. Cambridge, Massachusetts: MIT Press.

Wilson, William H. 1974. Moles and skylarks. In *Coming of Age: Urban America 1915-1945*. New York: Wiley, 124-161.

Wolfe, Margaret Ripley. 1981. Changing the face of southern Appalachia: urban planning in southwest Virginia and east Tennessee, 1890-1929. *Journal of the American Planning Association* 47, 3, July: 252-265.

Wurster, Catherine Bauer. 1965. The social front of modern architecture in the 1930s. *Journal of the Society of Architectural Historians* 24, 48-52.

5. Planning since World War II

Altshuler, Alan A. 1965. *The City Planning Process: A Political Analysis*. Ithaca: Cornell University Press.

Anderson, Martin. 1964. *The Federal Bulldozer: A Critical Analysis of Urban Renewal, 1949-1962*. Cambridge: MIT Press.

Beauregard, Robert A. 1976. The occupation of planning: a view from the census. *Journal of the American Institute of Planners* 42, 2, April: 187-192.

Bellush, Jewel and Murray Hausknicht, editors. 1967. *Urban Renewal: People, Politics, and Planning*. Garden City: Anchor Books.

Erber, Ernest, ed. 1970. *Urban Planning in Transition*. New York: Grossman Publishers.

Estall, Robert. 1977. Regional planning in the United States: an evaluation of experience under the 1965 Economic Development Act. *Town Planning Review*, 48, 4:341-64.

Fishman, Robert. 1980. The anti-planners: the contemporary revolt against planning and its significance for planning history. In *Shaping an Urban World*, edited by Gordon E. Cherry, pp. 243-252.

Godschalk, David R., ed. 1974. *Planning in America: Learning from Turbulence*. Washington, D.C.: American Institute of Planners.

Grabow, Stephen. The outsider in retrospect: E. A. Gutkind. *Journal of the American Institute of Planners* 41, 3, May 1975: 200-14.

Haar, Charles M. 1975. *Between the Idea and the Reality: A Study in the Origin, Fate and Legacy of the Model Cities Program*. Boston: Little, Brown and Company.

Hall, Peter. 1980. *Great Planning Disasters*. London: Weidenfeld and Nicholson.

Heskin, Allan David. 1980. Crisis and response: a historical perspective on advocacy planning. *Journal of the American Planning Association* 46, 1, January: 50-63.

Jacobs, Allan B. 1978. *Making City Planning Work*. Chicago: American Society of Planning Officials.

Judd, Dennis R. and Hendelson, Robert E. 1973. *The Politics of Urban Planning: The East St. Louis Experience*. Urbana: University of Illinois Press.

Krueckeberg, Donald A. 1978. Practical demand for analytic methods. In *Planning Theory in the 1980s: A Search for Future Directions*, edited by Robert W. Burchell and George Sternlieb, pp. 309-340. New Brunswick: Center for Urban Policy Research.

Lubove, Roy. 1969. *Twentieth-Century Pittsburgh: Government, Business, and Environmental Change*. New York: John Wiley & Sons.

Mandelbaum, S.J. 1980. Urban pasts and urban policies. *Journal of Urban History* 6, 4, August: 453-483.

Mann, Lawrence D. 1972. Social science advances and planning applications: 1900-1965. *Journal of the American Institute of Planners* 38, 6, November: 346-58.

Pressman, Norman E.P. 1976. Hans Blumenfeld: humanist and urban planner. *Plan Canada* 16: 25-35.

Schon, Donald E. et al. 1976. Planners in transition: a report on a survey of alumni of MIT's department of urban studies, 1960-1971. *Journal of the American Institute of Planners* 42, 2, April: 193-202.

6. Special Topics in Planning History

A. Planning and Housing

Bauer, Catherine. 1934. *Modern Housing*. Boston: Houghton Miffin Company.

Birch, Eugenie Ladner and Gardner, Deborah S. 1981. The seven-percent solution: a review of philanthropic housing, 1870-1910. *Journal of Urban History* 7, 4, August: 403-438.

Fish, Gertrude Sipperly, ed. 1979. *The Story of Housing.* New York: MacMillan Publishing Company.

Friedman, Lawrence M. 1968. *Government and Slum Housing: A Century of Frustration.* New York: Arno Press.

Jackson, Anthony. 1976. *A Place Called Home: A History of Low-Cost Housing in Manhattan.* Cambridge: The MIT Press.

Jackson, Kenneth T. 1980. Race, ethnicity, and real estate appraisal: the home owners loan corporation and the federal housing administration. *Journal of Urban History* 6,4, August: 419-452.

Keith, Nathaniel S. 1973. *Politics and the Housing Crisis Since 1930.* New York: University Books.

Lubove, Roy. 1962. *The Progressives and the Slums: Tenement House Reform in New York City, 1890-1917.* Pittsburgh: University of Pittsburgh Press.

Marcuse, Peter. 1980. Housing policy and city planning: the puzzling split in the United States, 1893-1931. In *Shaping an Urban World,* edited by Gordon E. Cherry, pp. 23-58. New York: St. Martin's Press.

Philpott, Thomas L. 1978. *The Slum and the Ghetto: Neighborhood Deterioration and Middle-Class Reforms, Chicago, 1880-1930.* New York: Oxford University Press.

B. Utopias, New Towns, and Garden Suburbs

Arnold, Joseph L. 1971. *The New Deal in the Suburbs: A History of the Greenbelt Town Program, 1935-1954.* Columbus: Ohio State University Press.

Batchelor, Peter, 1969. The origin of the garden city concept of urban form. *Journal of the Society of Architectural Historians* 28, 3, October: 184-200.

Birch, Eugenie Ladner. 1980. Radburn and the American planning movement: the persistence of an idea. *Journal of the American Planning Association* 46, 4, October: 424-439.

Conkin, Paul K. 1959. *Tomorrow a New World: The New Deal Community Program.* Ithaca: Cornell University Press.

Corden, Carol. 1977. *Planned Cities: New Towns in Britain and America.* Beverly Hills: Sage Publications.

Creese, Walter L. 1966. *The Search for Environment—The Garden City: Before and After.* New Haven: Yale University Press.

Fishman, Robert. 1977. *Urban Utopias in the Twentieth Century: Ebenezer Howard, Frank Lloyd Wright, and Le Corbusier*. New York: Basic Books.

Grabow, Stephen. 1977. Frank Lloyd Wright and the American city: the broad acres debate. *Journal of the American Institute of Planners* 43, 2, April: 115-124.

Hayden, Dolores. 1976. *Seven American Utopias: The Architecture of Communitarian Socialism, 1790-1975*. Cambridge: The MIT Press.

Jackson, Kenneth J. 1973. The crabgrass frontier: 150 years of suburban growth in America. In *The Urban Experience: Themes in American History*, edited by Raymond A. Mohl and James F. Richardson, pp. 196-221. Belmont, California: Wadsworth Publishing Company.

Lubove, Roy. 1952. New cities for old: the urban reconstruction program of the 1930s. *Social Studies* 53: 203-13.

McFarland, John R. 1966. The administration of the New Deal greenbelt towns. *Journal of the American Institute of Planners* 32, 4, July: 217-224.

Meyerson, Martin. 1961. Utopian tradition and the planning of cities. *Daedalus*, winter: 180-193.

Myhra, David. 1974. Rexford Guy Tugwell: initiator of America's greenbelt new towns. *Journal of the American Institute of Planners* 40, 3, May: 176-188.

Pommer, Richard. 1978. The architecture of urban housing in the United States during the early 1930s. *Journal of the Society of Architectural Historians* 37, 4, December: 235-64.

Stein, Clarence S. 1966. *Toward New Towns for America*, Cambridge: The MIT Press.

Stern, Robert A.M., and Massengale, John Montague, eds. 1981. The Anglo-American suburb. *Architectural Design* 50, 10/11: the entire issue.

Wilson, Richard Guy. 1979. Idealism and the origin of the first American suburb: Llewellyn Park, New Jersey. *American Art Journal* 11, 4, October: 79-90.

C. Zoning

Babcock, Richard F. 1966. *The Zoning Game: Municipal Practices and Policies*. Madison: The University of Wisconsin Press.

Bassett, Edward M. 1939. *The Autobiography of Edward M. Bassett*. New York: The Harbor Press.

Logan, Thomas H. 1976. The Americanization of German zoning. *Journal of the American Institute of Planners* 42, 4, October: 377-385.

Makielski, Stanislaw J., Jr. 1966. *The Politics of Zoning: The New York Experience*. New York: Columbia University Press.

Toll, Seymour I. 1969. *Zoned American*. New York: Grossman.

D. The New Deal

Beckman, Norman V. 1960. Federal long-range planning: the history of the National Resources Planning Board. *Journal of the American Institute of Planners* 26, 2, May: 89-97.

Clawson, Marion. 1981. *New Deal Planning: The National Resources Planning Board*. Baltimore: Johns Hopkins University Press.

Funigiello, Phillip J. 1972. City planning in World War II: the experience of the National Resources Planning Board, *Social Science Quarterly* 53, 1, June: 91-104.

Krueckeberg, Donald A. 1980. From the background garden to the whole U.S.A.: a conversation with Charles W. Eliot, 2nd. *Journal of the American Planning Association* 46, 4, October: 449-456.

Lepawsky, Albert. The planning apparatus: a vignette of the New Deal. *Journal of the American Institute of Planners* 42, 1, January 1976: 16-32.

Merriam, Charles E. 1944. The NRPB: a chapter in American planning experience. *The American Political Science Review* 38, 6, December: 1075-1088.

Sternsher, Bernard. 1964. *Rexford Tugwell and the New Deal*. New Brunswick: Rutgers University Press.

E. Planning Education

Adams, Frederick J. 1954. *Urban Planning Education in the United States*. Cincinnati: The Alfred Bettman Foundation.

Adams, Frederick J., and Hodge, Gerald. 1965. City planning instruction in the United States: the pioneering days: 1900-1930. *Journal of the American Institute of Planners* 31, 1, February: 43-50.

Gaus, John M. 1943. *The Education of Planners*. Cambridge, Massachusetts: The Graduate School of Design of Harvard University.

Perloff, Harvey S. 1957. *Education for Planning: City, State, and Regional*. Baltimore: The Johns Hopkins Press.

F. Documentary Collections

Dorsett, Lyle W. 1968. *The Challenge of the City, 1860-1910*. Lexington: D.C. Heath.

Glaab, Charles N. 1963. *The American City: A Documentary History*. Homewood, Illinois: The Dorsey Press, Inc.

Lubove, Roy. 1967. *The Urban Community: Housing and Planning in the Progressive Era*. Englewood Cliffs: Prentice-Hall, Inc.

Still, Bayrd. 1974. *Urban America: A History with Documents*. Boston: Little, Brown and Company.

Sutton, S.B., editor. 1979. *Civilizing American Cities: A Selection of Frederick Law Olmsted's Writings on City Landscape*. Cambridge: The MIT Press.

Tunnard, Christopher. 1968. *The Modern American City*. Princeton: D. Van Nostrand Company.

Walker, Robert H. 1976. *The Reform Spirit in America*. New York: G.P. Putnam's Sons.

Weimer, David R., ed. 1962. *City and Country in America*. New York: Appleton-Century-Crofts.

G. Bibliographies

Birch, Eugenie Ladner. 1981. Four perspectives on the history of urban planning. *Trends in History* 2, 1, fall: 79-92.

Gardner, Deborah S. 1981. American urban history: power, society and artifact. *Trends in History* 2, 1, fall: 49-78.

Guttenberg, Albert S. 1969. *Environmental Reform in the United States: the Populist-Progressive Era and the New Deal*. Council of Planning Librarians, Exchange Bibliography no. 85. Monticello: Council of Planning Librarians.

Heifetz, R. 1969. *Annotated Bibliography on the Changing Scope of Urban Planning in the U.S.A.* Council of Planning Librarians, Exchange Bibliography no. 86. Monticello: Council of Planning Librarians.

Hubbard, Theodora Kimball and Katherine McNamara. 1928. *Manual of Planning Information*. Cambridge: Harvard University Press.

Hulchanski, John David. 1977. *History of Modern Town Planning 1800-1940*. Council of Planning Librarians Exchange Bibliography no. 1239. Monticello, Illinois: Council of Planning Librarians.

McNamara, Katherine. 1936. *Bibliography of Planning*, 1928-1935. Cambridge: Harvard University Press.

Sutcliffe, Anthony. 1981. *The History of Urban and Regional Planning: Annotated Bibliography*. London: Mansell.

7. United States Urban History: General Works

Boyer, Paul. 1978. *Urban Masses and Moral Order in America, 1820-1920*. Cambridge: Harvard University Press.

Bremner, Robert H. 1956. *From the Depths: The Discovery of Poverty in the United States*. New York: New York University Press.

Chudacoff, Howard P. 1975. *The Evolution of American Urban Society*. Englewood Cliffs: Prentice-Hall.

Gluck, Peter R. and Meister, Richard J. 1979. *Cities in Transition: Social Changes and Institutional Responses in Urban Development*. New York: Franklin Watts.

Goldfield, David R. and Brownell, Blaine A. 1979. *Urban America: From Downtown to No Town*. Boston: Houghton Mifflin.

Gelfand, Mark I. 1975. *A Nation of Cities: The Federal Government and Urban America*, 1933-1965. New York: Oxford University Press.

Graham, Otis L., Jr. 1976. *Toward a Planned Society: From Roosevelt to Nixon*. New York: Oxford University Press.

Handlin, Oscar and Burchard, John, eds. 1966. *The Historian and the City*. Cambridge: The MIT Press.

Huthmacher, J. Joseph. 1968. *Senator Robert F. Wagner and the Rise of Urban Liberalism*. New York: Atheneum.

Klebanow, Diana; Jones, Franklin L.; and Leonard, Ira M. 1977. *Urban Legacy: The Story of America's Cities*. New York: The New American Library.

McKelvey, Blake. 1963. *The Urbanization of America, 1860-1915*. New Brunswick: Rutgers University Press.

McKelvey, Blake. 1968. *The Emergence of Metropolitan America 1915-1966*. New Brunswick: Rutgers University Press.

McShane, Clay. 1979. Transforming the use of urban space: a look at the revolution in street pavements, 1880-1924. *Journal of Urban History* 5, 3, May: 279-307.

Mann, Arthur. 1954. *Yankee Reformers in an Urban Age: Social Reform in Boston 1880-1900*. New York: Harper & Row.

Miller, Zane L. 1973. *The Urbanization of Modern America: A Brief History*. New York: Harcourt, Brace, Jovanovich, Inc.

Nash, Rodrick, ed. 1976. *The American Environment: Readings in the History of Conservation*, Second Edition. Reading, Massachusetts: Addison-Wesley Publishing Company.

Rose, Mark H. and Clark, John G. 1979. Light, heat, and power: energy choices in Kansas City, Wichita and Denver, 1900-1935. *Journal of Urban History* 5, 3, May: 340-364.

Schiesel, Morton J. 1977. *The Politics of Efficiency: Municipal Administration and Reform in America 1880-1920*. Berkeley: University of California Press.

Smith, Michael P. 1979. *The City and Social Theory*. New York: St. Martin's Press.

Stave, Bruce M., ed. 1975. *Socialism and the Cities*. Port Washington: Kennikat Press.

Tau, Joel A. 1979. The separate versus combined sewer problem: a case study in urban technology design choice. *Journal of Urban History* 5, 3, May: 308-339.

Tunnard, Christopher, and Reed, Henry Hope. 1956. *American Skyline*. New York: New American Library.

Warner, Sam Bass, Jr. 1972. *The Urban Wilderness: A History of the American City*. New York: Harper and Row.

INDEX

295